gene activity in early development

Eric H. Davidson

THE ROCKEFELLER UNIVERSITY

gene

activity

in

early

development

ACADEMIC PRESS   NEW YORK   LONDON

ACADEMIC PRESS, INC.
111 Fifth Avenue, New York, New York 10003

United Kingdom Edition published by
ACADEMIC PRESS, INC. (LONDON) LTD.
Berkeley Square House, London W1X 6BA

LIBRARY OF CONGRESS CATALOG CARD NUMBER: 68-8427

Second Printing, 1969

PRINTED IN THE UNITED STATES OF AMERICA

*   this book is dedicated to my teacher
and associate

Professor Alfred Ezra Mirsky

✳ preface

The purpose of this work is to review the current state of knowledge regarding genomic function in the programming and operation of what Bonnet, in 1762, described as "the miracle of epigenesis." The book is divided into four sections, each of which deals with a rather broad area of information. Section I is concerned with gene activity in early embryogenesis, with the time of onset and the nature of embryo genome control, and with recent attempts to analyze the shifting patterns of gene expression as development proceeds. In Section II various classic and recent studies relevant to the phenomenon of cytoplasmic localization of morphogenetic potential are reviewed, and the significance, from a contemporary vantage point, of this often neglected area of developmental biology is discussed. Section III deals with genomic function in oogenesis, beginning with a general survey of what could be described loosely as the natural history of the oocyte nucleus, and proceeding to current attempts to understand the character and the ultimate function of the oocyte gene products. In Section IV various aspects of the general problem of gene regulation in animal cells are discussed. Though indeed this represents a wide range of subject matter, it constitutes but a fraction of the vast science of developmental biology.

It is with great pleasure that I acknowledge the invaluable assistance which, in the form of penetrating discussions and careful critical reviews, I have received from my associate Professor Alfred E. Mirsky and from my colleague Dr. Bruce Voeller. This book is affectionately dedicated to Professor Mirsky, under whose guidance I first entered this field, and who persuaded me to undertake the writing of the book, which is based originally on a series of lectures delivered to the Graduate Fellows of The Rockefeller University. The encouragement and help of my wife Lyn have been essential ingredients of this enterprise. I am also extremely grateful to Miss Hanya Barth and Miss Llyana Landes for their conscientious and intelligent

vii

assistance, and to Miss Blazena Soskice for her painstaking work in the preparation of the manuscript. Finally, I would like to thank the staff of Academic Press for their understanding and cooperation in every phase of this project.

ERIC H. DAVIDSON

September, 1968

✳ contents

I

✴ gene activity in early embryogenesis

Cellular differentiation is at present interpreted in terms of the theory of variable gene activity, one of the most potent unifying theories to develop in the biological sciences during this century. This theory proposes that cell specialization results from the function of the appropriately selected group of genes in each specialized cell type, and the initial section of this book is devoted to consideration of early embryogenesis in relation to this concept and its corollaries. For several reasons the discussion is arbitrarily confined to *early* embryogenesis, by which one denotes development up through the immediate postgastrular period. These reasons include the relatively large amount of information we possess regarding gene activity and the fate of gene products in early embryogenesis, and the fact that later morphogenesis depends to a greater extent on complicated intertissue interactions than does early embryogenesis. Furthermore, the *onset* of cell differentiation early in development provides a unique set of opportunities for the study of genomic regulation in animal cells. The initial establishment of functional cell diversity and the appearance of spatially specified groupings of differentiated cell types where there were none before must depend basically on the *de novo* establishment of a mosaic of gene activity patterns in the nuclei of the differentiating cells, and this point of view leads directly to the problem of the gene regulation process by which these patterns are established.

Since the variable gene activity theory of differentiation is more or less to be taken for granted in what follows, it is useful to begin by noting briefly the logical structure of the argument upon which this theory now rests.

1

1

The variable gene activity theory
of cell differentiation

Several premises are required in arriving at the proposition that differentiation is a function of variable gene activity. First among these is the now well-understood molecular relationship between the genetic DNA and the structure of the various proteins found in the cell. Since the cell owes its definitive characteristics to the characteristics and functional attributes of its proteins, the cell requires the expression of genetic information coding for protein structure in order for these characteristics to materialize. Thus, the differentiated state must ultimately depend on the transcription of genomic information.

early evidence for the informational equivalence
of differentiated cell genomes

A second premise of the argument for the variable gene activity theory is the proposition that every living cell nucleus in a metazoan organism contains the same complete genome as was present in the zygote nucleus. Evidence for this has been accumulating ever since 1892, when experiments designed specifically to test this point were carried out by Driesch (1). Driesch, and later various other experimental embryologists (2), showed that at least in very early development (cleavage stages) given nuclei could be partitioned into cells other than those normally inheriting them without causing abnormal development. It was argued that since nuclei normally assigned to endoderm cells could also direct the development of mesoderm, and vice versa, these nuclei must contain the genes for mesoderm as well as the genes for endoderm properties. The evidence from these experiments implies that any cleavage-stage nucleus contains all the zygote genes. In these experiments the normal pattern of distribution of cleavage-stage nuclei into the diverse sectors of egg cytoplasm is transiently altered by forcing cleavage to occur under the pressure of a flat glass plate which is subsequently removed, and Driesch and his followers regarded the pressure plate experiment as a direct test of the 1883

3

qualitative nuclear division theory of Roux. The latter is in a sense a direct antagonist of today's variable gene activity theory, since it supposes that differentiation of cell function results from the partition of *qualitatively diverse genes* into the cell nuclei. According to this theory each cell contains in its nucleus only those genes needed for the programming of its particular set of functional activities, and developmental specialization would thus stem from the progressive establishment of a mosaic of diverse partial genomes.

Though the pressure plate experiments of Driesch and later workers were taken to indicate that this view is incorrect (2, 3) it can be argued that these experiments demonstrate the genomic equality of nuclei only at a period of development long antecedent to the actual onset of cell differentiation, or even to the onset of demonstrable control over morphogenesis by these nuclei. That even highly differentiated cells contain a complete genome equal to that in the zygote nucleus is suggested by a variety of later observations, however. It was recognized very early that the cells of an organism are normally equal in the number of distinct chromosomes which they possess. A significant clue came from the study of insect polytene chromosomes, where it is possible to recognize the major banding patterns in the chromosomes of diverse cell types, and chromosomal abnormalities associated with mutations affecting the structural characteristics of one tissue can be observed in the chromosomes of another tissue. A well-known case in point is furnished by the Bar gene in *Drosophila*, which affects the morphogenesis of the eye. Bridges (4) showed that a duplication in a certain band complex is visible in the polytene chromosomes of salivary gland cells in flies bearing this mutation, though the salivary gland cells are evidently not responsible for the details of eye morphogenesis. Other examples concern wing structure in the same organism; here again intrachromosomal abnormalities are cytologically detectable in the nuclei of cells of the salivary gland. The differentiated cells of one tissue thus seem to bear genetic information for the structure of other tissues.

altered cell fate experiments

An interesting experimental test of the idea that differentiated cells carry information normally expressed only in other cell types can be found in certain altered cell fate experiments, in which obviously differentiated cells are induced to change their specialized roles and to assume a new state of differentiation. Thus in the regeneration of the newt eye, as was shown unequivocally by Stone (5), the regenerated *neural retina cells* derive directly from cells which were formerly *pigment* cells, possessing a totally different structure and function, and from which they are not normally derived. Similar cases have come to light, for example, the transformation of blood lymphocytes first into phagocytotic macrophages, and then into collagen-secreting fibroblasts. This transformation was claimed to occur many years ago by Maximow (6) and others, and has since been observed in various experimental circumstances. Thus Petrakis, Davis, and Lucia (7) have shown that a culture of circulating mononuclear leukocytes sealed into a diffusion chamber is apparently able to give rise to a sheet of collageneous connective tissue fibroblasts, after passing through an intermediate macrophage stage. The identity of the collagenous fibroblasts with their macrophage precursors is certified by their retention of india ink particles originally incorporated by the macrophages. These cases, however, like most of the other examples of transformation in state of cell differentiation with which we are familiar, are vulnerable to the argument that they deal with only a small fraction of the total genomic information possessed by the organism, and thus with only a few functional traits. A priori, such traits could be regarded as "closely related" by virtue of the very fact they belong to the repertoire of functions normally resident in a single cell type. From a biochemical point of view this argument is scarcely persuasive in that the differences between a cell specialized for pigment synthesis and a neuron, or between a leukocyte and collagen-secreting fibroblasts, would seem no less than those between a liver and a kidney cell. Nonetheless, one must have recourse to a certain amount of generalization to conclude from such cases that a differential cell nucleus actually contains the *whole* genome, and the case for this now rests to a large extent on other evidence.

DNA constancy and the reversibility of differentiation

A critical element of evidence relevant to the nature of the nuclear changes underlying cell differentiation is the presence of twice the haploid amount of DNA in the nucleus *of every differentiated cell* (certain particular exceptions aside), except for the gametes, which contain half the somatic cell quantity. This fact, discovered in 1947–1948 by Mirsky and Ris (8) and Boivin, Vendrely, and Vendrely (9), has provided one of the major reasons for regarding DNA as the genetic material. Equality of DNA content among differentiated cell nuclei means that differentiation cannot in general be explained through the selective physical *loss* of unused DNA genes from the nucleus, but this does not preclude the possibility that differentiation involves the *inactivation* of DNA coding for properties not manifest in a given cell type by means of some mutationlike chemical alterations in the genetic material. The latter scheme is now virtually eliminated as well, unless the alterations in question are instantly reversible, for the experiments of Gurdon have shown that nuclei from a sizable proportion of the *differentiated intestinal cells* of a feeding *Xenopus* tadpole possess the capability of directing the whole course of development when implanted into enucleate eggs of the same species (10). That experimental *tour de force* was accomplished after a long succession of previous experiments with apparently less fortuitous material, experiments which had seemed to demonstrate that embryonic nuclei soon become irreversibly limited in their potentialities.

Gurdon's striking results, however, demonstrate that differentiation need not involve irreversible changes in any significant part of the genome, and therefore that irreversible gene inactivation mechanisms cannot be regarded as the fundamental cause of differentiation. As a postscript to this study, Gurdon and Uehlinger recently reported that some of the adult toads developing from enucleate eggs which had received differentiated cell nuclei have now matured and have shown themselves to be as fertile as are normal *Xenopus* (11). The nuclear transplant and the altered cell fate experiments agree in emphasizing one essential fact: Whatever the nature of the nuclear process leading to differentiation, it must be regarded as a reversible process. On this basis one must exclude proposals according to which molecular alterations of the DNA itself differentiate groups of inactive and active genes in the course of early development, for such models generally result in a mosaic of chemically altered genomes which is clearly refractory to reversal once active cell multiplication has taken place.

Various exceptions to the above generalizations exist, some of which we shall have occasion to consider at more length in other contexts. Striking variations in DNA content are known in nuclei bearing polytene chromosomes, where DNA accumulates far beyond the 2C (i.e., twice haploid) value, or, on the other end of the scale, in cases of total DNA loss in certain terminally differentiated cell types such as mammalian erythrocytes or eye lens epithelium cells. Here, as in the occasional haploid and tetraploid cells which occur at a regular low frequency (e.g., in liver), the whole chromosome set is lost or is duplicated, and these examples are therefore of little interest in interpreting the *differential* appearance of gene products. In the development of polytene chromosomes, however, certain regions of the genome appear to be replicated to a greater extent than other regions (12). In the large puffs of the polytene chromosomes of *Rynchosciara,* such an example exists, Breuer and Pavan (13) having reported an excess accumulation of DNA on these sites. Excess replication of certain genes occurs as well in the ribosomal RNA cistrons during oogenesis in amphibia (see Section III for a detailed discussion of this now well-known phenomenon).

Cases in which a certain portion of the genome is lost rather than being replicated also exist, the most famous being that of chromosome diminution in *Ascaris* (see Section II). Except for the case of the ribosomal RNA cistrons of the amphibian oocyte, all of these examples share a common characteristic: they are irreversible as far as the fate of the cells involved is concerned. Thus the cells bearing polytene chromosomes will never go on to divide, and the cells which have lost the chromatin extruded in the course of *Ascaris* germ cell stem line partition can never develop as germ cells. The ribosomal RNA gene system constitutes a bona fide case in which selective replication of the ribosomal cistrons represents one way of regulating the overall activity of ribosomal RNA synthesis, but it is clear that there must be other ways as well. However, this mechanism, if not unique, is at least unusual: Ritossa, Atwood, Lindsley, and Spiegelman (14) have shown that DNA extracted from various tissues of the chick always contains the same 0.03% of the genome homologous to ribosomal RNA even though the rates of ribosomal RNA synthesis vary sharply in these tissues.

The oocyte represents the only situation where selective replication of the ribosomal RNA cistrons is so far authenticated, and here selective replication results in the creation during oogenesis of characteristic extragenomic, i.e., nonchromosomal, nucleolar bodies. Nonetheless there may be other situations as well in which selective partial replication of the genome is used as a means to amplify the *quantitative* output of a particular class of gene product. It is evident, nonetheless, that the main cases of *qualitative* nonequivalence in DNA content among differentiated cell nuclei occur in the course of special patterns of differentiation which are by nature irreversible, and these cases are in general associated with certain once-in-a-lifetime circumstances (oogenesis, polytenization, or germ line segregation). Though more subtle variations among differentiated cell genomes may yet be detected, at present no evidence exists to challenge the general principle of the informational equivalence of most differentiated cell genomes.

failure to detect differences in the DNA sequences present in differentiated cells

A direct test of the concept of genomic equivalence is to be found in the DNA-DNA hybridization studies of McCarthy and Hoyer (15). The critical experiment is reproduced in Fig. 1, and it shows that DNA preparations extracted from mouse embryo, mouse brain, kidney, thymus, spleen, and liver are totally indistinguishable in their ability to compete with (labeled) mouse L-cell DNA for complementary binding sites in mouse embryo DNA. McCarthy and Hoyer concluded from this and similar experiments that "all polynucleotide sequences in DNA are present in each somatic cell . . . (and that) all the sequences represented appear in the same relative proportions" (15). This statement is manifestly true for all the DNA which participated in the hybridization reaction illustrated in Fig. 1, and the experiment of

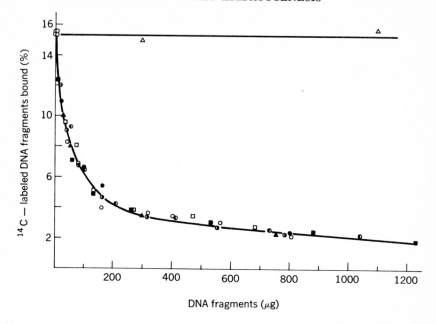

FIGURE 1. Competition by unlabeled DNA fragments in the reaction of labeled DNA fragments with DNA agar. One microgram of ¹⁴C-labeled DNA fragments (2500 counts/min/μg) from mouse L cells was incubated with 0.50 gm of agar containing 60 μg of mouse embryo DNA in the presence of varying quantities of unlabeled DNA fragments from various mouse tissues, from mouse L cells, or from *B. subtilis*. The percentage of ¹⁴C-labeled DNA fragments bound is plotted against the amount of unlabeled DNA present. (Open circle) mouse L cell; (filled circle) embryo; (open square) brain; (filled square) kidney; (circle, open left, filled right) thymus; (circle, filled left, open right) spleen; (filled triangle) liver; (open triangle) *B. subtilis*. McCarthy, B. J., and Hoyer, B. H., *Proc. Natl. Acad. Sci. U.S.* **52**, 915 (1964).

McCarthy and Hoyer thus strongly reinforces the conclusions already drawn from the diverse range of evidence which came before, viz., that the various differentiated cell nuclei present in an organism are not distinguished by a diverse content of genomic information.

Given the dependence of functional cell character on the cell genome and the equivalence within any one organism of these genomes, one is led directly to the proposal that selective variation in gene activity lies at the root of the differentiation phenomenon. Thus the small fraction of the organism's (or cell's) genetically borne capabilities which actually materialize in any one cell type must indicate the restriction of gene expression to only the appropriate small fraction of genes needed to direct that cell's special behavior. The rest of the genome in the cell is to be regarded as repressed, i.e., inhibited from synthesizing RNA. These two corollaries, that only a small portion of the genome is active and that in any differentiated cell most of the genome is repressed (reversibly), follow necessarily from the variable gene activity theory of cell differentiation. Though the theory was briefly discussed along with some other ideas by Morgan, in 1934 (16), the serious proposal that variable gene activity could underlie differentiation can be considered to date from the early 1950's, and the writings of Mirsky (17, 18), Stedman and Stedman (19), and others (e.g., 20).

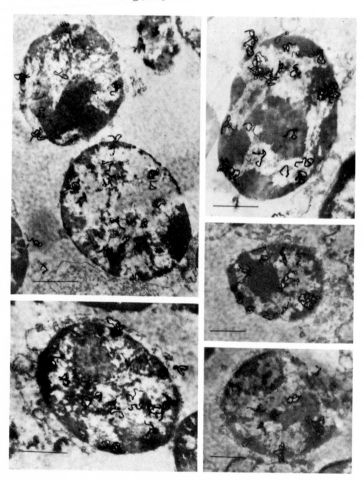

FIGURE 2. Electron microscope radioautographs of isolated calf thymus nuclei after incubation in uridine-^{3}H. Note location of silver grains chiefly over diffuse regions of the nuclear chromatin. ×21,000. The line in the lower left corner is 1 μ. Littau, V. C., Allfrey, V. G., Frenster, J. H., and Mirsky, A. E., *Proc. Natl. Acad. Sci. U.S.* **52**, 93 (1964).

direct evidence for the variable gene activity theory of differentiation

In the last decade the theory has been tested directly in many ways. Strong evidence now exists supporting the existence of an inactive chromatin fraction in differentiated cell nuclei which includes the major portion of the genomic DNA. Allfrey and Mirsky, for example, have demonstrated that more than 75% of the DNA in isolated calf thymus nuclei can be removed with DNase without impairing RNA synthesis, provided that the histones thus released are inactivated and an adequate ATP supply is ensured (21). This RNA synthesis, however, is dependent on the presence of the remaining minority fraction of the nuclear DNA (22). In the same laboratory the inactive chromatin of the thymus nucleus has been visualized in the electron microscope and has even been partially isolated (23). Figure 2 (24) displays electron microscope radioautographs of these nuclei, fixed after exposure to the RNA precursor uridine-^{3}H. This experiment, which was carried out by Littau, Allfrey, Frenster, and Mirsky (24), shows that RNA synthesis occurs mainly in the diffuse region of the chromatin rather than in the clumped electron-dense areas containing most of the nuclear DNA.

The fraction of the genome actually functional in differentiated cells has also been studied. Measurements based on RNA-DNA hybridization procedures and on chromatin template activity now exist for a number of differentiated cell types. In the hybridization experiments radioactively labeled, newly synthesized RNA extracted from various differentiated cell types is annealed with homologous DNA under conditions favoring hybrid formation between the RNA and complementary stretches of DNA. Comparison between the amount of DNA hybridized and the amount which could have engaged in hybridization under the conditions used have shown that in differentiated cells only about 10% or less of the genomic fraction assayed is actually active in RNA synthesis [(25–28); further references to experiments of this genre are to be found in Section IV]. Similarly, in a variety of tissues, only about 10% of the template activity displayed by pure DNA appears to be available in differentiated cell chromatin preparations. It has been shown in several such studies, furthermore, that the chromatin preparations employed function in a "normal" manner in that the spectrum of gene products which they produce *in vitro* correspond to those synthesized in that cell type *in vivo* (see Section IV).

Other RNA-DNA hybridization experiments demonstrate that the spectrum of genes active in each tissue is indeed distinct, exactly as the theory of variable gene activity necessitates, so that the RNA gene products of each cell type hybridize with partly overlapping but partly nonoverlapping regions of the genomic DNA. This experimental approach was first utilized to test the extent of *non*homology among the RNA populations of diverse tissues by McCarthy and Hoyer (15), and it has since been applied to this problem by various other workers [e.g., see Paul and Gilmour (29, 29a) or Miyagi, Kohl, and Flickinger (30); several such studies are discussed in detail in Section IV]. Furthermore, both template activity and hybridization studies demonstrate that the spectrum of gene activity changes as the state of cell differentiation changes, for instance in liver regeneration (30a) and in hormone response (e.g., 30b). The presence of partially diverse RNA populations specific to given differentiated cell types and to given states of differentiation clearly represents a direct verification of the variable gene activity theory of cell differentiation. Given the strong experimental support for the essential elements of this theory, its premises, and its consequences, it would seem an inescapable conclusion that it is in terms of variation in the pattern of gene function that we must understand cell differentiation, at least to a first approximation, and we turn now to the problems encountered in applying these concepts to the fascinating events of early development.

2

The onset of genome control in embryogenesis

It is now clearly established, at least for many deuterostome groups (echinoderms and lower chordates), that the initial, visible events of embryogenesis are *not* under the direct control of the embryonic cell genomes. These early events require active cell division, with all the complex biochemical processes thus entailed, including protein synthesis, membrane formation, mitotic spindle formation, chromosomal movements, DNA synthesis, etc. The earliest stages of embryonic life also involve a certain amount of actual morphogenesis, in particular the construction of characteristic pregastrular structures such as the hollow blastula of the echinoderm, or the structures demarcating the germinal layers from the nutrient syncytium in meroblastic eggs. Though specialized cellular structures thus exist even at these very early periods, pregastrular cells appear in general to be *functionally* nondifferentiated, at least in comparison to the situation following gastrulation when a variety of clearly specialized functional tissues has come into being. *Differentiation* in this discussion is defined as the active manifestation of a specialized or histospecific cell *function*. This definition excludes functionally inactive cells which are *different* from their neighbors merely by virtue of having passively inherited a different cytoplasm, or any cells which during a given period are carrying out no specialized function, irrespective of any possible synthesis of precursors for a future specialized function which might be taking place. The experiments we are now to review show in general that predifferentiation morphogenesis (which is to say, in lower deuterostomes, the major part of pregastrular morphogenesis) is independent of immediate control by the embryo cell genomes, while development from the onset of functional tissue level differentiation onward is directed by these same genomes. For the moment it is desirable to confine discussion to the submammalian deuterostomes, since by far the most is known about organisms belonging to this phylogenetic area, in particular sea urchins, ascidians, teleosts, and amphibians. The available data concerning protostomes and mammals in fact indicate that in

12

both groups serious deviation from the echinoderm-amphibian pattern of events may exist.

the species hybrid experiments and their conceptual background

Effective investigation into the role of embryo genome control in morphogenesis can be said to have begun in 1889, with the first interspecific sea urchin hybrid experiments of Theodor Boveri (31), several earlier unsuccessful or inconclusive attempts notwithstanding. Boveri fertilized normal eggs and enucleate egg fragments of *Spherechinus granulatus* with sperm of a species belonging to a different genus, *Echinus* (= *Parechinus* = *Psammechinus) microtuberculatus*. The experiment was undertaken to determine if the nuclear substance alone is the bearer of hereditary qualities. Boveri reported that while true (diploid) hybrids between these species developed skeletal structures of a phenotypically hybrid character the (haploid) hybrid merogones formed by fertilizing enucleate eggs developed strictly in accordance with paternal type. These results, he believed, demonstrated the nuclear nature of the hereditary determinants, since the sperm contributes the only nuclear components in the hybrid merogone, and also emphasized explicitly the fact of embryo genome control over developmental morphogenesis and differentiation. This experiment was repeated in later years by Boveri himself, and in his last paper, which was published posthumously in 1918 (32), Boveri partially qualified his earlier results, pointing out several sources of error unknown in the 1890's. Later workers, using far better methods, have learned much about hybrid sea urchin merogones that was not known in Boveri's time. Some of the most important of these investigations have been carried out by Boveri's former students such as Baltzer [see reviews in von Ubisch (33) and Hörstadius (34)]. If one takes into account the various artifacts and interpretative difficulties (33), Boveri's early conclusions are in general correct, though real androgenetic haploid hybrids between the species originally used by Boveri do not in fact possess the range of developmental capacities he originally reported. In any case the Boveri experiment opened the way to an intensive experimental attack on the role of the embryo genome in early development by means of the species hybrid experiment. In these experiments hybrids are formed between species whose normal development differs sufficiently from the start so that by inspection it is possible to determine whether the course of development follows a maternal, a hybrid, or a paternal pattern. Since the genomic contents of the blastomere nuclei are replicas of the initial zygote fusion nucleus, observations of this nature could be expected to indicate the extent of genomic control over morphogenesis at each stage of development.

Both the technical and the conceptual developments which made these brilliant experiments possible had taken place only a very short time previously. Technically, the species hybrid experiments rested on the work of

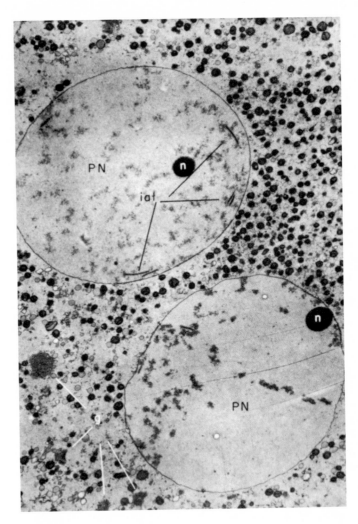

FIGURE 3. Region of the penetrated human ovum with male and female pronuclei (PN). Nucleoli (n) and intrapronuclear annulate lamellae (ial) are in evidence. Note the numerous organelles which populate the cytoplasm adjacent to the pronuclei. (g) Golgi complex. ×5400. Zamboni, L., Mishell, D. R., Jr., Bell, J. H., and Baca, M., *J. Cell Biol.* **30**, 579 (1966).

the Hertwigs, and it is interesting to note that it was during the period in which he was associated with the laboratory of R. Hertwig that Boveri carried out his first hybrid merogone studies. Only a few years earlier the Hertwigs had described the formation of normal and merogonal sea urchin hybrids; the conceptual background of the new line of investigation was almost as recent. At root in a theoretical (if not necessarily a historical) sense was the demonstration by Kölreuter, who, as early as 1761, showed that male and female parents contribute equally to the hereditary characters of the offspring (35). Kölreuter's demonstrations apparently did not influence later workers in cellular embryology, and it was not until the writings of Nägeli in the 1880's that the attention of developmental biologists was drawn to this incisive early experimental study. By this time the conclusions Kölreuter had drawn were already assumed by many investigators; in the absence of the basic concept of equal parental contribution to inheritance it is of course impossible to understand the nature of pronuclear fusion and fertilization. Pronuclear fusion was apparently reported first by Warneke, who observed it in a snail egg in 1850, and by Bütschli (1873) who reported fusion in both nematode and snail eggs. Auerbach (1874) independently described pronuclear fusion in *Ascaris*, as did Hertwig and Fol in 1879 in the sea urchin [see Fol (36) for an extensive consideration of earlier and contemporary references]. Shortly thereafter Strasburger described pronuclear fusion in plants. These observations were of the utmost significance in that they produced the conviction that the *nuclei* of the male and female gametes are in fact the vehicle in which are borne the parental hereditary determinants.

Figure 3 (37) shows the pronuclei of a human egg as viewed in the electron microscope and also illustrates the apparent equality of the egg and sperm pronuclei, the very feature which was so suggestive to the early observers. The true significance of the pronuclear fusion phenomenon did not become completely clear until 1883, with the publication of Van Beneden's careful observations of chromosomal movements before, during, and after fertilization in *Ascaris*.

In Fig. 4 several of the essential plates from Van Beneden's classic paper (38) are reproduced. The use of *Ascaris megalocephala* contributed enormously to the correct interpretation of fertilization, for reasons which are clear from Van Beneden's figures (Fig. 4): In contrast to the human being (Fig. 3) or the sea urchin (36) the individual chromosomes, which in *Ascaris megalocephala* are only two in number per haploid set, *can be seen clearly before, during, and after the actual fusion of the gamete pronuclei* even with the relatively primitive cytological procedures in use in the 1880's. With Van Beneden's study it became evident (*a*) that the particular nuclear components which are contributed equally by both parents to the zygote are the chromosomes per se, and (*b*) that perfect replicates of these chromo-

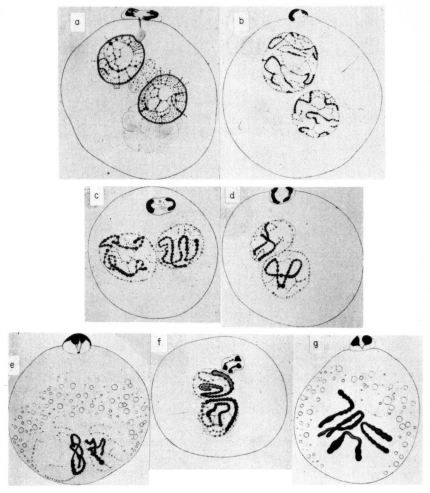

FIGURE 4a–g.

somes are immediately distributed in equal fashion to the two blastomeres as the first cleavage occurs. From this point onward the development of the chromosome theory of heredity occurred with great rapidity. The year after the publication of Van Beneden's paper (1884) Nägeli proposed that every cell contains an "idioplasm" which includes all the hereditary characters of the species, and Hertwig, who had studied the fusion of egg and sperm pronuclei in sea urchin fertilization, Strasburger, who had already seen meiosis in plant material, and Weismann all arrived at the conclusion that the "idioplasm" (i.e., the genome) must be located in the chromosomes

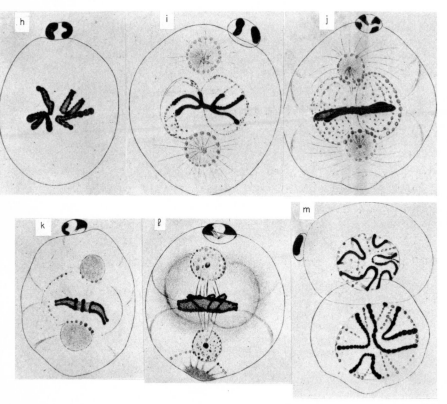

FIGURE 4. Successive stages of pronuclear fusion and first cleavage mitosis in *Ascaris* as given by Van Beneden. The chromosomes become visible while the pronuclei are still separate (a)–(e). As fusion occurs the four chromosomes remain clearly identifiable (f) and (g), and can still be observed as the first cleavage metaphase plate forms and mitosis is carried out (h)–(m). Van Beneden, E., *Arch. Biol.* **4**, 265 (1884).

themselves. In this manner the cellular theory of chromosomal heredity came into being, and the stage was set for the study of how the genomic determinants might operate in embryogenesis. This field of investigation, defined in contemporary terms, is precisely the subject of this book.

evidence for delayed onset of embryo genome control from echinoderm species-hybrid studies

Out of the hundreds of echinoderm hybrid experiments reported in the literature we can consider briefly only a few. Many of the hybrid crosses studied by Boveri and his followers resulted in the early death of the hybrids; it has been shown that in many cases the early arrest and death of hybrids is associated with mitotic failures and the elimination of a significant portion of the chromosomes. This phenomenon was first established by Boveri's student Baltzer, in 1910, in a study of hybrids formed by fertilizing *Spherechinus* eggs with *Strongylocentrotus* (*Parecentrotus*) sperm (39). These hybrids rarely survive up to the pluteus stage, and when they do they display maternal, rather than hybrid skeletal, characteristics. Baltzer showed that these results are due to the elimination of most of the paternal chromosomes in the course of the cleavage mitoses. Early arrest, lethality, and failure of true diploid hybrid formation stemming from similar mitotic irregularities

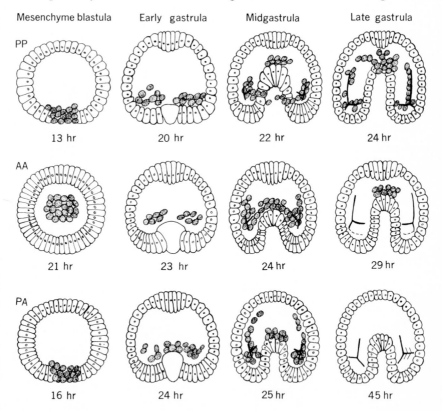

FIGURE 5. Development of hybrid and parental sea urchin embryos. (PP) Parental type *Paracentrotus lividus* (♀); (AA) parental type *Arbacia lixula* (♂); (PA) hybrid intermixture of parental types. Note primary mesenchyme cells appearing in blastulae, secondary mesenchyme, and invagination in gastrulae, with skeletal rod formation ensuing. Hybrid embryos may progress as far as skeletal rod formation (PA, 45 hr), but development beyond mesenchyme blastula stage (PA, 16 hr) is retarded. Hybrid mesenchyme blastula is of thin-walled, maternal form (PP, 13 hr). Whiteley, A. H., and Baltzer, F., *Pubbl. Staz. Zool. Napoli* **30**, 402 (1958).

occur in many other hybrid crosses as well [see Morgan (40) for a summary of early studies with sea urchin species hybrids]. However, in certain more viable sea urchin hybrid combinations these problems do not arise, and in such hybrids it is noted that early morphogenesis occurs strictly in accordance with the maternal patterns. Later development, on the other hand, results in the expected hybrid intermixture of parental types. An example is the cross between *Paracentrotus lividus* (♀) and *Arbacia lixula* (♂) which is diagramed in Fig. 5, reproduced from a recent study by Whiteley and Baltzer (41). These hybrids eliminate no chromatin and may proceed as far as the pluteus stage, with skeletal formation, before they arrest. Figure 5 illustrates the general early conformity in rate and form between the development of the hybrid and that of the normal maternal parent: No sign of the influence of the paternal genome is evident until well after the primary mesenchyme cells have been given off and gastrulation is under way. By this point development of the hybrids has started to become retarded with respect to either parent, though the developmental stage attained by the hybrid remains much closer to the maternal than to the paternal parent. Since pregastrular development is maternal rather than hybrid in nature it cannot be controlled by the embryo cell genomes because these are composed equally of maternal and paternal components. In recent reviews by Chen (42) and Fankhauser (43) a large number of other species hybrid experiments relevant to the point at which the hybrid genome begins to take effect are summarized. In general the conclusions drawn from diploid sea urchin hybrid experiments are consistent with those attained in studies of androgenetic hybrid merogones in that the particular influence of the foreign nucleus is evident only at or after gastrulation in both classes of hybrid.

An experiment designed explicitly to indicate the time of onset of embryo genome control over morphogenesis, i.e., the point at which morphogenesis ceases to follow a strictly maternal form, was carried out by Tennent in 1914 (44). Tennent fertilized eggs of *Cidaris tribuloides* with sperm of *Lytechinus variegatus* and compared the time required by the hybrids to form an archenteron, and the site of primary mesenchyme cell formation, with the corresponding developmental parameters in the parent species (Table I).

TABLE I. Development of *Cidaris* (♀) × *Lytechinus* (♂) Hybrids[a]

	Archenteron invagination (hr)	Mesenchyme formation (hr)	Site of origin of primary mesenchyme cells
Cidaris (♀)	20–33	23–26 (follows invagination)	Archenteron tip
Lytechinus (♂)	9	8 (precedes invagination)	Archenteron base and sides
Hybrid	20	24 (follows invagination)	Archenteron base and sides

[a] From Ref. 44.

The experiment apparently shows that up to the moment at which the primary mesenchyme cells are produced development is of the *Cidaris* pattern, which is to say that the course of morphogenesis fails to reflect the hybrid composition of the embryonic genome. It is precisely at this point, however, that the presence of the hybrid genome becomes manifest in its effect on the mode of primary mesenchyme delamination.

Table II presents data summarized from another set of experiments, one of the most elegant of the classical sea urchin species-hybrid studies, pub-

TABLE II. Primary Mesenchyme Cells in Sea Urchin Hybrids[a]

Egg		Sperm	Average No. primary mesenchyme cells
Echinus	×	*Echinus*	55 ± 4
Spherechinus	×	*Spherechinus*	33 ± 4
Echinus	×	*Spherechinus*	35 ± 5

[a] From Ref. 45.

lished by Driesch in 1898 (45). Among the many hybrids considered in this work are the relatively viable combinations between *Echinus* (= *Parechinus* = *Psammechinus*) *microtuberculatus* and *Spherechinus granularis*. Either reciprocal cross in this case yields a pluteus of *intermediate* skeletal form [a result verified subsequently by Hörstadius (34)]. Driesch counted the primary mesenchyme cells in the parental and hybrid species and showed that *only the number of primary mesenchyme cells characteristic of the maternal species is found in the hybrid* (Table II).

The experiment of Table II and other similar experiments to be found in the same work indicate that the onset of embryo genome control over morphogenesis in the sea urchin does not happen until after the partitioning off of the future mesenchyme cells. This is an important point, since it indicates the level of sophistication which must be attributed to the maternal program for early development; the experiment proves that it is this program which precisely regulates the initial details of primary mesenchyme delamination.

Modern studies of interspecific sea urchin hybrids have shown that many biochemical parameters appear to follow the same patterns as the morphological parameters so far mentioned. Thus pregastrular development appears to conform to maternal type, and direct control by the new embryo genome can be detected only after the onset of differentiation and gastrulation. Examples include respiratory rate and DNA synthesis rate, which have been studied by Whiteley and Baltzer (41), and RNA synthesis rate as well [(42); see the latter reference for an exhaustive and up-to-date review of biochemical studies on the sea urchin species hybrids].

embryo genome control in the development of species-hybrids in higher deuterostomes

Interspecific amphibian hybrids of both diploid and androgenetic haploid type have also been studied with respect to the time of onset of embryo genome control. An extensive series of hybrid crosses among various species of the anuran genus *Rana* has been described by Moore (46), who studied various parameters of early development in the hybrids, in particular the rate at which they attain given stages of development at various temperatures. Moore's hybrids fall into two major classes: those which arrest at the onset of gastrulation, and those which proceed beyond. Developmental arrest and death in the former group can probably be attributed to mitotic abnormalities (47, 48), as in analogous cases with sea urchin species hybrids. Moore showed that morphogenesis always conforms to the maternal rate until gastrulation in hybrids which arrest at this point. In hybrids progressing further deviations from the maternal rate of development are not observed until neurulation. According to the Boveri-Driesch interpretation of the species-hybrid experiments this would suggest that, at least at the gross level of observable morphogenesis, embryo genome control is not established until neural plate formation, well after the separation and appearance of the first differentiated cell types.

In the many other urodele and anuran crosses which have been described it is noteworthy that even in lethal combinations the embryos, if diploid, proceed through cleavage and blastulation, and do not arrest until gastrulation [see the summary tables presented in Chen (42) and Fankhauser (43)]. Thus androgenetic haploids formed between urodeles of separate genera, viz., *Triton palmatus* and *Salamandra maculosa,* actually manage to develop as far as the late blastula. Similarly, diploid hybrids between these species suffer massive mitotic disorders but nonetheless manage to proceed to the beginning of gastrulation (48). These data suggest that as in the sea urchin, pregastrular amphibian morphogenesis follows a maternal program and does not depend on embryo genome function. Even more striking than in the echinoderm hybrid experiments, moreover, is the delayed effect of the paternal genomic component: In amphibian hybrids phenotypically hybrid characters, whether of morphological or biochemical nature, are not observed until after gastrulation, and frequently not until much later. Throughout cleavage and blastulation, for instance, the respiration rate of lethally crossed hybrid frogs remains maternal, with deviations occurring only as the stage of arrest approaches. This is so even in the *Triton* × *Salamandra* cross alluded to above (49). Another parameter which has been studied, and which follows the same pattern as respiratory activity, is DNA synthesis. Thus, according to Gregg and Løvtrup (50), DNA accumulation in the lethal combination *Rana pipiens* × *Rana sylvatica* continues to occur at the normal maternal rate up to the time when the controls have begun to neurulate, despite the fact that development in these hybrids arrests hours earlier at gastrulation.

Species-hybrid experiments have played a very important role in alerting students of development to certain of the basic aspects of genomic function in early development, particularly the early development of amphibians and echinoderms. Extensive hybridization studies have also been carried out with teleost embryos [earlier work is reviewed by Morgan (40)], and the results, overall, bear close resemblance to the amphibian species-hybrid results. Thus the rate of early development is generally maternal. [Newman (51) showed that for teleost hybrids this criterion may be unreliable, however, and that in certain cases at least the cleavage rate may be altered in either direction by the foreign sperm.] Developmental arrest in either intrageneric or intergeneric teleost species hybrids occurs only at gastrulation, or later, according to Newman (52), and the initial signs of paternal genome influence are detectable only with gastrulation. Chromatophore development, the patterns of optic cup and circulatory system formation, and other aspects of later differentiation in teleosts suggest control by the hybrid embryo genome as expected (52).

Summarizing his own studies, Newman observed (51): "It is doubtless during the process of gastrulation that the first steps in differentiation take place, and it is very interesting to note that in so many heterogeneric crosses the developmental stoppages occur at the onset of or during the process of gastrulation. The conclusion would seem to be obvious that any teleost spermatazoon may play a role in cleavage equivalent to that of agents that are successful in artificial parthenogenesis . . . ," but the paternal genome "fails to exercise any really hereditary function until the embryo begins to differentiate tissues and organs." This summary would of course be equally pertinent to the interspecific amphibian hybrids we have already discussed. Another point of similarity between teleost hybrids, on the one hand, and both echinoderm and amphibian hybrids, on the other, is the fact that teleost crosses resulting in lethal developmental arrests frequently display massive chromosome elimination and other mitotic abnormalities (40).

According to the studies of Minganti (53) interspecific ascidian hybrids may show this behavior as well, with abrupt gastrular arrest following the onset of severe mitotic abnormalities and the elimination of what is probably the paternal set of chromosomes. Though developmental arrest in these cases could be ascribed to chromosomal loss and consequent interference with the essential timetable of cell divisions, this is doubtful, since according to Minganti (54) androgenetic haploid ascidian merogones may arrest at gastrulation even without loss of chromosomes. Other diploid ascidian hybrid combinations successfully traverse gastrulation, suffer no chromosome elimination, and encounter difficulty only later at the stage of larval differentiation. Ascidian embryos develop very rapidly, and it is perhaps a consequence of this fact that detailed maternal cytoplasmic influence extends comparatively far into morphogenesis. In Minganti's study of androgenetic hybrid merogones formed by fertilizing enucleate eggs of *Ascidia malaca* with sperm of *Phallusia mamillata*, for example, it is noted that the adhesive papillae of the *swimming tadpole* were of the maternal form, even though the only genes in the embryo were paternal in origin. In the species contributing the egg cytoplasm in this example the swimming tadpole appears as early as 9 hours after fertilization.

interpretation of the species-hybrid experiments

The contemporary biochemical approaches to which most of this review is devoted have vastly deepened our comprehension of the mechanisms involved in both the maternal programming of early development and the gene control of later cell differentiation. Viewed in this context the species-hybrid experiments nonetheless remain important for us in several ways. Historically these experiments played an extremely significant role in presenting the whole problem of gene action in embryological development, and thus foreshadowed some of the most essential of our present concepts, e.g., the idea of maternal templates, and the direct relationship between embryo genome function and the onset of differentiation. The species-hybrid experiments also provide some of the most precise data yet available on the moment of onset of embryo genome control and these data complement and corroborate the modern actinomycin experiments, increasing the biological significance of the latter. In addition, as will be pointed out in the discussion of the actinomycin studies below, they provide a much needed assurance that the actinomycin experiments can probably be taken at face value. The latter, however, serve a similar function in reinforcing the conclusions drawn from the species-hybrid experiments, for considered alone the interspecific hybrid method may be vulnerable to several kinds of objection. Consider, for example, the fact that intolerance of the paternal genome by the recipient egg cytoplasm causes the complete destruction and elimination of the paternal chromosomes in certain crosses: Failure to show paternal characters could result from similarly discriminatory, though less drastic, effects on the paternal chromosomes, which might preferentially inhibit their function until the responsible cytoplasmic factors disappear or are diluted out. In this case the absence of hybrid phenotype in early development would scarcely constitute a reliable index of maternal cytoplasmic control. Another argument concerns the effect of the taxonomic distance separating the crossed species.

Hybrids between closely related species which may be the most likely to succeed [this is not necessarily true, however (52)] are also the least likely to display early hybrid genome control over mophogenesis, since except for temporal distinctions the mechanics of early development will of course tend to be the more similar the more closely related are the species. An example may be at hand in the experiments of Driesch and of Tennent cited above: In Driesch's experiment the two genera involved, *Spherechinus* and *Echinus* (= *Parechinus* = *Psammechinus*), are members of different families belonging to the same order, *Camarodonta*, while in Tennent's experiment the parental genera, *Cidaris* and *Lytechinus*, belong to completely different orders with diverse patterns of development, viz., *Cideroidea* and *Camarodonta* (55). It thus seems logical that paternal genomic effect would become *manifest* earlier in the *Lytechinus* × *Cidaris* hybrids than in the *Echinus* × *Spherechinus* hybrids, as in fact it does in the altered mode of primary mesenchyme formation in the *Lytechinus* × *Cidaris* cross. It will be recalled that the *Spherechinus* × *Echinus* hybrid displayed a mode of primary mesenchyme elaboration identical with that of the maternal parent and that paternal genome effect is detected only later in this cross.

The results of sea urchin hybrid crosses are in some cases conflicting, with reference to the earliest point of hybrid genome control, and to some extent the apparent onset of genomic control in species-hybrid experiments may indeed be affected by the taxonomic distance separating the parents. Other possible difficulties with the species-hybrid technique could be mentioned, and partly in order to find independent corroboration for the conclusions indicated in the interspecific hybrid literature we turn now to other experiments, in which the embryo genome is destroyed, removed, or inhibited *in situ*. These experiments will on the whole enable us to sidestep all the potential objections to the interspecific hybrid method itself. Even more importantly, they have provided previously unimagined opportunities for investigation of the very questions raised so long ago by Boveri, Driesch, and their contemporaries, viz., the nature of the maternal programming of early development, and the functional role of the embryo genome in morphogenesis.

development in physically enucleated embryos

In order to investigate directly the need for genomic function in early embryogenesis, there have been attempts made to study the "development" of embryos lacking any nuclear genome whatsoever. Only those morphogenetic events which continue to occur despite the severe operative procedures to which these embryos are subjected are meaningful in experiments of such drastic nature, and it turns out to be one of the significant facts of developmental biology that certain complex early processes do continue to be carried out in the total absence of nuclei. The well-known 1936 report of Harvey (56) on the fate of parthenogenically activated enucleate sea urchin egg fragments prepared by centrifugation marks an important point in the history of this class of experiment, though there were many direct forerunners in lethal hybrid and early enucleation experiments. Harvey reported that the absence of the nucleus does not prevent a certain amount of cleavage from taking place. The complete lack of any nuclear material in the experimental eggs was verified by the absence of a Feulgen reaction (57).

In amphibians essentially similar observations have been reported by Fankhauser, who observed cleavage in abnormal embryonic cells of the salamander *Triton* which are completely without chromatin (58). Briggs, Green, and King (59) have more recently described a detailed study in which eggs of *Rana pipiens* are enucleated after fertilization (activation) with lethally irradiated sperm. The lethality of the irradiation was checked by fertilizing *pipiens* eggs with irradiated sperm of *Rana*. These eggs develop as typical gynogenetic haploids, showing that the lethal effect of the foreign chromatin normally to be expected in this particular interspecific cross is abolished by the irradiation. Enucleate eggs prepared in this fashion carry out extensive cleavage and even succeed in forming partial blastulae, one of which is shown in Fig. 6. As can be seen in this figure, cleavage amphiasters are

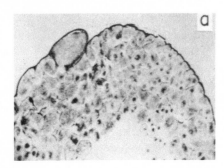 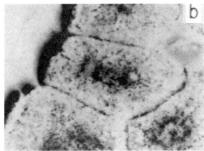

FIGURE 6. (a) Achromosomal partial blastula, 21 hours (enucleated *pipiens* egg × irradiated *pipiens* sperm). Section through cleaved animal hemisphere. Cells are intact and show well-defined boundaries throughout most of the cleaved area. ×65. (b) Enlarged view of amphiastral figure in same blastula as that shown in (a). The figure contains no Feulgen-positive material. Note alignment of pigment granules between the centers. ×500. Briggs, R., Green, E. U., and King, T. H., *J. Exptl. Zool.* **116**, 455 (1951).

formed in the blastomere cytoplasm despite the absence of chromosomes. The enucleation experiments (many more of which could be listed) have demonstrated that the division of the egg mass into cells separated by membranes, the most obvious function of the cleavage process, is dependent on maternal cytoplasmic factors rather than on the embryo genome.

"chemical enucleation": development of actinomycin-treated embryos

That eggs subjected to so severe an operation as physical enucleation do not cleave normally is scarcely surprising. With actinomycin, which binds *in situ* to the DNA, thus preventing RNA synthesis, it is possible to effect a more subtle, graded, *chemical enucleation*, as it were. Where technical conditions permit the dosage to be properly adjusted, this can be done without blocking DNA synthesis. At least for the initial hours after the onset of the treatment, side effects, if any, are probably minimal in actinomycin-treated eggs. The appropriate conditions are not always easily obtained, unfortunately, and various problems are encountered in attempting to apply actinomycin to eggs and early embryos. Actinomycin does not easily penetrate eggs and thus often fails to rapidly block RNA synthesis. This is mainly because of the impermeable outer membranes characteristically insulating fertilized eggs and embryos from the external environment. Other factors are no doubt involved as well, e.g., the relatively enormous quantity of cytoplasm to be penetrated, and the presence in eggs of excess cytoplasmic DNA, at least some of which may also be able to bind actinomycin (see Section III in this connection).

The first important utilization of actinomycin to investigate the role of gene action in early development was in the experiments of Gross and Cousineau (60, 61), who reported that sea urchin embryos could be treated with sufficient actinomycin to block 94% of the RNA synthesis during the first 5 hours of development without preventing cleavages from occurring. Cleavage in these heavily treated embryos is irregular and delayed; even at the high doses of actinomycin (24–100 μg/ml) used to effect this near complete repression of RNA synthesis DNA synthesis continues, though at a reduced rate. In these experiments the small fraction of the early RNA synthesis which is actinomycin resistant cannot be regarded as responsible for what morphogenesis does occur, since it has been shown that the actinomycin-resistant incorporation is merely end-group turnover in transfer RNA (62). At lower doses of actinomycin development advances beyond cleavage in the sea urchin and irregular blastulae form. Cellular differentiation never occurs in the actinomycin-treated embryos, however, and these are always unable to enter gastrulation.

Results similar in essence have been obtained with animals from every region of the phylogenetic map, except mammals. In the marine mud snail *Ilyanassa obsoleta*, Collier has reported that cleavage and gastrulation take place in the presence of high levels of actinomycin, but development proceeds no further than gastrulation (63). It is significant that in this organism gastrulation consists essentially of a process of epiboly by which the endoderm cells are covered by ectodermal derivatives, but gastrulation does not, in contrast to the general deuterostome case, involve the *de novo* differentiation of specialized tissue masses. It is the latter set of functions, which (at 18°C) does not take place until 2 days after gastrulation, that actinomycin-treated *Ilyanassa* embryos are unable to perform. Though the effect of actinomycin on RNA synthesis in the cleavage-stage embryos is not monitored in this experiment (63), the same doses used at a later stage suffice to block 65–95% of the RNA synthesis in the embryo. As early as the 16-cell stage in this organism, furthermore, actinomycin is able to penetrate and to severely inhibit RNA synthesis, according to radioautographic data from the author's laboratory. Recently Feigenbaum and Goldberg (63a) have reported further experiments on the effects of actinomycin (10–50 μg/ml) in early *Ilyanassa* development. According to these authors, mitotic rate remains normal in actinomycin-treated cleavage stage embryos, and the detailed events of early spiralian cleavage progress exactly as in the controls. It is clear that the actinomycin has actually penetrated the treated embryos, furthermore, for the nucleoli of the blastomere nuclei are condensed and abnormally basophilic, and the chromatin appears distributed in an irregular way. At the postgastrular onset of organogenesis, however, embryonic development becomes extremely sensitive to even a brief exposure to actinomycin (63, 63a).

Actinomycin has been microinjected into newly fertilized insect eggs by Lockshin (64). In these embryos development proceeds through the construction of the blastoderm in the presence of the actinomycin. Arrest occurs only at the onset of gastrulation, the stage where tissue differentiation becomes manifest in the controls.

The effect of actinomycin on amphibian eggs has also been studied with the microinjection method, necessary because of the extreme impermeability of these eggs. This experiment was performed by Brachet and his associates, using embryos of both *Pleurodeles* and *Xenopus* (65, 66), and a similar experiment with similar results has been described by Wallace and Elsdale (67). Brachet and Denis reported that cleavage is "completely unaffected" by actinomycin, though gastrulation and neurulation are blocked. A remarkable case, one which focuses attention on the distinction to be made in some animals between the blocking of gastrulation and the blocking of differentiation per se, has been provided by studies of Reverberi and his associates concerning development in actinomycin-treated ascidian embryos (68). We have already noted, in considering the interspecific ascidian hybrid experiments of Minganti, that the first effects of embryo genome function in these rapidly developing creatures may be detected no earlier than the swimming tadpole stage in nonlethal crosses. A similar pattern is recorded in Reverberi's Studies of actinomycin-treated ascidian embryos: If treated with an amount of actinomycin just sufficient to produce a morphogenetic effect these embryos successfully traverse cleavage, blastulation, gastrulation, neurulation, and tubulation, and even hatch out into swimming tadpoles, but then developmental arrest occurs. On the other hand, treatment with large doses of actinomycin (5–20 μg/ml) results in blockage of development at the blastula stage, according to Smith (69), but it is possible in this case that DNA synthesis has been interfered with as well.

A basic correspondence between the species-hybrid results and the actinomycin results is to be noted in the echinoderm, ascidian, teleost, and amphibian cases, in that data from both sources indicate that *development through cleavage and up to the point of the first functional, de novo differentiation is independent of embryo gene action,* whether this point occurs at the onset of gastrulation, or at some later, postgastrular stage.

The complexity of some of the cytoplasmically programmed processes of early morphogenesis is not to be underestimated. Viewed at the electron microscope level, it is clear that they entail numerous and detailed cytodifferentiations. To take one example, Lentz and Trinkhaus (70) have shown that pregastrular development in the teleost *Fundulus heraclitus* involves the development in the early blastomeres of lobopodia and of specialized intracellular apparatus for the digestion and transportation of yolk, the appearance in certain cells of characteristic endoplasmic reticular structures and of golgi apparatus, and the establishment of certain levels of polysomes as compared to monosomes. Some of the early cytodifferentiations distinguishing adjacent cytoplasmic areas of periblast and blastomere in *Fundulus* are portrayed in Fig. 7, which is reproduced from the paper (70) of Lentz and Trinkhaus. Figure 7 should be viewed with the fact in mind that exposure of *Fundulus* embryos to actinomycin during the first hour after fertilization does not interfere with normal cleavage and blastulation, though subsequent gastrular axiation is blocked (71, 72). Experiments demonstrating this have been reported by Wilde and Crawford, using actinomycin at levels which inhibit only 50% of total precursor incorporation into embryo RNA; but similar results are obtained if the embryos are poisoned with cyanide, which blocks 100% of the RNA synthesis (72). These observations, like Driesch's demonstration that the exact number of primary mesoderm cells in the sea

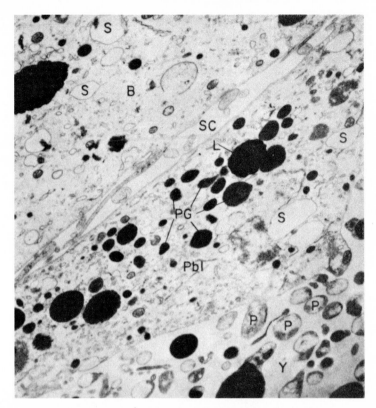

FIGURE 7. Eight-cell blastoderm of *Fundulus*. The periblast (Pbl) extends as a sheet of cytoplasm between the yolk (Y) and blastomeres (B). Villous projections (P) extend from the periblast into the yolk. The cytoplasm of the periblast and blastomere contains electron-transparent spaces (S), membranous profiles, a few small mitochondria, opaque lipid droplets (L), and dense protein or proteid granules (PG) of different densities. Villi extend from both periblast and blastomere into the segmentation cavity (SC). ×27,000. Lentz, T. L., and Trinkhaus, J. P., *J. Cell Biol.* **32**, 121 (1967).

urchin embryo may be cytoplasmically programmed, and the discovery that the elegant, asymmetric spiral cleavage pattern in *Ilyanassa* is insensitive to actinomycin, indicate the extremely detailed complexity of the maternal program carried in the egg cytoplasm.

For the cleavage divisions alone to take place requires protein synthesis, as was first shown explicitly by Hultin in 1961 through the use of puromycin (73). Puromycin also blocks cleavage in amphibian embryos (66). Cycloheximide, also a potent inhibitor of protein synthesis, is reported by Karnofsky and Simmel (74) to stop cleavage in *Echinarachnius* (sand dollar) eggs in much the same way as does puromycin, rendering unlikely any suspicions that the result of puromycin treatment could be attributable to one of the side effects known for this agent. It is now clear that all of the classes of gene product required for cleavage-stage protein synthesis are present in the egg cytoplasm from the start. Thus, in the cleavage-stage sea urchin nearly complete actinomycin blockade of RNA does not in the least affect the rate of protein synthesis hours later (61, 75), and similar data exist for other animals (e.g., 63, 69, and 71 cited above; also 76). The evidence on this matter is considered in detail below; for the present it is important only to make the general point that the presence in egg cytoplasm (irrespective of embryo genome action) of the complete protein synthesis machinery offers—in principle—an explanation for the maternal control of predifferentiation morphogenesis.

the timing of transcription for early genome-controlled morphogenesis

By administering actinomycin at progressively later periods of development it has been found possible to analyze the temporal relations between gene action and morphogenesis. This interesting approach has recently been employed by Barros, Hand, and Monroy (77) in a study carried out with the starfish *Asterias forbesi*, and a detailed analysis along similar lines for the sea urchin *Paracentrotus lividus* has been reported by Giudice, Mutolo, and Donatuti (78). Some of the experiments carried out by these workers are summarized in the diagrams reproduced in Fig. 8. In the starfish it is found that by interfering with RNA synthesis during the period from 5 to 6 hours after fertilization to 11 hours after fertilization gastrulation is blocked (Fig. 8a). Gastrulation does not normally begin in this organism until 15 hours after fertilization and midgastrula normally occurs at 18–19 hours, with the first primary mesenchyme cells being released after 20 hours. Yet if actinomycin treatment is delayed until after 11 hours, gastrulation is able to take place up to the stage of primary mesenchyme formation. The period of gene transcription for gastrulation, from about 6 to 11 hours postfertilization, is thus delineated. In *Paracentrotus* the normal sequence of events is the reverse of that in the starfish, and primary mesenchyme cells appear well in advance of gastrular invagination. The main conclusion to be extracted from the experiment of Fig. 8b is that transcription which is critical for gastrular morphogenesis occurs as early as 6–11 hours after fertilization, i.e., during the hatching blastula–early mesenchyme blastula period (experiments 4–6). Gastrulation does not take place until after 18 hours. A very interesting additional finding portrayed in Fig. 8b and verified in other experiments reported by Giudice *et al.* is the imperviousness of mesenchyme appearance to

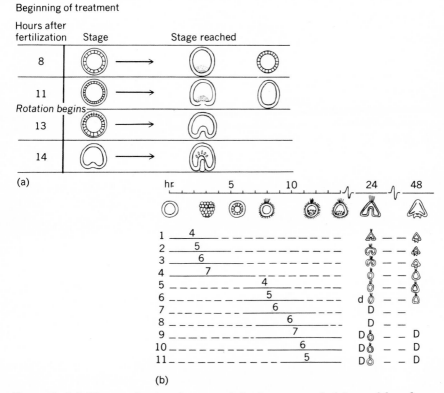

(a)

(b)

FIGURE 8. (a) Diagram showing the stage of development reached by starfish embryos when the treatment with actinomycin D (2 μg/ml) was started at various stages between the early blastula and the early gastrula. Barros, C., Hand, G. S., Jr., and Monroy, A. *Exptl. Cell Res.* **43**, 167 (1966). (b) Effect on development of "pulse" treatments with actinomycin D. At the top the developmental stages of control embryos are indicated. The continuous lines represent the period in which the drug was present; the length is expressed in hours by the numbers above the lines. In the last two vertical columns the stages attained at 24 and 48 hours after fertilization are schematically represented. Here "d" indicates degeneration of a minor fraction of the embryos, and D degeneration of a major fraction of the embryos. Giudice, G., Mutolo, V., and Donatuti, G., *Arch. Entwicklungsmech. Organ.* (1968) (in press).

actinomycin treatment sufficient to block 73–77% of all RNA synthesis. One is reminded in this connection of the early species-hybrid experiments indicating maternal rather than embryo genome control of primary mesenchyme determination (Table II). Collier has employed a similar method to ascertain the temporal relations between gene transcription and morphogenesis in *Ilyanassa* (63). As with the starfish, gene transcription for the early events of embryonic differentiation is complete well in advance of the period when these differentiations normally become manifest. Actinomycin treatment between the fourth and fifth day of development in *Ilyanassa* prevents the differentiation of eyes which normally appear at 6.5–7 days, for example, and if the embryos are only exposed to actinomycin after 5 days, eye formation is unaffected (though morphogenesis of other structures is now interfered with). The same pattern of events holds for shell gland, esophagus, intestine, and other organ primordia, with gene transcription occurring 1–2 days before the respective morphogenesis in every case.

There are in the literature several earlier studies which may be susceptible to interpretation along similar lines. In 1933 Gilchrist, for example, published an unusual experiment in which *Rana* eggs were exposed to lateral temperature gradients at various stages in early development (79). This was done by orienting the eggs in a water bath containing a constant hot-to-cold gradient. After given periods of exposure the gradient was reversed in order to compensate for faster cell division at the higher temperatures on one side of the egg, a procedure which is useful mainly at the earlier stages when the egg is symmetrical. As a result of the high temperature treatments, various abnormalities in specific areas of the embryo occur, but only much later. Figure 9 (79) summarizes the temporal pattern linking time of treatment with time and location of effect. The general resemblance between this pattern and that in Fig. 8 is evident, and at least in the case of the midblastula stage treatment which blocks gastrulation, the "determination" to which Gilchrist refers (Fig. 9) is perhaps the result of the battery

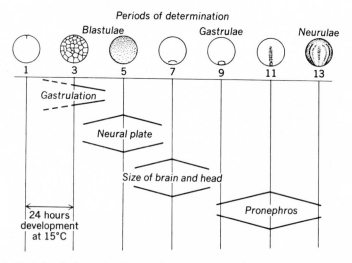

FIGURE 9. Periods of determination as shown by reversed thermal gradients. Gilchrist, F. G., *J. Exptl. Zool.* **66**, 15 (1933).

of early transcriptions underlying gastrular morphogenesis in amphibians. Another interesting experiment which is relevant here is that of Neyfakh, who used relatively low dosages of X-irradiation to "inactivate" the nuclei of teleost embryos, supposedly without interfering with cytoplasmic functions (80). This interpretation of the irradiation effect is supported in Neyfakh's account by the observation that androgenetic haploids formed by irradiating whole eggs (including both cytoplasm and nucleus) and then fertilizing develop exactly the same as do gynogenetic haploids formed by irradiating the sperm only. That is to say, the irradiation of the egg does not interfere with the ability of the cytoplasm to direct cleavage and blastulation, though in either case it does destroy one parental genome and result in a haploid individual. From experiments in which embryos of the teleost *Misgurnus fossilis* are irradiated at successive intervals Neyfakh concludes that in the course of a 2.5-hour period ending 8.5 hours after fertilization, nuclear function required for the whole of gastrulation in this organism takes place, though gastrulation itself does not occur until the period 9–18 hours of development.

All of the studies last cited, in particular the actinomycin studies, are self-controlled in the sense that the inactivating agent cannot be considered to cause a general destruction or poisoning of the embryo. This is so because applications of the inhibiting agent *after* a certain point in these experiments permits the same morphogenesis to occur as would have been blocked had the agent been applied earlier; the possibility that the later application is ineffectual because of some change in susceptibility can be ruled out by the observation of some particular subsequent effect on morphogenesis. In the case of several of the actinomycin studies we have considered (63, 77), the authors showed that the dosages used are not high enough to block all RNA synthesis; evidently this is not necessary in order to block an essential portion of the transcription needed for subsequent morphogenesis. It is clear that in deuterostomes it is during the blastular period, when the events of morphogenesis are totally independent of contemporaneous genomic direction, that readout for future embryo genome-dependent morphogenesis (gastrulation) occurs, and a further implication of these experiments is that the gene products thus created may be stored over a considerable period of time before they are actually utilized. The latter is clearly true for postgastrular deuterostome embryogenesis and for *Ilyanassa*, a protostome, as well.

In summary of the data we have considered to this point: The complex processes of predifferentiation morphogenesis appear to be carried out independently of embryo genome control, and, in fact, in the animals we have considered, they show no requirement for embryo genome function. Gene action does take place during this phase of development, however, and one major role of the gene products then synthesized is clearly the programming of gastrular and postgastrular differentiation, or more generally, of the initial set of *de novo* tissue primordial differentiations at whatever stage these occur. Since early morphogenesis is evidently programmed through biological information stored in the egg cytoplasm, while the program for subsequent differentiation is synthesized in the embryo genome, the switchover from cytoplasmic to nuclear direction is a fundamental step in early life. It is at this point, the point at which many lethal hybrids arrest and die and morphogenesis becomes sensitive to prior actinomycin treatments, that the new organism can truly be said to have assumed control of its own immediate destiny.

3

Early molecular indices
of differentiation

So far we have dealt primarily with evidence concerning the presumed
function of the genome, and with the overall biological end product of that
function, viz., embryonic differentiation. At this point, without becoming
immersed in the enormous and general literature on enzymic activity in
embryogenesis, it is desirable to glance briefly at the onset of differentiation
per se, as viewed from the molecular level. Differentiation, by definition,
is associated with change in the population of protein molecules in the
differentiating cells, and the first of the several illustrative studies selected
here consists of a direct assay of change in the patterns of protein synthesis.

protein synthesis in actinomycin-treated
sea urchin embryos

The qualitative nature of the proteins synthesized in normal and actinomycin-
treated sea urchin embryos has been compared by Terman and Gross (81)
and Gross (82), and a similar study has been reported by Spiegel, Ozaki,
and Tyler (83). In Fig. 10 (81) is reproduced an electrophoretic distribution obtained by separating the total saline-extractable proteins of cleavage
stage and gastrular *Arbacia* embryos by disc electrophoresis, under basic
conditions. As the figure legend indicates, both total protein present and
newly synthesized proteins are displayed, the first by amido black staining
(strips 1 and 6) and the latter by means of radioautographs (strips 2, 3,
4, and 5). The radioautographs are made by placing the gel strips under
radiosensitive film after the newly synthesized pulse-labeled proteins have been
subjected to electrophoresis. Strips 1, 2, and 3 represent proteins extracted
from 2-cell cleavage-stage embryos, and strips 4, 5, and 6 represent proteins
extracted from gastrulae. Comparing adjacent control strips 1 and 2 and
similarly strips 5 and 6, it is obvious that the spectrum of newly synthesized
proteins does not tend to resemble that of the bulk protein components

35

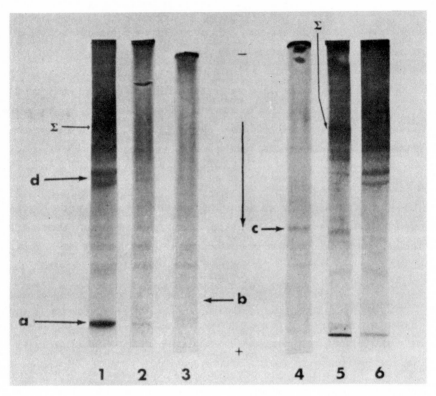

FIGURE 10. Stained band patterns and radioautographs from electrophoresis of *Arbacia* soluble proteins: 1 and 6 are stain patterns from 1-hour (2 cell) and 18-hour (gastrula) control embryos; "a" is the fastest (anodically) migrating component; "d" is a bulk doublet in which little radioactivity is detected during cleavage, but which becomes more radioactive later; 2 is the radio-autograph obtained from a 1-month exposure of a dried slice from 1; 5 is similarly obtained from 6; 3 is a radioautograph from proteins of actinomycin embryos corresponding in time to 2; 4 is from an actinomycin culture corresponding to 5; "b" is an early radioactive band that has no bulk counterpart; and "c" is a band that increases in prominence with time, both in controls and in actinomycin. Σ denotes a diffuse region of staining probably represent-ing a large number of unresolved protein species. Exposure to labeled amino acids was for 20 minutes (2, 3, and 5) or 40 minutes (4). Terman, S. A., and Gross, P. R., *Biochem. Biophys. Res. Commun.* **21**, 595 (1965).

present in the embryos, the latter consisting essentially of the same proteins as were originally present in the egg when it was fertilized. Throughout cleavage, blastulation, and gastrulation the patterns describing the distribu-tion of these bulk proteins alters little. Inspection of the radioautographs portrayed in strips 2 and 5, on the other hand, shows that a completely new pattern of protein synthesis has been established by gastrulation. At the 2-cell stage actinomycin blockage of embryo gene activity fails to affect the spectrum of proteins in synthesis, as comparison of the actinomycin-treated synthesis pattern (strip 3) with the control (strip 2) shows, but a sharply different result is obtained in the parallel comparison at gastrulation. Thus, the spectrum of proteins in synthesis in actinomycin-treated gastrulae (strip 4) is qualitatively very different from that in the controls. It is evident that by the onset of gastrulation, and in fact as early as the swimming blastula stage (81, 82), the embryo genome affects the protein synthesis pattern. The studies of Gross and his co-workers have shown that even in actinomycin-treated sea urchins certain alterations in the pattern of protein synthesis occur, but the magnitude of these changes is small compared to those taking place in control embryos which have been allowed to proceed normally into gastrulation. The mechanisms responsible for these alterations in the distribution of proteins synthesized in the presence of actinomycin are evidently not genomic in a direct sense; i.e., they are not the result of change in the populations of template RNA made available at different times through activation and repression of the respective embryonic genes [the actinomycin treatment used in these experiments is such as to inhibit essentially all *de novo* RNA synthesis (61, 62)]. As Gross and his associates have pointed out (81, 82), such regulation of protein synthesis as occurs in the actinomycin embryos must be attributed to translation level control over protein synthesis rather than to control at the level of gene transcription. The existence of translation level control systems in embryogenesis, super-imposed on the fundamental control over template RNA populations exercised by the genomic regulatory apparatus is an undoubted fact, but to what extent such controls are qualitatively selective remains unknown. The main conclusions deriving from these studies of Gross and his colleagues are that early development, even prior to the onset of gastrulation, involves the appearance of a novel molecular pattern of protein biosynthesis, and that this change, the index of early cell differentiation, is directed mainly by the embryo genomes. These experiments illustrate at the molecular level the switchover from maternal egg cytoplasmic control to embryo genome control.

Data leading to essentially similar conclusions have been presented by workers using other methods and material as well. Ellis (82a) has described the effects of actinomycin on protein synthesis in sea urchin hatching blastulae and gastrulae, as assayed by incorporation of amino acids into various protein fractions separated by DEAE-Sephadex chromatography. Actinomycin inhibits the synthesis of most of the gastrular proteins, while interfering less extensively with the pattern of protein synthesis at the hatching blastula stage. This study also demonstrates a large increase in the diversity of the proteins synthesized as development progresses. Using immunological methods, Westin, Perlmann, and Perlmann (83a) have also shown that new proteins appear in sea urchin embryos after the hatching blastula stage, and that the complexity and novelty of the proteins synthesized increases through gastrulation and pluteus formation. A shift from actinomycin insensitivity of protein synthesis to actinomycin sensitivity has also been demonstrated in amphibian material by Denis (76). As in the sea urchin, this change occurs only as development progresses beyond cleavage, and visible differentiation sets in.

the appearance of histospecific proteins

Though it is clear that a novel set of proteins is assembled by gastrulation, what functions these proteins actually perform or what enzymic activities they include is for the most part not known. A number of particular enzymic activities have been observed to increase sharply, beginning at gastrulation, but in most such studies it is difficult to be certain that what is measured is *de novo* synthesis of new protein molecules, rather than activation or recombination of enzyme subunits which had perhaps been stored in the egg cytoplasm from the time of oogenesis. There are certain cases, however, in which it is demonstrable that new histospecific proteins do indeed make their appearance as the tissues requiring their function differentiate. Consider, for example, the inductive appearance of enzymes for the synthesis of melanin pigments in differentiating amphibian neural crest cells studied by Wilde (84). These differentiated cells appear as a consequence of neurulation, a stage of development known through the actinomycin studies of Denis (66, 76, 85) to depend on embryo genome function and on genome-controlled protein synthesis. Numerous other cases could be cited, including the appearance of hemoglobin in blood island differentiation, the appearance of myosin in differentiating somites, etc. A beautiful example is illustrated in Fig. 11, which depicts the early stages of skeleton formation by the differentiating

FIGURE 11. Serial photographs showing early stages of matrix formation in larvae of *Mespila globulus*: (a) c^1d^1 is a matrix in the youngest stage; (b) a fine process coming out of a^1 is passing across the upper left process of c^1d^1 and just touching, at the lower left, another process of c^1d^1. This contact is indicated by the arrow. Though not evident in the photograph, the process a^1 touched the lower process c^1d^1 and moved along that process toward c^1d^1 until it touched the tip of the third process. Hereupon the process from a^1 fused with c^1d^1 (c). (d) Further growth of the matrix. All the cells (A-G) are involved in matrix formation, as shown by the processes (labeled a-f with superscript numbers) in the figure. Numerals in upper left-hand corner of each photograph indicate the times of photographing ×950. Okazaki, K., *Exptl. Cell Res.* **40**, 585 (1965).

mesenchyme cells of a sea urchin. These photographs are reproduced from a recent investigation of skeletal matrix formation by Okazaki (86). They describe a particular biosynthetic specialization, the synthesis and secretion of the calcareous matrix material, which is a specific early function of the mesenchyme cells. As in the other cases cited, it is known that this new biosynthetic activity cannot take place if embryo gene action has been blocked or otherwise interfered with (78).

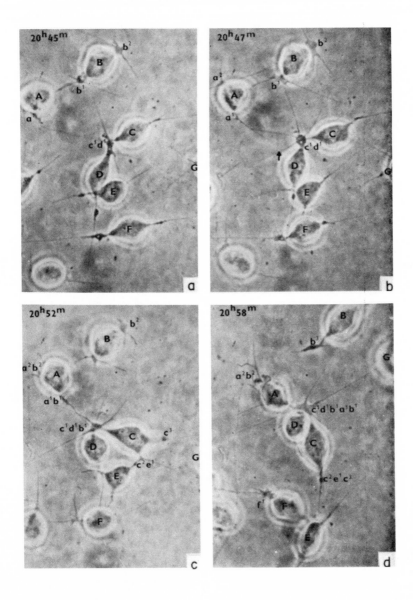

In order to obtain a balanced view of the degree of alteration in patterns in enzyme activity as development proceeds, it is useful to be able to compare the activities of a number of enzymes at different stages. Morrill and Norris have provided such a comparison for hydrolytic enzymes in *Ilyanassa,* the results of which are presented in Table III (87). Though here, too, enzyme *activities* rather than enzyme protein synthesis per se, is measured, Table III illustrates nicely the presence of three general classes of hydrolase: an initial group of enzymes the activities of which remain constant throughout; a group of enzymes which are present early in development but at the time of onset of differentiation disappear; and a group of enzymes which makes its first

TABLE III. Distribution of Hydrolytic Enzymic Bands during the Development of *Ilyanassa obsoleta*[a]

Enzyme	Band No.	Days of development										
		0	1	2	3	4	5	6	7	8	9	10
Esterase	2	x	x	x	x	x	x	x	x	x	x	x
Esterase	4	x	x	x	x	x	x	x	x	x	x	x
Esterase	5	x	x	x	x	x	x	x	x	x	x	x
Esterase	6	x	x	x	x	x	x	x	x	x	x	x
LNase[b]	1	x	x	x	x	x	x	x	x	x	x	x
ANase[c]	1	x	x	x	x	x	x	x	x	x	x	x
α-Glucosidase	1	x	x	x	x	x	x	x	x	x	x	x
LNase	2	x	x									
ANase	2	x	x	x	x							
Acid phosphatase	1	x	x	x	x							
Acid phosphatase	3	x	x	x	x							
Esterase	3	x	x	x	x	x						
β-Glucuronidase	1	x	x	x	x	x						
LNase	3					x	x	x	x	x	x	x
Acid phosphatase	2					x	x	x	x	x	x	x
Acid phosphatase	4					x	x	x	x	x	x	x
Acid phosphatase	5					x	x	x	x	x	x	x
Acid phosphatase	6					x	x	x	x	x	x	x
β-Glucuronidase	2						x	x	x	x	x	x
Esterase	7							x	x	x	x	x
Esterase	8								x	x	x	x
Esterase	9								x	x	x	x
Alkaline phosphatase	1								x	x	x	x
Esterase	1									x	x	x
Sulfatase	1									x	x	x
ANase	3									x	x	x

[a] From Ref. 87.
[b] Leucyl naphthylamidase.
[c] Alanyl naphthylamidase.

appearance at exactly this same time. These changes in the hydrolytic enzyme population are probably associated with the genome-dependent appearance of the first tissue primordia in *Ilyanassa*, since it is in the critical day 4–5 period of development that they begin to take place.

These examples show that new biosynthetic patterns are set up with the onset of visible differentiation, and the requirement for a new set of templates to support the new histospecific synthesis follows from this association. This relation is, of course, the natural result of the variable gene activity theory of cell differentiation as applied to the events of early development. An interesting aspect of this interpretation is that it provides a natural evaluation of the relative usefulness and potentiality of the cytoplasmic control systems as opposed to transcription level control. The complex cytoplasmic control systems of the early embryo, including translation level control over protein synthesis, is the product of lengthy preparative processes in oogenesis, and, as we have seen, these systems appear to be capable of directing intracellular cytodifferentiation, of maintaining a certain program of protein synthesis, of specifying the position and division rates of hundreds or thousands of cells, etc. The demands of *de novo* functional differentiation are beyond even these remarkable capabilities, however, and it is evident that in order to direct the appearance of new tissue primordia transcription level control must be brought into play.

4

RNA synthesis in the early embryo

The bulk RNA of the embryo, like that of other cells, is ribosomal RNA, and throughout the early stages of embryogenesis the bulk RNA content remains essentially constant or in some species (88, 89) even declines slightly. Thus the patterns of RNA synthesis discussed in what follows refer to what is only a minute fraction of the total RNA in the embryo, the latter consisting almost exclusively of RNA inherited from oogenesis. In considering RNA synthesis during early embryogenesis we are again to be confined mainly to the lower deuterostomes, since only scattered data are yet available either for protostomes or for the higher chordates. Some radioautographic and actinomycin studies with mammalian embryos exist (these are reviewed below), but the difficulty of handling mammalian embryos *in vitro* has so far precluded biochemical analyses of RNA synthesis patterns in this material. The problems posed by such experiments are further exacerbated by the presence in mammalian embryos of actively growing accessory trophic tissues. As in much of what we have already discussed, therefore, the major part of the available information concerns echinoderms and amphibians.

informational and ribosomal RNA synthesis in early Xenopus embryos

In *Xenopus laevis*, at present the most intensely studied amphibian species, embryo gene activity begins early in cleavage. *Xenopus*, like other amphibians, sheds an egg which is virtually impermeable to all RNA percursors except

FIGURE 12. Sedimentation pattern of RNA from sibling embryos at different developmental stages. Each density gradient centrifugation was performed on RNA isolated from 150 embryos. The stages and hours after fertilization of each group of embryos are: (a) early cleavage stages 2 to 7, 1.5 to 3 hours; (b) midblastula stages 8 to 9, 5 to 6 hours; (c) gastrula stages 10 to 11, 28 hours; (d) neurula stages 13 to 14, 34 hours; (e) muscular response stages 25 to 26, 54 hours; (f) heartbeat stages 33 to 34, 74 hours; (open circles) OD at 260 mμ (filled circles) radioactivity. Brown, D. D., and Littna, E., *J. Mol. Biol.* **8**, 669 (1964).

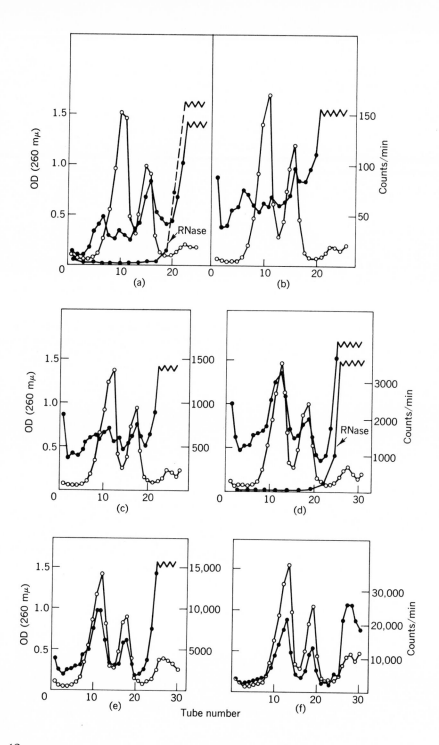

43

CO_2, and in experiments in which it is desired to employ a labeled precursor the isotope can be administered only by one of three routes. One method, initially described by Kutsky (90), consists of injecting the isotope (usually ^{32}P phosphate) into the peritoneal cavity of the gravid female. In this way the eggs may be loaded with the percursor before the permeability barrier, which forms as the eggs traverse the oviduct, can be set up. A second group of procedures involves circumventing the external permeability barrier physically, by cutting the embryo open, dissociating the cells, or microinjecting the isotope into the embryo. Third, it is possible to label directly with $^{14}CO_2$, introduced as $Na_2{}^{14}CO_3$ dissolved in the buffered salt solution in which the eggs develop.

Ribonucleic acid synthesis in cleavage-stage *Xenopus* embryos has been demonstrated by Brown and Littna, who for this experiment utilized the first of these labeling methods (91); ^{32}P-labeled RNA synthesized during cleavage is heterogeneous in molecular size and possesses a base composition which tends to resemble that of the total *Xenopus* DNA. Sucrose gradient analyses of the RNA synthesized at cleavage and later stages in *Xenopus* are reproduced in Fig. 12 from this study of Brown and Littna (91). Since the embryos of Fig. 12 are labeled from the ^{32}P-precursor pool present from the beginning of ovulation, the radioactive RNA is that which has been synthesized cumulatively from the time of ovulation up to each stage. It can be seen that a much larger amount of heterogeneously sedimenting RNA is synthesized in the blastula stage than is synthesized in cleavage, and even more is made during gastrulation. Note that the amount of ribosomal RNA in these comparative gradients remains relatively invariant, as shown by the solid traces. Furthermore, the experiments of Brown and Littna demonstrate that it is not until gastrulation in *Xenopus* that ribosomal RNA begins to be synthesized. This is indicated by the appearance at this stage of a radioactive RNA distribution paralleling the position of the ribosomal RNA peaks in the gradients (Fig. 12) and by the presence, for the first time, of a non-DNA-like,* high G-C base ratio in the 28S fractions of the newly synthesized RNA. The absence of ribosomal RNA synthesis in the period antecedent to gastrulation and the sudden activation of ribosomal RNA synthesis with the onset of gastrulation (94) have been corroborated for amphibian material in several laboratories, including our own (92–94). According to Woodland and Gurdon (94) ribosomal RNA synthesis begins in the endoderm several hours

---

* The term "DNA-like" refers to the overall base composition of the RNA in question. All animal DNA's known are rich in adenine and uracil, and "DNA-like" RNA shares this characteristic. The significance of this parameter is that an RNA which mimics the overall or average base composition of the DNA is statistically likely to be the product of a large number of diverse genes rather than the product of only one or two types of gene as, e.g., is ribosomal RNA.

after its onset in other regions of the embryo. This fiinding is based on methylated albumin-kieselguhr (MAK) analysis of RNA extracted after microinjection of tritiated nucleosides into the living embryos. In addition it is reported by these authors that early heterogeneous, or informational, RNA synthesis is carried out at a greater rate in the endoderm cells.

The fate of the maternally stockpiled egg ribosomes has been elucidated in experiments of Brown and Gurdon (95, 96). These investigations utilize the anucleolate (o-nu) mutant of *Xenopus*, homozygous bearers of which lack the capability to synthesize ribosomal RNA. In the homozygous form

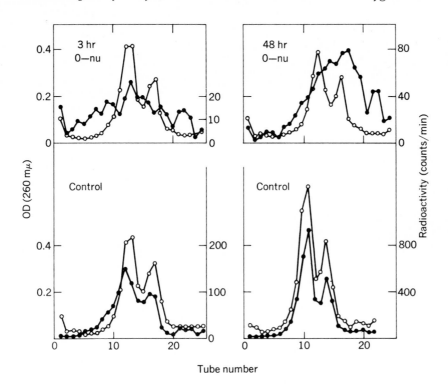

FIGURE 13. Sedimentation pattern of ^{14}C-RNA at 3 and 48 hours after labeling: o-nu and control embryos were incubated for 3 hours with $^{14}CO_2$ (from stage 22 to 24) and then allowed to develop in nonradioactive medium. Embryos (26 per sample) were collected at 3 hours (stage 27) and 48 hours (stage 40) after the end of the chase. Ribonucleic acid was extracted without the addition of carrier and purified by passage through Sephadex G-100. The RNA contained in the unretarded fraction was concentrated *in vacuo* and centrifuged in a sucrose gradient. The upper two curves are the plots of o-nu RNA and the lower ones of control RNA. (Open circle) OD at 260 mμ (filled circle) radioactivity. Brown, D. D., and Gurdon, J. B., *J. Mol. Biol.* **19**, 399 (1966).

this mutation, which was first described by Elsdale, Fischberg, and Smith (97), is lethal, but heterozygous individuals are able to develop and function normally. The mutation can be detected cytologically in heterozygotes by the presence of cells bearing only one nucleolus rather than the usual two or more. It is now known that the o-nu mutation is actually a deletion of the chromosomal nucleolar organizer region. The latter is recognizable as a secondary constriction in a certain pair of chromosomes in *Xenopus*, and heterozygotes lack the region bearing this constriction in one of these chromosomes, homozygotes in both (98). The studies of Wallace and Birnsteil (99) show, furthermore, that the genome of o-nu homozygotes contains no detectable DNA hybridizable with ribosomal RNA.

Thus it is clear that chromosome sets bearing the o-nu mutation lack the organizer ribosomal RNA cistrons. Heterozygous +/o-nu females mated with +/o-nu males give rise to the expected Mendelian fraction of o-nu homozygotes, and these animals survive only until the swimming tadpole stage (97). The heterozygous mothers of the o-nu homozygotes are quantitatively normal with respect to their capacity to synthesize ribosomal RNA, and they shed eggs which apparently contain a normal complement of ribosomes and ribosomal RNA's (96). The homozygous o-nu embryos therefore provide an opportunity to study the fate of maternal ribosomal RNA and, conversely, the requirement for new ribosomal RNA as embryogenesis progresses. Figure 13, from the study of Brown and Gurdon (95), describes RNA synthesis patterns in normal embryos and in o-nu homozygotes. This and similar experiments show that the latter fail to synthesize ribosomal RNA, though they do synthesize heterogeneously sedimenting informational RNA. Nonetheless, the o-nu homozygotes differentiate and develop all the way to the swimming tadpole stage, and this constitutes a direct demonstration of the extended conservation and use of maternal ribosomes. Although new ribosomal RNA synthesis begins relatively late, it is evident that there is still a long period thereafter during which new ribosomes are not actually necessary, for the development of o-nu homozygotes becomes retarded only after hatching (96).

The discovery that ribosomal RNA synthesis begins only with gastrulation dovetails with older observations regarding the time of appearance of nucleoli in amphibian embryos. Observable first as aggregations of fibrous, electron-dense material in the blastomere nuclei (99a), the nucleoli develop a typical nucleolar fine structure and, according to radioautographic studies, begin to engage in RNA synthesis only at gastrulation. Figure 14 is reproduced from one such investigation, that of Karasaki (100). Note that even the incompletely formed "primary nucleoli" shown in Fig. 14 are active in RNA synthesis. Prior to gastrulation RNA synthesis is confined to the nonnucleolar regions of the nucleus. Cytological observations of the onset of nucleolar activity in the early gastrula provide a corroboration for the conclu-

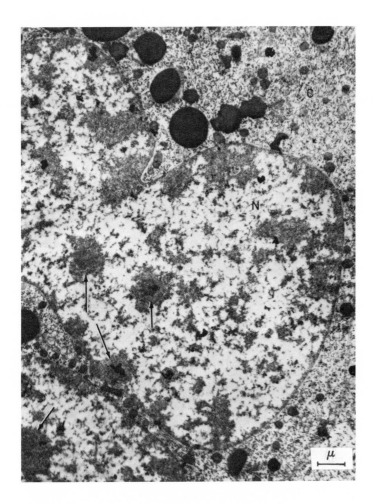

FIGURE 14. Portion of an ectodermal cell from the gastrula of the newt cultured for 3 hours after treatment with tritiated uridine. The chromatin components are found as strands and clumps. Within the chromatin clumps, nucleolus-like bodies can be found (arrows). Silver grains are found over the peripheries of chromatin clumps and the primary nucleoli. Twenty-one days' exposure. ×12,000. Karasaki, S., *J. Cell Biol.* **26**, 937 (1965).

sions regarding the onset of ribosomal RNA synthesis based on biochemical data. Thus in *Xenopus*, where ribosomal RNA synthesis begins later in endoderm cells than in the rest of the embryo, the nucleoli also appear later in these cells, as shown by Woodland and Gurdon (94).

In the delayed onset of ribosomal RNA synthesis we have an unequivocal case of the precisely timed activation of a particular set of genes, the ribosomal RNA cistrons. It is apparent that these genes are in some way inhibited from functioning until after the late blastula stage. At least three molecular species of ribosomal RNA are involved here, 28S, 18S, and low molecular weight 5S or 6S ribosomal RNA's; Brown and Littna show that these are all synthesized in the postgastrular embryo (91, 101). Quantitatively the activation of the ribosomal RNA gene system is to be regarded as an important event since, as in other organisms, ribosomal RNA genes are multiple in *Xenopus* with the 28S and 18S ribosomal RNA cistrons present at least 450 times per genome, according to Brown and Weber (99).

The fact that new ribosomal RNA synthesis is not initiated until gastrulation means that the amphibian embryo must rely exclusively on the ribosomes it has inherited from the fertilized egg, for the whole period antecedent to the activation of its own ribosomal RNA synthesis. In *Xenopus* the earliest ribosomal RNA synthesizing gastrula contains perhaps 30,000 cells, and experiments with microinjected puromycin (66) prove that protein synthesis is necessary for the production of those cells during cleavage and blastulation, just as is the case in sea urchins (73). In other words, all the protein synthesis required for the elaboration of an embryo of some 30,000 cells is obligatorily carried out on the ribosomes synthesized during oogenesis. This constitutes a specific example of an important general relationship: the synthesis of a gene product (ribosomal RNA) during oogenesis for utilization during embryogenesis.

The synthesis of low molecular weight ribosomal RNA (5S) and of transfer RNA has also been investigated by Brown and Littna (101), who used Celite and Sephadex G-100 columns to separate these species of RNA, rather than relying solely on sucrose gradients. These authors calculated that the egg, when newly shed, contains 1–2 molecules of 5S RNA per ribosome and less than 1 molecule of 4S RNA per ribosome. By the tail-bud stage the transfer RNA to ribosome ratio has increased to about 15. In contrast, 5S ribosomal RNA synthesis appears to be controlled in accordance with synthesis of the other species of ribosomal RNA so that throughout development a more or less constant ratio of 5S RNA per ribosome seems to be maintained.

FIGURE 15. Amounts of DNA, dRNA (DNA-like RNA), and rRNA (ribosomal RNA) synthesized cumulatively in the *Xenopus* embryo by each stage of development. The total radioactivity in dRNA at each stage was calculated knowing the total radioactivity in high molecular weight RNA and the proportions of dRNA and rRNA in the total radioactive high molecular weight RNA. Since specific activities of the α-phosphates of the nucleoside phosphate precursors were determined for each sample of embryos, the total radioactivity in each class of RNA could be converted to millimicrograms of RNA. Brown, D. D., and Littna, E., J. Mol.

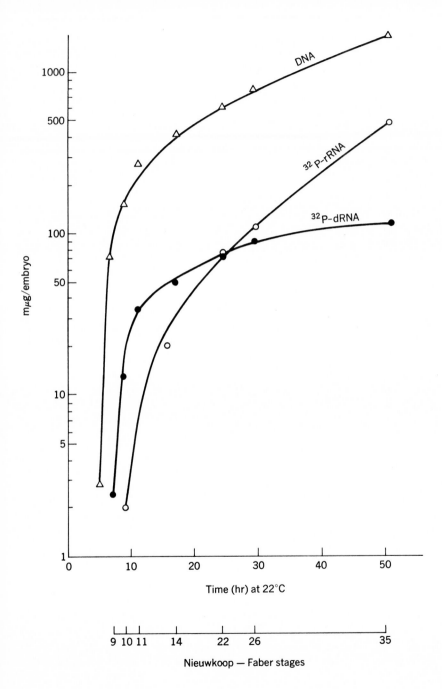

Figure 15 (102) summarizes the observations of Brown and Littna with regard to the quantity and rate of accumulation of ribosomal RNA (rRNA), DNA, and DNA-like RNA (dRNA) in the developing *Xenopus* embryo. The per embryo DNA-like RNA values plotted in Fig. 15 are calculated from the amount of radioactive label (^{32}P phosphate) incorporated in this heterogeneous class of apparently informational RNA's. To make this calculation, Brown and Littna labeled the animals by intraperitoneal injections of isotope into the gravid female, and determined the specific activity of the nucleotide precursor pool, which does not change greatly throughout early development. The results indicate that during the ovulation process the oocyte synthesizes a minimum of 1 mμg of DNA-like RNA, and that the content of newly synthesized RNA of this class has risen to a little over 10 mμg by midgastrulation. After this a more or less constant amount of DNA-like RNA per cell is established, as shown by the ratio of total newly synthesized DNA-like RNA to DNA. These data suggest that in terms of the quantity of informational RNA synthesized by the average nucleus the embryo genomes have assumed their most active state by midgastrulation.

By this stage, however, the differentiation of certain tissue primordia has already occurred, and on the basis of the evidence reviewed earlier we should expect to find that prior embryo gene activity is needed if the onset of gastrulation and cell differentiation is to take place. An investigation of pregastrular RNA synthesis rates carried out by Bachvarova, Davidson, and Mirsky has shown that a sharp increase in the level of gene activity in fact occurs in a large proportion of the embryonic cells as early as the mid-to-late blastula period. In these experiments (93, 103), *Xenopus* embryos of different stages were individually bisected into dorsal and ventral halves and labeled with uridine-5-^{3}H, which thus has free access to the cells. Radioautographic assay of the RNA synthesis rate per nucleus at successive stages revealed that the embryo nuclei undergo a sudden activation of RNA synthesis in the mid-to-late blastular period, well before the first morphological signs of gastrulation. This activation occurs within a period of ½–1 hour in some areas of the embryo, and as a result RNA synthesis rates increase at least 20-fold. A large proportion of the several thousand cells in the embryo is involved.

Figure 16 (103) illustrates the radioautographic assay of RNA synthesis in the nuclei of two embryonic cell types, each of which is seen before and after the mid-to-late blastular activation period. Ribonucleic acid labeled during a 1–hour period in bisected embryos of various stages was also extracted and subjected to sucrose gradient analysis and Sephadex gel filtration, with results illustrated in Fig. 17 (93). The Sephadex separation (Fig. 17a) permits comparison of the synthesis rates of high molecular weight RNA and transfer RNA in embryos of successive stages, a comparison which demonstrates precisely the magnitude of the nuclear activation phenomenon occur-

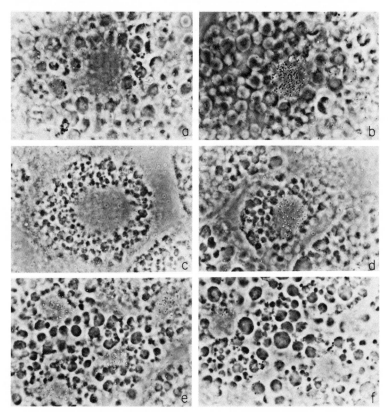

FIGURE 16. Radioautographs of RNA synthesis in *Xenopus* embryo cells. Intranuclear labeling is demonstrated in various regions at various stages: (a) presumptive endodermal cell, stage 7; (b) endodermal cell, stage 8½; (c) equatorial cell, stage 8; (d) equatorial cell, stage 8½; (e) inner equatorial cell, stage 9; (f) same as e, except treated with ribonuclease. Bachvarova, R., and Davidson, E. H., *J. Exptl. Zool.* **163,** 285 (1966).

ring between mid- and late blastulation. Pulse-labeled, high molecular weight RNA from the early gastrula sediments in a heterogeneous, nonribosomal fashion, as shown in the gradient (Fig. 17b) and as found also by Brown and Littna (91). This RNA tends to be DNA-like in base composition. It seems likely that in the widespread and sudden arousal of the embryo revealed by these studies we are observing the pregastrular genomic readout on which gastrulation depends. From the point of view of embryo genome function this is clearly a very significant step; utilization of the genetic messages elaborated as a result of blastular activation will slowly establish the directional relation between genome function and cell differentiation which is to last from that point forward. In the late blastula, as both the radioautographic

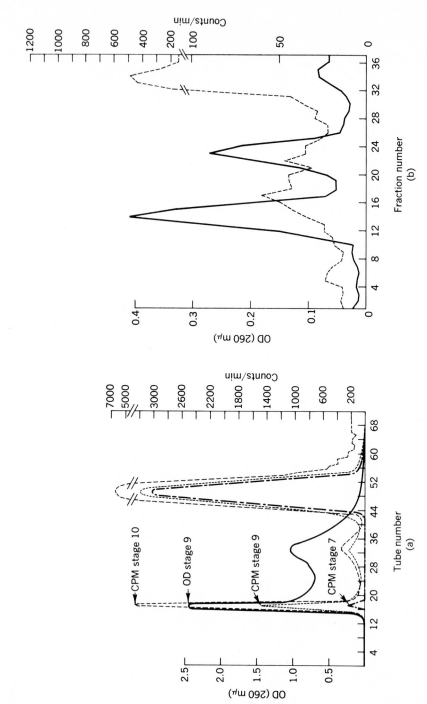

studies of Bachvarova *et al.* (93, 103) and the biochemical investigations of Woodland and Gurdon (94) indicate, the various regions of the embryo are already carrying out RNA synthesis at their own characteristic and different rates, and this in itself is a clear index of differential early gene expression.

It can be seen from Fig. 17a that transfer RNA synthesis as well as high molecular weight RNA synthesis is activated between stage 8 (midblastula) and stage 9 (late blastula). This observation has been corroborated by Brown and Littna (101) and by Woodland and Gurdon (94).

the amount of the genome active in the early morphogenesis of Xenopus: RNA-DNA hybridization studies

From the data we have so far reviewed it is impossible to ascertain the range of genomic information represented in the RNA's synthesized in the early embryo. It is known only that these RNA's are sufficiently diverse and numerous to give the population of newly synthesized RNA molecules an average nucleotide base composition tending to resemble that of the total DNA, and that all molecular size classes are demonstrable in the usual sucrose gradients. A significant addition to this knowledge has recently been provided by Denis (104), who has attempted to measure the actual percentage of the genome functional at successive stages of embryogenesis in *Xenopus*. These experiments are carried out with a RNA-DNA hybridization technique in which denatured DNA is immobilized in agar, and at the appropriate salt concentration and temperature labeled RNA is permitted to anneal with the DNA. Ribonucleic acid molecules bearing polynucleotide sequences complementary to sequences in the agar-bound DNA are able to form stable hybrids, a condition which will evidently be fulfilled when the DNA molecules present in the annealing mixture include replicas of the genes serving originally as the DNA templates for the RNA's. If labeled RNA is added to excess, i.e., until no further hybridization occurs with increasing RNA input, and if the specific activity of the hybridizing RNA is known, the mass of RNA hybridized per unit amount of DNA can be calculated from the hybridized counts. This value serves as a measure of the percentage of the genome

FIGURE 17. (a) Sephadex G-100 elution pattern of uridine-^{3}H-labeled RNA from embryos of different stages. The first optical density peak is primarily owing to carrier yeast bulk RNA, and the second to yeast transfer-RNA marker which had been added to the final RNA solution. (b) Sedimentation pattern of uridine-^{3}H-labeled RNA from early gastrulae in a 5–20% sucrose gradient. (Dashed line) acid-insoluble counts/min.; Solid line (OD at 260 mμ). Modified from Bachvarova, R., Davidson, E. H., Allfrey, V. G., and Mirsky, A. E., *Proc. Natl. Acad. Sci. U.S.* **55**, 358 (1966).

functional in the cells from which the labeled RNA has been extracted. In the case of the informational RNA synthesized in the embryogenesis of *Xenopus* the specific activity and quantity of this class of gene products can be determined by measuring the specific activity of the precursor pool, as shown by Brown and Littna (102; cf. Fig. 15).

TABLE IV. Hybridizable RNA Present in Embryos of Different Stages[a]

Stage	Type of labeling	Saturation of DNA (%)
12 Gastrula	^{32}P	2.4
	^{14}CO$_2$ 11 hr	2.4
26–28 Tail-bud embryo	^{32}P	5.0
	^{14}CO$_2$ 11 hr	3.0
39–42 Swimming tadpole	^{32}P	8.5
	^{14}CO$_2$ 11 hr	1.8

[a] From Ref. 104.

Denis has utilized such calculations to convert embryo RNA counts hybridized with *Xenopus* DNA at saturation to percent of DNA hybridized, and the results for various stages of development are presented in Table IV (104). The table shows the percentage hybridization for RNA preparations labeled cumulatively by ^{32}P injection into gravid females from ovulation onward, and for RNA labeled within an 11–hour exposure to ^{14}CO$_2$ at the stages of development noted. To obtain the *percentage of the genome functional* from the percentage of DNA hybridized it is necessary to double the latter values, since only one strand of DNA is functional in RNA synthesis (105–107). If taken literally the data of Table IV show that as the embryo proceeds from gastrulation through neurulation to the tail-bud stage and beyond, there is a progressive increase in the total amount of genomic information used. The cumulatively labeled tadpole appears to have utilized some 17% of the information in the genome, as opposed to only 5% utilized by late gastrulation. However, the values obtained for the more briefly labeled (^{14}C) embryos fail to show this increase, and it is to be concluded that different sets of genes must be used at different stages of development. Thus even though according to Table IV no more than 4–6% of the genomic information is in transcription at any one time (i.e., during an 11–hour labeling period), the sum of the diverse active DNA fractions over time amounts eventually to 3–4 times the value for any one period.

In considering these experiments the crucial question is the degree of confidence one can attach to the quantitative results of the RNA-DNA hybridization procedures employed. Throughout this book we shall be referring to data obtained with this powerful technique, and it is thus of some value to pause briefly in order to discuss the strengths and limitations of the current hybridization methodology. In general, RNA-DNA hybridization has been the subject of various criticisms, and it is certainly clear that if improperly used it can yield misleading results. Objections to the use of RNA-DNA hybridization procedures in studies dealing with informational RNA fall into several categories. One objection is that RNA-DNA hybridization may not be specific. Comparison of the ability of RNA's from different organisms to form stable hybrids with DNA from one organism shows that RNA-DNA hybrids are specific, however, at least at the level of familial discrimination.

Denis, for instance, in a paper accompanying that cited above (107a), has demonstrated that with the technique he employs, RNA from *Xenopus* hybridizes poorly with DNA from animals of other genera, even from other organisms of the same order (Salientia) such as *Rana pipiens*, and not at all with DNA from distantly related organisms. Observations to the effect that RNA from distantly related organisms fails to hybridize appreciably with DNA from some given organism under conditions permitting homospecific RNA to hybridize well have been reported by many other investigators. On the other hand, the specificity of the RNA-DNA hybridization reaction can scarcely be considered absolute; i.e., the method cannot be expected to distinguish among almost but not quite completely complementary RNA and DNA stretches. The actual quantitative limits of the hybridization method remain to be determined in terms of the average number of noncomplementary base pairs which can be tolerated for a given length of polynucleotide without resulting in hybrid instability under set conditions of temperature and salt concentration.

It has recently become apparent that the DNA of metazoan organisms contains extensive regions of *partial internal homology,* a discovery of basic interest resulting mainly from the work of Britten and his associates (108). This conclusion follows from the observations that denatured animal cell DNA reassociates at rates which are orders of magnitude greater than the rate of reassociation of nonredundant ("single-copy") DNA (108). Furthermore, the rapidly reassociating hybrids tend to possess relatively low thermal stability compared to native DNA (108–110). It is evident that in animal cells *an important fraction of the DNA is organized into large families of nearly homologous genes* in which most but not all of the nucleotide sequence is repeated in each member of the family. There also exist certain highly repetitive DNA fractions, e.g., mouse satellite DNA, which reassociates to form DNA-DNA hybrids of high thermal stability, and the more perfect base pairing in such hybrids can be taken as an index of a higher degree of homology within the families of genes constituting the DNA fraction. Britten and Kohne have found that regions of partial internal homology are present in the genomes of every animal and plant investigated, but repetitive regions apparently do not exist in bacterial genomes (108). Like the total DNA of *E.coli* the nonrepetitive or single copy DNA of animal cells reassociates slowly to form hybrids whose stability, i.e., perfection of base pairing, approximates that of native DNA. In the mouse nonrepetitive DNA accounts for some 70% of the DNA in terms of quantity per genome, and the partially homologous fraction accounts for about 15%. These values vary widely, however, depending on the organism (108): The single-copy fraction of bovine DNA amounts to less than 60% of the total, while in salmon DNA it appears that less than 10% is nonrepetitive.

Several investigators have pointed out that RNA-DNA hybrids might form between the gene products of any portion of an internally homologous family of genes and the DNA of other genes within this family (e.g., 108, 111). It thus becomes important to judge whether a significant part of the RNA-DNA hybridization registered in excess RNA saturation experiments could result from partial matching of RNA with DNA which is of the same internally redundant family of genes but is different from the particular member of that family which served originally as template for the hybridizing RNA. The true percentage of DNA functional in the synthesis of the RNA's tested might then be lower than that calculated from the saturation experiment. The extent to which DNA-RNA hybrids obtained in any given experiment will belong to the redundant as opposed to the single-copy class depends on many variables. These include the genomic characteristics of the organism employed, the copy number of the hybridizing RNA species, the nucleic acid concentrations, the salt concentration, the time and temperature of annealing, and the use of ribonuclease after annealing to destroy imperfectly hybridized RNA stretches. Higher nucleic acid concentrations and longer annealing times are required in order for single-copy genomic sites to hybridize (108), simply because of the greater diversity of the information involved and the consequently greater rarity of each matching nucleic acid species. Furthermore, the size and informational complexity of the genome *in toto* (and in RNA-DNA hybridization the complexity of the *active* fraction of the DNA) will affect the conditions required to obtain maximum hybridization, as Britten and Kohne have clearly pointed out (108).

In hybridization experiments carried out in the presence of excess DNA the major part of the RNA hybridized is likely to consist of the most frequent RNA species, the latter term denoting any RNA molecules able to hybridize with a given gene or with a given internally homologous family of genes. If, however, the hybridization is carried out as in Table IV, with a saturating excess of RNA, distortion of the distribution of hybridizing RNA species because of inequalities in the copy number of the species is minimized. Nonetheless, much or all of the DNA hybridized will belong to the redundant portion of the genome, and the percent of DNA hybridized in the saturation experiment therefore cannot be translated directly into the number of diverse genes expressed. Such a translation would require at minimum knowledge of the degrees of redundancy of the hybridizing families of genes. It is evident that in all of the RNA-DNA hybridization studies with animal cells cited in this review the hybridization conditions actually employed are such that at least the major part of the RNA hybridized is bound to redundant rather than single-copy portions of the genome (108).

The conclusions drawn from these studies thus refer mainly or exclusively to the activity of the internally redundant fraction of the genome. Now it is clear that changes of gene activity associated with differentiation are detectable with these same RNA-DNA hybridization procedures, both in comparisons among different tissues (e.g., 15, 29, 29a, 30) and among different states of the same tissue (e.g., 110, 112). Qualitative changes in the informational RNA content of differentiating cells therefore cannot be attributed solely to changes in the spectrum of gene products produced *within* partially homologous families of genes; were this the case the RNA populations associated with diverse states of differentiation could probably never have been distinguished under the annealing conditions customarily employed. It is thus evident that differentiation involves change in activity *among* the internally redundant families of genes, so that the *function of a different set of internally homologous gene families is associated with each state of differentiation.* The demonstration of this is in the striking alterations in pattern of gene activity actually observed in the hybridization studies cited above, in various other investigations described in Section IV, and in the hybridization experiments to be discussed here (e.g., see Figs. 20 and 21). Such experiments cannot have detected *intra*family changes in gene activity and they are relatively (or completely) unlikely to have monitored alterations in the spectrum of activity of the single-copy portion of the genome.

Given adequate annealing time, RNA concentration, etc., the single-copy portion of the animal cell genome of course hybridizes with its RNA gene products just as does the redundant portion at shorter times and lower concentrations (108b). Specific DNA-DNA reassociation in single-copy animal cell DNA has been demonstrated by Britten and Kohne (108, 108a), and cases of RNA hybridization with single-copy DNA are available in studies with bacterial material. As noted above the bacterial genome appears to lack the large, internally redundant regions common to all higher organisms, but because of the smaller size and lesser complexity of the bacterial genome, reassociation of its single-copy DNA occurs at a rate hundreds of times faster than does reassociation of animal cell single-copy DNA (108). Reassociation, or RNA-DNA hybridization, can therefore be monitored in bacterial material without employing the very high concentrations and long annealing times required in order to study the hybridization of animal cell single-copy DNA. Furthermore, it can be demonstrated that hybridization of homologous RNA with bacterial DNA proceeds until the maximum theoretical saturation ratio of RNA to DNA in the hybrids is attained. Thus saturation of bacterial DNA with metabolically labeled RNA at close to a 0.5 RNA/DNA ratio has been reported for at least two species of bacteria [(113, 114): see Section IV for detailed discussion of these studies]. Since only one strand of the DNA is functional in RNA synthesis, 50% saturation of the DNA indicates that 100% of the genomic information is present in the hybridizing RNA populations. It is empirically clear, therefore, that hybridization can proceed to absolute saturation in the annealing systems used, even where the DNA is of the single-copy class.

To summarize this digression: The RNA-DNA hybridization procedure is sufficiently specific to distinguish sharply the RNA populations of genera as closely related as *Xenopus* and *Rana*, just as it can distinguish the spectra of informational RNA's present in different tissues of the same organism. The technique cannot, however, be expected to distinguish among nearly identical polynucleotides. This limitation could conceivably affect the absolute accuracy of determinations by the excess RNA saturation method of the percentage of the genome which is active in a given circumstance, since the RNA could hybridize with genes of an internally replicate gene family other than those genes actually responsible for its synthesis. Redundancy in the hybridizing DNA fraction could thus result in a limited overestimation of the proportions of the genome actually active. However, except in saturating experiments in which higher concentrations and longer annealing times than usual are employed, the proportion of the genome active may be considerably underestimated because of failure to monitor single-copy DNA hybridization. The length of annealing time and nucleic acid concentration required in order to obtain hybridization within the single-copy portion of the genome will depend, if other parameters are held equal, on the genome size of the organism. Thus failure to discriminate at the *intragene* family level and partial failure to monitor hybridization of the single-copy portion of the genome both affect the interpretation of experimental data regarding the apparent percentage of the genome active. Neither source of difficulty, however, need directly affect comparisons of the relative amount of the genome active at successive stages of differentiation in the same tissues. Though it is primarily the activity of the internally redundant gene families which is monitored in the hybridization studies we are now to consider, *it is clear that sharp changes in the pattern of activity among these families occur in differentiation.* Analysis of the spectrum of activity in the redundant portion of the genome is therefore of fundamental importance in the study of differentiation.

These arguments lead to the conclusion that the data of Table IV provide a useful index of the relative diversity of gene transcription as development proceeds. As the variable gene activity theory of cell differentiation would predict, development involves the utilization of different sets of genes at different times. Recent measurements in the writer's laboratory suggest that about 55% of the *Xenopus* genome consists of unique sequences, the remaining 45% being composed of internally redundant sequences. Hybridization in the experiments of Table IV is confined to this redundant fraction. The data of Table IV show that under half (17%/45%) of this 45% of the genome could have been functional by the swimming tadpole stage (if all the genes of each active family were active), i.e., that even with all the hundreds of thousands of cells of the embryo cumulatively considered, a large fraction of the redundant gene families has so far remained repressed. Similarly, at any one stage, at least 80 or 90% of the genomic information included in the redundant portion of the genome appears not to be in use. Another interesting point illustrated in Table IV is the fact that the amount of DNA registered as functional during gastrulation (2.4%) is already close to the highest level recorded for any period up to the tadpole stage. This recalls the finding of Brown and Littna (102) that the mass of newly synthesized informational RNA per cell also attains its maximum value during gastrulation (Fig. 15).

change in the informational content of the newly synthesized embryo RNA's

In an effort to gain further insight into the patterns of gene expression during early development, Denis has performed competition hybridization experiments in which the degree of homology between the population of RNA's present at one stage and the population of RNA's in synthesis at another stage is tested. These experiments are carried out by annealing a constant amount of labeled RNA from a given stage of development with a large excess of DNA in the presence of increasing amounts of unlabeled RNA from embryos of different stages. If the unlabeled or competing RNA contains molecules homologous with those of the labeled preparation, then "competition" for the DNA sites will occur and this will result in an apparent decrease in the hybridization of the labeled RNA, the extent of which is a direct function of the ratio of competing to labeled or "reference" RNA in the annealing mixture.

Denis' experiments indicate that the degree of competition increases as the newly synthesized reference RNA and the unlabeled competing RNA preparation are drawn from embryos at closer stages of development. Thus there appears to be more homology in the RNA populations from adjacent than from distant stages. Radioactive reference RNA from the swimming tadpole stage is not competed with at all by RNA from blastulae, for example, while RNA from gastrulae, neurulae, and tail-bud stage embryos competes with increasing success. Similarly, the hybridization of RNA in synthesis during gastrulation is not affected by the presence of blastular RNA, illustrating the novelty of the gene activity patterns which set in at gastrulation, and RNA from neurulae competes with the gastrular reference RNA better than RNA from later stages. It is concluded from this set of experiments that some genes (or members of internally homologous families of genes) are functional throughout embryogenesis, from gastrulation on; that some are functional in gastrulation and neurulation but are not functional at later stages; and that in each later stage a certain group of genes (or families of genes) is functional for a while but is later repressed as development advances.

The competition experiments of Denis are not carried out under saturation conditions, and therefore excess DNA sites are present even after all the possible reference RNA is hybridized. This is an interesting point, for it renders the meaning of the experiments somewhat different than would be the case were the experiment carried out in the presence of saturating RNA and limited DNA. In the presence of excess DNA reference RNA species present in a large number of copies will be hybridized in an amount disproportionately greater than the percentage of the genome complementary to them. Since the amount of reference RNA replaced by competing unlabeled RNA is strictly a function of the ratio of unlabeled to reference RNA, a competition experiment carried out under conditions of excess DNA mainly portrays competition for those genomic sites represented in the RNA population in the largest number of copies. While this is perhaps useful in comparing overall homology between RNA populations, it evidently distorts the competition results in the direction of relative insensitivity to relatively rare species in the reference RNA population, and oversensitivity to frequent species in the reference RNA population.

The results of nonsaturation competition experiments, as Denis himself has pointed out [(104); see also the discussion of this problem by Crippa et al. (115)], are for this reason somewhat "ambiguous" in that the degree of competition observed depends on both the qualitative diversity of the RNA molecules present and the quantitative frequency of appearance of each species of RNA. A safe conclusion from the competition experiments of Denis would be that progressive changes occur in the distribution of at least the more frequently present species of RNA as embryogenesis proceeds. That these changes indeed reflect alterations in the pattern of gene activity characteristic of each particular stage of development is made likely by the saturation experiments summarized in Table IV. Additional evidence is provided by another set of experiments in which a small amount of DNA is presaturated with unlabeled gastrular RNA, then exposed to labeled RNA in nonsaturating amounts from tail-bud and tadpole stages. The apparent hybridization level is found to be decreased by the presaturation treatment by 54% and 18%, respectively, a finding which again suggests that some genes functional at gastrulation are still represented in the tail-bud embryo, while less are represented in the tadpole.

Another study employing hybridization to investigate changes in the spectrum of genes functional during amphibian embryogenesis has been reported by Flickinger, Greene, Kohl, and Miyagi (116). Here embryos are bisected at the blastula stage into animal and vegetal halves, and the RNA is extracted after a 24-hour labeling period. Bisected embryo halves continue to carry out the processes of gastrular morphogenesis, at least in *Xenopus* (103). A small quantity of DNA is saturated with RNA from either animal or vegetal halves under annealing conditions in these experiments, and the filters bearing the DNA are then exposed to additional labeled RNA from the same or the opposite embryo halves. The results constitute a demonstration that partially different sets (families) of genes are functional in the animal and vegetal halves during the 24-hour labeling period, for in each case addition of the RNA preparation other than that used to presaturate the DNA results in an increase in total hybridization, while the controls show no increase. In other words the dissimilar RNA preparation, whether from animal or vegetal halves, contains gene products not represented in the presaturating preparation. These data further strengthen the view that the basic regulatory phenomenon in early embryonic differentiation is the regulation of patterns of gene transcription, as Flickinger and his associates have pointed out, since different genes are evidently active in embryonic tissues undergoing different courses of differentiation.

Recent findings in *Xenopus* demonstrate that totally novel patterns of gene activity are imposed as early as the mid-to-late blastular period. Hybridization experiments carried out in the writer's laboratory (117) with the saturation competition procedure prove that the RNA species in synthesis at this time are qualitatively novel to the embryo, not being represented in the populations of RNA present in the unfertilized egg or in the early blastula. Furthermore, most of the species of informational RNA in synthesis between mid- and late blastula are special to that stage of development, only a minority fraction remaining present in the early gastrula. A stage-specific pattern of gene activity thus exists several hours before the onset of visible differentiation in *Xenopus*, and this pattern is evidently subject to rapid alteration. These features correlate with the evidence from actinomycin and other experiments demonstrating that the program for gastrular differentiation begins to be transcribed during blastulation.

At this point, before entering on discussion of the equivalent studies with echinoderms, it is perhaps useful to summarize the main points of information deriving from these direct investigations of gene action during amphibian embryogenesis:

(1) There exists an early synthesis of informational RNA, which increases slowly in intensity from cleavage to midblastulation. After this, during blastulation, an abrupt, embryo-wide increase in gene transcription occurs, and informational RNA synthesis rates increase at least 20-fold. The newly synthesized RNA's contain a novel program of genetic information. By mid-gastrulation informational RNA content per cell has attained the values which will persist through the remainder of early development. Transfer RNA synthesis becomes activated as well during the mid-to-late blastular activation period.

(2) With gastrulation the previously quiescent synthesis of ribosomal RNA is initiated. Before this time the embryo depends exclusively on ribosomes inherited from oogenesis, and these continue to constitute the bulk of the working ribosomes until much later in development. New ribosomal RNA does not become an essential requirement until the hatching tadpole stage.

(3) As early as the mid-to-late blastular period, qualitative differentiation of the patterns of gene activity has set in in the various embryonic cell nuclei. The progression of embryogenesis is thus associated with changes in the distribution of gene products, only partly overlapping from stage to stage, and with the utilization of an ever greater range of genomic information as measured cumulatively.

(4) During the pregastrular period morphogenesis appears to be carried out independently of the simultaneously occurring synthesis of new RNA's in the blastomere nuclei, and it is apparent that the embryo inherits from the unfertilized egg whatever species of gene products are needed for the programming and execution of early morphogenesis.

FIGURE 18. Proposed scheme for the coordinated consumption of egg ribosomes and the synthesis of new ribosomes in the course of development. (Solid line with crosses) ribosomal RNA content; (solid line with filled circles) surviving egg ribosomal RNA content, obtained as the product of the total ribosomal RNA (solid line with crosses); the proportion of 13S ribosomal RNA taken to represent RNA of egg origin (insert). The difference between these curves is the estimate of new ribosomal RNA synthesis (dashed line). Insert: semilog plot of the content of surviving egg ribosomal RNA. After the 20-hour stage, the rate of decay of this content obeys first-order kinetics with a half-life of 18 hours. Nemer, M., and Infante, A. A., J. Mol. Biol. 27, 73 (1967).

informational and ribosomal RNA synthesis in the early sea urchin embryo

The course of early morphogenesis in the sea urchin is very different from that in amphibians, the form of the echinoderm blastula and gastrula bearing little resemblance to that generally characteristic of higher deuterostomes.

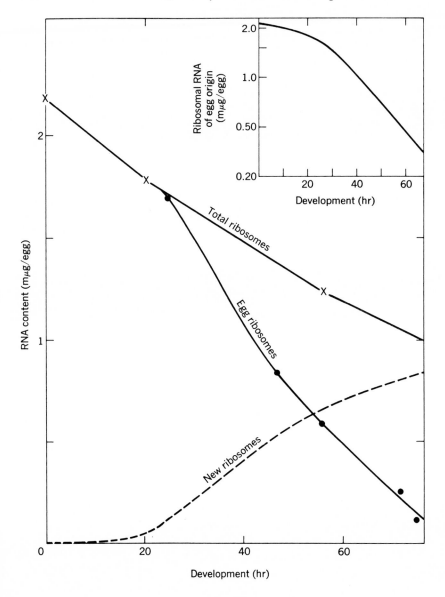

Furthermore, at least in some species of echinoderm, differentiated primary mesenchyme cells delaminate long in advance of gastrulation per se, and this event has no obvious parallel in chordate blastulation. The total number of cells in the embryo is also orders of magnitude greater at gastrulation in amphibians than in echinoderms. It is remarkable, therefore, that the underlying patterns of gene activity in these two groups display as strong a conformity to the same general pattern as they do. Having considered in some detail the nature of early RNA synthesis in amphibian embryos we turn now to parallel studies which have been carried out with early embryos of the sea urchin, in order to document the generality of this pattern.

In the sea urchin embryo the maternal ribosomal RNA content (i.e., the bulk RNA of the egg) declines until the onset of new ribosomal RNA synthesis. This decline has been noted by Comb and his associates (118, 119) and by Nemer and Infante (120), who have utilized what is possibly a mutant genetic trait carried by certain individual females of *Stronglocentrotus purpuratus* to study directly the fate of the inherited ribosomal RNA. Eggs from these females contain ribosomal RNA in which the 18S component can be split into two 13S fragments by heating briefly to 60°C; since the embryos developing from these eggs synthesize normal ribosomal RNA, this thermal fragility characteristic may be used as a marker with which to study the eventual disposition of maternal ribosomal RNA. Nemer and Infante found that the *concentration* of the aberrant ribosomal RNA species does not alter from cleavage to the mesenchyme blastula stage, showing that there is no dilution of the maternal ribosomal RNA by newly synthesized embryo ribosomal RNA during this period. Thereafter, however, such a dilution appears to take place, and by the late gastrula stage only about 50% of the embryo ribosomes are of egg origin. These relationships are diagrammed in Fig. 18, taken from the study of Nemer and Infante (120).

A direct implication of this investigation is that ribosomal RNA synthesis is absent or insignificant during the cleavage and premesenchyme blastula stages. In the sea urchin the embryo genome begins to carry out a small amount of heterogeneously sedimenting, DNA-like RNA synthesis early in cleavage, which increases in rate with the progress of development. Sedimentation analyses of this early informational RNA synthesis have been described by Wilt (121, 122), Nemer (123, 124), and various other investigators (e.g., 62, 125). In Fig. 19 (125) the heterodisperse nature of the RNA in synthesis in the mesenchyme blastula of *Sphaerechinus granularis* is displayed, and the cited studies show that the rate of synthesis of this class of molecule increases with gastrulation, as in the amphibian embryo. Gross, Kraemer, and Malkin (126) and Comb, Katz, Branda, and Pinzino (119) have reported base compositional analyses of the RNA in synthesis at various stages of development

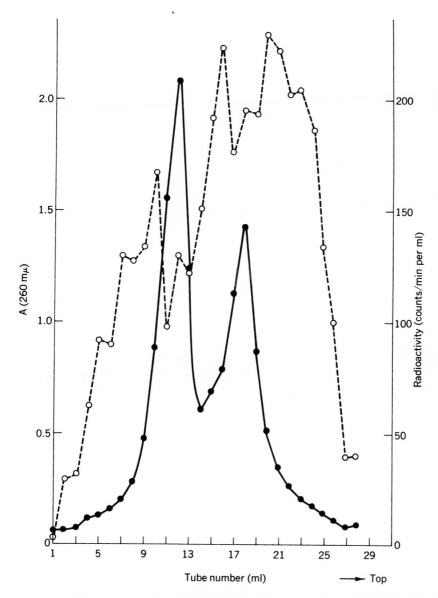

FIGURE 19. Density-gradient centrifugation of radioactive RNA. Mesenchyme blastula embryos were incubated for 23 minutes with 16 μC of uridine-^{3}H and cytidine-^{3}H, and the RNA extracted. Centrifugation at 25,000 rpm for 14 hours. (Dashed line with open circles) radioactivity; (solid line with filled circles) A$_{260}$. Siekevitz, P., Maggio, R., and Catalano, C., *Biochim. Biophys. Acta* **129**, 145 (1966).

in sea urchins, and their data show that it is impossible to detect significant ribosomal RNA labeling during cleavage and blastulation.

Furthermore, Comb (127) has demonstrated that newly incorporated methyl groups (using methionine-$^{14}CH_3$ as donor) are not detectable in ribosomal RNA until postgastrulation (pluteus), a further item of evidence in favor of the delayed onset of ribosomal RNA synthesis. In this important characteristic, then, the pattern of gene activity in the echinoderm embryo appears to parallel that demonstrated for the amphibian embryo: The protein synthesis required for cleavage and blastulation must be carried out solely on maternal ribosomes, and the embryo genome begins to produce its own ribosomal RNA only after the completion of cleavage and the formation of a blastula. Exactly when ribosomal RNA synthesis in the sea urchin embryo is initiated remains somewhat unclear, however. Perhaps the most direct evidence is that derived by Nemer and Infante in the study cited above (120) in which maternal ribosomal RNA is found to be diluted (with new ribosomal RNA) from the mesenchyme blastula stage onward. Base composition and sedimentation studies show clearly that synthesis of ribosomal RNA is active after gastrulation (122, 123, 127a). Comb and his associates, utilizing MAK columns for the analysis of RNA's extracted directly from the ribosomal cell fraction, likewise observe synthesis of RNA's eluting with the ribosomal peak and bearing a high G-C base composition in gastrulation (119).

All studies agree that by the pluteus stage RNA with the sedimentation, MAK elution, and base composition characteristics of ribosomal RNA is a major component of the newly synthesized RNA. Neither sucrose gradient nor MAK column chromatography permit the clear separation of ribosomal RNA from other high molecular weight RNA's, however, and the extent to which the ribosomal components must predominate before they can be detected by these methods cannot easily be determined. The direct biochemical studies thus fail to provide evidence for ribosomal RNA synthesis quite as early as the mesenchyme blastula stage, the initiation point for this species of gene activity according to the dilution experiments of Nemer and Infante (120). A further important item of evidence here is the observation of Cowden and Lehman (128) that nucleoli first make their appearance in the sea urchin embryo at the very early gastrula stage, and this shows that the cytological basis exists for the onset of ribosomal RNA synthesis only this early in development, at least in *Lytechinus variegatus*. However, in another species, *Arbacia lixula*, nucleoli are reported much earlier, according to Millonig (129).

Comb and his associates have also studied transfer RNA synthesis in the sea urchin and have demonstrated clearly that the onset of synthesis of this species of RNA occurs at gastrulation (119). The 5S ribosomal RNA synthesis appears to follow the same pattern (119). These observations also depend on the application of the MAK column, which yields a complete separation of these low molecular weight RNA's.

To the extent that the comparison can be made, certain detailed differences between the echinoderm and amphibian exist in the timing of onset of the various classes of RNA synthesis. In the echinoderm embryo ribosomal RNA synthesis appears at least in certain species to begin before gastrulation, at the mesenchyme blastula stage, while transfer and 5S RNA synthesis start during gastrulation. In the amphibian *Xenopus*, however, ribosomal RNA synthesis begins in the gastrula and transfer RNA synthesis occurs earlier, at the time of massive gene transcription occurring in the mid-to-late blastular period. Nonetheless, the main impression is one of basic similarity. Thus blastular gene activity in the amphibian plays the same role in programming gastrular morphogenesis as does gene activity during the midblastula stage in the echinoderm; informational RNA synthesis begins early in cleavage in both groups; and the onset of ribosomal RNA synthesis is delayed, as is the onset of transfer RNA synthesis. Furthermore, if we consider that the mesenchyme blastula of the sea urchin is the stage at which *de novo* differentiation of a mesodermal cell type first occurs, then the beginning of ribosomal RNA synthesis at this time is actually in accordance with the amphibian example since the corresponding event, appearance of mesoderm, begins only with gastrulation in amphibians.

change in the patterns of transcription during early echinoderm development

There exist at present two reports which provide some insight into the qualitative nature of the changes in informational RNA synthesis occurring during sea urchin embryogenesis, viz., Glisin, Glisin, and Doty (130) and Whiteley, McCarthy, and Whiteley (131). The first of these is among the few RNA-DNA hybridization studies in the embryological literature carried out under saturating RNA conditions. In this investigation saturating levels of labeled RNA from the hatching blastula stage are hybridized with DNA in the presence of increasing quantities of competing, nonlabeled RNA from other stages. Homology between the unlabeled and the labeled preparations is thus displayed as an apparent decrease in the amount of labeled RNA hybridized. The results of the experiment are shown in Fig. 20 (130). The competition curves indicate that genes functional in the hatching blastula stage had been functional even before fertilization, since RNA's homologous to those in synthesis at blastulation are present in unfertilized eggs, and it is also evident that the same genes (or internally homologous families of genes) continue to be functional throughout the rest of blastulation. It is important to note in

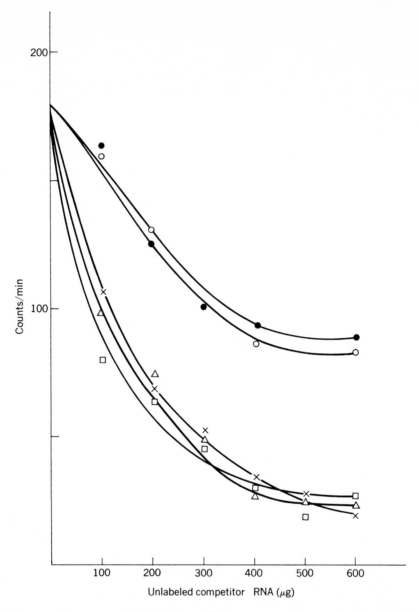

FIGURE 20. Comparison of RNA's from different stages of sea urchin development. Unlabeled RNA samples prepared from different stages of development were compared by determining their apparent inhibition of hybridization between 100 μg of labeled hatching blastula RNA and 2 μg of DNA: (Open triangle) hatching blastula; (open square) 2 hours after hatching; (cross) unfertilized egg; (filled circle) gastrula; (open circle) prism stage. Glisin, V. R., Glisin, M. V., and Doty, P., *Proc. Natl. Acad. Sci. U.S.* **56,** 285 (1966).

this connection that the patterns of *protein synthesis* in the sea urchin are also essentially the same in late oogenesis as in early embryogenesis. Ozaki, Piatagorsky, and Tyler (132) have shown this in an electrophoretic comparison of the proteins labeled in oocytes by intracoelomic injection of radioactive amino acids and the proteins made in the early embryo. Figure 20 also indicates that as development progresses some of the early genes active in both oogenesis and cleavage are shut off and the RNA they have produced

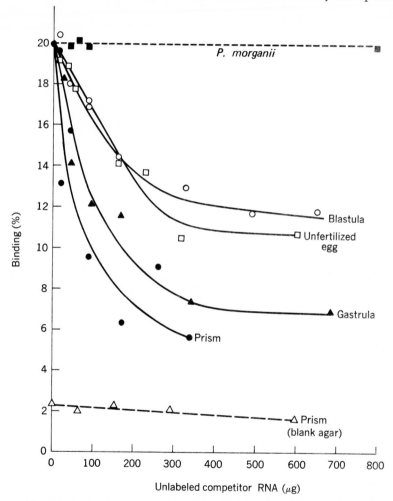

FIGURE 21. Competition by unlabeled RNA from various developmental stages in the binding of ³²P-labeled prism RNA to DNA-agar. Four micrograms ³²P-labeled *S. purpuratus* prism RNA, unlabeled competitor RNA as shown, *S. purpuratus* DNA-agar containing 110 μg DNA, or agar lacking DNA (bottom curve). Whiteley, A. H., McCarthy, B. J., and Whiteley, H. R., *Proc. Natl. Acad. Sci. U.S.* **55,** 519 (1966).

is degraded, since unlabeled gastrular and prism stage RNA fails to compete as efficiently with newly synthesized blastular RNA. The results obtained by Whiteley *et al.* (131) correlate well with these conclusions, although their competition experiments are carried out in the presence of excess DNA, and are consequently more likely to measure changes in relative frequency (i.e., number of copies) of the more common RNA species present as well as qualitative changes in the spectrum of RNA's available. Using radioactive prism-stage RNA as the reference RNA, Whiteley *et al.* found that unlabeled RNA from increasingly later stages competes increasingly well, so that the RNA's present in the gastrula compete almost as well as unlabeled prism-stage RNA. The experiment is shown in Fig. 21 (131). It can be concluded from this experiment that the qualitative plus quantitative distribution of RNA molecules, ultimately a function of gene activity, is specific for each passing stage of development in the sea urchin. According to other experiments published in the same report (131) a set of genes (or families of genes) exists which is functional during the prism stage and is also functional in a variety of adult tissues. In a closely related study the template activity of sea urchin embryo chromatin has been shown to increase as development proceeds. Marushige and Osaki (132a) have reported that pluteus chromatin supports significantly more RNA synthesis with exogenous polymerase than does blastula chromatin. Thus, as in the amphibian, more genomic information would appear to be made available for transcription at later stages of development than is in use in the pregastrular period.

In general the sea urchin hybridization experiments show that the prism and the hatching blastula stage are both characterized by a particular, though partially overlapping, spectrum of gene activity, and this will obviously be true for other stages as well. A paticularly interesting point revealed by the experiment of Fig. 20 is the existence of early genes functional only before gastrulation, and apparently even before fertilization, in oogenesis. No parallel observations yet exist for amphibian material. Except for this, however, the conclusions of Glisin *et al.* and of Whiteley *et al.* are essentially similar to those drawn from Denis' more extensive studies with *Xenopus*.

patterns of early gene activity in other deuterostomes

Ribonucleic acid synthesis patterns in the early development of teleosts have also been investigated, mainly by Spirin and his associates. In general the same patterns of RNA synthesis appear to exist as in amphibian and echinoderm material, just as the phylogenetically intermediate position of the teleost might lead one to expect. Thus Belitsina, Aitkhozhin, Gavrilova, and Spirin (133) have demonstrated an early informational RNA synthesis during the blastula stage; according to these authors no RNA synthesis at all takes place earlier than the blastula stage. Methylated albumin-kieselguhr column and sucrose gradient separations of the newly synthesized RNA's at successive stages of development show that informational RNA synthesis increases continuously through the late gastrula period. However, synthesis of ribosomal RNA cannot be detected until after gastrulation by these methods. Aitkhozhin, Belitsina, and Spirin (134) have verified the absence of ribosomal RNA synthesis during earlier stages by demonstrating the failure of adenine-^{14}C and uridine-^{14}C to be incorporated into ribosomal RNA extracted directly from the embryo ribosome fraction, isolated after labeling from cleavage, blastula and gastrula stage embryos.

Under the conditions used in these experiments informational and transfer RNA label actively from these precursors (133). In the organism used for these studies, *Misgurnus fossilis*, nucleoli do not appear until the midblastula stage, according to Pankova (135), and it can be safely concluded that ribosomal RNA synthesis in *Misgurnus* conforms to the now familiar pattern of delayed onset until after the beginning of differentiation. Teleost development, as the reader will recall, occurs in a different manner than does most amphibian or echinoderm development. Rather than being included in large entoblasts which participate in cell division and morphogenesis, in teleosts the comparatively enormous yolky mass of the egg remains separated and noncellular during the period of germ layer formation. Aitkhozhin *et al.* (134) have shown that the ribosomal content of the embryo per se increases constantly throughout pregastrular development, but during the same period the *total* ribosomal RNA content of yolk plus embryo remains constant at about 2.2 μg/egg. The explanation of this apparent paradox is that during cleavage and blastulation ribosomes are transported from yolk to embryo. With the electron microscope, Aitkhozhin *et al.* have demonstrated an actual gradient of maternal ribosomes in the yolk, culminating in a densely packed ribosomal boundary layer continguous to the embryo. Transport of ribosomes from yolk to embryo in teleosts can be regarded as a special case of the general phenomenon of maternal ribosome utilization during early embryogenesis, one which represents a particular adaptation to the circumstances of meroblastic development.

Only sketchy data exist for other deuterostomes. We are lacking detailed biochemical studies of RNA synthesis pattern equivalent to those reviewed above for reptilian embroygenesis; nor do such studies exist for any of the hemichordates or cephalochordates. One report, that of Smith (69), indicates that heterogenously sedimenting RNA is synthesized as early as the 4-cell stage in the urochordate *Ascidia nigra*, while protein synthesis up to gastrulation in this species appears to be independent of early gene function. Organisms widely studied in other respects, such as the cephalochordate genus *Amphioxus*, have not lent themselves to molecular level investigations of RNA synthesis. The reasons for this include the difficulty of extricating the embryos from metabolically active accessory tissues, the presence of impermeable membranes rendering radioactive labeling of large numbers of embryos difficult, and various other more capricious factors such as the direction of interest of the workers who happen to be familiar with the organisms in question, etc. Somewhat more attention has been directed toward mammals and birds, however, and even on the basis of the few available studies of gene activity in mammalian and avian material it has become apparent that to assume that the echinoderm-teleost-amphibian pattern represents the whole of the deuterostome world is a serious error. One example is the timing of onset of ribosomal RNA synthesis in the chick. Lerner, Bell, and Darnell (136) have described the extraction and sedimentation analysis of RNA synthesized in the developing chick embryo, and their experimental results reveal an unmistakable and striking discrepancy with the lower chordates we have considered thus far: Ribosomal RNA in the chick is synthesized as early as 4–18 hours after fertilization, during early cleavage.

Three varieties of relevant evidence are so far available for mammalian material: actinomycin experiments, radioautographic observations of RNA synthesis, and observations on lethal mutants, in particular certain of the well-known t mutants in the mouse. Because the mammalian embryo is normally implanted in the uterine wall at a relatively early stage in development, most of the relevant studies concern only the cleavage and blastular stages. Techniques now exist permitting embryos of these stages to be maintained in vitro in the presence of relatively simple media (137, 138). Embryos temporarily maintained in this way can later be returned to the uterine environment, where they will successfully undergo implantation and continue their development, apparently unaffected by their brief sojourn in the artificial environment.

As is the case with amphibians and echinoderms, RNA synthesis begins at once in cleaving mammalian eggs. Figure 22, taken from a radioautographic investigation by Mintz (139), illustrates nuclear incorporation of uridine-^{3}H into RNA in the 2-cell embryo of the mouse. After this the rate of RNA synthesis increases continuously. Here, however, any resemblance to the other organisms we have so far mentioned ends. Mintz has shown that application of actinomycin to mammalian embryos at concentrations as low as those effective on tissue culture cells (e.g., < 0.1 μg/ml) blocks development at the 4-cell stage [(139); see also the study of Silagi (140)]. Cleavage and blastular morphogenesis in the mammal therefore appear to depend directly on the very early activity of the embryo genome and this represents a significant departure from the amphibian-teleost-echinoderm model. A second, and equally important, difference revealed by the radioautographic studies of Mintz is the appearance of nucleoli active in RNA synthesis as early as the 4-cell stage of cleavage (139). Actinomycin treat-

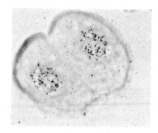

FIGURE 22. Two-cell mouse egg labeled with uridine-³H for 4 hours, ×480, Mintz, B., *J. Exptl. Zool.* **157**, 85 (1964).

ment appears preferentially to affect nucleolar RNA synthesis in cleaving mouse embryos just as it does in L cells (141). Thus 2-cell embryos treated with actinomycin fail to develop nucleoli, and nucleolar RNA synthesis in embryos exposed to marginally low levels of actinomycin is inhibited while extranucleolar RNA synthesis continues. Nucleolar activity in the early mouse embryo is shown in Fig. 23, taken from a recent study by Skalko (142). Mintz has also described shrinkage of nucleoli and loss of bulk

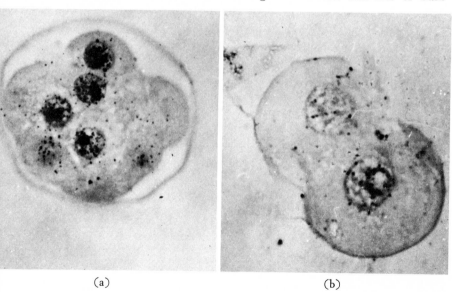

(a)   (b)

FIGURE 23. Radioautograph of (a) very early mouse embryo and (b) a morula exposed to uridine-³H for 1 hour *in vitro*. Note in (a) the immature cleavage nucleoli, with uptake of uridine into the RNA generally restricted to the heterochromatic nucleolar shell. The morula (b) contains intensely basophilic nucleoli, with intensive uridine incorporation. Skalko, R. G., Personal communication (1967).

nucleolar RNA in 8-cell embryos treated with actinomycin. Conceivably, therefore, the precocious sensitivity of the early mammalian embryo to actinomycin is related to the precocious synthesis of nucleolar RNA (presumably ribosomal RNA) in these embryos.

Studies with the lethal t^{12} mutation support the proposition that mammalian embryogenesis depends on embryo genome action throughout the pregastrular period (after the 2-cell stage, that is). This mutation, first described by Dunn and Glueckshohn-Waelsch (143), blocks the development of homozygous carriers earlier than the blastocyst stage (144), which in the mouse begins after only 5 cleavages. Thus t^{12}/t^{12} homozygotes arrest by the 30-cell stage. Mintz has shown that the bulk RNA content of t^{12}/t^{12} blastomeres fails to reach the level normally attained in cleavage (145) which indicates that the t^{12}-bearing genome is incapable of maintaining a normal level of ribosomal RNA synthesis during cleavage. Corroborating this interpretation is the observation that the rate of nucleolar RNA synthesis in cleavage stage t^{12}/t^{12} embryos is depressed (139). The t^{12} studies of Mintz thus serve to underline the dependence of bulk ribosomal RNA content in cleavage-stage mouse embryo blastomeres on early ribosomal RNA synthesis.

We thus have several lines of evidence which indicate that early gene products, including ribosomal RNA, are required by the mammalian embryo as soon as the 4-cell stage, and certainly by the 32-cell stage. This is not to say that the mammalian egg lacks the stores of maternal informational and ribosomal RNA verified for other eggs. Mintz reports that protein synthesis in the mouse embyro is extremely resistant to inhibition by actinomycin even at high doses, and this in itself suggests the ultization by the embryo of maternal template RNA and ribosomal RNA. The latter in any case cannot be synthesized by the embryo genome during the uncleaved or 2-cell stage, since nucleoli have not yet made their appearance, and the embryo is therefore obliged to depend exclusively on maternal ribosomal RNA for the first 2 days of its development. Note, incidentally, that 2 days is a much longer time than the period preceding the onset of ribosomal RNA synthesis in many amphibians or echinoderms, where gastrulation is under way or completed by 24 hours.

The correspondence between nucleolar appearance and the onset of ribosomal RNA synthesis has been clearly verified for amphibian, teleost, and echinoderm embryogenesis. If this relationship is a general one, we have access to a phylogenetically wider range of data in considering the embryonic activation of ribosomal RNA genes, for cytological observations on the stage at which nucleoli first appear have been published for virtually all major groups of deuterostome. A useful collection of relevant references is to be found in a recent paper by Brown (146). In tunicates (urochordata) the nucleolus fails to appear until quite late in development, in *Ascidia nigra* not until the whole larval period has elapsed and metamorphosis has begun (147). This provides a fascinating correlation, for as mentioned above both the species-hybrid and the actinomycin experiments of Reverberi (68) indicate that a very late stage of development, metamorphosis, is the point of onset of control over development by the embryo genome. In higher chordates (teleosts, amphibians) nucleoli appear earlier, either at or shortly before gastrulation. In light of this comparative data it is evident that the appearance of nucleoli in mammalian embryos early in cleavage, and of active nucleoli at that, represents a sharp deviation from the general deuterostome pattern. We shall return to the provocative differences which distinguish the course of gene activity in mammalian embryogenesis from that in their lower deuterostome relatives in a later section (Section IV).

pattern of early gene activity in protostomes

Except for cytological information regarding the appearance of nucleoli, one is again faced with a dearth of information in considering gene activity in the early development of protosomes. The available information, however, is sufficient to provide immediate notice that it is unsafe to generalize to protostomes conclusions drawn from studies on deuterostomes. For example, in at least four genera of mollusk, nucleoli have been observed during cleavage stages, viz., *Limnaea* (148), *Limax* (148), *Cyclops* (149), and *Ilyanassa* (150). Radioautographic data show that in the case of *Ilyanassa* these nucleoli are functional in RNA synthesis as early as the 16-cell stage. In other mollusks (*Helix*) nucleoli do not appear and become functional until the blastula stage (151) and the same is true in *Drosophila* where their appearance corresponds with the formation of the cellular blastoderm (152). There does not seem to be a general protostome pattern for the timing of nucleolar appearance, nor even a general molluskan pattern.

So far the lowest protostome in which embryonic RNA synthesis has been studied is *Ascaris lumbricoides,* the subject of an investigation by Kaulenas and Fairbairn (153). These workers have shown that synthesis of informational RNA, as defined by its identification as the ribonuclease-sensitive RNA of the embryonic polysomes, begins even before first cleavage in *Ascaris* eggs. As in other organisms transcription of genetic information accelerates in *Ascaris* embryos as development proceeds, judging from the increase in newly synthesized polysomal template RNA detected in blastulae. A striking deviation from the usual molecular pattern of events exists in *Ascaris,* however, according to more recent studies of Kaulenas and Fairbairn (142a). Active ribosomal RNA synthesis begins in this embryo immediately after fertilization, and even more remarkable, the site of this synthesis is the male pronucleus. Pronuclear fusion in this species (*Ascaris lumbricoides*) is not complete until some 50–60 hours after the eggs enter the uterus and are fertilized, and an additional 5 hours elapse before the first cleavage occurs. During the 12–24 hour intrauterine period the female pronucleus is occupied with its reduction divisions, and the RNA synthesis observed to occur is attributable to the male pronucleus. As the egg traverses the uterus the total RNA content increases by some 50% of the starting value. The bulk RNA content of the egg at fertilization, i.e., the quantity of ribosomal RNA inherited from oogenesis, is extremely low, about 60×10^{-6} μg per egg. Electron micrographs of the male pronucleus shortly after fertilization reveal a dense accumulation of newly formed ribosomes in the contiguous regions of egg cytoplasm. Kaulenas and Fairbairn have verified the ribosomal nature of the RNA synthesized immediately after fertilization with base composition and sedimentation analyses. Their data also show that informational RNA synthesis becomes dominant as the eggs move through the uterus. Accumulation of newly formed template active RNA is also demonstrated directly in this interesting investigation by means of a cell-free *E. coli* protein synthesis system. It is apparent that both the template and the ribosomal RNA synthesized by the male pronucleus are to be utilized in postcleavage development, probably in the form of the stable polysomes previously identified in cleavage and blastula stage embryos (142a, 153).

Experiments relevant to early patterns of gene activity have also been performed with insect eggs. Lockshin (64) described a radioautographic study of RNA and protein synthesis carried out by microinjecting labeled precursors into coleopteran eggs under special conditions which render harmless this otherwise difficult operation. No RNA synthesis could be detected during cleavage. At this stage insect embryo nuclei are typically distributed throughout the interior of the egg cytoplasm, where they form a kind of nucleated syncytium. Not until these nuclei appear at the periphery of the egg do they become active in RNA synthesis. The onset of gene activity, however, precedes the appearance of cell membranes and the actual formation of the blastoderm, according to Lockshin (64). As in other organisms, cleavage and blastulation here depend on protein synthesis, and puromycin halts development within minutes. Injection of actinomycin, however, fails to interfere with morphogenesis until just previous to gastrulation.

A recent biochemical study of RNA synthesis in the milkweed bug (*Oncopeltus fasciatus*) by Harris and Forrest (154) corroborates this report and adds important new information as well. These workers also find that cleavage-stage embryo nuclei fail to synthesize any RNA. In gastrulating eggs ribosomal RNA synthesis is detectable with the usual gradient and base composition methods, and at later stages net increase of total ribosomal RNA as well as incorporation of precursor into ribosomal RNA are recorded.

In addition, at least from the gastrular stage onward species of RNA heavier than ribosomal RNA are also in synthesis. Following the beginning of organogenesis in *Oncopeltus,* by which time many clearly differentiated cell types are in process of appearing, almost all high molecular weight RNA synthesis seems to cease. This result cannot result from the late erection of permeability barriers against the labeled precursors, since the total tissue radioactivity is greater or equal during the period of declining synthesis than in the previous periods of increasing synthesis. The burst of heavy RNA synthesis (mainly ribosomal RNA synthesis) observed during gastrulation and the onset of segmentation, and the subsequent abrupt decline in synthesis rate, are portrayed in Fig. 24 (154), expressed on a per unit amount DNA basis. Interestingly enough, DNA synthesis declines at just the same time as RNA synthesis. We can conclude from these two studies that the embryos of coleopteran insects do not initiate RNA synthesis until the

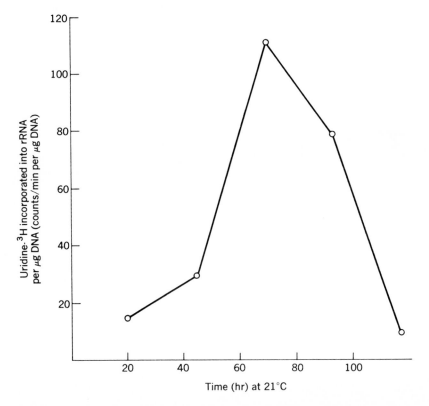

FIGURE 24. Rate of RNA synthesis per unit amount of DNA in embryos of *Oncopeltus.* Harris, S. E., and Forrest, H. S., *Science* **156,** 1613 (1967). Copyright © 1967 by the American Association for the Advancement of Science.

process of blastoderm formation, and that they do not initiate ribosomal RNA synthesis until gastrulation. After a period of intense synthesis in evident preparation for organogenesis the rate of assembly of new nucleic acid molecules falls off sharply. In earlier stages the complete maternal protein synthesis apparatus is present and the protein synthesis necessary for cleavage, etc., is carried out with these maternal components. Finally, the actinomycin experiments show that embryo genome function is needed for gastrular and later differentiation, but it is not required for blastoderm formation.

Another protostome for which radioautographic and biochemical observations exist is the gastropod *Ilyanassa obsoleta,* at present under study in the writer's laboratory. According to both criteria embryo gene activity begins very early in cleavage. In this species (155, 156) active nucleoli appear during early cleavage, as mentioned above, and by gastrulation (30 hours) high molecular weight RNA is in synthesis. The rate of RNA synthesis shows a sharp increase when calculated on a per cell basis, beginning just before gastrulation. After gastrulation, though the total amount of newly synthesized RNA per embryo continues to increase, the *per cell* rate of RNA synthesis begins to decrease (155). Actual analyses of the species of RNA formed at these early stages have not yet been carried out, however, except for the observations that the newly synthesized molecules are excluded by Sephadex G100 and therefore are too large to represent 4S or 5S RNA's. Collier has shown that the bulk (presumably ribosomal) RNA of the *Ilyanassa* embryo increases detectably only after gastrulation (157).

Ribosomal RNA of this gastropod is high in A-U content rather than G-C content, according to the careful analyses carried out by Collier (158). This is known to be true for several other protostomes as well, e.g., *Drosophila* (159, 160) and *Chironomus* (161) (but for no deuterostomes). In still other protostomes, for example, *Oncopeltus* (154), the ribosomal RNA is of the high G-C type. Ribosomal RNA synthesis in *Ilyanassa* achieves a peak value at 5 days of development, which is 3 days after the completion of gastrulation. The embryo by this point contains various differentiated cell types and organogenesis is well under way. Collier's experiments show that a class of RNA's of informational nature is actively synthesized by the 5-day embryo as well, judging from its MAK elution characteristics and its DNA-like base composition. Synthesis of informational RNA molecules can also be observed at 3 days of development, according to Collier's report (158). It is likely that informational RNA actually begins to be synthesized much earlier, probably within the first few hours of cleavage (156).

The necessity of reliance on data as scattered as those we have reviewed in the last few pages testifies to the fact that the molecular biology of protostome development represents one of the great unworked areas of developmental biology. The relative neglect of protostomes by contemporary investigators is remarkable in view of the long standing, earlier interest in protostomes, which is to be included among the most fruitful traditions of developmental cell biology. Aside from cytochemical and other measurements of bulk nucleic acid content and distribution, there remains little experimental information of aid in unraveling the patterns of gene activity in early protostome embryos. In view of the ancientness of the evolutionary separation between protostome and deuterostome lines, comparative knowledge of the details of genome function in protostome embryogenesis, when it becomes available, promises to be of very great interest.

summary of biochemical data regarding onset of various classes of RNA synthesis in the embryogenesis of diverse animals

In Table V is summarized some of the information presented in this section regarding the time of onset of each class of RNA in various animals, where known. Also shown are the quantities of RNA initially present in the egg of each species. We are to consider the DNA content of various unfertilized eggs at a later point (in Section III).

TABLE V. Starting Values and Time of Onset of RNA Synthesis in Various Organisms

Animal[a]	RNA content of egg[b] (μg)	Stage of onset of RNA Synthesis, where known[e]			Ref.
		Ribosomal RNA's	Informational RNA's	Transfer RNA's	
Deuterostome Echinoderms (numerous genera)	~.002	Gastrula; perhaps as early as mesenchyme blastula in some species	Early cleavage	Gastrula	119, 120, 122, 123, 125, 127, 127a
Ascidian (Ascidia)	—	—	Early cleavage	—	69
Teleost (Misgurnus)	2.2	After gastrulation	Blastula	—	133, 134
Amphibian (Xenopus)	4.0	Gastrula	Cleavage	Mid-to-late blastula	91, 92, 93, 94, 101
Bird (Gallus)	~2000[c]	Cleavage	—	—	136, 422
Mammal (Mus)	0.0016–0.0020	4–8 Cell stage[d]	Early cleavage, or prior to first cleavage[d]	—	139, 145

Protostome					
Nematode (*Ascaris*)	0.000060	Before pronuclear fusion	Prior to first cleavage	—	142, 142a
Mollusk (*Ilyanassa*)	0.004	Definitely by post gastrular period; possibly as early as 16-cell stage[f]	Definitely by post gastrular period; possibly early in cleavage[f]	—	150, 156, 157, 158, 163
Insect (*Oncopeltus*)	0.3[g]	Gastrula	By gastrulation	—	154

[a] Phyletic or class affiliation given, together with genus, in parenthesis. In the case of the echinoderm many genera have been studied, including *Lytechinus*, *Sphaerechinus*, *Strongylocentrotus*, *Arbacia*, and *Paracentrotus*. In other cases, mainly because of paucity of information, the representative single genus for which largest amount of biochemical information exists has been cited.

[b] This value serves as a general approximation of maternal ribosomal RNA content.

[c] Value for whole egg (white plus yolk). How much of this RNA finds its way into the embryo cannot be stated.

[d] In the absence of other information the evidence cited here is mainly indirect; viz. radioautographic observations of nucleolar function and of prenucleolar nuclear RNA synthesis, action of actinomycin, and studies with t¹² mutants. See text.

[e] Except where otherwise noted only data based on extraction and characterization of RNA species is cited.

[f] Indirect evidence cited as well as direct biochemical determinations which, however, were not designed to detect time of onset of each class of RNA synthesis: Early appearance of nuclear and nucleolar RNA synthesis in radioautographs, and high molecular weight nature of this RNA according to its behavior in gel filtration.

[g] According to these authors, over a third of the total egg RNA, as extracted, is of low molecular weight rather than ribosomal nature.

81

5

The fate and function
of early informational RNA

We have already alluded to the paradox stemming from the demonstration, on the one hand, that in most known organisms pregastrular morphogenesis is independent of embryo genome function, while, on the other, the embyro genome is nonetheless carrying on transcription throughout the pregastrular period. In molecular terms this paradox resolves into two separate problems: (a) the nature of whatever informational control does operate to direct pregastrular morphogenesis, and (b) the actual fate and function of the early synthesized informational RNA. To a highly limited extent the latter of these questions can be approached at the present time, though unfortunately the relevant experiments are almost wholly confined to the sea urchin.

evidence suggesting that early gene products
serve as templates for early embryo proteins

Direct evidence that informational RNA synthesized very early in development affects the pattern of early protein synthesis has come from the actinomycin experiments of Terman and Gross described above (81) and from later experiments employing both gel electrophoresis and DEAE columns reported by Gross (82). The reader will recall that analysis of the spectrum of the soluble proteins assembled during complete actinomycin blockade of early RNA synthesis showed that more change occurs in the distribution of the proteins synthesized during cleavage and blastulation in the absence of actinomycin than in the presence of actinomycin. Embryo-programmed change in the protein synthesis pattern can be detected as early as the swimming blastula stage (82). This is to say that control over the pattern of early protein synthesis is not *completely* based on maternal information, though the latter is clearly the overwhelmingly important element at these stages. These findings probably mean that some early informational RNA molecules are normally utilized during the premesenchyme blastula period of development for protein synthesis. The proteins synthesized at this point need not be destined for instantaneous use, however, and instead could be held in reserve for later morphogenesis.

Another case which may have relevance in this connection comes from a recent study of Silver and Comb (164), who described a specific group of nuclear proteins which begin to be synthesized in sea urchin embryos early in blastulation. These proteins are synthesized at differentially high rates established abruptly at the onset of blastulation. They are soluble in cold acetic acid, and Silver and Comb tentatively suggest that these proteins may be histones. Whether or not this is the case (they do not resemble vertebrate histones in amino acid composition) the precocious onset of their synthesis in the predifferentiation hatching blastula is suggestive in that this schedule of synthesis deviates from that characteristic of maternal template-coded protein synthesis (see below). It is to be noted that synthesis of these acid-extractable proteins begins at just the point when advance gene transcription for subsequent differentiation is taking place in echinoderms (77, 78).

Other provocative items of indirect evidence exist in the recent literature. One case of interest is that presented by Scarano, de Petrocellis, and Augusti-Tocco (165), who studied the effect of actinomycin on deoxycytidine (dCMP) aminohydrolase activity during early sea urchin development. Actinomycin was used at concentrations which permit development to the blastula stage but block further morphogenesis. As illustrated in Fig. 25, which is reproduced from this report, dCMP aminohydrolase activity fails to follow the normal course of *decline* in the presence of actinomycin. This surprising effect can be detected as early as the onset of blastulation at the higher actinomycin concentrations used, and it becomes more and more marked as the embryos proceed through the mesenchyme blastula and gastrula stages. The authors show that actinomycin has no effect on their enzyme assay per se, and the results portrayed in Fig. 25 are thus most simply interpreted as the consequence of interference by actinomycin with an early genomic function which is normally engaged in the control of dCMP aminohydrolase activity.

Another case has recently been published by Gontcharoff and Mazia (166), who have shown that BUdR treatment within the first 5 hours of sea urchin cleavages (8-cell stage, under their conditions) results in unequally sized blastomeres, lack of animal-vegetal differentiation, and failure of correct development of blastular form. Subsequent gastrular morphogenesis is also severely affected. Other experiments demonstrate that in order to produce these effects the BUdR must be incorporated into the DNA. Among the interpretations considered by the authors is BUdR interference with an

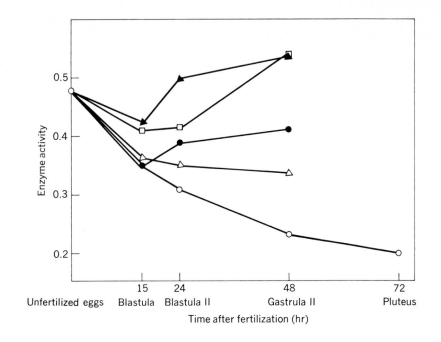

FIGURE 25. Action of actinomycin on dCMP activity during the early embryonic development of *Sphaerechinus granularis*. On the ordinate are plotted the micromoles of dCMP deaminated per milligram of proteins and per 10 minutes. Incubation mixture: 2 mM of dCMP, 100 mM of phosphate buffer (pH 7.3). The treated embryos remained at blastula stage. (Open circle) controls; (open triangle) embryos grown in 5 mg/liter of actinomycin; (filled circle) embryos grown in 10 mg/liter of actinomycin; (open square) embryos grown in 20 mg/liter of actinomycin; (filled triangle) embryos grown in 40 mg/liter of actinomycin. Scarano, E., de Petrocellis, B., and Augusti-Tocco, G., *Biochim. Biophys. Acta* **87**, 174 (1964).

early genomic function required normally for cleavage and blastulation. In order for this interpretation to remain consistent with the conclusions drawn from experiments on the same material with actinomycin it is necessary to suppose that this early genomic activity is relatively impervious to actinomycin, if BUdR does actually affect the transcription of the genetic message rather than acting in some other manner. Since it is just conceivable that species-hybrid experiments could fail to reveal the very early expression of genetic characters governing the form of cleavage and blastulation, because of the similarity among close species with respect to the earlier stages of morphogenesis, there remains a small gap in the otherwise formidable assembly of evidence, and in this niche there is perhaps still room for the hypothesis that a fraction of the early informational RNA is used as it is made, at the earliest stages of development. This would seem from the present vantage point unlikely, however.

evidence that early gene products are stored for later utilization

Most of the evidence regarding the fate and usage of early informational RNA leans toward the suggestion that these molecules are mainly stored for subsequent utilization, rather than being utilized as templates at the same stage as that in which they are synthesized. In both amphibian and echinoderm embryos early informational RNA is localized with the embryo ribosomes (91, 124, 165), but in neither case is there evidence for its immediate utilization as template for early protein synthesis. Brown and Littna have isolated from cleavage-stage *Xenopus* ribosomes a heterogeneously sedimenting class of newly synthesized RNA's (91), but it is not known whether the ribosomes containing these new RNA's are active in protein synthesis at this stage. It is certain, however, that they need not be, since both enucleate and actinomycin-treated frog eggs synthesize as much protein as do control eggs (76, 167). The studies of Spirin and Nemer (168) and Infante and Nemer (125, 169) have shown clearly that polyribosomes of cleavage-stage sea urchin embryos contain newly synthesized RNA, and the informational nature of this RNA is indicated by its polydisperse sedimentation characteristics and also by its relatively high capability (compared to ribosomal RNA) of forming hybrids with excess DNA. The size heterogeneity of the polysomal informational RNA of sea urchin embryos is evident in Fig. 26, in which is also displayed for comparison the sedimentation distribution of marker ^{32}P-labeled ribosomal and 4S RNA's. In addition the sedimentation profile of the relative hybridizing ability of the newly synthesized ^{3}H-labeled polysomal RNA is plotted in Fig. 26. When treated briefly with ribonuclease (10 μg/ml for 1 minute) these polyribosomes disintegrate (168), as active polyribosomal structures are expected to do. For the sea urchin, however, there exists strong evidence against the immediate participation in protein synthesis of polysomes bearing newly synthesized informational RNA, at least during cleavage. For one thing, as we have already seen, the pattern of soluble protein synthesis during sea urchin cleavage is almost the same in the presence and absence of near-total actinomycin blockade (81), and this is also true for the total quantity of protein synthesized (61, 170). Malkin, Gross, and Romanoff have demonstrated that the actinomycin-resistant protein synthesis occurs on polysomes which do not differ from

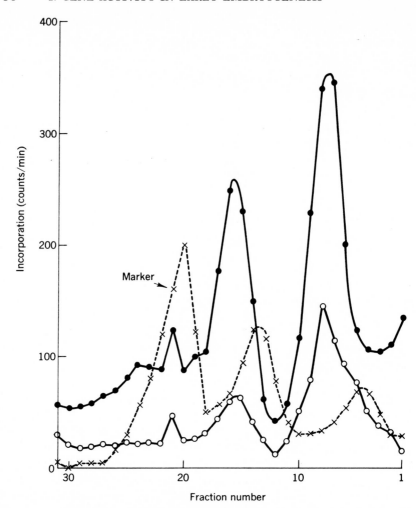

FIGURE 26. Sedimentation diagram of RNA of sea urchin embryo polyribosomes. Two parallel gradients are compared. Incorporation of uridine-^{3}H (solid line with filled circles) in the RNA of polyribosomes and of ^{32}P (dashed line with cross) in marker ribosomal and 4S RNA are plotted with the incorporation of uridine-^{3}H in the DNA-RNA hybrids (solid line with open circles) formed from each corresponding fraction. Nemer, M., and Infante, A. A., *Science* **150**, 217 (1965). Copyright © 1965 by the American Association for the Advancement of Science.

those of untreated embryos (170). In Fig. 27 is presented another experiment of Spirin and Nemer (168) which is directly relevant to the question of whether polysomes bearing newly synthesized informational RNA participate in early protein synthesis. Here cleavage-stage embryos are labeled for 2 hours with uridine-^{3}H, and in the final 2 minutes with leucine-^{14}C as well. The polysomes are extracted and displayed in the usual manner in a sucrose gradient (Fig. 27). The optical density trace indicates the location of the monosome peak, and it is evident that much of the labeled RNA sediments in polysomes ahead of the monosome peak. The significant point is that the labeled nascent protein in the polysomal area of the gradient is distributed in a completely different manner from the new informational RNA. Thus the protein synthesis carried out by the embryo appears to take place on polysomes heavier than those bearing the new RNA, though the two isotope traces certainly overlap. The lability of all the polysomal structures in Fig. 27a to ribonuclease is shown in Fig. 27b. On the basis of these and other experiments of a similar nature Spirin and Nemer have concluded that cleavage-stage protein synthesis takes place in heavy polysomal structures programmed with maternal messenger, while newly synthesized embryo informational RNA is bound in temporarily inactive lighter polysomes. In a recent addition to this picture Infante and Nemer have shown that the maternally coded polysomes are insensitive to actinomycin treatment, in contrast to those bearing newly synthesized RNA. The latter form only gradually, reaching a peak level at the blastula stage, and in actinomycin this level declines after several hours (169).

The researches of Spirin and his associates have resulted in the proposition of another class of cellular particulate in which newly synthesized embryo informational RNA may be sequestered and stored for use later in embryogenesis. These are the particles named by Spirin "informosomes" (168, 171), and their existence has been reported in early embryos of both sea urchins and teleosts. The key observation here is the sedimentation in sucrose gradients of a significant fraction of the newly synthesized informational RNA behind the monosome peak, but ahead of the free proteins and nucleic acids (133, 168, 171, 172). A sedimentation pattern of this nature is shown in Fig. 28 (171). These postribosomal RNA-containing particles have been further characterized by equilibrium (rather than sucrose gradient) sedimentation analysis. As resolved in CsCl density gradients, informosomes appear to exist as a heterogeneous group of particles characterized by a somewhat varying RNA to protein ratio. The separation in CsCl of several classes of informosomes extracted from embryos of the teleost *Misgurnus fossilis* is shown in Fig. 29, which is reproduced from studies of Belitsina (171). The informational particles of Fig. 29a are labeled in their RNA, and those of Fig. 29b are labeled in their protein. From the specific densities obtained in these equilibrium density-gradient studies, Spirin calculated that the informosomal particles contain only

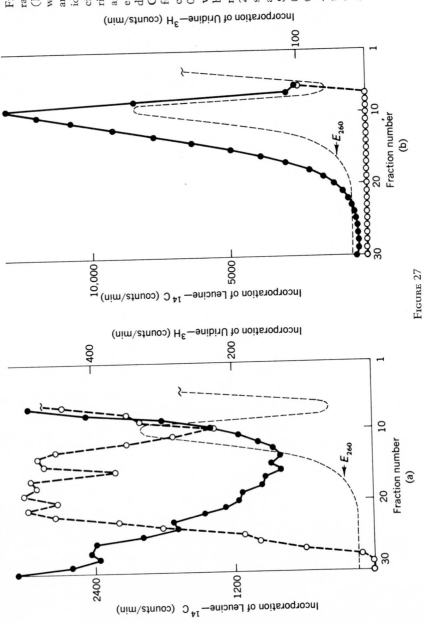

FIGURE 27. Incorporation of uridine-³H (heavy dashed line with open circles) and leucine-¹⁴C (solid line with filled circles) in the polyribosomes of cleavage stage sea urchin embryos. (Fine dashed line) control. Centrifugation was for 3 hours: (a) control; (b) the 12,000-g supernatant was treated with ribonuclease (10 μg/ml) for 1 minute at 25°C before analysis. Spirin, A. S., and Nemer, M., *Science* **150,** 214 (1965). Copyright © 1965 by the American Association for the Advancement of Science.

FIGURE 27

25–43% RNA assuming that the remainder of their total mass is protein. The RNA's extractable from these particles are very clearly of informational nature: They are synthesized during the early period of embryogenesis when informational RNA's are the only high molecular weight RNA's synthesized; when purified they sediment heterogeneously in a manner similar to that

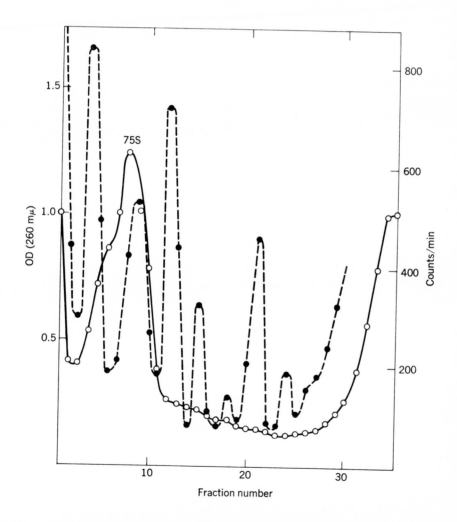

FIGURE 28. Sucrose gradient sedimentation of labeled cytoplasmic (nuclei-free) extract of loach (teleost) embryos. (Solid line with open circles) UV absorption; (dotted line with filled circles) radioactivity in RNA synthesized during blastulation. Spirin, A. S., *Current Topics Develop. Biol.* **1,** 1 (1966).

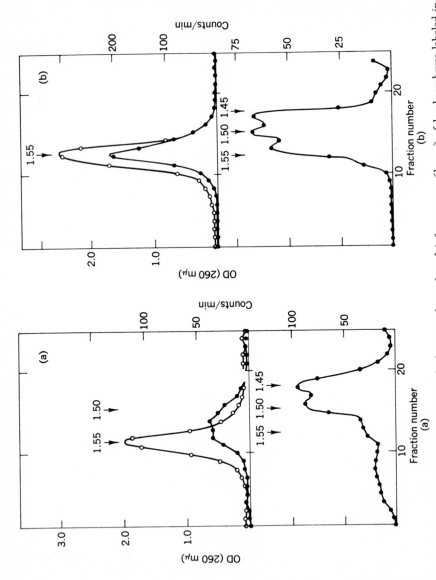

FIGURE 29. CsCl density-gradient centrifugation of ribosomes (upper) and informosomes (lower) of loach embryos labeled in (a) RNA or (b) protein. (Solid line with open circles) UV absorption; (solid line with filled circles) radioactivity. Spirin, A. S., ⸻ ⸻ ⸻ (1966).

of the informational RNA extracted directly from polyribosomes; and also like polyribosmal informational RNA, informosomal RNA hybridizes relatively well with DNA (168). In addition Spirin, Belitsina, and Aitkhozhin (172) have demonstrated that extracted informosomal RNA is able to act as template for protein synthesis in a cell-free ribosome system. Presumably the function of the protein components of the informosomal particles is to protect their informational RNA from nuclease action in order to preserve them until later in embryogenesis when they are to be utilized together with more recently synthesized RNA molecules for the programming of the initial acts of differentiation. In the absence of any knowledge as to the particular program carried in the informosomal RNA it is difficult to reach a judgment as to the special significance of the informosome. Is this particle to be regarded simply as an antinuclease device or, as Spirin *et al.* suggested (172), as a means for transporting messenger RNA from the nucleus to the cytoplasm? Spirin has recently presented a more complex and sophisticated view (171), viz., that the informosome might function as a device for qualitatively selecting certain genetic messages for delayed as opposed to immediate ultization, and thereby a selective mechanism regulating gene expression and differentiation at the translational level.

Another class of structure known to contain newly synthesized template RNA in a protected, inactive condition is the ribonuclease-resistant stable polysome. The apparently inactive polysomes from early sea urchin embryos discussed above are all nuclease sensitive (Fig. 27). No nuclease-resistant polysomes have in fact been reported in early embryos of either echinoderms, teleosts, or amphibians. A number of cases have come to light in other embryological systems, however, in which a stable template for some histospecific tissue product is bound into a ribonuclease-resistant inactive polyribosomal structure. Loss of stability to ribonuclease in these structures is correlated with their activation and the onset of synthesis of the histospecific proteins for which their messenger RNA codes. The main examples of this phenomenon are discussed individually in Section IV, and the reader is referred to that discussion for references to cases lying outside the province of early embryogenesis. Though ribonuclease-resistant inactive polysomes apparently do not play a role in the pregastrular development of any of the deuterostomes which have been studied from this point of view (bird, amphibian, fish, echinoderm) the *Ascaris* study of Kaulenas and Fairbairn cited above (153) provides just such a case. The experiments of these authors show that in *Ascaris* newly synthesized informational RNA is associated with very stable polysomal structures. These are resistant to endogenous nucleases and to the usual treatments with ribonuclease at 5 μg/ml, but this resistance disappears if the polysomes are treated with trypsin. Furthermore, the inability of these polysomes to carry out protein synthesis is abolished by trypsin, the trypsin-sensitive proteins of the polysomes evidently serving both as an antinuclease device and as a protein synthesis inhibitor. At the cleavage stages both precleavage template RNA and newly synthesized embryo template are bound in the stable polysomes. By the onset of blastulation the situation has changed, and all the polysomes bearing embryo genome synthesized template RNA have become both nuclease sensitive and functional in protein synthesis. At this stage no further increase over the endogenous protein synthesizing activity can be obtained by trypsin treatment.

Whether nuclease-resistant inactive polyribosomes are a general feature of the highly determinant pattern of development charactistic of lower protostomes is not known (this would indeed constitute an interesting distinction between protostomes and deuterostomes). Whatever the mode of early informational RNA storage, however, the net effect is the same; early embryo genome function appears in large part to represent the production of a program for subsequent events (except perhaps in mammals). The informational molecules are protected and stored until the time of their utilization in one of several ways. During this period the increasing rate of synthesis of the embryo RNA program depends in part on the increasing number of nuclear synthesis sites as cleavage and early blastulation progress, and the need for temporal stability of the informational RNA is a corollary of its unavoidably gradual accumulation. The coleopteran insect embryo, as we have seen, seems to have saved itself the trouble, or at least part of the trouble, in that early informational RNA synthesis is simply absent until many nuclei have appeared and blastoderm formation is clearly under way (154). The mouse embryo, however, requires its own newly synthesized RNA in order to develop beyond the 4-cell stage. In a sense both of these cases represent extreme adaptations to the special characteristics of the extraembryonic environment, the insect developing rapidly from preformed nutrient within a sealed, impermeable carrier, and the mammal developing very slowly in a condition of obligatory dependence on the fallopian environment for nutrients as basic as substrates for its bioenergetic machinery.

6

Maternal template RNA

There is now a variety of direct evidence supporting the proposition that the egg contains template RNA synthesized during oogenesis, and the object of what follows is merely to provide sufficient details to balance the picture of early genomic transcription so far presented and to provide a background for the discussion of oogenesis in Section III. This area has been well reviewed in several places (82, 171, 173), and the reader is referred to these sources for more detailed information. Since RNA synthesis is almost quiescent in the unfertilized egg, it is clear than any maternal template RNA present in the egg at the moment of fertilization is the product of gene activity occurring during ovarian oogenesis or in the course of ovulation.

the demonstration of maternal template RNA

The important experiments have fallen into two general categories: those proving that maternal template does indeed exist, and those in which the maternal template RNA is actually isolated and characterized. The first category includes the actinomycin studies which we have already discussed in detail and which demonstrate that protein synthesis in the early embryos of a variety of creatures is not affected by inhibition of embryo RNA synthesis with actinomycin (60, 61, 64, 69, 76, 139, 167). Of particular importance are the findings of Terman and Gross (81) and Gross (82), and of Spiegel *et al.* (83), who showed that the spectrum of proteins synthesized during early sea urchin embryogenesis is mainly independent of embryo genome function (Fig. 10). Proof of this independence, at least with respect to the quantity of protein synthesis per unit time, has been obtained by physically enucleating the eggs and assaying protein synthesis in the activated cytoplasmic fragments. The first such experiment was carried out by Denny and Tyler (174) with sea urchin eggs, and a similar demonstration has been reported by Brachet, Ficq, and Tencer (175). In both cases enucleate halves of unfertilized sea urchin eggs are found to possess the capability of synthe-

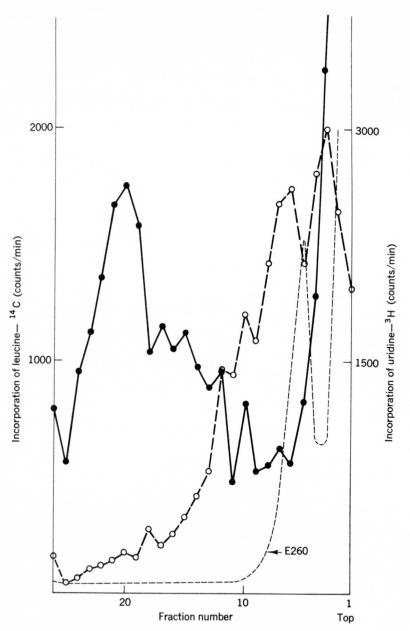

FIGURE 30. Incorporation of uridine-³H (dashed line with open circles) and leucine-¹⁴C (solid line with filled circles) in the polyribosomes of cleavage-stage sea urchin embryos. Embryos at the 4-cell stage were incubated at 19°C in seawater for 2 hours with uridine-³H. At the end of this period L-leucine-¹⁴C was added for 2 minutes. Embryos were homogenized, and the 12,000-g supernatant was analyzed by sedimentation. Centrifugation for 2 hours at 24,000 rpm. Spirin, A. S., and Nemer, M., *Science* **150,** 214 (1965).

sizing protein at control rates when parthenogenically activated. Furthermore, Tyler has shown that the relative amino acid composition of the total proteins synthesized in enucleated sea urchin egg fragments is the same as that of normal eggs (176). A parallel observation has recently been made for amphibian eggs as well, by Smith and Ecker (167). The latter microinjected a radioactive protein precursor into individually enucleated *Rana* eggs and showed that enucleation makes no difference in the rate of protein synthesis carried on in the egg cytoplasm.

The existence of the complete polysomal apparatus for protein synthesis, including template RNA, has now been certified directly for cleavage-stage embryos as diverse as amphibians (178), teleosts (133), echinoderms (169, 175, 176), and nematodes (153). As noted above, Malkin *et al.* found that normal polyribosomes can be extracted from early sea urchin embryos suffering 90% inhibition of new RNA synthesis (170), suggesting that the polyribosomes of early embryogenesis do not depend on embryo gene action for any essential components. In Fig. 27 a polysomal preparation from cleavage-stage sea urchin embryos labeled in both the polysomal template RNA and the nascent protein is portrayed. Figure 30 (168) describes an exactly similar preparation, except that the time of centrifugation is shorter. The light polysomes bearing the newly synthesized informational RNA are under these conditions clearly separated from the heavy polysomes upon which the mass of the protein synthesis is being carried out. It is clear that the latter are the polysomes bearing the functional template-active maternal RNA.

extraction of maternal template RNA and the nature of its program

Template-active maternal RNA has now been extracted directly from unfertilized eggs of both sea urchins and amphibians (25, 179, 180). The first successful attempt to extract from unfertilized eggs an RNA which would manifest template activity in a cell-free protein synthesis system was that of Maggio, Vittorelli, Rinaldi, and Monroy in 1964 (179). More recently, Slater and Spiegelman have isolated the RNA of unfertilized sea urchin eggs and assayed its template function in comparison with that of viral reference RNA of known template activity (180). By this means an estimate that some 4% of the total RNA of the unfertilized egg is template active was arrived at. Similar experiments were being carried out at the same time with informational RNA extracted from the mature ovarian oocyte of *Xenopus* in the writer's laboratory. According to the latter measurements (25) about 2–3% of the total RNA in the *Xenopus* oocyte is template active, meaning that there is at least some $0.5–1 \times 10^2$ mμg template-active RNA per egg. If only the order of magnitude of this estimate is correct (see discussion in Section III) a very large number of individual messenger RNA molecules could be included in such mature *Xenopus* eggs: If the molecules are assumed to be the size of those coding for the β-chain of hemoglobin, the messenger RNA content of the egg would be eqivalent to 10^5-10^6 individual templates.

The existence of maternal template in the egg at fertilization is thus at present firmly established. Except for one or two cases, however, we re-

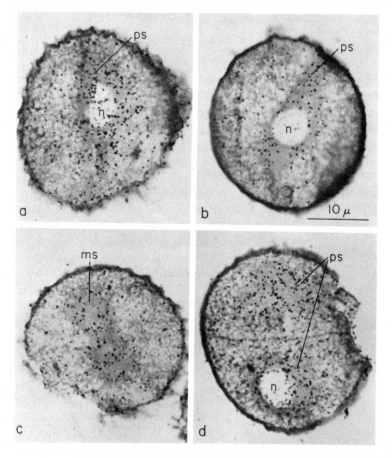

FIGURE 31. Radioautographs of sea urchin eggs during the first two cleavages, continuous incorporation of DL-leucine-³H. (a), (b), and (c): first division; early prespindle, prophase, and metaphase, respectively; (d) prophase of the second division. (ps) Prespindle; (ms) metaphase figure; (n) nucleus. Silver grains identify radioactivity incorporated into newly synthesized protein. Sections stained through the emulsion with azure B. Gross, P. R., and Cousineau, G. H., *J. Cell Biol.* **19**, 260 (1963).

main ignorant of the nature of the proteins which are so actively synthesized on these maternal templates. In general these proteins are known only as bands on electrophoretic gel strips or as counts incorporated in the protein synthesis study. Since cleavage halts abruptly if the synthesis of maternal template-directed proteins is blocked, a reasonable hypothesis is that structural proteins required for new cell wall formation and for mitosis itself, e.g., mitotic spindle proteins, are among the early protein products of the embryo. Early protein synthesis might also be required for the assembly of the enzymic apparatus required for the maintenance of an active metabolism by the ever-increasing cell population. In other words, it seems likely that maternal template RNA programs the synthesis of ubiquitously required "housekeeping" proteins.

A successful effort has been made by Gross and his associates (61, 181–183) and by Stafford and Iverson (184) to study the synthesis of one of the most likely such candidates, the mitotic spindle proteins of cleavage (61). Figure 31, reproduced from the radioautographic study of Gross and Cousineau (182), shows a heavy concentration of grains incorporated as leucine-^{3}H into what is clearly the spindle apparatus at mitosis. These proteins label preferentially in the cleaving egg, though the total incorporation into mitotic proteins is never in excess of 10% of that into the whole egg, and after a short pulse of leucine-^{3}H amino acid incorporation into spindle proteins is observed to be 3–4 times higher than in other cell proteins. Wilt, Sakai, and Mazia, however, have shown that this preferential relationship does not exist for the very first cleavage mitosis in the sea urchin egg (184a). First cleavage occurs even after severe inhibition of protein synthesis, and though newly synthesized protein is normally included in the mitotic apparatus at first cleavage, the latter is not preferentially labeled. Amino acid label incorporated into an isolated mitotic apparatus, from a preparation of Stafford and Iverson (184), is shown in Fig. 32. A second example in which a known functional protein is probably synthesized from stored template RNA derives from an investigation by Auclair and Siegel (185). This study concerns the ciliary proteins which appear in sea urchin blastulation when the embryo becomes motile. It was found that *Paracentrotus* gastrulae, if deciliated with hypertonic seawater solutions, reassemble cilia rapidly, at the expense of a pool of preexistent ciliary proteins. Incorporation of amino acids into these specific structural proteins occurs at exactly the same rate in embryos treated with high dosages of actinomycin as in control embryos. Although it is theoretically possible that the stored template bearing the program for ciliary protein synthesis is actually that synthesized by the embryo itself earlier in development, this is made unlikely by the recent study of Runnstrom and Manelli (186), who reported that in both *Paracentrotus* and *Sphaerechinus* exposure of early (prehatching) blastulae to actinomycin fails to interfere with the *initial formation* of motile cilia (though the later formation of stereocilia is actino-

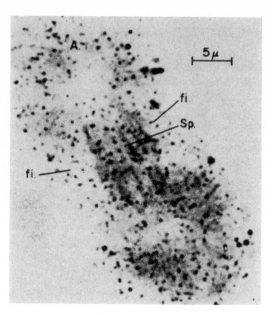

FIGURE 32. Radioautograph of a 1-μ section of the centrifuged pellet containing isolated mitotic apparatus. Stained with toluidine blue. Ilford L-4 emulsion exposed for 7 days. (A.) Aster, (Sp.) spindle. The mitotic apparatus shown is at very early anaphase. Fibers (fi.) stain more darkly than the matrix, and silver grains tend to be distributed along their length. Stafford, D. W., and Iverson, R. M., *Science* **143,** 580 (1964).

mycin sensitive). Furthermore, ciliary neoformation in blastulae of *Arbacia* is also actinomycin resistant, according to earlier work of Auclair and Meismer, though ciliary precursor synthesis is slightly depressed by actinomycin according to these workers (187).

It thus appears that the maternal template stockpile may indeed include information for various structural proteins required by the early embryo; evidence for maternal message for housekeeping enzymes, on the other hand, is still lacking. If we assume that the function of the template stockpile is to direct the synthesis of structural and housekeeping enzyme proteins, a limited number of qualitatively diverse messages should be present in a very large number of copies. The diversity of the genomic information represented in the maternal template RNA stockpile in this case might be small compared to that expressed in a differentiated growing cell which has not only to carry on the same housekeeping activities as the cleaving embryo cells but also to program and operate its characteristic histospecific functions. The correctness of such speculations is not known as yet, although evidence exists which is relevant to them, if only obliquely (Section III).

fertilization and the activation of the maternal program

As is now well known, protein synthesis is activated sharply at fertilization [see Monroy's articles (173, 188) and the more recent review of Tyler (189) for a detailed discussion of this activation phenomenon and references]. Large increases in protein synthesis rate occur as a result of either fertilization or parthenogenic activation in the sea urchin and also in amphibians, and these increases are totally independent of the presence of the nucleus since they occur in parthenogenetically activated, physically enucleate eggs. This is clear from the investigations of Denny and Tyler (174) and Brachet et al. (175) on protein synthesis in enucleate sea urchin egg fragments and the study of Smith and Ecker with enucleate frog eggs (167), all cited above. Protein synthesis before fertilization or activation does not appear to be completely quiescent, though various results are obtained with different species. Pre-fertilization incorporation of amino acids into protein clearly occurs in *Spissula*, a lamellibranch mollusk (190), in some sea urchins (189, 191, 192), in the frog (193), and in certain worms [(189); see this review of Tyler for references and thorough examination of the evidence relevant to prefertilization protein synthesis].

The activation phenomenon itself, as it affects the protein-synthesizing mechanism at fertilization, remains somewhat mysterious. In the organism which in these respects is best studied, the sea urchin, it is clear that increase in protein synthesis is by no means the initial response to fertilization. Epel (192) has shown that the step-up of protein synthesis after fertilization requires, in *Lytechinus* eggs, certain prior metabolic events, including increase in respiratory rate, breakdown of cortical granules, and activation of certain enzymes. This sequence was elucidated for eggs which had been preloaded with labeled amino acids in order to avoid complications resulting from precursor penetration time. Epel reports that some 5–7 minutes elapse after fertilization before the protein synthesis rate begins to accelerate in this sea urchin. This finding is of interest in that it leads to the question of the mechanisms of maternal template release and the activation of protein synthesis.

A significant clue as to what is going on in the first minutes after fertilization is provided by the discovery of Monroy and Tyler (177), Stafford, Sofer, and Iverson (194), Malkin, Gross, and Romanoff (170), and Infante and Nemer (169) that the fraction of ribosomes present as polysomes changes soon after fertilization. In unfertilized sea urchin eggs few of the ribosomes are present in polyribosomal aggregates, while after 40 minutes to 2 hours 25–40% of the ribosomes are recorded in polysomes. Polysomes can be detected as early as 15 minutes after fertilization, according to Cohen and Iverson (194a). One result of fertilization, then, is the rapid formation of active polysomal structures, an event which does not take place instantaneously but which is ultimately responsible for the increase in protein synthesis level occasioned by fertilization (or parthenogenic activation). This conclusion implies not only that all the necessary components of the protein synthesizing machinery are present in the mature egg but also that either ribosomes or template RNA, or both, are sequestered in such a manner as to account for their inability to form polysomes until after fertilization.

It is thus unlikely that inadequacies of egg transfer RNA's (or other soluble factors) could account for the relative quiescence of protein synthesis prior to fertilization, and direct investigation of the ability of the soluble factors present in unfertilized eggs to support protein synthesis has in fact shown them to be perfectly functional (195–197). Nor can the ribosomes of the unfertilized egg be blamed, for they appear to be able to accept various synthetic polynucleotide messengers and to carry out the synthesis of the polypeptides coded for by these artificial templates (75, 179, 197–200). By a process of exclusion, therefore, it seems necessary to conclude that it is the maternal template RNA in the egg which is precluded from participation in the formation of polyribosomes until after parthenogenetic activation or fertilization. Two possibilities exist here: either the template RNA's are blocked on the ribosomes themselves or they are located in some other particulates. Although the answer to this problem is not as yet clear, the current evidence leans toward a nonribosomal site for template storage in that contrary to what might be expected if the ribosomes were the site of storage for large template molecules unfertilized egg ribosomes fail to display any differences in sedimentation properties from those of much later embryos (122, 201). Irrespective of the site of template storage, the sequestration mechanism by which the maternal template is inactivated is probably a protein coat. This follows from the interesting experiments of Monroy, Maggio, and Rinaldi (202), who demonstrated that the endogenous protein synthetic activity of a crude ribosomal preparation from unfertilized eggs is increased markedly by a mild trypsin treatment.

A recent investigation by Mano, furthermore, has shown that in the sea urchin a protease distinguished by an optimum at pH 8 appears in the heavy particulate fractions of the cytoplasm at fertilization only to disappear later (203); see also the earlier report of Lundblad (204). At present the most likely site for maternal template storage appears to be a class of very heavy cytoplasmic particle which has been visualized in the electron microscope by several investigators. Heavy, RNA-containing particles were originally observed in sea urchin egg cytoplasm by Afzelius (204a). Recently Harris (205a) has found that these bodies, which prior to fertilization are located in the vicinity of the oocyte nucleus, disperse into the cytoplasm at time of germinal vesicle breakdown. The presence of maternal template RNA in heavy cytoplasmic aggregates has been demonstrated directly by Stavy and

Gross (205), who report that the major part of the endogenous template activity extractable from the unfertilized sea urchin egg is located in rapidly sedimenting particles. Though they contain ribosomes these particles are apparently not polyribosomal in nature. Tyler (189) states that the messenger RNA of the heavy ribosomal aggregates in unfertilized eggs is rendered RNase sensitive by mild trypsin treatment. Other possibilities are the storage of maternal messenger in informosome-like postribosomal particles and/or in (possibly inactive) polyribosomes. Some evidence for these alternatives has been presented by Piatagorsky (206) in experiments in which the location of RNA labeled during late oogenesis is studied by sucrose gradient analysis of extracts from mature eggs bearing this RNA.

To summarize, maternal template RNA molecules are stored in unfertilized eggs within protein shields, which are ruptured through the controlled action of proteases, the responsible enzymes being released on fertilization. Stable polyribosomes then form by combination of the maternal template with maternal ribosomes, and synthesis of the structural and other proteins needed for early morphogenesis begins. According to Infante and Nemer maternally coded polysomes persist at the original level into gastrulation in sea urchins (169).

CONCLUSIONS

The genomic program for early development is complicated, in the temporal pattern of its appearance, and in the information it bears. Embryo genome function, at first expressive of only a small fraction of the genomic information borne by the organism, begins immediately after fertilization, the gene products being stored in one of several apparently inactive forms for later utilization. Thus an informational program is slowly accumulated during the early period of "nonresponsibility" enjoyed by the multiplying embryo genomes. Throughout this period embryo cell functions are operated primarily according to the program embodied in the maternal templates synthesized during oogenesis and located in the active polyribosomes of the blastomeres. During blastulation, however, a further embryo program begins to be synthesized in the blastomere nuclei (perhaps as a result of the previous intercession of both maternal and early embryo gene products). The new set of informational RNA's is essential for gastrular morphogenesis, but at least in some organisms the pattern of protein synthesis during blastulation continues to be qualitatively and quantitatively directed in the main by preformed maternal templates. In amphibians and echinoderms the embryo gene products synthesized during blastulation assume direct control of gastrular morphogenesis and of the distribution of proteins in synthesis. The point of embryo genome control occurs far earlier in the development of mammals than in lower deuterostomes, and this may be true for certain other forms as well. From gastrulation onward the diversity of genomic information utilized appears to increase, and cell-specific patterns of differentiation are established. The maximum length of time maternal informational RNA's remain present is unknown, and it is possible that like maternal ribosomal RNA's the informational RNA inherited from oogenesis continues to function far beyond gastrulation; suggestive examples are to be found in actinomycin and species-hybrid experiments with ascidians and mollusks. The accession to control by the embryo genome is thus a gradual process, occuring in several steps. In the remainder of this book we shall be concerned basically with the nature of the regulative mechanisms of selective gene activation which govern this process.

II

✻ cytoplasmic localization and the onset of differentiation

The phenomenon of cytoplasmic localization of morphogenetic potentiality poses some of the most interesting—and deep-seated—problems in developmental biology. In recent times this aspect of the developmental process has attracted very little attention, probably because most of the relevant evidence is of a nonbiochemical nature, and investigation of the localization problem at the molecular level is just beginning. We can be certain, nonetheless, that the crucial significance of this area to the biology of early development will lead increasingly to biochemical attempts at understanding. In the following pages we take up the salient points of evidence upon which the concept of cytoplasmic localization of morphogenetic potential at present rests, with the advantage of several remarkable recent advances. This review will lead to a consideration of the theoretical implications of the localization phenomenon as the earlier writers sought to explain it, and as it can be treated in terms of our contemporary understanding of differentiation. Unfortunately, a documented discussion of cytoplasmic localization oriented around the fundamentals of differentiation and gene function has not been published since Chapter XIV of the 1925 edition of E. B. Wilson's monumental treatise *The Cell in Development and Heredity* (207). Wilson's insight into this problem remains in large part apropos today, and, consequently, the organization of this essay, particularly the first section of it, draws heavily on this incomparable work.

103

I

The localization phenomenon

Localization is the phenomenon of precocious specification of future cell
fate and precocious limitation of morphogenetic potential very early in
embryogenesis, long before the cells in question manifest their morphogenetic fates. In cases of localization the differentiation of a given line of
cells can be regarded as a function of the particular areas of cytoplasm inherited early in embryogenesis by the stem cells of that cell lineage. Localized areas of future cell fate can often be mapped out on the uncleaved
egg cytoplasm and can be tested for at the earliest cleavage stages; where
localization precedes fertilization it is sometimes referred to as "prelocalization." Consider, for example, the study of ascidian embryogenesis published
by Conklin in 1905 (208) in which the development of *Styela* (*Cynthia*)
is described. In this egg pigmented areas of cytoplasm corresponding to
the morphogenetic fate map for the cells presently inheriting these areas
can be distinguished. Figure 33, reproduced from Conklin's elegant hand-
drawn figures, displays the relationship between the various cytoplasmic
regions of the embryo, as recognized by their unique pigmentation, and the
tissues ultimately formed from these regions of egg cytoplasm. In this egg
five kinds of egg cytoplasm can be observed: (*a*) a dark yellow cytoplasm
eventually included in the tail muscles of the larva, (*b*) a light yellow material later segmented into the coelomic mesoderm of the larva, (*c*) a light
gray substance inherited by notochord and neural plate cells, (*d*) an opaque
gray material segregated into the endoderm cell lineage, and (*e*) a transparent cytoplasm later present only in ectodermal cells.

105

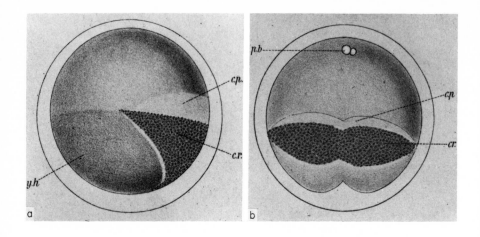

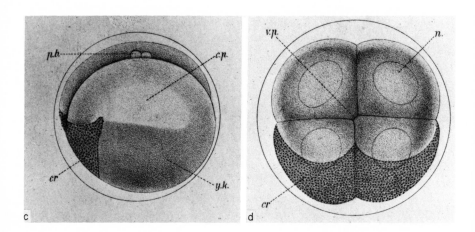

FIGURE 33a–d. Living eggs of *Cynthia (Styela) partita*: (a) side view of egg showing the formation of the crescent (*cr.*) from the yellow hemisphere (*y.h.*); in figures (a–c) the animal pole is above, the vegetal pole below. Above the yellow crescent is an area of clear protoplasm (*c.p.*). (b) First cleavage of an egg, viewed from the posterior pole and showing the forms taken by the yellow crescent during the division, and also, the enlargement of the area of clear protoplasm and its extension toward the animal pole. (*p.b.*) polar bodies. (c) End view of egg of same stage as (b) showing the lateral limits of the yellow crescent, the clear protoplasm in the upper hemisphere, and the yolk (*yk.*) in the lower. The anterior portion of the lower hemisphere is composed of light gray material; this is the gray crescent and gives rise to chorda and neural plate. (d) Four-cell stage seen from the vegetal pole (*v.p.*); the crescent covers about half of the posterior blastomeres.

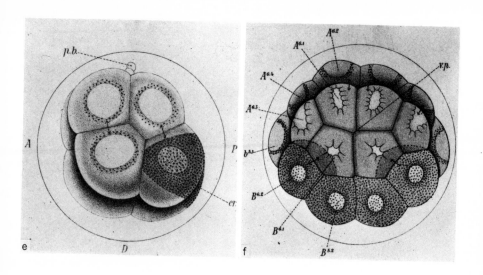

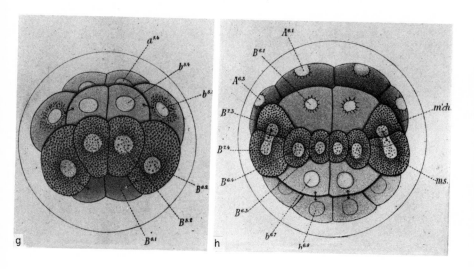

FIGURE 33e–h. (e) Eight-cell stage viewed from the right side showing a small amount of yellow protoplasm around all the nuclei. Note the crescent. (A) Anterior; (P) posterior; (V) ventral; (D) dorsal. (f) Twenty-two-cell stage, from the vegetal pole; 4 mesoderm cells (yellow), 10 endoderm chorda and neural plate cells (gray), and 8 ectoderm cells (clear). (g) Same stage viewed from the posterior pole. (h) Forty-four-cell stage, posterior view, showing separation of another mesenchyme cell (*m'ch.*) from a muscle cell (*ms.*).

107

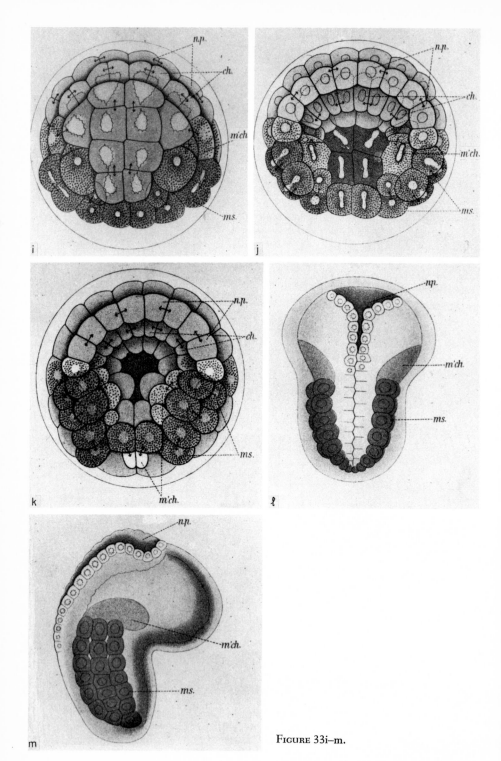

FIGURE 33i–m.

108

The total cytoplasmic mass of the embryo remains constant through gastrulation, which is well under way by the 180-cell stage. *Delineation of the presumptive tissue areas* appears to be accomplished simply through the partitioning of the cytoplasmic materials early in embryogenesis. As early as the 64-cell stage, in fact, the separation of the five recognizable kinds of egg cytoplasm into their respective cell lineages has been completed. The definitive distribution in the uncleaved egg of these cytoplasmic substances is set up within a few minutes after fertilization, not being present when the egg is first shed. This cytoplasmic localization process is shown in Fig. 34 (208). The unfertilized egg already possesses polarity in one axis so that the sperm is able to enter only at the bottom, but the demarcation of the anterior-posterior axis depends on the acentric movement of the two pro-nuclei. Thus the site toward which the fusion nucleus comes to lie is the future posterior end, and here is localized the yellow cytoplasm later in-corporated in the embryo's first mesodermal stem cells. The localization problem was defined for the developmental cell biologists of the turn of the century by cases such as that illustrated with *Stylea*: What is the nature of the mechanism by which inheritance of a particular sector of egg cytoplasm can determine the future fate of an embryonic cell lineage?

FIGURE 33i–m. (i) Seventy-four-cell stage, dorsal view, showing division of 4 chorda (*ch.*) and 4 neural-plate (*n.p.*) cells; there are 10 mesenchyme and 6 muscle cells, besides 10 endoderm cells. (j) One-hundred-sixteen-cell stage showing the beginning of gastrulation, and also, the neural plate, chorda, muscle, and mesenchyme cells. (k) Late gastrula; the yellow cells in the midline are mesenchyme cells, the others, muscle cells. (l) Young tadpole seen from dorsal side, neural groove open in front and closed behind, small-celled mesenchyme in front of large muscle cells. (m) Same stage as preceding seen from the right side, showing neural groove, mesenchyme, and three rows of muscle cells. Conklin, E. G., *J. Acad. Natl. Sci.* (*Philadelphia*) **13,** 1 (1905).

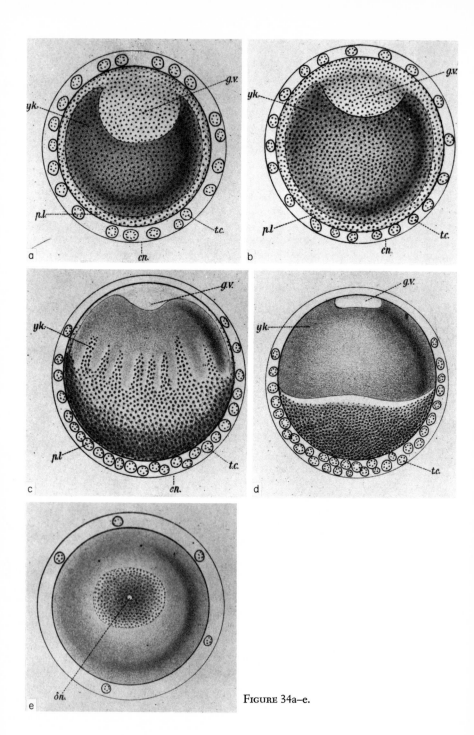

FIGURE 34a–e.

110

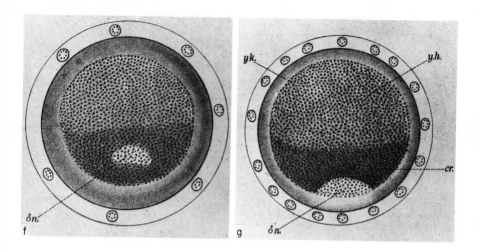

FIGURE 34. Figures of the living eggs of *Cynthia (Styela) partita;* maturation and fertilization: (a) Unfertilized egg before the fading of the germinal vesicle (*g.v.*), showing central mass of gray yolk (*yk.*), peripheral layer (*p.l.*) of yellow protoplasm, test cells (*t.c.*), and chorion (*cn.*). (b) Similar egg during the disappearance of the nuclear membrane, showing the spreading of the clear protoplasm of the germinal vesicle at the animal pole. (c) Another egg about 5 minutes after fertilization, showing the streaming of the peripheral protoplasm to the lower pole where the spermatozoon enters, thus exposing the gray yolk (*yk.*) of the upper hemisphere; the test cells are also carried by this streaming to the lower hemisphere. (d) Later stage in the collection of the yellow and clear protoplasm at the vegetal pole; clear protoplasm lies beneath and extends a short distance beyond the edge of the yellow cap. (e)–(g) Successive stages of the same egg drawn at intervals of about 5 minutes; viewed from the vegetal pole. In (e) the area of yellow protoplasm is smallest, and the sperm nucleus, (♂ *n.*) is a small clear area near its center. (f) and (g) show stages in the spreading of this yellow protoplasm until it covers nearly the whole of the lower hemisphere [yellow hemisphere (*y.h.*)]; at the same time the sperm nucleus and aster move toward one side of the yellow cap and a crescent (*cr.*) begins to form at this side. Conklin, E. G., *J. Acad. Natl. Sci. (Philadelphia)* **13**, 1 (1905).

2

Localization and preformationism

Wilson (207) has pointed out the close conceptual re. tions which linked
the earlier experimental investigations of the localization phenomenon with
the then contemporary controversy over preformationist vs epigenetic developmental theory, a controversy carried on by a number of eminent biologists engaged personally with the design and execution of experiments
aimed at the localization problem. O. Hertwig (209), Bourne (210), Whitman (211), Spencer (212), and Huxley (213) all published explicit discussions of the preformation question, as it applied in their minds to the
contemporary state of their science. This controversy obliquely affected the
design of the experiments outlining the localization problem, some of which
we are to review in this section, and for this reason the arguments centering
around the "neopreformationism" of the 1890's remain significant for the
contemporary student of localization.

the origins of late-nineteenth-century "neopreformationism"

Toward the end of the nineteenth century certain striking observations on
the part of embryologists concerned with the cell theory of devolpment led
to the espousal of theories of ontogeny which were regarded at the time as
antithetical to the principle that development occurs in an epigenetic manner,
i.e., by means of the progressive construction of more complex systems from
less complex levels of organization. These theories, here referred to as
"neopreformationist," stemmed mainly from the impressive experimental evidence demonstrating cytoplasmic localization of morphogenetic potential in
a variety of organisms. The essence of neopreformationism was the belief that
the embryo is in some mysterious manner *foreshadowed* in the egg, and it
was this concept which was found so uncomfortable by most of the writers

112

cited above. Wilson has excerpted from O. Hertwig's 1894 essay *Präformation oder Epigenese* (209) a quotation which perfectly exemplifies this attitude:

> The doctrine of cytoplasmic determinants has thrown back the mystery, which we might hope at least partially to resolve by investigation of the properties of visible forms, into an invisible region where there is absolutely no point of attack for research. Thus by its very nature it remains unfruitful for research, to which it can offer no possible way of advance. In this respect it resembles its predecessor, the preformation theory, of the 18th century.

A similar utterance by Bourne (210) also pubilshed in 1894, reveals the real source of discomfort:

> It is certainly a striking fact that the most minute and elaborate researches of the past few years have led the course of biological speculation back to the point of view of Haller and Bonnet in the 18th century, and have threatened to discredit altogether the opposite doctrine of epigenesis. . . . The evolutionary (preformationist) doctrine, after being thoroughly discredited by the labors of the embryologists of the last 50 years, is now with us again, not perhaps in its old form, but in a form which differs from the old one only because of the more numerous accumulation of facts . . . the theory is called on to explain.

Bonnet's preformationist theory served as a target throughout much of the nineteen century. The arguments which dethroned the rigid doctrines of Bonnet are for us today as dry and distant as a Napoleonic guide to manners, but that accomplishment was evidently too recent and too significant for any possible hint of a return toward preformationism to be regarded without heat by the late nineteenth-century investigators. According to Bonnet's ovist theory of preformation [published initially in 1745 (214)] a complete embryo is patterned in every egg, and each such embryo contains an ovary, with eggs, which in turn bear smaller embryos within, etc.; this is the doctrine of *"emboitement."* Bonnet calculated that 27,000,000 embryos must have existed in the ovary of Eve. Bonnet, however, is not an unsympathetic figure, intellectually speaking, and at least in his earlier work he stated that the preformationist theory is only "an escape from the greater miracle of epigenesis." Thus a certain personal sophistication is expressed in the following quotation:

> All that I have said upon generation may be taken for a nonsense if you like. I am myself strongly disposed to regard it from that point of view. . . . But I will ask if other hypotheses are found to be more satisfactory . . . what is the use, indeed, of putting one's soul to torture in seeking mechanical solutions, which do not satisfy the case . . . in the actual state of our knowledge of the physical world we do not discover any way of explaining mechanically the formation of an animal, or even the least organ. I therefore think it more consonant with sound philosophy, because more consonant

with the facts, to admit as at least highly probable, that *organized bodies pre-exist from the beginning.* [Translated by Whitman (215).]

The accumulation of evidence in favor of epigenetic developmental mechanisms had already begun while Bonnet was writing on preformationism. Epigeneticists insisted that organism and organs increase in complexity of organization as they develop rather than simply increasing in size without further "differentiation or essential modification," the heart of Bonnet's position [see Whitman's 1895 discussion (216)]. Among the early investigations which directly support epigenetic interpretations of development were the demonstrations by Wolf in 1759 that leaves and flowers develop from undifferentiated tissues, Panter's 1817 description of epigenetic development in the chick from primitive germ layers, and the studies of von Baer (1828–1837), as a result of which the germ layer theory was generalized to other animals. Von Baer showed unequivocally that skin develops epigenetically from ectoderm, muscular and skeletal systems from mesoderm, etc. Finally, in 1867, Kowalewsky demonstrated that the germ layers themselves are formed epigenetically, and preformationism appeared to be dead.

A neopreformationist doctrine closer to the tastes of certain late nineteenth century experimentalists soon arose, however. Significantly, it was developed by men like His, the teacher of Miescher, and a proponent of the theory that satisfactory explanation of biological phenomena can only be obtained at the molecular level. His suggested in 1874 that the epigenetic character of early chick development is only apparent, the underlying phenomenon being the "coalescence of preformed germs." His wrote:

It is clear on the one hand that every point in the embryonic region of the blastoderm must represent a later organ or part of an organ, and on the other hand, that every organ developed from the blastoderm has its preformed germ in a definitely localized region. *The material of the germ is already present, but is not yet . . . directly recognizable* (217).

A similar statement by Lankester a few years later (1877) carries the "molecular preformation" hypothesis even further (218):

Though the substance of an egg cell may appear homogeneous under the most powerful microscope, excepting the fine granular matter suspended in it, it is quite possible, indeed certain, that it may contain *already formed and individualized*, various kinds of physiological molecules. The visible process of segregation is only the sequel of a differentiation already established. . . . Thus, since the fertilized egg already contains hereditarily acquired molecules, . . . invisible though differentiated, there would be a possibility that these molecules should part company, *not* after the egg-cell had broken up into many cells as a morula, but at the very first step in the multiplication of the egg-cell. . . . We should not be able to recognize these molecules by sight; the two cleavage cells would present an identical appearance, and yet the segregation . . . has already taken place. This hypothesis may be called that of *Precocious Segregation*.

neopreformationism and development in lower protostomes

The concept of precocious segregation of morphogenetically significant egg cytoplasmic substances and other allied hypotheses led to the growth of interest in the embryology of animals in which, unlike the case in the chick, the fate of each cell lends itself to study. This is probably one of the reasons why localization phenomena have for so long been generally regarded as characteristic mainly of invertebrate development of the so-called mosaic type, e.g., molluskan and annelid development. Protostome embryos of lower and median grades of organization are characterized by an exceedingly fortuitous early structure, from the investigator's point of view, and it was possible very early to work out complete cell lineages for several such

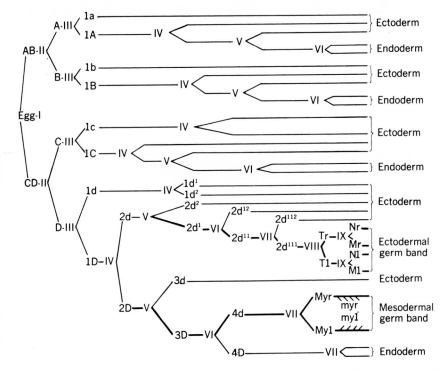

FIGURE 35. Chart of the cell lineage of *Tubifex*. The heavy lines in the lower part of the chart give the history of the ecto- and mesodermal germ bands. The designations represent names of individual cells; e.g., Myr stands for right myoblast. Reproduced by T. Morgan, ed., *Experimental Embryology*. New York: Columbia University Press, 1927, p. 371; after A. Penners, *Zool. Jahrb. Anat.* **43**, 223 (1922).

creatures, e.g., for the annelids *Clepsine* (219), *Arenicola* (220), and *Tubifex* (221), for the mollusk *Crepidula* (222), and for a large number of organisms belonging to other groups as well. [References to many early cell lineage studies are given in Wilson (207); see also Costello (223).] This is because the cells are relatively few, and are visually easy to distinguish, and because the embryos develop asymmetrically with cells of various recognizable special shapes or positions playing an important role.

In Fig. 35 a diagram of the complete cell lineage of *Tubifex rivulorum* is reproduced, after the work of Penners (221). The diagram shows that ectoderm, endoderm, mesodermal "germ band," and ectodermal "germ band" develop from early segregating cell lineages. Thus, one can trace the lineage of a particular specialized cell, say, a cell of the coelomic mesoderm column, back to one specific blastomere, in this case the 4d blastomere. This blastomere lineage in turn is always carved out of a certain portion of the egg, the orientation of which is established before first cleavage. In this *Tubifex* resembles a variety of organisms, as the axis of the egg coincides with the body axis of the animal owing to some process of cytoplasmic localization resulting in the establishment of polarity even before fertilization or at the onset of cleavage. Neopreformationist hypotheses clearly called for experiments in which the potential of isolated cells to carry out their fated differentiation would be questioned directly, and in this way an empirically testable question took form. Thus to a certain extent it can be considered that the course of experimental investigation was shaped by the disagreement between the epigeneticists and the neopreformationists, those who believed that differentiation really appears *de novo* as the blastomeres multiply, as opposed to those who believed that this appearance is only the visible manifestation of underlying molecular preformations, and therefore that no new increase in the underlying degree of organization occurs in embryogenesis.

3
Definitive experimental
evidence for localization

the capabilities of isolated blastomeres

Isolated blastomere experiments were undertaken initially to test whether the early embryo is indeed a "mosaic of preformational areas," and their eventual result was to establish localization as one of the primary phenomena of embryogenesis. A spectacular and influential case of isolated blastomere behavior is illustrated in Fig. 36, which is compiled from Wilson's 1904 report on experiments with embryos of the mollusk *Patella coerulea* (225).

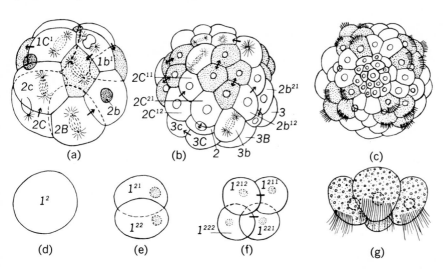

FIGURE 36. Normal development of Patella: (a) 16-cell stage, from the side (primary trochoblasts shaded); (b) 48-cell stage; (c) ctenophore stage, about 10 hours, from upper pole, primary trochoblasts ciliated. (d)–(g) Isolated primary trochoblasts: (d) primary trochoblast ($\frac{1}{16}$, 1^2), obatined by successive isolation; (e) result of first division; (f) after second division; (g) product of (f). After Wilson, E. B., *J. Exptl. Zool.* **1**, 197 (1904).

In this study Wilson isolated a number of different presumptive cell types in low calcium seawater and observed their subsequent course of development, as compared to the course of development expected for these blastomeres had they remained in the context of the normal whole embryo. His observations indicate that the isolated blastomere lineages in fact follow their normal developmental fate, as is shown perhaps most clearly by the trochoblast isolations portrayed in Fig. 36. The drawings here indicate that isolated blastomeres destined to give rise to primary trochoblasts carry out the correct number of cell divisions, and then, at the appropriate time, the definitive trochoblasts become ciliated in accordance with the same schedule they would normally have followed. Wilson concludes (225): "The history of these cells gives indubitable evidence that they possess within themselves all the factors that determine the form and rhythm of cleavage, and the characteristic and complex differentiation that they undergo, wholly independently of their relation to the remainder of the embryo." Results consistent with this statement were obtained in this work with other similarly isolated cell types, and with multicellular embryo sectors, e.g., isolated $\frac{1}{16}$ embryo macromeres which produced endodermal gut rudiments, or isolated apical progenitors which differentiate *in vitro* into apical sensory and ectodermal cells.

Another remarkable example has been provided by Penners (226, 227), working with the annelid *Tubifex rivulorum*. It will be recalled (Fig. 35) that in this organism both the neural ectodermal germ band and the mesodermal germ band stem from the D quadrant of early cleavage. At the 4-cell stage the D macromere is the largest and its products remain asymmetric far into development, with respect to both size and rate of division, compared to the A, B, and C quadrants. Penners found that each of these blastomeres would continue its normal course of development even if all the others are killed *in situ* by ultraviolet microbeam irradiation. Thus if A, B, and C are killed the D macromere nonetheless adheres to its unique cleavage pattern, gives rise to the primary neural ectoderm germ band stem cell 2d (Fig. 35) and to the primary mesoderm stem cell 4d (Fig. 35), and after this to the ectodermal and mesodermal germ bands themselves. Similarly, if 4d or 2d (Fig. 35) are individually killed the ectodermal germ bands form, but the embryo lacks coelomic mesoderm. The converse experiment, however, shows that the mesodermal stem cell (4d) derivatives possess the capability of producing the ectodermal germ band even if 2d has been eliminated (228).

In other organisms, both protostomes and lower deuterostomes, retention of the normal developmental fates by isolated blastomere cell lineages has also been investigated, and experimental demonstrations of early self-differentiation exist, among others, for the mollusks *Ilyanassa* (229, 230) and *Dentalium* (231), the nematode *Ascaris* (232), the annelids *Nereis* (233)

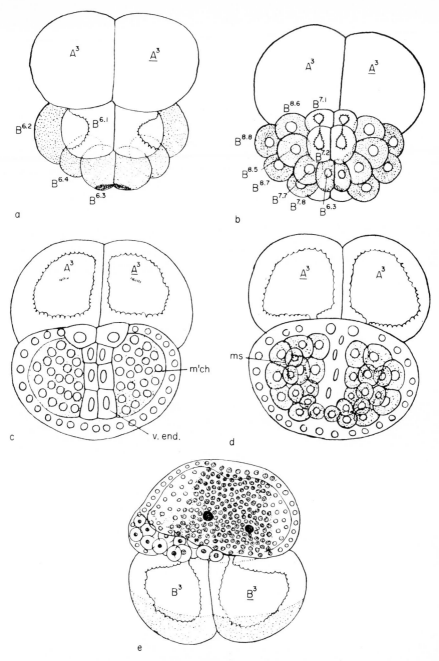

FIGURE 37a–e.

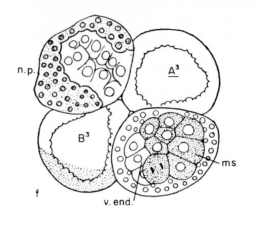

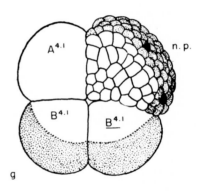

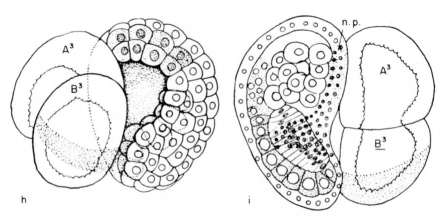

Figure 37f–i.

and *Sabellaria* (234), the ascidian *Styela* (235), and the ctenophore *Beröe* (236). The latter two cases deserve a brief description.

A precocious morphogenetic event occurring in the development of *Beröe* is the appearance of the "swimming plates," and Fischel, following other early experimentalists, published an investigation in 1898 of the distribution of swimming-plate-forming ability among the early blastomeres of this embryo. Swimming plates are normally formed by the descendants of an octet of animal pole cells, and Fischel showed that isolated blastomeres of *Beröe* give rise to embryos containing exactly that number of swimming plates which correspond to the number of presumptive swimming-plate-producing cells included in the lineage normally descendant from the isolate. In other words, the program for this morphogenetic function is present in just those early blastomeres which are normally ancestral to the swimming plate producers and can neither be substituted for through the function of other cells nor indeed affected in a major way by the presence or absence of other cells.

FIGURE 37. (a) Posterior half of 32-cell stage of *Styela* dorsal view. The cleavage of this half is altogether normal. Anterior blastomeres (A_3) killed by spurting from a pipette in the 4-cell stage, fixed 1 hour later. (b) Posterior half of 76-cell stage. Spurted in the 4-cell stage, fixed 2 hours later. Two rows of yellow crescent cells are present, the inner being mesenchyme, the outer muscle cells; the anterior pair of mesenchyme cells ($B^{8.6}$) are larger than normal. There are two pairs of caudal endoderm cells ($B^{7.1}$ and $B^{7.2}$). A pair of ventral ectoderm cells is visible in the midline behind B. (c) An embryo, spurted in the 4-cell stage, fixed at 4 hours, deep focus, showing the double row of ventral endoderm cells (v end) in the midline, and on each side of this a mass of mesenchyme cells (m'ch.). (d) Ventral view of posterior half embryo of the same stage as the preceding, showing the muscle (ms.) and mesenchyme cells beneath the ectoderm and on each side of the strand of ventral endoderm. (e) Anterior half embryo, dorsal view. Spurted in the 4-cell stage, fixed 22 hours later. The yellow crescent is plainly visible in the injured cells. Sense spots are present, but the neural plate never forms a tube. The chorda cells lie in a heap at the left side. There is no trace of muscle substance or of a tail in this anterior half embryo. Normal larvae of this stage are undergoing metamorphosis. (f) Left anterior and right posterior (diagonal) quarter embryo, dorsal view; spurted in the 4-cell stage, fixed 5 hours later. The anterior quarter shows thickened ectoderm cells, probably neural plate (np) around the endoderm cells; in the posterior quarter are 8 muscle and 3 caudal endoderm cells. (g) Right anterior dorsal eighth embryo, 14 hours after injury, showing endoderm, chorda, and neural plate cells with sense spots. (h) Right half gastrula of about 220-cell stage; spurted in the 4-cell stage and fixed 3 hours later. The neural plate, chorda and mesoderm cells are present only on the right side *and in their normal positions and numbers.* (i) Living left half embryo, dorsal view, showing the endoderm cells forming exogastrulae and the yellow crescent cells at the surface. Conklin, E. G., *J. Exptl. Zool.* **2**, 145 (1905).

The ascidian experiments cited are the remarkable partial embryo studies published by Conklin in 1905 (235). Some of Conklin's experiments are summarized in the drawings reproduced from his paper in Fig. 37 (235). It is evident from this figure that every embryo fraction, from the early cleavage stages at which the blastomeres are mechanically singled out, contains the potentiality of forming certain presumptive tissue types (notochord, mesoderm, neural plate, gut, ectoderm, etc.), and that these basic potentialities are independently expressed by the living blastomeres in Conklin's experiments.

Certain examples thus exist in which long in advance of the actual manifestation of differentiation, the cleavage planes separate cells whose descendants bear given morphogenetic potentialities from cells whose descendants bear other morphogenetic potentialities. In these cases the embryo, by early cleavage, manifests a determinate character, or, at the level of future organ and tissue delineation, a "preformational" character. For the materialization of at least some of the organs and tissues which can be formed by isolated blastomeres embryo genome function will ultimately be required, as in the tadpole stage ascidian embryos of Conklin (cf. Section I), and probably in the growth of coelomic mesoderm and neural ectoderm in *Tubifex*. The partial blastomere experiments, therefore, direct our attention to the nature of that "preformational" character resulting from the localization in the blastomeres of something which is ultimately going to affect the qualitative nature of genome function in the blastomere lineages.

blastomere specification as a consequence of factors present in the egg cytoplasm

The brief discussion of localization in *Styela* above (Figs. 33 and 34) suggest that it is inheritance of a special part of the original egg cytoplasm which endows the embryonic cell lineages with their special character. Though postfertilization movements (Fig. 34) are responsible for the definitive localization pattern of the pigment-marked egg cytoplasm in *Styela* this localization is apparently a matter only of rearrangement of preformed substances already present in the egg. Furthermore, the arrangement process follows a pattern which is partly independent of the sperm entrance point, suggesting the existence of "invisible" prelocalized demarcations in the egg cytoplasm even before fertilization. The most obvious example of this, and one that is common to the eggs of a great many organisms, is the prefertilization specification of the future dorsoventral axis of the egg.

In Penners' study of *Tubifex*, where the "D" quadrant lineage is the only one able to give rise to coelomic mesoderm, it is possible to discern exactly which part of the cytoplasm of the uncleaved egg is going to be distributed into the D quadrant. In this organism the uncleaved egg possesses two areas of "pole plasm" clearly distinguishable by eye, and these are normally inherited only by the CD blastomere at the first cleavage. The pole plasms fuse around the blastomere nucleus at this stage and are shunted into the D blastomere at the second cleavage. The morphogenetically important 2d and 4d cells, according to Penners, owe their specific character to their inheritance of the original pole plasms present in the unfertilized egg. This position, while unproven for *Tubifex,* is demonstrably true in certain similar cases discussed in detail below, and thus it is not unlikely that Penners' interpretation is accurate. However, an unequivocal demonstration that morphogenetic blastomere potency is owing to the inheritance of substances present in the egg cytoplasm is difficult to achieve, and caution is in order. Commenting on Penners' studies Morgan has pointed out, for example, that the microscopically visible cytoplasmic inclusions in the egg of *Cumingia,* a bivalve mollusk, can be moved about in various orientations by centrifugation without in the least affecting subsequent morphogenesis (237). Early localization in *Cumingia* is as sharp and as determinate as in *Tubifex.* Arguments of this nature scarcely affect one's main interest in such cases, however, for irrespective of whether the morphogenetic substances involved are the *visible* polar plasms or are movable at low centrifugal forces (as they seem to be in *Tubifex*) it remains clear that these substances are cytoplasmic and that they are present in the egg before cleavage begins.

A set of precise demonstrations to the effect that specific regions of egg cytoplasm qualitatively *determine* the subsequent patterns of blastomere lineage differentiation exists in early studies on the determination of germ cells in various protostomes [early references are collected in Hegner (238)]. Two cases from this early literature are particularly striking. In *Ascaris megalocephala (Parascaris equuorum)* Boveri showed that for five successive cleavages elimination of a certain part of the chromatin occurs in one of the two offsprings in one particular cell lineage at each division (239). At each division the cell not suffering chromatin diminution is the germ-line stem cell, the other is a somatic cell. After fifth cleavage, i.e., the 32-cell stage, there are 31 somatic cells and one germ-line stem cell. Figure 38 portrays in section the appearance of the early cleavages of the *Ascaris* embryo as given by Boveri (239), and it is apparent that from the beginning the germ-line stem cell possesses a distinct cytological appearance. Not only do chromosome diminutions occur in the other cells and not in this one, but in the early cleavages the germ cell mitotic spindles are oriented perpendicularly to those of the somatic cells [orientation of cleavage stage mitoses is well known to be a function of cytoplasmic organization in the egg: *vide* actinomycin-insensitive spiral cleavage (63)].

Boveri and his associates found that in eggs undergoing abnormal cleavage induced either by polyspermy or by centrifugation the number of germ-

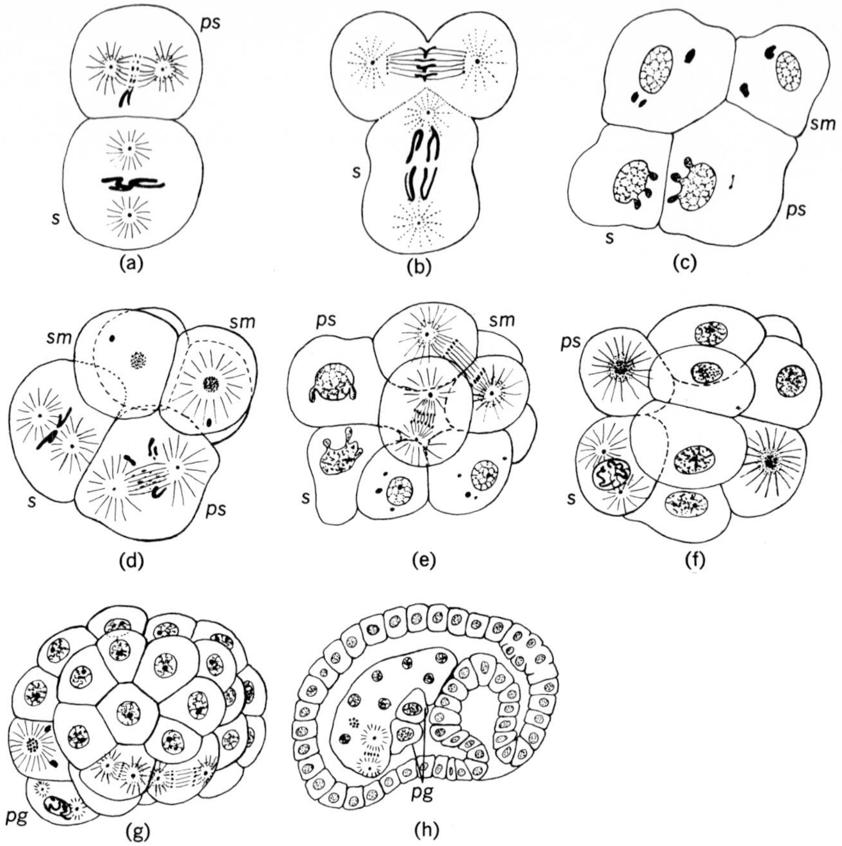

FIGURE 38. Germ-line stem cells and primordial germ cells in *Ascaris megalocephala*, early stages showing diminution. (ps) primordial somatic cell, yet to undergo diminution; (sm) somatic cell; (s) germ-line stem cell. (a) Second cleavage in progress; the somatic cell, showing diminution in progress; (b) later stage, elimination-chromatin at equator of upper spindle (T stage); (c) 4-cell stage showing eliminated chromatin in upper two cells. (d) Third cleavage in progress, second diminution at ps; (e) 10-cell stage showing mitosis of somatic cells with diminished nuclei; (f) 12-cell stage, third diminution in progress at ps; (g) about 32 cells, fourth diminution in progress, leaving primordial germ cell (pg) (in prophase); (h) gastrula completed with two primordial germ cells. Wilson, E. B., *The Cell in Development and Heredity*. New York: Macmillan, 1925, pp. 322–324.

line stem cells depends on the number of cells into which is distributed the polar egg cytoplasm normally bequeathed to the single initial germ-line stem cell (239). Examples are diagramed in Fig. 39 (240). The polyspermy and centrifugation experiments complete the demonstration that it is a component of the egg cytoplasm which specifies the germ cells, a function which in a most direct way is observed to involve an immediate effect on the nuclear apparatus. Nuclei presented with the special germ cell determinant cytoplasm are protected from diminution, while all nuclei distributed into the remainder of the cytoplasm undergo chromosome diminution. The conclusion of this process is marked by the cessation of diminution mitoses at the 32-cell stage, the point beyond which no further somatic cells are given off from the germ cell line.

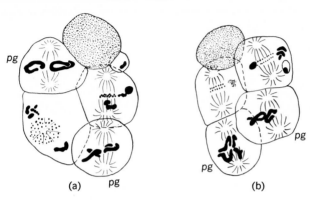

FIGURE 39. Centrifuged *Ascaris* eggs with two rather than one primordial germ cells (pg) owing to redistribution of cytoplasmic germ cell determinants before cleavage. The stippled ball of cytoplasm at the top of the embryo is the result of centrifugation. Diminution is observed in the somatic cells. Hogue, M. J., *Arch. Entwicklungsmech. Organ.* **29**, 109 (1910).

Another striking case of egg cytoplasmic determination of germ cell differentiation is that investigated by Hegner in the eggs of chrisomelid beetles (228). Development of germ cells in these eggs can be said to initiate when the cleaving nuclei reach the periphery of the egg and blastoderm organization begins. Nuclei arriving at the polar region of the oblong egg enter a specially demarcated area of cytoplasm localized there which appears to function as the germ cell determinant so that only the cells formed from these nuclei and their polar cytoplasm differentiate as germ-line stem cells. Hegner succeeded in selectively destroying the germ cell determinant cytoplasm with a hot needle before the peripheral movement of the nuclei had brought them to the polar germ cell determinant region of the egg (Fig. 40). The injury so induced is rapidly walled off by the forming blastoderm, as shown in Fig. 40, and normal development of a differentiated gastrula and ultimately a hatching insect takes place. Only one thing is wrong with the insects which develop from these eggs: They lack germ cells.

It is clear that the genomic information for germ cells is present in the undisturbed nuclei of the treated embryos, since all the nuclei bear all the

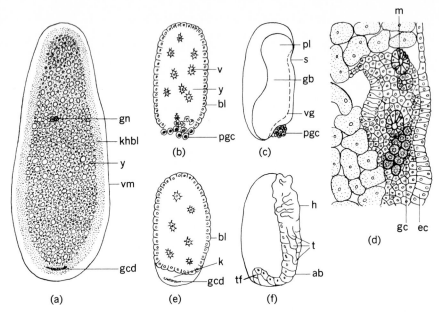

FIGURE 40. (a) A longitudinal section through an egg of *Calligrapha bigsbyana* 4 hours after deposition. (b)–(f) *Leptinotarsa decemlineata*: (b) A longitudinal section through an egg 1 day after deposition when in the blastoderm stage. (c) Superficial view of the right side of an egg 36 hours after deposition. Note mass of primordial germ cells. (d) Longitudinal section through the tail fold of a normal embryo 60 hours old, showing germ cells. (e) Longitudinal section through an egg, the posterior end of which was killed with a hot needle just after the egg was laid; the egg was then allowed to develop for 24 hours. (f) Side view of an egg similarly treated. The posterior end was killed with a hot needle just after deposition, and the egg was then allowed to develop for 60 hours. (gc) Germ cells; (gcd) germ cell determinants; (gn) germ nuclei copulating; (khbl) *Keimhautblastem*; (vm) vitelline membrane; (y) yolk; (bl) blastoderm; (pgc) primordial germ cells; (v) vitellophag; (gb) germ band; (pl) procephalic lobes; (s) stomodeum; (vg) ventral groove; (k) portion of egg killed; (ab) abdomen; (h) head; (t) thoracic appendages; (tf) tail fold; (ec) ectoderm; (m) malpighian tubules. Hegner, R. W., *Biol. Bull.* **20**, 237 (1911).

genomic information of the organism, but with the destruction of the *germ cell determinant cytoplasm* the capacity of the embryo to *elicit* this information is evidently lost. This is not an isolated case, and, as reviewed in more detail in Section III, germ cell determinants are known in numerous phylogenetically distant groups of animals. The fortuitous geometry of the insect egg with its striking early characteristic of syncytial nuclear replication, its frequently large size, and its clearly marked polarity have made it a favorite subject of early research on germ cell determinants, and more recent investigations have corroborated the provocative results of Hegner and his predecessors. An indicative case is owing to Geigy, who showed that ultraviolet irradiation of the polar region of *Drosophila* egg cytoplasm previous to blastoderm formation results in the formation of agametic but otherwise normal organisms. Other similar studies are discussed below. In the eggs of *Drosophila*, as in many other organisms, there are certain cytoplasmic granules which appear to be intimately involved with germ cell determination. These granules are incorporated bodily in the germ line progenitor cells, the pole cells. If the polar granules are displaced by centrifugation, pole cells fail to form (244a). However, the morphogenetic determinants do not appear to be localized solely in the polar granules since the latter do not possess the capability of causing pole cells to form in the new locations to which they are shifted in centrifuged eggs (contrast the centrifugation experiments with *Ascaris* eggs, Fig. 39). Pole cell formation thus requires not only the presence of the polar granules but their correct location in the vegetal germ cell determinant cytoplasm as well. We are concerned here with the germ cells considered merely as a particular differentiative cell line and with the implication of egg cytoplasm elements (the germ cell determinants) as critical factors necessary for their differentiation.

cytoplasmic localization in the embryogenesis of Dentalium and Ilyanassa

In one of the most remarkable of his papers, Wilson, in 1904, described a series of experiments with early embryos of the scaphopod mollusk *Dentalium* designed to demonstrate the extensive qualitative control over morphogenesis which may be resident in the egg cytoplasm. These experiments (225) made use of a peculiarly convenient phenomenon which occurs early in cleavage in *Dentalium*, and in several other protostomes, including some annelids and the gastropod mollusk *Ilyanassa*. This is the transient extrusion during the first cleavage of a "polar lobe" containing vegetal pole egg cytoplasm. The lobe is attached by only a thin strand of protoplasm to one of the blastomeres, the CD blastomere, into which it flows as the cleavage is completed. A photograph of the living trefoil-like structures resulting from first cleavage polar lobe extrusion in *Ilyanassa* is presented in Fig. 41. As in the annelids, e.g., *Tubifex*, the CD blastomere alone carries the capacity to give rise to the mesodermal columns on which the development of various organs and ultimately of body form depends. At the second cleavage a polar lobe is once more transiently extruded, and as the cleavage terminates, it flows back into the D cell. Of the four blastomeres now present only the D quadrant

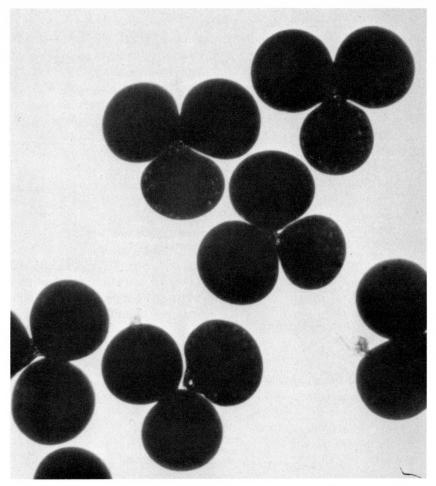

FIGURE 41. Typical *Ilyanassa* "trefoils." At this stage of first cleavage the cytoplasmic polar lobe can be removed, leaving the AB and CD cells.

lineage bears the mesoderm-producing ability. The lobe is again briefly extruded at several subsequent cleavages, always returning to the D macromere. In 1896, Crampton, then a student of Wilson, had found that in *Ilyanassa* the polar lobe could be easily separated from the remainder of the embryo without interfering with the ability of the embryo to continue cell division, but that the resulting embryos appeared to lack the mesodermal germ bands (229). Since removal of the polar lobe involves the removal of absolutely no nuclear components, this striking, though preliminary, result seemed to warrant further investigation. The most advanced of the lobeless embryos described by Crampton in his brief account attained the age of 48 hours: In this species differentiated organ primordia do not appear until much later (cf. Section I). A clear result of Crampton's study was that the extirpation of the polar lobe at first cleavage causes the permanent loss of the special division schedule and the uniquely asymmetric position of the D blastomere lineage. After delobing all four blastomere lineages behave exactly alike.

Following this suggestive exploratory investigation, Wilson took up his study of these phenomena in *Dentalium* and developed what remains one of our most unequivocal cases of cytoplasmic localization of morphogenetic potential. Isolated blastomere experiments showed that the *Dentalium* embryo is of a typically determinate nature in that the morphogenetic character of each individual blastomere lineage is set from the beginning, i.e., from some point antecedent to the appearance of the cleavage planes which separate the early blastomeres. If the egg cytoplasm sequestered in the first polar lobe at the trefoil stage is removed, by separating the nucleated blastomeres from the cytoplasmic polar lobe, the morphogenetic value of the D blastomere and its descendants is altered, and Wilson found that lobeless *Dentalium* embryos fail to develop the main coelomic mesoderm bands. Examination of postgastrular lobeless embryos revealed the absence of major organ primordia which are directly or indirectly derivative from this mesoderm, e.g., mouth, shell gland, and foot as well as of the coelomic primordium itself. As Wilson pointed out, the lobeless embryos develop in exactly the same way (or fail to develop in exactly the same way) as embryos deriving from the isolated A-B blastomeres or from single A, B, and C blastomeres.

The latter embryos cannot produce mesoderm either, since they lack the cytoplasm contained in the D blastomere. The conclusion can be drawn, therefore, that the cytoplasm extruded in the polar lobe is that which contains the mesodermal determinants endowing the D quadrant lineage with its particular morphogenetic potentialities: Since the nuclei in the embryo are equal in their genomic content, the nucleus of the AB cell must contain information for the creation of mesodermal cells, just as does the nucleus of the CD cell; therefore, it is the cytoplasm special to the CD cell which determines the eventual utilization of this nuclear information. Since the only difference between normal and lobeless embryos is the absence of cytoplasmic components normally localized in the D quadrant in the latter, the factors eliciting mesodermal differentiations must be included in the polar lobe cytoplasm. Wilson showed that the polar localization of the morphogenetically significant cytoplasm is estabilshed by means of a series of cytoplasmic movements a few minutes before the onset of first cleavage. The significant cytoplasm is thus already present in the egg when it is shed, but its ultimate pattern of localization, just as in *Styela,* depends partly on fertilization.

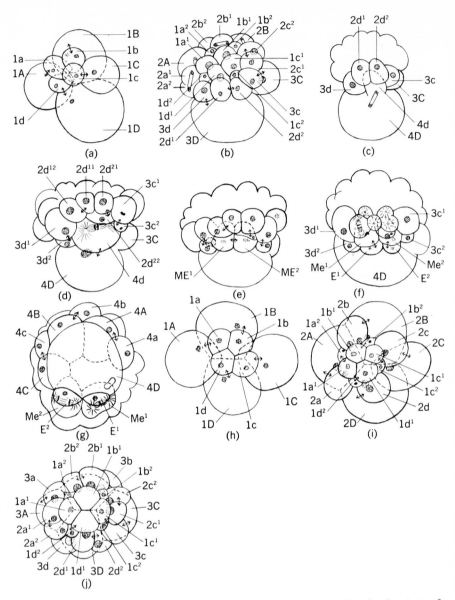

Figure 42. (a)–(c) Normal cleavage of *Ilyanassa*. From camera lucida drawings of stained whole mount preparations. ×326. (d)–(f) Normal cleavage showing the early derivatives of the mesentoblast cell (4d). (g) The egg has been oriented so that the vegetal pole is toward the observer. The division of Me[1] and Me[2] will produce the primordial mesoderm. (h)–(i) Cleavage after removal of the polar lobe at the trefoil stage. Clement, A. C., *J. Exptl. Zool.* **121,** 593 (1952).

Clement (230, 241–244) has recently repeated and greatly amplified Wilson's 1904 experiments, using *Ilyanassa*, the organism originally studied by Crampton. Figure 42 describes the later cleavage of *Ilyanassa*, with special emphasis on the morphogenetically significant D quadrant descendants from which arise the primary mesentoblasts and ultimately their derivatives, the organs forming with the participation of coelomic mesoderm. Clement's careful histological studies of the veligers developing from eggs from which the polar lobe has been removed at the trefoil stage show that these organs, e.g., heart and intestine, are missing from the lobeless larvae. The latter, shown in comparison to normal larvae in Fig. 43 (241), also fail to organize velum, shell, eyes, foot, and otocyst. On the other hand, lobeless larvae do possess active muscle, nerve ganglia and nerve endings, stomach, velar tissue with cilia, and pigment and ectomesodermal mesenchyme cells, evidently the progenitors of muscle in the lobeless larvae. [Ectomesoderm, which is to be distinguished from coelomic or endomesoderm, arises from the second and third micromere quartets and is regarded as a vestige of the remote evolutionary origins of mesoderm in precoelomate radial animals (245).] Removal of the polar lobe cytoplasm thus does not simply block all differentiation, only *certain* differentiation.

By removing the D macromere at successively later stages of development, Clement has been able to locate the points at which the morphogenetic materials originally present in this macromere are shunted into its lineal descendants, and particularly into those which are themselves the direct ancestors of tissue types for which the lobe carries determinants (243). As this operation is carried out at progressively later cleavages the degree of differentiation displayed by the embryos improves. By the time the fourth derivative of the D macromere, 4d, is given off, removal of the whole macromere has no *qualitative* effect on later differentiation, the resulting embryo being normal except for its small size. This experiment also serves to eliminate the possibility that the effects of polar lobe removal are due to some general injurious effect on the embryo, e.g., starvation for substrates carried in the lobe. Further evidence on this point comes from recent experiments of Clement (244a), which show that centrifugally produced vegetal pole egg fragments containing only a small fraction of the original yolky cytoplasm are able to produce lobe-dependent differentiated structures. Thus the morphogenetic substances transiently present in the polar lobe are not movable by centrifugal forces sufficient to displace yolk, nuclei, lipid droplets, etc. Removal of the D macromere before the 2d cell is given off results in as severe an inhibition of morphogenesis as removal of the first cleavage polar lobe or of the whole D quadrant. The morphogenetically significant polar lobe contents therefore appear to be shunted into 3d and particularly into 4d, the latter being the lineal ancestor of the primary

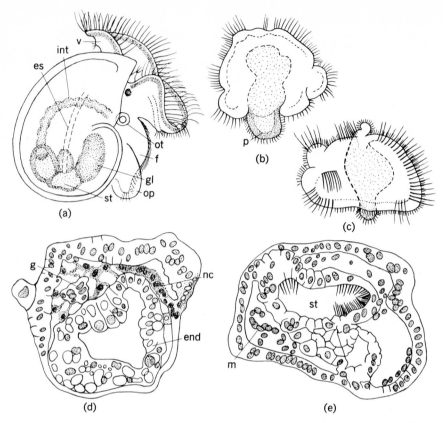

FigURE 43. Comparison of lobeless and normal larvae. From camera lucida sketches of
living specimens. ×171. The outline of the endoderm is indicated with a
broken line in the lobeless larvae. (a) Normal veliger about 9 days old.
(v) Velum; (int) intestine; (es) esophagus; (ot) otocyst; (f) foot; (gl) digestive gland; (st) part of stomach; (op) operculum. A round mass of
undigested yolk is at the junction of stomach and intestine. (b) Nine-day-
old lobeless larva, posterior view (p) posterior protrusion. (c) Nine-day-old
lobeless larva, anterior view. (d) and (e) Sections of lobeless larvae. (d)
Six-day-old larva. Endoderm with considerable yolk. Note the mesenchyme-
like cells between endoderm and ectoderm; nc is probably a nerve com-
missure and g, a ganglion; (end) endoderm, (e) Nine-day-old larva showing
ciliated stomach chamber (st). The numerous nuclei (m) between ectoderm
and endoderm probably belong to mesodermal cells. Clement, A. C., J. Exptl.
Zool. **121**, 593 (1952).

mesentoblasts (Fig. 42). Only embryos including 4d form heart and intestine.
Although embryos from which the D macromere is deleted after the formation of 3d but before the formation of 4d show velum, eyes, and foot and
some shell development, most of these tissues are not formed directly from

the 3d cell lineage and an indirect inductive effect based on 3d descendants is the most likely cause of this result. Inductive effects are known explicitly to be involved in eye differentiation in *Ilyanassa* (244), and it is clear from the detailed experiments of Cather (246) that this is also true of shell formation. Two classes of morphogenetic effect are thus exerted by the polar lobe cytoplasm: (*a*) determination of the cell lineage specifically responsible for coelomic mesoderm and derivatives thereof such as heart, and (*b*) determination of structures descendant from other cells but inductively affected by coelomic mesoderm derivatives.

Clement's detailed analysis is useful in pointing out this distinction, which is a general one. On the one hand, we have self-differentiation of cell lineages, as so well illustrated by isolated blastomere experiments. On the other hand, we have a class of phenomena more complex in nature, since they involve interactions between diverse cell types, which is to say *between cells which are already to some extent self-differentiated*. Differentiations depending on the juxtaposition of diverse cell layers, e.g., chordamesoderm induction in amphibian embryos, are clearly of the latter group. Though in a broad sense any appearance of a new cell type during embryogenesis is the result of an "induction" event, the distinction exists that in the one case the induction is of a second order of complexity, requiring the previous ontogeny of the interacting cell types, while in the other the primary "inducing" agents are simply inherited by the blastomere and its lineal descendants as the pre-existent egg cytoplasm is partitioned in the course of cleavage. The subject of inductive interactions between embryonic cell types is not within the scope of this discussion [see the recent reviews by Tiedemann (247) and Yamada (248) for overall summaries of this area and pertinent recent references], while the specification of differentiative fate by what is originally inherited in the egg cytoplasm is central to it. The case of the *Ilyanassa* and *Dentalium* polar lobe is at present among the strongest examples of the latter phenomenon in the literature, thanks to the investigations of Crampton, Wilson, and Clement.

4

Regulative and mosaic development, and the universality of morphogenetic determinants in egg cytoplasm

It will be noted that except for the urochordate *Styela* all the examples of localization so far considered occur in protostomial animals. It is obviously of paramount importance to know whether localization is a universal phenomenon or a peculiarity of certain large but nonetheless confined phylogenetic groupings. One could suspect, for instance, that localization is associated with development in those creatures which gastrulate after forming only a few dozen or a few hundred cells (rather than thousands, as in the amphibians), or that it is confined exclusively to organisms with extremely determinate cleavage patterns, particularly those with spiral cleavage. The question of the generality of localization is frequently answered rather tentatively in the affirmative with the assertion that almost all eggs seem to show some localization of morphogenetic potential by the onset of cleavage if only in the assignment of dorsoventral and anterior-posterior or (at least) animal-vegetal gradients in the egg. It is pointed out in this connection, however, that such polarity assignments are in some eggs extremely labile, e.g., in amphibian eggs, and in such instances cytoplasmic localization seems to take on a somewhat ephemeral character.

In other organisms, by contrast, the localization patterns are anything but easily disturbed (*see* Morgan's example of centrifuged *Cumingia* eggs, cited above), and these organisms happen frequently to be just those in which development is described as "mosaic," after the early conception of the embryo as a "mosaic of self-differentiating parts." We are dealing here with separate questions, which, however, are unfortunately rarely resolved as such, for the "mosaic" or "regulative" quality of a given organism's development is not necessarily an index of the existence or nonexistence of cytoplasmic localization of morphogenetic potential in the egg. Diverse factors contribute to the mosaic or regulative character of development in any particular organism. These include (*a*) the geometrical relations between the early cleavage planes and the distribution of the morphogenetically significant cytoplasm in the egg; (b) the point in development at which the localization patterns actually become established; (c) the relative extent to which the events of early embryogenesis depend on cellular interactions; and (d) the physical lability of the cytological structures on which the localization phenomena may depend.

The first two of these factors are discussed with great clarity by Wilson (207); for emphasis on the third see Watterson (249). In order to clarify the question of the generality of cytoplasmic localization—and therein the extent to which localization is a fundamental aspect of development, as opposed to a quirk of evolutionary specialization—it is useful to consider briefly each of these four points.

the orientation of cleavage and the mosaic vs regulative dichotomy

It became known early in the history of experimental embryology that isolated blastomeres of certain organisms are capable of giving rise to *qualitatively normal dwarf embryos*. No tissues appear lacking in such embryos, and in the more fortuitous cases there is no evidence of any qualitative failure of differentiation. Such organisms contrast sharply with those in which isolated blastomeres produce only the fractional embryonic structures to which their lineal descendants are normally destined to give rise. The first unequivocal demonstration that a single blastomere possesses the potential of forming a qualitatively complete embryo was that of Driesch in 1891 (250). Driesch and, subsequently, Boveri showed that in sea urchins the first two blastomeres and the individual blastomeres of the 4-cell stage possess the capability of forming a complete embryo. Furthermore, certain of the 8-cell stage blastomeres can develop far enough to produce a pluteus. Other examples include the CD cell (but not the AB cell) of *Tubifex* (227), any of the first 4 and in certain species the first 8 of the blastomeres in hydromedusa embryos (251), either of the first 2 cells and some of the first 4 cells of the cephalochordate *Amphioxus* (252), any of the first 2 or 4 blastomeres in some teleosts (253), and under some conditions either of the first 2 blastomeres in urodeles (254, 255) and anurans (256). In all of these cases it is clear that the developing blastomere lineage performs activities not normally assigned to it, e.g., the formation from a right-hand blastomere of both a left and a right side of the embryo, exactly the opposite of what occurs when either the left- or right-side blastomeres of *Styela* are allowed to develop (Fig. 37).

Striking as it may be, however, this contrast is essentially irrelevant to whether or not the eggs in question display cytoplasmic localization, a point of view which can scarcely be more precisely indicated than by the diagrams devised by Wilson for this purpose and reproduced here in Fig. 44 (257). The drawings of Fig. 44 map out on the uncleaved eggs of four diverse organisms the experimentally demonstrated regions of morphogenetic sig-

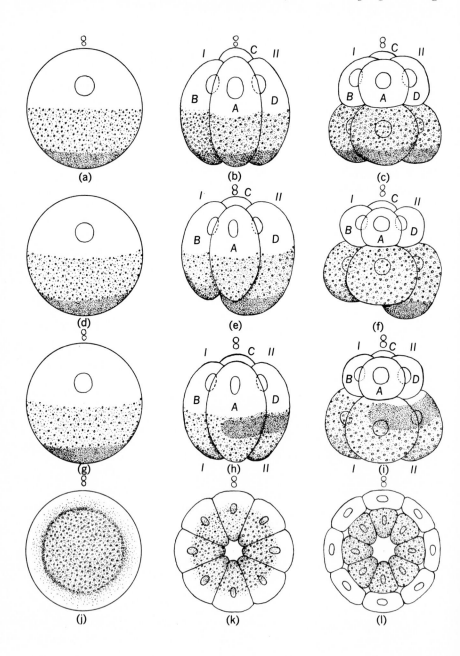

nificance and describe in each case the partitioning of these cytoplasmic regions among the early blastomeres. This exercise shows that the developmental potency of the early blastomeres can be understood primarily as a function of the relation between the planes of cleavage and the distribution of the morphogenetically significant regions in the egg. If the mesodermal determinants, for example, are asymmetrically distributed with respect to the cleavage planes, all of the blastomeres cannot be totipotent since possession of a qualitatively complete set of germ layer determinants is limited to certain specific blastomeres (e.g., Figs. 44d–f).

To quote Wilson:

> Totipotence on the part of the early blastomeres is dependent primarily on a symmetrical or merely quantitative distribution of the protoplasmic stuffs of the cleavage. In the hydromedusa (Figs. 44j–l) the original grouping of these materials is, broadly speaking, concentric about the center of the egg, and all of the radial cleavages accordingly are quantitative . . . since the first five cleavages are of this type complete dwarfs may be produced from any of the blastomeres up to the stage when the first qualitative divisions begin by the delamination—cleavages parallel to the surface. In the sea urchin the ooplasmic stuffs are polarized, displaying a symmetrical horizontal stratification at right angles to the axis of the egg. Since the first two cleavages pass exactly through the axis and cut all the strata symmetrically (Figs. 44a–c) the first four or two blastomeres receive equal allotments of these strata in their normal proportions and hence remain totipotent . . . we should expect the third cleavage to be qualitative; this is borne out by both observation and experiment (257).

Similarly, in annelids and many mollusks and other allied creatures undergoing spiral cleavage the mesoderm substances initially located in the polar region of the egg are distributed only to that cell which alone retains the capacity to develop into a qualitatively complete dwarf embryo (Figs. 44d–f), e.g., the CD cell of *Tubifex* or the D cell of *Ilyanassa*. In the ascidian egg (Figs. 44g–l) only the posterior blastomeres A and D retain the mesodermal determinants initially present in the egg cytoplasm, but other essential determinants not figured (e.g., neural ectoderm) are missing from these cells (Figs. 33 and 37). As Conklin showed in *Styela*, no one blastomere gives rise to a complete embryo in this form. The mere presence of the

FIGURE 44. Diagrams of the primary stratification in the eggs of the sea urchin (a)–(c) and the annelid or gastropod (d)–(f). The first two cleavage planes designated as I or II. The upper or white zone is ectoblastic, the middle or granular one the entoblastic, the lower or lined one the mesoblastic. In (a)–(c) all the zones are equally divided; in (d)–(f) only the two upper zones are thus divided, the lower one passing entirely into the D quadrant. (g)–(i) Primary stratification in the ascidian and (j)–(l) in the hydromedusa. In the ascidian the lower (mesoplasmic) stratum is equally divided between the A and D quadrants. In the hydromedusae this stratum is absent, and the remaining two are equally distributed up to the time of delamination (1). Wilson, E. B., *The Cell in Development and Heredity.* New York: Macmillan, 1925, pp. 1072–1076.

necessary cytoplasmic materials in a blastomere of course will not ensure the qualitatively normal development of a dwarf embryo if the blastomere should be isolated, since other factors are involved, but it is clearly a necessary prerequisite for such a development. Thus the blastomere lineages of all embryos in Fig. 44 depend on cytoplasmic localization patterns, those characterized as regulative (sea urchin and hydromedusa) and those characterized as mosaic (annelid) alike. It is clear, therefore, that blastomere totipotency cannot be used as an index of the existence of cytoplasmic localization.

time of appearance of definitive cytoplasmic organization in various eggs

A second source of the confusion in part responsible for the erroneous identification of localization with the mosaic form of development (and the absence of localization with regulative development) is the differential timing in the establishment of the localization patterns in different organisms. We have already mentioned the progressive localization which occurs between fertilization and the initiation of the cleavage division in *Styela* and *Dentalium*. In both of these eggs this phenomenon is clearly visualized (see Fig. 34). Numerous experimentalists have sought to correlate precleavage cytoplasmic movements with the ontogeny of localization itself by sectioning eggs under the microscope at various times between release from the ovary and cleavage, fertilizing the fragments, and recording the effect of the operation on later development. In the primitive worm *Cerebratulus,* for example, Wilson (257) showed that removal of a large non-nucleated sector of egg cytoplasm in any plane whatsoever fails to interfere qualitatively with development, and egg fragments as small as one-fourth the original mass of the egg can be fertilized and induced to develop after the germinal vesicle has broken down. This egg, once entered into cleavage, forms a typical, determinate, spirally cleaving embryo whose blastomeres, if isolated, manifest little more than those morphogenetic potencies displayed by them in their normal context (257).

Yatsu carried out similar operations on *Cerebratulus* eggs (258), extirpating portions of the egg cytoplasm at three successive points in the precleavage maturation process: before germinal vesicle dissolution, at the metaphase of the first reduction division, and at pronuclear fusion. These operations fail to interfere with subsequent development when undertaken before germinal vesicle breakdown, but about half the larvae resulting from egg fragments cut at first meiotic metaphase lack either apical or digestive organs; this is true of almost all embryos resulting from eggs cut at the pronuclear fusion

stage. Yatsu concluded that localization begins with germinal vesicle dissolution and becomes definite in the period between fertilization and fusion. Various evidence suggests that in the sea urchin, on the other hand, the future animal-vegetal blastomere values are not determined until the onset of the first cleavage, and that the localization of the micromere-forming cytoplasmic elements may occur even later than this (259, 260). A great many demonstrations of *progressive* localization could be cited (207, 260); the conclusion to be drawn is the same as that suggested by the visible redistribution of egg substances in *Styela* and *Dentalium,* viz., that localization is a temporally dependent phenomenon in which egg substances already present earlier are gradually moved into their appropriate definitive locations. Thus the extent to which the development of an embryo seems to conform to the model of a "mosaic of self-differentiating parts" depends partly on when the test is made, for organisms differ in when and how the cytoplasmic materials responsible for the qualitative determination of blastomere lineage fate are distributed.

intertissue interactions and the mosaic vs regulative dichotomy

It can be questioned whether considerations such as the foregoing are relevant only to known examples of self-differentiating blastomere lineages, rather than being of general applicability. Thus in some organisms overall development apparently depends more on a fixed program of self-differentiation inherited by the various cell lineages than in others, where intertissue interactions are apparently of greater significance. In this empirical distinction lies part of the significance of the mosaic vs regulative embryo dichotomy. An exhaustive series of experiments by Hörstadius (261) shows that after the 8-cell stage the embryos of *Cerebratulus* can be dissected into any groups of blastomeres whatsoever, and recombined in any way whatsoever, but irrespective of its new context each blastomere lineage in the recombinants differentiates precisely as it would have in the intact egg: the perfect mosaic embryo. There is an extensive literature of ingenious recombination and "relocalization" experiments designed to detect corrective early interblastomere inductive effects if they exist.

It is clear that in many animals, as in *Cerebratulus,* the progressive self-differentiation of each group of blastomeres continues with near-complete independence even in the most bizarre situations, where the result of this characteristic is inevitably the production of an inviable monster. Notable examples include the fusion-recombination studies of Novikoff (262) and Hatt (263) with the annelid *Sabellaria;* the observations of Penners showing that in *Tubifex* double embryos form from eggs whose coelomic mesoderm determinants are distributed into two D cells rather than one (264) and the similar experiments of Novikoff (265) and Tyler (266) with other annelids and mollusks; and the recombination experiments of Reverberi and Minganti with fragments from 8-cell ascidian embryos (267). In these cases the nature of the morphogenesis carried out by each blastomere lineage is independent of the lineage or course of morphogenesis of the adjacent blastomeres. Nevertheless, in some organisms of groups which have always been regarded as exemplars of the mosaic developmental character, interlineage interactions have been unequivocally demonstrated to be involved in morphogenesis as well, particularly, though not exclusively, in postgastrular morphogenesis. Examples are shell gland induction in gastropod mollusks (243, 246, 268) and induction of anterior neural structures in ascidians (267, 269). Cather's recent study of shell formation in *Ilyanassa* (246) illustrates this point convincingly. The shell gland is of ectodermal derivation, and the experiments of Cather demonstrate that any combination of ectoderm and endoderm can form shell, though neither can carry out this histospecific function alone. The innate ability of A, B, and C quadrant ectoderm to give rise to shell is repressed by the presence of the polar lobe cytoplasm borne in the D macromeres, however. Shell formation is normally confined to the D quadrant ectoderm derivatives, but induction of this activity must be initiated during the third quartet stage by the 3D macromere. A complex and temporally precise pattern of intercellular inductions directed from the D quadrant of the *Ilyanassa* embryo thus exists with respect to the formation of the shell gland, and there is evidence that the inductive role of the D quadrant extends as well to various other courses of differentiation in *Ilyanassa* and in allied embryos of the spiralian type.

Cellular interaction clearly plays an even more prominent role in the early embryogenesis of other organisms, however, and this property is essential for what is meant by regulative development. In the newt, for instance, it was shown clearly by Mangold (following earlier workers) that giant though otherwise normal single embryos can be formed by uniting two separate eggs (270). In order for this result to occur it is necessary that intercellular interactions, including of course the induction of gastrular structures, must have exercised an extremely important influence over the behavior of each cell lineage, and the newt result stands in direct contrast to similar experiments with *Sabellaria* (263) where double embryos are reported to form from two fused eggs. Intercellular interaction is a potent and decisive factor in the early development of the sea urchin, a striking demonstration of which is the ability of a longitudinally cut sea urchin half *blastula* to round up, gastrulate, and form a qualitatively complete pluteus (271). The extensive recombination experiments of Hörstadius (259) demonstrate this characteristic many times over in that the recombinant blastomere lineages are induced to behave in numerous different ways depending on the nature of the adjacent blastomeres. For example, Hörstadius showed that an artificially assembled juxtaposition of animal pole blastomeres and micromeres induces the central blastomere tiers to function as equatorial and endodermal cells, rather than continuing to develop as animal hemisphere cells.

Recent experiments of Giudice, Mutolo, and Moscona (271a) and of Pfohl and Giudice (272) have documented at the molecular level the significance of intercellular interaction in early sea urchin development. Giudice (273) had previously shown that the cells of dissociated sea urchin embryos will under appropriate conditions reaggregate and eventually give rise to differentiating pluteus-like larvae. Giudice and his associates (271a) have now demonstrated that the activation of ribosomal RNA synthesis fails to occur in dissociated sea urchin blastomeres if dissociation is carried out at the mesenchyme blastula stage or earlier. Embryonic cells dissociated at the midgastrula stage, however, synthesize ribosomal RNA as do control embryos. Early intercellular interaction thus appears to be necessary for the normal activation of ribosomal RNA synthesis. A similar result is obtained in other experiments (272) where alkaline phosphatase activity is measured in re-aggregating sea urchin blastomeres. As shown in Fig. 45, the activity of this enzyme increases sharply during normal development, and in dissociated reaggregating cells a similar increase is recorded if dissociation is carried out at the early pluteus stage, just before the actual increase in alkaline phosphatase activity. If dissociation is carried out at the mesenchyme blastula stage, however, alkaline phosphatase activity fails to be activated at the proper time, again showing the necessity of intercellular interactions in normal early development. Further indications of this nature come from the work of Markman (274), who has found that isolated animal half embryos synthesize RNA at higher than normal rates and also increase their cell number at higher than normal rates. Transplantation of micromeres into the isolated animal halves, according to Markman, results in moderation to control levels of the abnormal RNA synthesis rates, just as it results morphologically in amelioration of the extreme "animalization" syndrome.

Nonetheless, even in organisms in which regulative abilities are as highly developed as in the embryos of the newt and sea urchin, cytoplasmic localization of morphogenetic potential has been clearly demonstrated (this statement is documented below), just as inductive effects exist in embryos displaying relatively little regulative ability. Self-differentiation of blastomere lineages, on the one hand, and the inductive differentiation of blastomere lineages which underlies regulative ability, on the other, probably operate

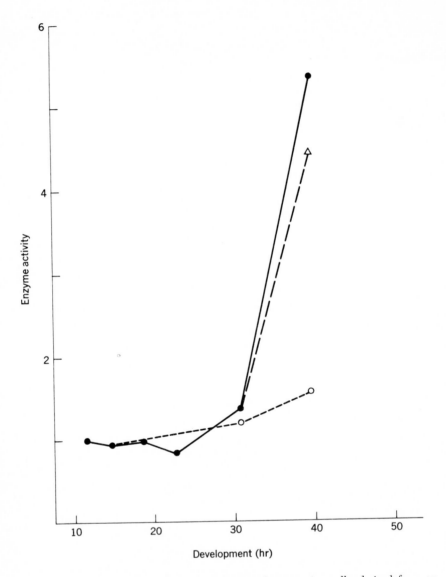

FIGURE 45. Relative alkaline phosphatase activity of aggregating cells, derived from an average of five experiments, is plotted together with values for control embryos: (solid line with filled circles) control embryos; (short-dashed line with open circles) cells dissociated from mesenchyme blastulae; (long-dashed line with open triangle) cells dissociated from early plutei. Pfohl, R. J., and Giudice, G., *Biochim. Biophys. Acta* **142**, 263 (1967).

in the embryogenesis of all animals, though the variations in the relative importance of each mode of development among animal groups is indeed striking. We conclude that the differences in the significance of blastomere interactions for early morphogenesis are real, but that this parameter is directly relevant to the *regulative ability* of an embryonic system rather than to the presence or absence of cytoplasmic localization.

lability of localization patterns

A related source of confusion is the variation in lability displayed by the localization patterns as one compares diverse eggs (249). In the frog, as Ancel and Vintemberger (275) have shown, for example, the basic polarity imposed on the egg from the time of its initial appearance is very easily changed merely by the force of gravity, but this is scarcely meant to imply that this polarity was not present in the first place, ensconced in the original contents and structure of the egg cytoplasm. Drastic alterations in the preassigned morphogenetic values of the early blastomeres and of the particular sectors of egg cytoplasm which they inherit have been experimentally induced in a number of ways and in a great variety of animals. Perhaps the best known examples are those dealing with the effects of lithium chloride and sodium thiocyanate on the course of differentiation in early sea urchin embryos (259, 276). Lithium chloride treatment induces prospective ectoderm cells to behave as endoderm, so that a LiCl-treated embryo develops a disproportionately enormous gut. In LiCl-treated embryos, furthermore, different cell types appear to be involved in primary mesenchyme production than are normally so engaged.

Thiocyanate produces the opposite effect, causing cells normally carrying out other functions to behave as apical tuft cells. These agents, the overall effects of which are extremely complex, operate in ways as yet unknown, and the physiological site of their primary action remains mysterious. Recent experiments of Runnstrom and Markman (277) show that the effect of LiCl treatment is blocked by parallel actinomycin treatment of the embryos, which suggests that directly or indirectly this vegetalizing agent functions via the embryo genomes. This in turn implies that LiCl treatment interferes with the operation of the program according to which the correct patterns of gene activity are normally imposed in each cell and its descendants. The lithium experiments and the vast literature regarding other demonstrations of lability show that at least in some organisms both the location in the egg of morphogenetically significant cytoplasmic substances and their ability to function can be externally affected.

localization, regulative development, and mosaic development

This brief digression has been undertaken merely for the purpose of pointing out that no logical incompatibility exists between the mass of evidence which lends itself to the characterization of development in some animals as regulative and the proposition that cytoplasmic morphogenetic determinants are of universal occurrence. It is evident that mosaic and regulative embryos differ with respect to various interesting and important properties, but *none of these preclude the normal operation of egg cytoplasmic factors in the assignment of morphogenetic roles to the various blastomere lineages.* In certain animals isolated blastomeres give rise to partial embryos, while in others they may give rise to whole embryos; in certain animals blastomere interactions are relied upon for critical early steps in morphogenesis, while in other animals inductive responses become significant only later; in some animals the morphogenetic patterns of blastomere assignment are more labile than in others, or are established later rather than earlier. In all animals the character of development is partly mosaic and partly regulative but not completely either.

Though there is indeed no logical incompatibility between the presence of morphogenetic cytoplasmic determinants and any of the characteristics usually associated with regulative development, the role of these determinants is far more obvious and overtly impressive in animals whose development tends more toward the mosaic character, and where relatively simple patterns of precocious localization are evident. For this reason most (though not all) of the relevant early studies have dealt with animals whose embryos may be characterized in this way, i.e., with urochordates, annelids, and mollusks. The phylogenetic distribution of obtrusively mosaic patterns of development in itself constitutes a warning against taking that characterization very seriously. Thus, to consider a protostomial example, certain insect groups display generally determinate, mosaic patterns of development (e.g., *Coleoptera*), while other insects display extremely regulative characteristics, for instance, the *Diptera* studied by Seidel (278). Similarly, consider the development of ascidians, which in deuterostome phylogeny lie between the echinoderms on the one hand and the cephalochordate, teleost, and amphibian levels of organization on the other. The highly mosaic character of ascidian development is evidently completely isolated, phylogenetically speaking, since echinoderms, cephalochordates, teleosts, and amphibians have in common a far greater apparent regulative capacity than do ascidians.

5

Demonstrations of localization
in regulative embryos

In the years following the brilliant investigations which defined the cyto-plasmic localization phenomenon, and which certainly represent some of the finest achievements of developmental biology, demonstrations that morpho-genetically significant cytoplasmic determinants are localized in the egg have extended to material more or less refractory to earlier investigations, in par-ticular to the eggs of amphibians and echinoderms. We now review some of these demonstrations, which are of a certain added interest in that, as we have seen, these eggs display strong regulative abilities in isolated blastomere experiments and in experiments testing the lability of the blastomere assignments.

cytoplasmic determinants in the eggs of echinoderms

The earliest detailed observations indicating that morphogenetic determinants exist in the cytoplasm of the sea urchin egg are owing to Boveri (279). This study was carried out in 1902, with *Paracentrotus lividus,* a species in which a median band of pigment granules marks the location of the cytoplasm which will be needed for the formation of the archenteron. Boveri's demon-strations of this correspondence was achieved by shaking the eggs into pieces and fertilizing the fragments: Only fragments containing the pigment-marked cytoplasm gastrulate and form archenteron. These results were con-firmed by Hörstadius in 1928 (280) who, like Boveri, found that the initial axial orientation apparent from the time of pigment layer formation marks the eventual definitive orientation of the embryo. Thus animal half-egg fragments develop in a manner similar to the animal halves of 16-cell cleav-age-stage embryos, and the morphogenesis carried out by vegetal egg frag-ments likewise corresponds to that observed in 8- or 16-cell vegetal-half em-bryos. The potentials for micromere, skeleton, and archenteron formation appear to be localized in the vegetal region of the egg cytoplasm even before fertilization, and the orientation and distribution of these materials remain unchanged as the egg substance begins to be divided up among the cleavage

145

blastomeres. Hörstadius extended these findings to *Arbacia punctulata* (281), orienting the eggs individually soon after fertilization, and cutting them in half at the pronuclear fusion stage. Haploid and diploid animal and vegetal halves are all obtained in this manner. The animal halves cleave equally, producing no micromeres, and form spherical structures with enlarged apical tufts, the typical extreme animalization syndrome. The vegetal halves, however, form micromeres and gastrulate with archenteron and skeleton formation ensuing. The results are independent of the presence of the genomic contribution of the egg. As with polar lobe removal in *Dentalium* and *Ilyanassa*, both the animal and vegetal fragments possess the full genomic complement and yet develop only partially, lacking certain qualitatively distinct courses of differentiation. Hörstadius' experiments thus illustrate with great clarity the localization of morphogenetically determinant cytoplasmic factors in sea urchin egg cytoplasm. Furthermore, they prove that this localization is under normal conditions the permanent one, so that the nature of the cytoplasm inherited by a given blastomere depends on its position vis-à-vis the initial pattern of morphogenetic localization established before cleavage. It is further reminiscent of the annelid and gastropod examples that the initial effects of the egg cytoplasm determinants on morphogenesis are manifested early in cleavage. Thus *Arbacia* fragments containing cytoplasm destined for the archenteron-forming cells produce micromeres, while fragments lacking the archenteron determinants fail to do so; of course, only the former gastrulate (281).

Hörstadius, Josefson, and Runnstrom have extracted some proteins from unfertilized sea urchin eggs which resolve on Dowex-50 into components displaying animalizing and vegetalizing activity, and which the authors consider to include the cytoplasmic agents responsible for the morphogenetic location patterns revealed by the earlier studies (282). Although micromere appearance early in cleavage is clearly mediated by the cytoplasm and is totally independent of embryo genome function (Section I), the ultimate *function* of the micromere lineage in archenteron formation depends directly on embryo genome function. [See the discussion in Section I and the recent review by Runnstrom concerning evidence implicating embryo genome action in both animalization and vegetalization (283).] In the sea urchin, therefore, the same relations between cytoplasmic localization, asymmetric cleavage pattern, and ultimate nuclear differentiation exist as in the more obtrusively mosaic lower protostomes.

cytoplasmic localization in amphibian eggs

Recent experiments on localization in amphibian eggs have much increased our knowledge of cytoplasmic determinants in this key group, the only really well-known chordate class. An unequivocal demonstration of cytoplasmic localization in the amphibian egg exists in the experiments of Smith on germ cell determination in *Rana pipiens* (284). It has been known for many years that the amphibian germ-cell stem line originates early in cleavage from blastomeres forming at the vegetal pole of the egg. Smith has shown that ultraviolet irradiation of vegetal pole cytoplasm at first cleavage in *Rana pipiens* results in the subsequent absence of germ cells from otherwise normal metamorphosed embryos, a finding in accord with the results of earlier studies on germ cell determination in amphibians (see Section III for references in this connection).

The deficient germinal ridges of irradiated and control larvae are shown in Fig. 46. The experiments reported by Smith indicate that irradiation must occur before the 8-cell stage is reached; by this point the germ-line stem cells have already been specified, and later irradiation does not interfere with the appearance of germ cells. Parallel irradiation of the animal pole cytoplasm produces no visible defects and certainly none in the germ cell line. According to Smith's study, the deficiency in the cytoplasmic factors responsible for germ cell determination which results from ultraviolet irradiation can be compensated for by the injection into the vegetal pole of an irradiated egg of cytoplasm from the vegetal pole of an unirradiated egg. The recipient eggs are able, in a significant fraction of cases, to give rise to an embryo containing germ cells, while controls receiving no normal vegetal cytoplasm or cytoplasm from the animal pole never develop germ cells. These experiments are presented in Table VI. The early stage by which germ cell determination in *Rana pipiens* has at least begun to occur, so that the specifying cytoplasm is no longer a requirement (third cleavage), associates this process with the first equatorial segregation of particular nuclei into the vegetal sector of the egg. It will be noted how similar is the process of germ cell determination in *Rana* to that described above for creatures as phylogenetically remote as the insects studied by Hegner.

Other evidence regarding cytoplasmic localization in amphibian eggs has recently been developed by Curtis (285), who has exploited a method of his invention for transplanting small ($150 \times 150 \mu$) sections of egg cortex to other eggs and embryos. A sequence of previous studies dating back to early experiments of Spemann [(286); see also Holtfreter and Hamburger (287) and Briggs and King (288) for a summary of foregoing evidence] indicates that chordamesoderm-specifying, or more generally, dorsalizing material is localized prior to first cleavage in the gray crescent area of amphibian eggs, though the positioning of the latter is not invariably a reliable guide. Curtis has shown that transplantation of a cortical graft from the gray crescent area of an 8-cell embryo to the ventral side of a fertilized but not yet cleaved *Xenopus* egg results in double gastrulation and axiation. This experiment is diagrammed in Fig. 47 (experiment c). Figures 47a and d show that excision of the gray crescent cortical cytoplasm before (d) but not after (a) the 8-cell stage results in failure of gastrulation and subsequent development. Thus the cytoplasm whose location is indicated by the pigmentation of the crescent appears to have performed some act of determina-

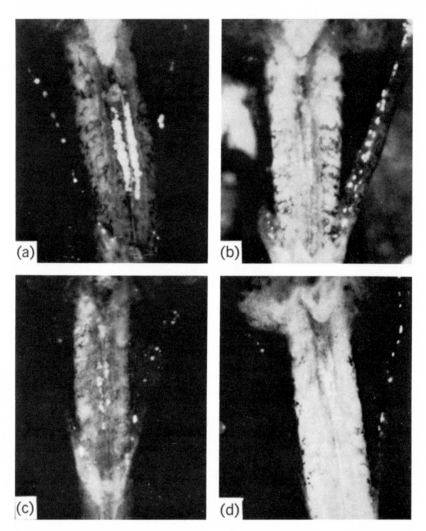

FIGURE 46. (a) Dissected stage-25 larva showing the primordial germ cells in a normal unirradiated control. (b) and (c) Two stage-25 larvae which developed from eggs that were irradiated with a UV dose of 5300 ergs/mm^2. (d) Stage-25 larva which developed from an egg which was irradiated with a UV dose of 15,000 ergs/mm^2 (cephalic end at top of photograph). Smith, L. D., *Develop. Biol.* **14**, 330 (1966).

TABLE VI. Transfers of Normal Cytoplasm into the Vegetal Hemisphere of Irradiated Eggs[a]

Type of transfer[b]	Stage	No. injected	No. displaying no leakage	No. of normal stage 25	No. or % of animals with germ[c] cells	No. or % of animals without germ cells
Vegetal pole-vegetal pole	2-cell	110	64	51	15 (10) 23%	49 77%
Animal pole-vegetal pole	2-cell	45	31	28	0	28
Irradiated uninjected controls		–	–	40	0	40
Fertilized controls		–	–	40	40 (82)	0
Vegetal pole-vegetal pole	4–8-cell	40	15	11	7 (12) 47%	8 53%
Animal pole-vegetal pole	4–8-cell	19	14	13	0	13
Irradiated uninjected controls		–	–	20	0	20
Fertilized controls		–	–	20	20 (61)	0

[a] From Ref. 284.
[b] The first region listed is that from which donor cytoplasm was obtained, and the second region is that into which the cytoplasm was injected.
[c] The number in parentheses indicates the mean number of germ cells; i.e., 15 (10) indicates 15 animals with primordial germ cells and the mean number of germ cells per animal was 10.

tion as early as third cleavage, an impression which is strengthened by the experiment described in Fig. 47b. Here it is shown that double axiation can no longer be induced by unfertilized egg gray crescent cytoplasm in eggs as old as third cleavage.

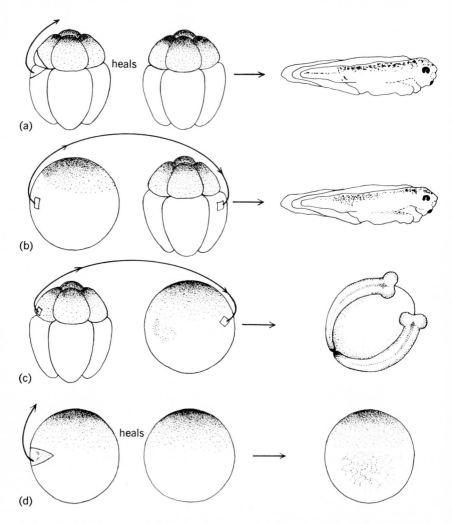

FIGURE 47. (a) Excision of the gray crescent cortex from a stage-4 embryo results in a normal embryo being formed [compare with (d)]. (b) Grafting gray crescent cortex from stage 1 to the ventral margin of stage 4 does not result in the induction of a second embryonic axis. (c) Grafts of gray crescent cortex from stage-4 embryos to the ventral margins of stage-1 embryos induce secondary embryonic axes. (d) Excision of gray crescent cortex from stage-1 embryos prevents morphogenesis though cleavage and mitosis continue. Curtis, A. S. G., J. Embryol. Exptl. Morphol. **10**, 410 (1962).

These findings are most simply regarded as direct evidence for the precocious determination by cortical egg cytoplasm of the blastomere nuclei. Note that as shown in Fig. 47c the responsible cytoplasmic determinants are still present in the 8-cell stage, even though determination has occurred by then, since the cortical cytoplasm from the gray crescent area of the 8-cell embryo is able to induce double axiation when transplanted back to an unfertilized egg. The significance of the 8-cell stage as the point of no return in the determination of the blastomere lineages which are to construct the

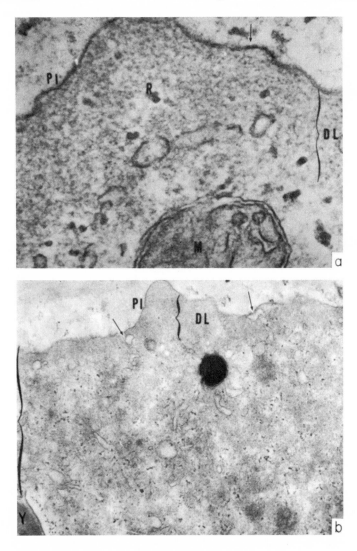

FIGURE 48a, b.

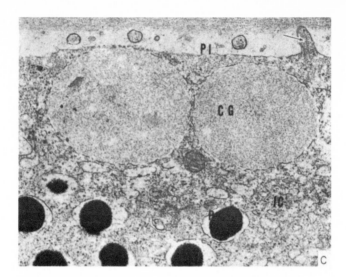

FIGURE 48. (a) First cleavage zygote of *Xenopus*: animal pole. 100,000 ×. Plasmalemma (PL) has a unit membrane structure (arrow). Texture of dense layer (DL, brackets) differs from that of ground cytoplasm; 250-Å particles (R) are present in both dense layer and background cytoplasm. (b) First cleavage zygote: dorsal surface. 25,000 ×. Note presence of discontinuities in the dense layer (arrows) and width of yolk-free cytoplasmic band (large brackets). (c) Unfertilized egg: animal pole. 30,000 ×. Plasmalemma is quite smooth except for periodic outpocketings (arrow). Cortical granules (CG) are detached from plasmalemma. Note the lack of specialized peripheral cytoplasm that is different in texture from more internal cytoplasm (IC). Hebard, C. N., and Herold, R. C., *Exptl. Cell Res.* **46**, 553 (1967).

dorsal axes of the embryo is very likely the same as in the case of germ cell determination; with the first *transverse cleavage* the most general blastomere assignments have to have been specified. Whether or not the cytoplasmic determinants present originally in the egg are themselves mobilized into a gradient of some form during early cleavage as Curtis believes his experiments to indicate is a separate question. In neither case is the demonstration that *morphogenetically significant cytoplasmic materials* are localized in the cortex of the uncleaved egg affected.

The cortical layer of the *Xenopus* egg is characterized by a special structure, according to the recent electron microscope studies of Hebard and Herold (289). A dense layer of about the same thickness as the cortical grafts transplanted by Curtis envelopes the main mass of cytoplasm in this egg (Figs. 48a and b), lying directly beneath the plasma membrane. It is interesting and significant that this layer forms only after fertilization, when the definitive dorsoventral localization patterns of the amphibian egg are

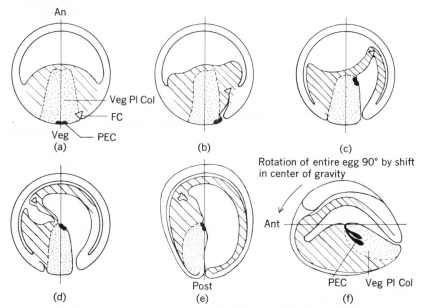

FIGURE 49. Diagrammatic median sections of *Ambystoma maculatum* embryos from (a) the beginning of gastrulation to (f) midneurulation. The triangle represents the flask cells which initiate invagination. The dark spots represent experimentally stained polar endoderm cells. (An) Animal pole; (FC) flask cells; (PEC) polar endoderm cells; (Veg) vegetal pole; (Veg Pl Col) vegetal plasm column; (Ant) anterior; (Post) posterior. Harris, T. M., *Develop. Biol.* **10**, 247 (1964).

established. The absence of the dense cortical layer in the unfertilized egg is shown in Fig. 48c. Though centrifugation and other types of experiment have indicated that in many forms the morphogenetically significant cytoplasmic determinants are probably located in the egg cortex, it has in general been very difficult to detect cortical cytodifferentiation such as that shown here.

Another recent study yielding information on localization in amphibian eggs is that of Harris (290), who has investigated the disposition and fate of the pigmented vegetal cytoplasm recognizable even before fertilization in the urodele *Ambystoma*. In early cleavage this material is partitioned into vegetal pole cells, the descendants of which can be identified throughout blastulation. These cells constitute the lineages which are apparently responsible for the orientation of gastrular invagination. Thus in the blastula they form a column aligned with the future dorsoventral axis of the embryo, and it is along this column that the flask cells which initiate gastrulation move. The physical relationships which exist during gastrulation between the forming archenteron, the invaginating polar cells, and the lineages bearing the original pigmented vegetal egg cytoplasm are shown in Harris' diagram, reproduced in Fig. 49. After gastrulation the vegetal plasm-containing cells become the site of intestine morphogenesis, the intestinal lumen forming within the center of this cell mass along the path denoted by the marked polar endoderm cells of Fig. 49f. Here again we have a case in which the later morphogenetic fate of an important blastomere lineage is associated with the inheritance of a particular sector of the original egg cytoplasm. Thus the localization of this cytoplasm in the uncleaved *Ambystoma* egg foreshadows the axial orientation of the future gastrula, and the differentiation of the cells ultimately inheriting it implements the building of that orientation.

the universality of cytoplasmic localization

The evidence summarized in the last few pages shows that morphogenetic determinants are localized in the cytoplasm of amphibian and echinoderm eggs no less than in the eggs of other organisms. We are now in a better position to judge the generality of the localization phenomenon in the animal kingdom: *It seems clear that cytoplasmic localization, at least up to a median grade of chordate evolution, is universal.* Though cytoplasmic localization has been claimed to exist in mammalian eggs, the evidence surrounding this question remains controversial (291). A striking aspect of the generality of localization is the occurrence of detailed similarities with respect to cytoplasmic determination among animals separated by enormous evolutionary space and time. Consider germ cell determination. We have seen that in a nematode, a frog, and in an insect, germ-line stem cell determination occurs just when the cleaving nuclei arrive in a certain region of polar cytoplasm (further examples are cited in the next section). The nearest common ancestor of these organisms was probably an extremely primitive coelomate worm, and localization, as we have noted, is clearly identifiable even in the eggs of coelenterates such as *Beröe*. Cytoplasmic localization is thus evolutionarily more ancient than even the coelomic grade of organization, and in fact it appears to be older than the bilateralia. In the absence of information to the contrary, it is scarcely absurd to suppose that localization is as old as the process of metazoan embryogenesis.

6

Interpretations of the localization phenomenon

The interest aroused in the late nineteenth century by the discovery and documentation of cytoplasmic localization, and the resulting stimulation of a neopreformationist viewpoint were discussed earlier. Neopreformationism in a sense led to the isolated blastomere experiments, as noted above. In more general terms, however, the neopreformationism-epigenesis debate is of significance because it forced the formation of new theories of biological information flow in development. Thus Whitman, in his Woods Holl * Lecture of 1895 (211) concluded that it is a mistake to place oneself in the position of choosing between preformationist and epigenetic explanations for embryogenesis. From his point of view preformationism is anathema. He characterized it as "a negation wrapped in negations to a depth that is absolutely hermetic to positive reality . . . the greatest error that ever obstructed the progress of our knowledge of development . . . ending in one infinite negation—NO CHANGE" (216). Whitman considered that the real problem posed by the discovery of cytoplasmic localization of morphogenetic potential is the problem of explaining localization and prelocalization while at the same time preserving the idea that the nucleus contains genetic determinants through whose action epigenetic development must take place. The ideas stemming from this resolution of the problem lead directly to the present period of biological thought. It is thus useful to touch briefly on several of these earlier treatments of the localization phenomenon before turning to a more contemporary view of this fascinating problem.

the "embryo in the rough"

For some years after 1900 a theory espoused by Boveri, Loeb, and Morgan among others was current which proposed that the egg cytoplasm and its regions of localized determinants is responsible for the form of the "embryo in the rough." It was proposed that the role of Mendelian (i.e., nuclear genomic) factors is to determine merely the details of the *individual's* de-

* Correct spelling in 1895.

155

velopment, such as color, size, and detailed shape of skeleton. In 1903, for example, Boveri listed among the "preformed" characters determined by the structure of the cytoplasm the tempo of development, polarity, axis of symmetry, pattern of cleavage, and the crude areas of morphogenetic localization, e.g., the location of the mesoderm stem cells (292). He proposed that those characters which are determined by the nuclear genes, e.g., the skeleton of the sea urchin pluteus, are the ones which develop *epigenetically,* in contrast to the "embryo in the rough" characters already preformed in the cytoplasm. Thus an equivalency was drawn, on the one hand, between epigenesis and those developmental processes stemming from the action of the embryo genome, and, on the other, between preformation and morphogenesis independent of embryo genome action, the whole pregastrular period of development (in the sea urchin) belonging to the latter. As early as 1895–1896, however, it had been pointed out by Driesch and by Wilson that even these preformed characters can be regarded only as the product of an *earlier epigenetic process originating in the oocyte nucleus* during oogenesis.

In an appendix to Crampton's study of localization in *Ilyanassa,* Wilson wrote (1896): "Cytoplasmic organization, while affording the immediate conditions for development, is itself a result in the last analysis of the nature of the nuclear substance which represents by its inherent composition the totality of heritable potence. Logically carried out this view inevitably involves the conclusion that the specific plasma structure of the egg is acquired during its ovarian maturation" (293). This line abolishes the distinction between epigenetic, genome-directed morphogenesis and the preformational morphogenesis of the "embryo in the rough" mediated by the egg cytoplasm. Instead, cytoplasmic preformation is regarded as the result of an earlier ovarian epigenetic process in which *oocyte gene action* results in the assembly of the morphogenetically significant components of the egg cytoplasm. The only real preformation is that of the genome itself: "Heredity is effected by the transmission of a *nuclear preformation* which in the course of development finds expression in a process of cytoplasmic epigenesis" [Wilson, in 1925 (294)]. The startling 1896 insight of Wilson and Driesch is a fruitful basis for further advances in the treatment of the localization problem, but further than this statement writers of the classical period of developmental cell biology did not go. The morphogenetic determinants present in the egg cytoplasm were always referred to simply as "organ-forming substances."

localization and cell differentiation

Since localization affects the course of differentiation it would seem clear, as we have already indicated, that it must be explained in terms of the regulation of embryo genome function. It was generally believed in Wilson's time that all cells contain the complete genome and also that genes direct the cellular construction of properties. Nevertheless, as we have seen, it was not until much later that the theory of variable gene activity was clearly enunciated as an explanation for cell differentiation. The failure to take this conceptual step prevented the earlier writers from proceeding beyond the idea of organ-forming substances. Considered in the light of the variable gene activity theory of cell differentiation it is clear that localization cannot be due exclusively to a deposition in the egg of "organ-forming stuffs," as understood literally, be they either histospecific proteins or histospecific template RNA's, even though the latter might indeed exist in egg cytoplasm. This is because new embryo genome action is needed in order for differentiation to occur. *Therefore any explanation for the localization of morphogenetic potential must account for the novel patterns of embryo genome action if it is to account for differentiative specification of blastomere lineages,* above and beyond any storage of preformed tissue characteristic products in these blastomeres.

One is thus led to the proposition that localization of morphogenetic potential is the visible end product of the deposition in egg cytoplasm of molecules whose function is to elicit specific patterns of gene activity in blastomere nuclei, as these molecules are partitioned among the nuclei along with other cytoplasmic components in the course of early cleavage. The blastomere nuclei are affected differentially according to which sector of egg cytoplasm they inherit. As first stated by Wilson, the active cytoplasmic components must themselves stem from prior gene function during oogenesis, on the part of the oocyte genome per se and/or the accessory cell genomes. Thus the interaction between blastomere nuclei and egg cytoplasm displays taxonomic specificity, as the results of species-hybrid (Section I) and interspecific nuclear transplant experiments (288) unequivocally indicate.

The a priori arguments employed by Wilson are in fact sufficient, for it is indeed true that in order to avoid any preformation except that of the genomic information in the chromosomes the molecules affecting the blastomere genome must result indirectly or directly from gene transcription. In this way an informational feedback is postulated: oocyte and/or accessory cell genome to egg cytoplasm, to the blastomere genomes, which by any theory are essentially replicas of the oocyte genome prior to the occurrence of blastomere specification. Various speculations as to the identity of the molecules participating in the terminal (i.e., specification) step of this process are considered in Section IV, to which we therefore defer discussion of the nature of the "organ-forming stuffs" of the classical authors. It is not feasible, on the basis of current evidence, to distinguish the possibility that the responsible molecular species are synthesized on maternal templates after fertilization from the simpler alternative that the responsible molecules are synthesized directly during oogenesis. In the latter connection it is to be noted that active protein synthesis occurs in the polar lobe cytoplasm of the *Ilyanassa* egg. Thus, according to recent experiments of Clement and Tyler (295), isolated polar lobes contain maternal template RNA and are able to support protein synthesis for as long as 24 hours after isolation. Another case in which egg cytoplasmic elements known to participate in morphogenetic determination have been shown to engage in protein synthesis is that of the polar granules of the *Drosophila* egg. These granules, whose presence is requisite for primordial germ cell formation (see above), have been the subject of a recent electron microscope study by Mahowald (295a). The granules, which themselves contain RNA, become dispersed at the time of pole cell formation, and during this critical period they are associated with dense clusters of polyribosomes. Thus it is likely that protein synthesis is involved with polar granule function.

To summarize this discussion, it would appear that *storage in the egg cytoplasm of molecules whose function is the selective specification of embryo gene activity is an extremely general and probably universal mechanism in animal development.* Were it understood in molecular terms such a mechanism would go far to explain the initial set of mysteries facing the development biologist, viz., the onset of embryo genome control and the appearance of the first patterns of embryonic differentiation.

recent evidence for the selective
gene activation
theory of localization

Direct experimental evidence that egg cytoplasm can indeed exercise startling effects on the patterns and level of nuclear gene function is not lacking. The most direct demonstration is owing to Gurdon and Brown (296), who transplanted *Xenopus* neurula and gut nuclei active in ribosomal RNA synthesis into enucleate, activated eggs. Within a few minutes remarkable changes are detected: The nuclei swell from $160 \, \mu^3$–$4500 \, \mu^3$ (the size of the normal zygote fusion nucleus), their nucleoli disappear, and ribosomal RNA synthesis is halted. A new and complete pattern of RNA synthesis must be induced by the contextual egg cytoplasm, since the injected nuclei are able to direct the construction of a normal gastrula, an operation which we know to require novel embryo genome function. The RNA synthesis patterns observed experimentally in the transplanted embryos bear out this supposition, as shown in Fig. 50. Here it is seen that in the donor gut tissue, as in the rest of the embryo, precursor is mainly incorporated into ribosomal RNA after a 1-hour labeling period, while in the transplant embryos heterogene-

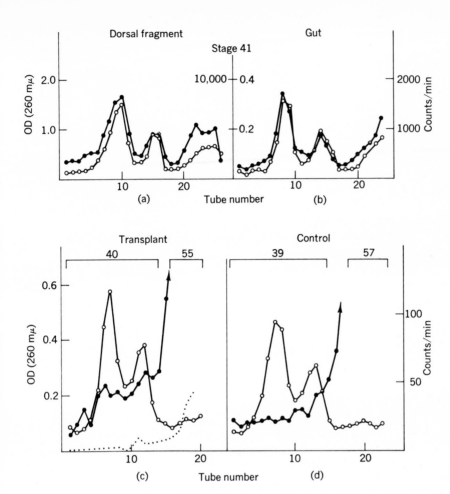

FIGURE 50. (a) and (b) Comparison of RNA synthesized by 160 *Xenopus* embryos during a 6-hour pulse with $^{14}CO_2$ in the gut (b), and in the rest of the tadpole (a). Total RNA was extracted within 1 hour after the pulse. The results are plotted on the same relative scale (OD versus counts/min) to show that the specific activity of the RNA in the gut is similar to that of the rest of the tadpole. (c) and (d) Sedimentation pattern of total RNA synthesized, (c) by 66 blastula nuclear transplant-embryos from stage-41 (tadpole) gut nuclei, and (d) by 66 blastulae reared from fertilized eggs. The lower line in (c) shows the ^{32}P-labeled RNA content of 66 sibling unfertilized eggs; the numbers at the top of each graph show the percentage of guanylic plus cytidylic acid in the bracketed radioactive RNA. The greater number of heterogeneous counts in (c) compared to (d) is probably because the transplant embryos in (c) were frozen at stage 9, whereas the controls in (d) were frozen at stage 8. (Solid line with open circles) OD; (solid line with filled circles) radioactivity. Gurdon, J. B., and Brown, D. D., *J. Mol. Biol.* **12**, 27 (1965).

ously sedimenting RNA similar to that made by normal late blastulae is synthesized instead. The experiment thus indicates that the *recipient egg cytoplasm has elicited qualitatively new informational RNA synthesis patterns while at the same time halting ribosomal RNA synthesis,* and the latter resumes in the transplant embryos at the same time as in normal controls.

Another nuclear function for which evidence of control by egg cytoplasm exists in amphibians is that of DNA synthesis. Experiments of Graham (297) have shown that microinjected sperm nuclei undergo DNA synthesis in phased cycles which are perfectly synchronous with DNA synthesis in the sperm and egg pronuclei and the zygote nucleus. Moreover, Gurdon has recently demonstrated that nuclei from a tissue which normally does not synthesize DNA at all, adult brain, will actively carry out DNA synthesis if introduced into the cytoplasm of ovulated *Xenopus* eggs (298). The capacity to induce DNA synthesis is acquired by the egg cytoplasm only after the germinal vesicle has broken down in the course of the pituitary hormone-dependent ovulation processes. One can only speculate as to how general in metazoan cells may be the phenomenon of genomic control by the cell cytoplasm, in view of the spectacular demonstrations by Harris that totally dormant red cell nuclei, when introduced into living HeLa cell cytoplasm, resume the synthesis of both RNA and DNA (299).

Recently, Thompson and McCarthy (300) have reported studies with isolated liver and avain erythrocyte nuclei which appear to demonstrate directly the presence of cytoplasmic factors able to activate both RNA and DNA synthesis. Isolated mouse liver nuclei are shown in these experiments to respond to an extract of ascites cell cytoplasm with an immediate 15- to 20-fold increase in DNA synthesis rate. A similar response occurs when L-cell cytoplasm is added to isolated hen erythrocyte nuclei incubated *in vitro* with ^{3}H-thymidine triphosphate. Cytoplasmic extracts derived from an essentially nondividing-cell-type, normal liver, however, fail to stimulate DNA synthesis in either erythrocyte or liver nuclei. Even more striking is the effect of cytoplasm on RNA synthesis by the isolated nuclei, as illustrated in Fig. 51. Here it can be observed that cytoplasm from an actively dividing liver tumor line carried in ascitic form is capable of stimulating normal liver nuclei to increase their rates of RNA synthesis sharply, while normal liver cyptoplasm again causes essentially no change in the intrinsic level of RNA synthesis. Ribonucleic acid synthesis in isolated erythrocyte nuclei (Fig. 51b) is in the same manner stimulated strongly by the addition of L-cell cytoplasm. These experiments indicate explicitly the presence of cytoplasmic substances which possess the capability of activating the genomic apparatus. The presence of such substances is correlated with the state of activity of the donor cells, and this fact would appear to diminish the possibility that some

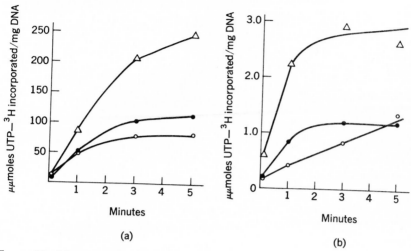

FIGURE 51. (a) Ribonucleic acid synthesis in isolated mouse liver nuclei. Total volume 0.29 ml, 5 μCi/incubation mixture (^{3}H-UTP): (open circles) nuclei alone, (filled circles) nuclei plus mouse liver cytoplasm, (open triangles) nuclei plus ascites cytoplasm; 600 μg protein per sample. (b) Ribonucleic acid synthesis in isolated hen erythrocyte nuclei: (open circles) hen nuclei alone, (filled circles) nuclei plus mouse liver cytoplasm, (open triangle) nuclei plus L-cell cytoplasm; 340 μg protein per sample. Thompson, L. R., and McCarthy, B. J., *Biochem. Biophys. Res. Commun.* **30**, 166 (1968).

ubiquitous, indirectly stimulatory factor (e.g., a metabolic substrate) could be responsible for these interesting results.

Another study specifically consistent with the interpretation of the localization phenomenon which we have given here is a recent investigation into the effect of polar lobe removal on nuclear activation during the embryogenesis of *Ilyanassa* (155). Though the bulk (ribosomal) RNA content of the *Ilyanassa* embryo remains constant until after the completion of gastrulation (157), RNA synthesis becomes activated soon after fertilization. The early RNA synthesis is actinomycin sensitive, and the RNA's synthesized are of high molecular weight (156). Assume that, as proposed, the morphogenetically significant polar lobe cytoplasm contains factors which selectively elicit histospecific gene activity in the cells descendant from the D blastomere; the failure of certain differentiations in lobeless embryos, despite the presence in these embryos of the undisturbed nuclei bearing the total genomic information carried in the organism, would then be interpreted as stemming from *failure to set up the mesoderm-specific patterns of gene activity* required for differentiation of the D blastomere lineage into coelomic mesoderm. A consequence of polar lobe deletion in this case would be a

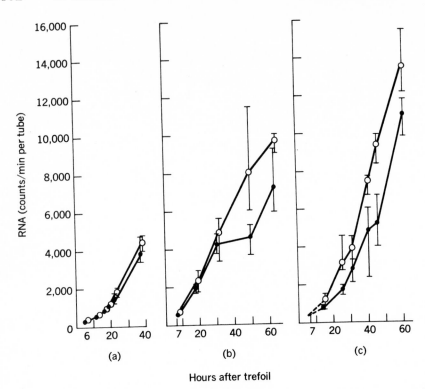

Hours after trefoil

FIGURE 52. Three experiments in which (filled circles) lobeless and (open circles) normal embryos are compared. Uridine-^{3}H uptake into the RNA of the embryos during a 2-hour labeling period is plotted against the number of hours which have elapsed between trefoil, when delobing is performed, and the time of labeling. Trefoil occurs about 3.5 hours after the eggs are shed. Each point represents the average of triplicate (experiments I and II) or quadruplicate (experiment III) determinations for each class of embryo. The brackets give the *absolute range* of the values recorded. Davidson, E. H., Haslett, G. W., Finney, R. J., Allfrey, V. G., and Mirsky, A. E., *Proc. Natl. Acad. Sci. U.S.* **54**, 696 (1965).

decrease in the level of gene activity, measurable as a decrease compared to controls in the rate of RNA synthesis, at the time when gene activity in preparation for early mesodermal differentiation is to occur. In Fig. 52 an experiment carried out in the writer's laboratory and designed to detect such a decrease is plotted, and Table VII summarizes data obtained in this study regarding the RNA synthesis rate per nucleus per unit time in normal and lobeless embryos. These experiments show that in the absence of polar lobe cytoplasm the activation of RNA synthesis fails to attain normal proportions as development proceeds. Thus the per cell RNA synthesis rates displayed in the lobeless embryos described in Table VII are significantly subnormal

TABLE VII. RNA Synthesis per Nucleus in Lobeless and Normal Embryos[a]

| Post-trefoil (hr) | No. of cells per Embryo | | RNA (av count/min/cell) | | | | | |
| | Lobeless | Normal | Experiment I | | Experiment II | | Experiment III | |
			Lobeless	Normal	Lobeless	Normal	Lobeless	Normal
6–7	15.4	12.2	0.61	1.05	2.0	3.0	—	—
18	24.0	22.4	2.5	2.9	5.2	6.8	3.3	5.6
30–31	32.3	31.6	7.3	8.6	8.7	10.3	6.0	8.4
38	62.8	63.2	5.6	6.3	4.7	6.6	5.1	7.1
60–62	126.0	125.8	—	—	3.9	5.2	5.9	7.3

[a] Cell counts were performed on 8–10 embryos at each time point. Ribonucleic acid synthesis per nucleus very likely varies according to which part of the cell cycle is assayed, and the values given in the right half of the table may not be median values. Nevertheless, the results are in accord with those of Fig. 52, which shows that the greatest change in rate occurs between 18 and 30 hours. From Ref. 155.

during the critical 24–30-hour activation period. Since the number of cells in lobeless and normal embryos increases at approximately equal rates it is difficult to regard polar lobe removal as the cause of some nonspecific injury which secondarily damages gene activity, e.g., depletion of some necessary substrates or energy supply sources. Further evidence against this possibility is available in Clement's studies (243, 244a) in which, as will be recalled, it is shown that the whole D macromere containing the bulk of the polar lobe contents can be removed without interfering with the subsequent development of a *qualitatively* normal veliger. Moreover, total bulk (ribosomal) RNA increases in lobeless embryos at the same rate as in normal embryos from 4 days after delobing, according to Collier (63). The effect of delobing would therefore seem to be qualitatively confined, since it does not include repression of normal ribosomal RNA synthesis rates; however, further study is obviously needed to clarify the qualitative nature of the genomic response to polar lobe deletion. The data of Table VII and Fig. 52 provide a direct indication, nonetheless, that gene activation occurring many hours after the trefoil stage requires the presence of the morphogenetically significant polar lobe cytoplasm.

CONCLUSIONS

It is useful, before proceeding to a different, though immediately related topic, to summarize the main conclusions deriving from this brief review of the extensive literature on localization of morphogenetic determinants. We have concluded that cytoplasmic localization is a fundamental aspect of development and is probably of universal occurrence. The nature of the localization phenomenon suggests that what are localized are molecules whose role is to selectively specify the patterns of gene activation in the early embryo. Synthesis of these determinants occurs during oogenesis, and they are stored until their final topological distribution in the egg cytoplasm just before or shortly after fertilization. The diverse patterns of gene activity required for the initial appearance of differentiating cell lineages are established in part through the interaction of these determinants with the totipotent blastomere genomes distributed among them during cleavage. It is noted that this proposition is the lineal descendant of a long line of theories regarding the transmission and operation of biological information for ontogeny, extending as far back as the traditional debate over preformationism.

In order to proceed further with the problem posed by the onset of differentiation in early development, it is clearly necessary to deal with oogenesis. In the sense that the maternal templates and the morphogenetic determinants stored in the egg from oogenesis direct early development, it is fair to state that embryogenesis begins with gene activity during oogenesis, and we turn now to a consideration of this subject.

III

✳ Gene function in oogenesis

We have now considered two independent areas of evidence which lead to the study of gene function in oogenesis. In the preceding discussion of cytoplasmic localization we arrived at the conclusion that the morphogenetically significant elements in the egg cytoplasm derive from prior gene action during oogenesis. One rationale for the investigation of gene activity during oogenesis is thus the possibility that the key to the mechanism of localization is to be found in analysis of the gene products synthesized during oogenesis and in their eventual disposition and function. Second, according to a variety of recent evidence (see Section I), the newly shed egg contains a large stockpile of preformed RNA molecules destined to serve as templates for most of the new proteins whose synthesis is required in early embryogenesis. These inherited templates too are the legacy of gene action during oogenesis. In general terms it is clear that the informational program present in the egg cytoplasm at fertilization originates in oogenesis, whether that program is defined with reference to the localization phenomenon or to the maternal messenger stockpile. We turn then to the subject of the present section in the hope of obtaining some further insight into the fundamental processes of early development.

The oocyte, like various other adult cell types, is the product of a long course of cell differentiation. The activities carried out in the oocyte genome are in general not different from those occurring in other cell nuclei. Both informational and ribosomal RNA are synthesized during oogenesis. The scale on which these classes of RNA molecule are synthesized, however, is often unique to the oocyte, as is the form taken by the genomic apparatus during oogenesis and the fate and function of its gene products. In what follows the nature of gene activity during oogenesis is taken up, with the understanding of the relation between the gene products formed in oogenesis and the events of early embryogenesis our eventual object—mainly, of course, an unfulfilled object. We begin with a brief review of certain general aspects of oogenesis, which will bear directly on the nature of gene activity during the preparation of the egg.

165

I

Origin and differentiation
of the female germ line

the origin of germ cells

It is desirable, in order that the biology of germ cell differentiation may be considered in its proper perspective, to begin with the origin of the germ cell stem line itself. Information is available regarding the origin of germ cells in animals representing the most widely separated groups [for references pertaining to germ cell origin see the reviews of Hegner (238), Franchi, Mandl, and Zuckerman (302) and Buonoure (303)]. In the organisms which have been studied germ cell lineage is usually traceable to the pregastrular period of development. In some organisms, in fact, it is traceable to the first few cleavages; we have already dealt with such cases in considering the determination of germ cells at blastoderm formation in insects (228, 304), their specification prior to the 8-cell stage in the frog (284), and the demarcation of germ cells in the *Ascaris* diminution cleavages (239). These examples have in common the specification of the germ cell lineage through localization of an egg cytoplasm determinant for germ cells. In each case the existence of localized germ cell determinants has been demonstrated experimentally by showing that agametic organisms develop from eggs in which the determinant egg cytoplasm is selectively destroyed prior to the onset of cleavage. In the frog this can be accomplished by ultraviolet irradiation, as first shown for amphibian eggs by Buonoure (303), and the ultraviolet method has also been applied to *Ascaris* (232) and *Drosophila* eggs (304), among many others.

As will be recalled, it is observed that the embryos resulting from these operations appear normal except that they lack the germ cell lineage. More rigorous proof of the existence of cytoplasmic germ cell determinants in *Rana* comes from the demonstration of Smith that germ cell formation can be restored by the transferral of vegetal pole egg cytoplasm into the cytoplasm of an irradiated egg which would otherwise be incapable of producing germ cells (see Table VI). Boveri's centrifugation and polyspermy experiments with *Ascaris* eggs (Section II) show with equal clarity that there is a sector of egg cytoplasm which specifies the lineages inheriting it as the germ line, since the exact number and location of the primordial germ-line stem cells depend on the number of blastomeres into which the cytoplasmic determinants are distributed. Though comparable demonstrations of germ cell determination by means of cytoplasmic localization are lacking for most other groups of animals, there is a range of descriptive and experimental observation which suggests that this mode of germ cell specification is actually a widespread phenomenon. Thus in the eggs of many organisms the cytoplasm which functions as the germ cell determinant is marked by distinctive pigmentation or by the inclusion of distinctive granules, and the segregation of this cytoplasm into the germ-line stem cells is easily observed.

The germ cells are often easy to recognize, standing out from the adjacent cells by virtue of their larger size and prominent nuclei. In those cases where the egg cytoplasm incorporated in the primordial germ cells bears some visible special character, the development of the whole germ cell lineage can often be traced. An example of this is illustrated in the drawings of Fig. 53, which represent the early history of the germ line in a copepod

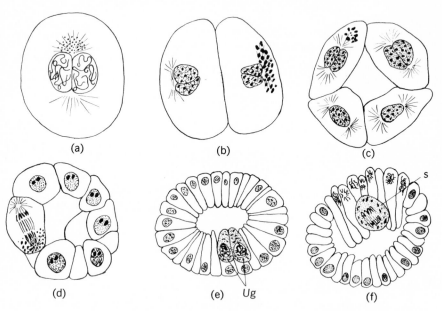

FIGURE 53. Early development of (a)–(e) *Cyclops* fuscus and (f) *Cyclops viridis* showing germ plasm granules localized to germ-line stem cell. (a) First cleavage at stage when germ plasm granules first became visible. (b)–(d) Later cleavage stages; the germ plasm granules have coalesced to form larger granules and can be observed to be localized in one particular cell, the primordial germ-line stem cell. (e) After seventh cleavage, the primordial germ cells (Ug) are clearly distinguished. (f) Eighth cleavage, a single germ-line stem cell (s) in plane of section. Note persistence of germ plasm granules. Amma, K., *Arch. Zellforsch.* **6**, 497 (1911).

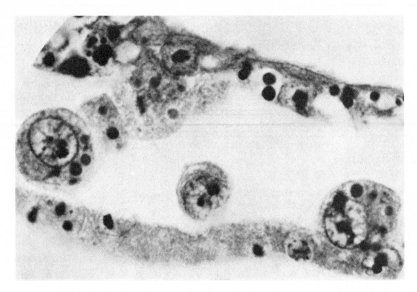

FIGURE 54. Photograph of primordial germ cells situated between the ectoderm and endoderm of a 3-somite blastoderm. × 1500. Willier, B. H., *Anat. Record* **70**, 89 (1937).

(*Cyclops fuscus*) studied many years ago by Amma (305). Here the germ cells inherit a striking accumulation of large cytoplasmic granules originally observable at one pole of the first mitotic spindle (Fig. 53a) and distributed only to cells of the germ line. They are still visible in the primordial germ cells after seven cleavages (Fig. 53e). Animal groups in which phenomena of this nature have been described include crustaceans, insects, and the primitive deuterostome phylum Chaetognatha (see 238).

Even where the primordial germ-line stem cells have not been traced back to the very beginning of embryogenesis, they are reported in most cases to be established at least as early as gastrulation. Germ cells have been identified at pregastrular stages of development in mollusks (306), chaetognaths (307), and many other invertebrates, and their appearance by gastrulation is described in virtually every higher chordate class [detailed references are to be found in the extensive review of Franchi *et al.* (302)]. In most cases the germ cells are noted "segregating" from the primitive endoderm or mesoderm, but germ line specification may actually occur much earlier in development, as in the anurans, and by a similar mechanism. In the chick, to take one well-studied example, primordial germ cells are initially detected scattered about the anterior extremity of the area pellucida at the primitive streak stage, as was shown clearly by Swift (308). Figure 54, reproduced from the definitive study of Willier (309), displays these large and distinctive cells lying between endoderm and ectoderm near their presumed site of origin at an early stage when mesoderm has not yet extended into this region. Benoit (310) has demonstrated that ultraviolet irradiation of the yolk-ectoderm border as early as 18–22 hours of incubation deprives the chick embryo of primordial germ cells.

For us the main points of interest deriving from studies of germ cell origin are: (a) that germ line specification occurs very early in embryological life so that the germ-line stem cells are already present by the time the basic mold of gastrular differentiation has been established; and (b) that in some organisms, and probably in many others as well, germ cell specification is accomplished through interaction between localized egg cytoplasm determinants and embryo genomes within the first few cleavages.

Thus there are an impressive number of cases where development of the germ cell lineage begins as a typical phenomenon of self-differentiation, dependent, like the differentiation of coelomic mesoderm in *Styela* or *Ilyanassa* and of swimming plates in *Beröe,* on cytoplasmic localization. Their further differentiation is, however, a function of inductive stimuli from other cell types (311). In other words, germ cells appear to differentiate like any other early embryonic cell line, with the specification of their particular patterns of nuclear activity dependent first on egg cytoplasmic factors and then, increasingly, on intercellular influences. The later course of differentiation in the female germ line is in various respects unique, and we now turn to the history of this cell lineage in the postembryonic period of development.

general aspects of the timing of oogenesis in the chordate life cycle

Between germ cell determination and the actual processes of oogenesis lie several complex events, among them the execution of a certain number of oogonial divisions, and the construction of specialized ovarian structures. The position of these events in the life history of the female is for us a point of considerable interest. Though it is difficult to perceive comparable patterns in dealing with oogenesis in highly diverse organisms, it is useful here to consider briefly the temporal position of *oogenesis,* as distinguished from oogonial multiplication and other preparatory functions, in the life cycle of various animals.

Following their early determination and the establishment of a primordial germ cell population, the germ cells in both protostome and deuterostome embryos migrate to the position of the forming gonad. This process has been the subject of intensive investigation and controversy, and only recently has it become fairly clear that in chordates the only germ cells in the definitive gonad are lineal descendants of the original primordial germ cells. [The evidence for this statement is reviewed by Franchi *et al.* (302) and by Nelsen (312).] In any case it is during larval life, or the embryonic equivalent thereof in forms lacking a process of metamorphosis, that a definitive gonad with nests of proliferating germinal cells is established. From this point until the stage when the organism attains sexual maturity and the gametes are shed a considerable period of time may elapse, during which two general processes occur. These are the replication of oogonia, the ultimate mitotic products of the germ-line stem cells, and the process of oogenesis per se, the special course of differentiation which ends with the fertilizable egg.

In amphibians and some teleosts, oogonial divisions and the creation of new oocytes appear to continue even after sexual maturity is attained, but the major part of the available evidence indicates that in other chordate groups the total number of oogonia ever to be possessed by an individual has already been formed at the onset of sexual maturity, or, in many cases, well before sexual maturity. New methods have been useful in clarifying this question. In the mouse, for example, it has recently been demonstrated by Borum (313) that synthesis of the DNA in the chromosomes of all the oocytes ever to be present in the adult ovary is completed during fetal life. The radioautographic experiments of this author reveal that no labeling of germinal vesicle DNA occurs after birth, showing that the definitive oocytes of the mouse have already carried out meiotic DNA synthesis by birth. Thus any further *de novo* production of oocytes or oogonia in neonatal life is ruled out. This point of view actually dates back to the 1870 studies of Waldeyer, who arrived at the same conclusion for mammals and birds on the grounds that mitotic figures are absent in the germinal ovarian tissues of these animals during neonatal life (314). The point in the life cycle at which oocyte neoformation ceases is significant because from this it is sometimes possible to deduce the minimum length of the period during which the female germ cells remain in storage and/or engaged in the actual process of oogenesis. This statistic, as will be shown below, turns out to be of considerable interest when viewed comparatively. The situation in higher vertebrates is analogous to that pertaining to central nervous system neurons, for once neonatal life has begun and all the potential oocytes ever to be present are on hand, the individual germinal cells must be preserved, in the case of long-lived species for many years.

In certain lower vertebrates where no neoformation of oogonia occurs after metamorphosis the oogonia may themselves persist into the period of sexual maturity, or at least into neonatal life, and oogenesis can thus be initiated from these stored reserves at later times. In the birds and mammals,

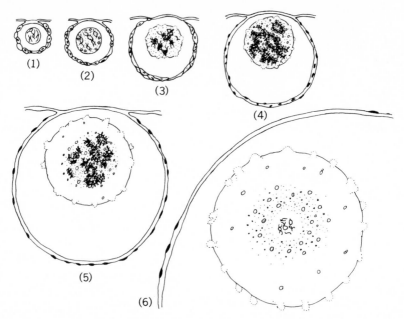

(1)

(2)

(3)

(4)

(5)

(6)

FIGURE 55. Schematic diagram of nuclear growth stages during the later development of frog eggs. Modified from Duryee, W., *Ann. N. Y. Acad. Sci.* **50**, Art. 8, 920 (1950).

however, the initial acts of meiosis (viz., DNA synthesis and synapsis) have already occurred in all the oogonia by the time of birth or hatching (302). Since the first meiotic metaphase does not occur until approximately the time of ovulation, it would appear that in these forms, throughout the whole of juvenile and adult life, the oocytes are arrested in the prophase of the first meiotic division.

In Fig. 55 we present a diagram modified from Duryee (315) to illustrate the substages of the long meiotic prophase typically traversed by the amphibian oocyte. The earliest postoogonial oocytes figured already contain a tetraploid genome. Throughout the initial stages the relative amount of cytoplasm remains low. Only at stages 3 and 4 does vitellogenesis, the deposition and accumulation of yolk, begin. Meanwhile the chromosomes synapse (stage 1, zygotene) and enter into the pachytene stage, where the bivalents condense and shorten. In adult anuran amphibians, many of the oocytes present at any one time in the ovary are in pachytene, i.e., Duryee's stage 2, which is a reserve or resting stage. In stage-2 oocytes which are selected to proceed further with oogenesis the chromosomes begin to lengthen, and the first signs of vitellogenesis can be noted in the substitution of an opaque cytoplasm (stage 3) for the transparent cytoplasm of the stage-2 oocytes. This development accompanies the beginning of the diplo-tene, which persists throughout stage 4 as well.

Stage 3, however, can also be regarded as a form of resting stage, at least in anurans such as *Xenopus*, since the oocyte nuclei at stage 3 are metabolically less active than those of stage 4, and the number of stage-3 oocytes is always greater than the number which at any one time are in stages 4 and 5 (316). It is the oocytes which enter stage 4, the maximum diplotene stage, that are definitively embarked on the course of differentia-tion leading to the production of a mature egg. During stage 4 pigment deposition begins, and in the nucleus the lateral loops of the lampbrush chromosome structures attain their maximum extension. In stage 5 the chromosomal bivalents tend to lose their lateral loops, and the lampbrush structures gradually disappear. In the course of this period the animal-vegetal pole pigment differentiation typical of those amphibian eggs which bear pigment becomes clearly visible. Stage 6 represents the end product of the process, the terminal ovarian oocyte. In the nucleus of the stage-6 oocyte the bivalents are now contracted and rodlike, in preparation for their ulti-mate mobilization in the metaphase movements which will occur with ovula-tion and fertilization.

The sequence of events diagramed in Fig. 55 has several fascinating and significant aspects. For one thing it requires a long time to take place, and during this whole time the chromosomal apparatus contains the 4C amount of DNA. Furthermore, it involves the transient existence of a re-markable chromosomal configuration, the lampbrush chromosome structure. With certain informative exceptions (see below), the same general pattern of events appears to be characteristic of oogenesis in animals of the most remote phylogenetic connection. The aspects of these processes which are of key interest here are the temporal location of the resting phases in the meiotic sequence, the occurrence of lampbrush chromosomes at the diplotene stage, and the actual duration of the lampbrush stage, in the few cases where that is known.

In all vertebrates some portion of the diplotene stage, and to some extent the pachytene, serves as a storage or arrest stage for oocytes during the long pauses which intervene between the onset of meiotic prophase and sexual maturity. In cyclostomes the oogonia carry out their divisions early in larval life and form nests of primary oocytes before the onset of metamor-phosis, and the diplotene lasts several years (317). Females of the sea lamprey *Petromyzon marinus* lay only one clutch of eggs in their lifetime, after which they die; since these eggs mature more or less together, it is possible in this species to study the temporal extent of each stage of oogenesis without the usual complications encountered in animals in which several stages of oogenesis occur simultaneously. Thus Lewis and McMillan (318) have shown that *Petromyzon* oocytes remain in diplotene for 5 years, the period required for the females to attain sexual maturity; the oocytes have all entered diplotene prior to larval metamorphosis. Spawning takes place in the spring, and during the last winter the oocytes increase sharply in size by the massive addition of yolk. Considered in terms of the staging diagramed for amphibians in Fig. 55, stages 1–4 occur in *Petromyzon* prior to metamorphosis, and 5 years later, after virtually the whole of adult life has elapsed, stages 5 and 6 occur in the course of the terminal winter and spring. Hardisty and Cosh (319) have recently pointed out that in lampreys the final number of egg cells shed, which varies from $1-3 \times 10^3$ in *Lamprey planeri* to $21-107 \times 10^3$ in *Petromyzon*, depends mainly on the number of oogonial divisions, rather than on the initial number of primordial germ cells, which is approximately the same in all the species studied. These relationships are displayed in Table VIII. Another striking fact evident in Table VIII is the enormous attrition in the number of usable egg cells in the ovary: About two-thirds of the oocytes which initiate meiosis are discarded before the diplotene is completed in *L. Planeri* and *A. marinus,* and those actually completing diplotene represent less than one-fifth of the available number of oogonia. The definitive mature oocyte population is thus the product of a lengthy course of differentiation which evidently involves a stringent selective process survived by only a small minority of the starting population.

In teleosts the situation is more difficult to study because here oogenesis occurs cyclically in accordance with spawning seasons, and at least in some species oogonial divisions continue into adult life (302). In amphibians oogenesis is also cyclic and again is keyed to spawning seasonality. However, it has proved possible, in a few cases at least, to arrive at estimates of the duration of the meiotic prophase in amphibian oocytes, and of some of the various prophase substages and resting stages. In *Rana temporaria* (320), oogenesis requires 3 years to complete (one should perhaps subtract from this figure the months spent in hibernation during cold weather). In this animal the diplotene part of the process occurs in the second and third years (stages 3–6 in Fig. 55), and the final addition of yolk (stages 5 and 6 of Fig. 55) takes place only in the final portion of the last year. In *Xenopus,* oogenesis is typically asynchronous and continuous so that oocytes of all stages are present at all times in the adult ovary. Sexually mature females in this species frequently bear a reserve of stage-5 and stage-6 eggs significantly larger than the number of mature stage-6 eggs shed at any one time. Thus stage 6 can be used as a resting or storage condition, the maximum duration of which it is difficult to estimate.

After a certain amount of time unovulated stage-6 oocytes become atretic and are resorbed. The minimum time required for a *Xenopus* female to re-

TABLE VIII. Fecundity and Primordial Germ Cell Numbers in Three Species of Lampreys[a]

Species	Fecundity			Counts of primordial germ cells		
	Adult egg numbers	Larval oocyte numbers	Estimated total germ cell numbers	Numbers of animals	Mean and SE	Range
L. planeri	1,000–3,000	5,000–10,000	30,000	44	51.4 3.3	10–94
L. fluviatilis	11,000–26,000	7,000–42,000	—	13	26.5 4.2	7–49
P. marinus (landlocked form)	21,000–107,000	114,000–165,000	500,000	7	54.1 5.6	27–69

[a] From Ref. 319.

place the mature stage-6 oocytes shed at a given ovulation from the preterminal stage-6 or late stage-5 stockpile is a matter of weeks only. However, estimates based on the rate of RNA accumulation and on vital stain experiments indicate that the earlier stage-4 period alone lasts at least 4–8 months in *Xenopus* (316). There are amphibians which carry out oogenesis more rapidly, however, according to some recent investigations into the kinetics of oogenesis in tropical rain forest anurans carried out in the writer's laboratory (321). The example of one species is particularly instructive. This is *Engystomops pustulosis*, a temporary water breeder able to produce several clutches of eggs during each rainy season. In the laboratory, egg clutches may be produced by a female every 2½–3 months under conditions in which oogenesis is both phased and synchronous. Thus in *Engystomops* all those stage-3 oocytes moving ahead into stage 4 do so together after ovulation of the previous batch of mature (stage-6) oocytes has taken place. No further oocytes then leave the stage-3 storage reserve until the more mature oocytes in the ovary have together traversed stages 4, 5, and 6 and been ovulated. Under these conditions the interval between successive ovulations can be used to provide a direct measurement of the length of time required for stages 4, 5, and 6 to be completed, here 2½–3 months. Of this about 30 days are occupied with stages 5 and 6, meaning that stage 4 of the diplotene, i.e., the lampbrush stage, occupies 1½–2 months in this species.

According to the 1906 account of Loyez (322) and various later studies summarized by Zuckerman *et al.* (302), oogenesis in reptiles involves an extremely protracted diplotene period lasting in some species for months or years. A prolonged resting or storage period occurs in reptile oogenesis during late diplotene. This is also true in birds (chick) where all the oocytes ever to develop have entered meiotic prophase soon after hatching. While the prediplotene stages of meiosis require only a few days, the lampbrush stage of the diplotene in the chick extends for several weeks after hatching (323, 324). In eutherian mammals a different picture emerges, however [a summary of references relating to oogenesis in mammals is given in Franchi *et al* (302)]. In the rat, one of the few mammals in which nuclear changes during oogenesis have been subjected to careful scrutiny (326a), it is clear that lampbrush chromosomes do not exist. Oogenesis (meiotic prophase) begins during intrauterine life, a few days before birth, and by a few days after birth the oocytes have passed through diplotene. Thus, unlike the case in many other vertebrate forms, in rodents the typical diplotene stage, as identified cytologically, appears to be completed within a few days (325, 326). Despite the brief duration of both pachytene and diplotene the oocyte population undergoes a severe selection process (326a), so that the number of oocytes which ultimately survive represent only 30% of the starting number (about 75,000 in the rat). After this the oocytes enter into a resting stage, the dictyate, in which the chromosomes become very diffuse, and in fixed sections tend to be difficult to visualize. The dictyate persists until sexual maturity and the onset of ovulation in rodents, and it has also been described for a variety of other mammals. Dictyate is a mode of late diplotene existence: The chromosomal homologs remain paired throughout, and the germinal vesicles in dictyate oocytes contain the 4C quantity of DNA (328). In a general sense, therefore, the dictyate stage appears analogous to the late stage-6 oocyte of the amphibian and to the post-lampbrush-stage oocyte of the juvenile bird and reptile. To verify this analogy, which is based prima facie on the fact that the stages in question are all late diplotene resting stages, it would be necessary to show that dictyate chromosomes are inactive in RNA synthesis, as are the stage-6 chromosomes of the amphibian oocyte. In the human the situation is again different. Baker and Franchi (327a) have recently reported the exciting discovery that diplotene human oocytes possess lampbrush chromosomes. In addition, they have shown that no dictyate-like stage exists in human oogenesis (327b). The diplotene configuration persists after birth, and it is worth remembering in this connection that in a species as long-lived as ourselves more than 40 years can separate the initiation from the termination of meiotic prophase (327). During diplotene, the number of oocytes suffers a drastic decline in the human, as in the other chordate species we have discussed. Baker (327c) has shown that the oocyte population in the fetal human ovary declines from a little over 2×10^6 at termination of pachytene (pachytene is essentially completed at 7 months of pregnancy) to about 0.3×10^6 at 7 years after birth. An earlier and equally severe attrition of the oocyte population takes place during the pachytene stage, and the final oocyte population is only about 5% the size of the peak population, 6.8×10^6 at 5 months of pregnancy (327c).

Several generalizations can be extracted from these comparative data regarding the essential sequence of events in chordate oogenesis. In all known chordates the oogonia are lineal descendants only of the primordial germ cells. The oogonial divisions, except in some teleosts and amphibians, have been in general completed by birth or metamorphosis. The chordates can be divided into two groups, with respect to the relation between oogenesis and the life cycle; those in which the processes of the meiotic prophase recur cyclically, with each breeding season, as in some fish and reptiles and all amphibians (302); and those in which meiotic prophase takes place at a very early stage just after or before hatching, metamorphosis, or birth in all the oocytes which are ever to mature. The latter group includes eutherian mammals, cyclostomes, birds, some fish, and elasmobranchs (302), and in these animals the late diplotene resting stage may last for an exceedingly long time (many years). In the former groups, on the other hand, although a late diplotene resting stage also exists, prediplotene resting stages are quantitatively more significant. Such early resting stages can occur in earlier phases of the meiotic prophase or after the oogonial divisions but before any of the chromosomal movements denoting the onset of meiotic prophase. In most cases, however, the following statements are applicable: Diplotene is by far the longest stage of prophase; severe attrition in the number of viable oocytes occurs between the end of pachytene and the end of diplotene; oocyte growth, vitellogenesis, and the growth of accessory structures (follicles) occur mainly after early diplotene has taken place, sometimes being separated from early diplotene by a long resting phase.

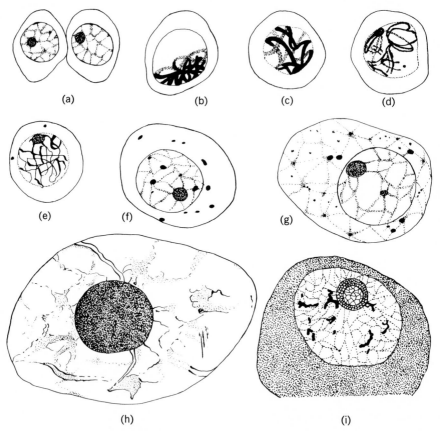

FIGURE 56. (a) Premeiotic primary oocytes of the sea urchin *Mespila globulus*. (b) Synapsis completed. (c) Moniliform but longitudinally double chromosomes. (d) Thick chromosomes separating into two thin chromosomes. (e) Decrease in basophilicity of diplotene chromosomes. (f) Resting period of diplotene oocyte. Note prominent nucleolus. (g) Slightly basophilic cytoplasm. (h) Nucleus of primary oocyte; diplotene threads. (i) Germinal vesicle with nucleolus; prochromosomes, again condensed, now visible in nucleus. Tennent, D. H., and Ito, T., *J. Morphol.* **69**, 347 (1941).

oogenesis in sea urchins

Information regarding the time relations of oogenesis in invertebrates is scarce. Two examples are briefly considered here, and these are chosen essentially for their comparative interest. Our first case concerns oogenesis in echinoderms. In the sea urchin *Mespila globulus* the various stages of meiotic prophase in growing oocytes have been described by Tennent and Ito (329), and illustrations from their account are reproduced in Fig. 56. Interesting similarities in the sequence of stages are evident in Fig. 56, comparing *Mespila* with chordates of the amphibian type, in which oogenesis is also cyclic and continuous throughout life. Following the premeiotic resting phase shown in Fig. 56a, the oocytes progress through the early meiotic prophase stages and enter diplotene. At this point the chromosomes decondense, and the oocyte cytoplasm increases in volume. There follows a prolonged late diplotene resting phase in which decondensation of the chromosomes renders them difficult to perceive, at least with the conventional procedures employed by Tennent and Ito. At the very end of this period vitellogenesis occurs and the eggs become mature. According to Gross, Malkin, and Hubbard, the small (previtellogenesis) oocyte nuclei are all active in RNA synthesis, while the late oocytes are relatively inactive except for a few which under certain conditions can be induced to enter a final 2-week period of preparation for shedding (330). That the younger oocytes are the ones mainly responsible for RNA accumulation is also the conclusion drawn by Verhey and Moyer on the basis of cytological estimations of the increase in ribosome content during the previtellogenesis stages (331). This pattern of events is in general similar to that characteristic of amphibian oogenesis; the late amphibian oocyte nucleus is also relatively quiescent, and most of the RNA present in the mature oocyte is the product of earlier synthesis occurring prior to the deposition of the major part of the yolk (see below). An important difference between the echinoderm and most of the chordates considered above, however, is that neoformation of echinoderm oocytes by continuous oogonial divisions occurs even in the adult ovary (329).

Like the early diplotene oocytes of many higher deuterostomes, previtellogenesis and "resting stage" oocytes of sea urchins appear to contain lampbrush chromosomes. Probable examples can be seen in the phase photomicrograph presented in Fig. 57, which represents a section of a young *Lytechinus* oocyte (332). Lampbrush chromosomes were first reported to be present in sea urchin oocytes by Jörgenssen in 1913 (333).

Most sea urchins have annual breeding cycles, even in tropical areas where water temperature remains high all year long [see the review of breeding habits presented by Hyman (334)]. At the end of each breeding cycle

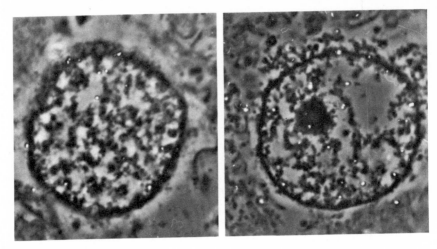

FIGURE 57. Radioautographs of immature *Lytechinus variegatus* oocytes, exposed *in situ* to uridine-³H. Lampbrush chromosomes and the oocyte nucleolus can be distinguished in the 1-μ Epon sections beneath the stripping film. The scattered grains denote the incorporation of uridine into oocyte RNA.

the ovaries appear to contain only "immature cells" (334), i.e., previtellogenesis oocytes. The most mature of these off-season oocytes, however, are already in the early diplotene stage, at least in *Lytechinus variegatus,* since they apparently contain lampbrush chromosomes. Furthermore, the diplotene winter oocytes of *Lytechinus* are not at rest, metabolically; in fact, they display active RNA synthesis (332). Combining this information with that provided by Tennent and Ito, the diplotene of meiosis would seem to be a temporally lengthy, synthetically active process in echinoderms, just as it is in the chordates.

panoistic and meroistic insect oogenesis

Particularly interesting examples of oogenesis in invertebrates exist in insects. We now consider one aspect of this area, the illuminating contrast between the panoistic and meroistic modes of insect oogenesis. In the meroistic type of oogenesis the oocyte is literally fed through large open channels which link it with a certain number of *nurse cells,* themselves differentiated from the same oogonial stem cell as has given rise to the oocyte. Two types of meroistic oogenesis are diagramed in Fig. 58, which is reproduced from a recent article of Bier (335). Panoistic oogenesis, in which the oocyte accessory tissues are of the more familiar follicular variety and true nurse cells are absent, is also illustrated in Fig. 58. According to Bier, insect oocytes of the meroistic type do not possess lampbrush chromosomes and either do not synthesize RNA during the oocyte growth phase or synthesize it at an exceedingly low rate. In the latter feature meroistic oocytes are unique; most oocyte nuclei carry out an intense RNA synthesis during the growth phase of oogenesis. The studies of Bier have shown that in polytropic meroistic ovaries (Fig. 58b), however, *the oocyte RNA is actually synthesized in the nurse cells and is transported directly into the oocyte* via the cytoplasmic bridges linking the latter with the nurse cells (further details of this phenomenon are provided below in the discussion of accessory cell function).

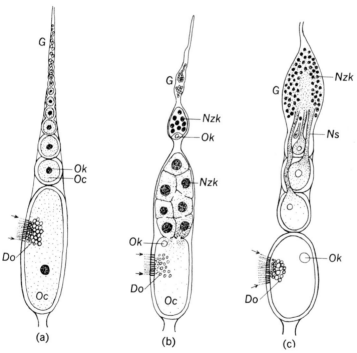

FIGURE 58. Diagram of the three types of insect ovary. Panoistic oogenesis is portrayed in (a), polytropic and telotropic meroistic oogenesis in (b) and (c), respectively. Cell nuclei which synthesize RNA are figured in black, and concentrations of labeled RNA in cytoplasm are represented by fine black dots. Yolk proteins (Do), derived originally from the blood, are pictured entering the oocyte (Oc) via the follicular epithelium. (Nzk) Nurse cell nucleus; (Ns) nutrient chord; (G) germarium; (Ok) oocyte nucleus. Bier, K., *Naturwissenschaften* **54**, 189 (1967).

Figure 59, a radioautograph of Bier (336), illustrates the inactivity of the oocyte nucleus in RNA synthesis, as compared to the associated nurse cell nuclei, in a meroistic ovariole. A striking aspect of this form of oogenesis is the rapidity with which it is typically completed. In *Drosophila*, for example, the whole of the meiotic prophase, from beginning to end, is carried out within 8–9 days. The evidence in this case comes from an experiment of Grell and Chandley (337), who labeled the ovariole with thymidine-^{3}H. The latter is incorporated into oocyte DNA not later than the final synthetic period preceding meiotic prophase, and mature oocytes bearing this label appear only 8–9 days later. In sharp contrast, insect oogenesis of the panoistic type (Fig. 58a) is a lengthy process. Oocyte development in the cricket takes 3–6 months, for instance, and the growth phase of the cricket oocyte is characterized by prominent lampbrush chromosome structures. It

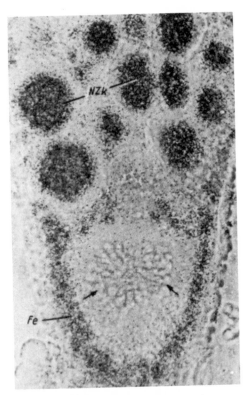

FIGURE 59. Radioautograph of oocyte, nurse cells, and follicular epithelium of *Vespa vulgaris* incubated 45 minutes with uridine-^{3}H. The oocyte nucleus (marked by arrows) synthesizes virtually no RNA during the labeling period in contrast to the nurse cell nuclei (NZk) and follicular epithelium (fe) cell nuclei. Bier, K., *Zool. Jahrb. Physiol.* **71**, 371 (1965).

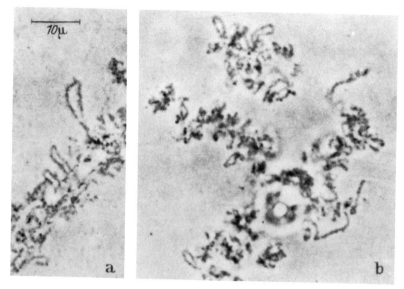

FIGURE 60. (a) Isolated, unfixed lampbrush chromosomes of *Decticus albifrons*. (b) Same as part a, enlarged. Kunz, W., *Chromosoma* **21**, 446 (1967).

has been demonstrated by Kunz (338), moreover, that RNA synthesis is carried on actively in lampbrush-stage orthopteran oocytes.

Figure 60 displays isolated lampbrush chromosomes of an orthopteran, *Decticus albifrons*, photographed by Kunz (339). The contrast between the meroistic and the panoistic type of oogenesis is highly instructive, for it suggests that there is a good reason, aside from marking time while the animal matures sexually or the season changes, for the generally long duration of the meiotic prophase in animal oogenesis. An illuminating exception, the example of meroistic oogenesis in insects suggests that synthetic activities requiring the meiotic prophase condition are needed in order to supply the oocyte with something which it takes an oocyte nucleus alone a long time to accumulate, but which the polyploid nurse cell nuclei can generate cooperatively within a few days. The molecules in question cannot be yolk, since yolk and other such products are typically accumulated in the course of a relatively brief final period of the diplotene stage. Furthermore in insect ovaries of all types yolk is primarily transported into the oocyte from external sites of synthesis rather than being synthesized by the oocyte (Fig. 58). *Both meroistic and panoistic oogenesis evidently require the functioning of a special nuclear apparatus in which more than the somatic (2C) amount of genetic material is present*: The diplotene lampbrush-stage chromosomes contain the 4C amount of DNA, and each of the polyploid nurse cell nuclei contain many times more than that. This is a peculiar and universal aspect of oogenesis. Coupled with the requirement for either a lengthy period of oocyte genome action, or, alternatively, a brief but intense multicellular effort, the participation of excess genetic material emphasizes the importance of large-scale genomic activity in the preparation of the oocyte.

An interesting hypothetical explanation for the absence of lampbrush chromosomes in rodents and some other mammals is suggested by the example of meroistic oogenesis in insects. Zamboni and Gondos (339a) have recently published electron micrographs which demonstrate membrane-bound, open cytoplasmic bridges connecting adjacent meiotic oocytes in the rabbit. The germ cells, according to these authors, are arranged essentially in syncytial clusters. The participating cellular elements are evidently all of germ line origin, providing a formal similarity between this multicellular system and the nurse cell-oocyte system of Fig. 58b. We know, furthermore, that a huge majority of the early oocytes of the rodent will become atretic and ultimately disappear as oogenesis progresses, as do the nurse cells of protostomes. Perhaps within each syncytial cluster most of the cells are actually functioning as feeders for the one among them which is destined to differentiate as an oocyte, thereby obviating the requirement for a protracted synthetic phase in mid-diplotene (i.e., lampbrush phase), in a manner directly analogous to that in which the meroistic insect system operates.

the occurrence of lampbrush chromosomes and the duration of the lampbrush stage

In Table IX some data regarding the distribution of lampbrush chromosomes in animal oocytes are collected (315–318, 321–324, 332, 333, 338–346). It is clear that lampbrush chromosomes occur in animals of every major group, both deuterostome and protostome. Though phylogenetically very widespread, lampbrush chromosomes are not found in all organisms, at least as far as observations to date indicate. The organisms in which they seem not to exist fall into two classes: those in which the chromosomes, after rapidly traversing diplotene, become highly diffuse and then enter into a lengthy dictyate resting stage, and those in which the chromosomes remain clumped or otherwise visible but clearly do not develop a lampbrush type of structure. The latter is the case in some protostomes (347); the former is apparently the case in some mammals (302). Where compact oocyte chromosomes can actually be observed throughout diplotene it is possible to state with certainty that there is no lampbrush stage. However, the difficulty of visualizing lampbrush chromosomes, especially if they are very fragile or very small, renders many earlier negative reports questionable. Consider the contrast in

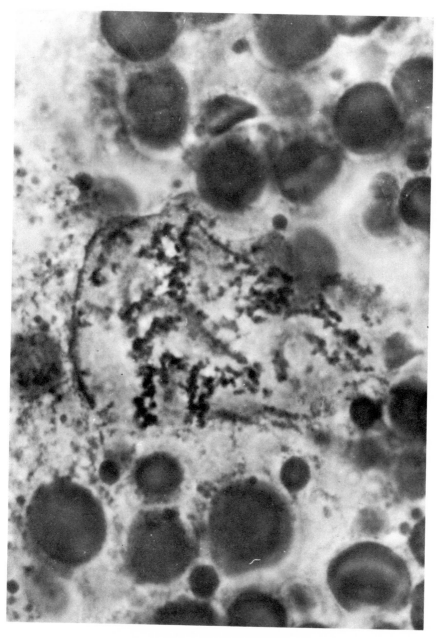

Figure 61. Lampbrush chromosomes of *Ilyanassa obsoleta* seen in the nucleus of growing oocyte, fixed and embedded in epon. Large spherical bodies adjoining the nucleus are yolk platelets.

185

dimensions illustrated in Figs. 61 and 62. Figure 61 shows the relatively tiny lampbrush chromosomes of an early vitellogenesis oocyte from the snail *Ilyanassa,* and in Fig. 62 is reproduced a phase photomicrograph of the lampbrush structures isolated from a urodele oocyte nucleus. It is evident that lampbrush chromosomes vary enormously in size. That variation, to a first approximation, is a function of DNA content, and thus striking differences may exist even among related organisms. Oocytes of the anuran amphibian *Xenopus,* which possesses a diploid DNA complement of 6 $\mu\mu$g (348), are reported to bear lampbrush chromosomes with an average loop length of only 1 μ and a maximum loop length of only 10 μ (344), and these dimensions can be compared with those of the urodele lampbrush chromosomes shown in Fig. 62. The diploid DNA complements of two species of the urodele genus *Triturus* are 67 and 89 $\mu\mu$g (349). Since the minute dimensions of some lampbrush chromosomes may have prevented their discovery in certain creatures, the distribution of lampbrush chromosomes indicated in Table IX must be regarded as a minimum index of their ubiquity. Nonetheless, if only from what is known at present of their phylogenetic distribution, it is clear that lampbrush chromosomes must play some fundamental and general role in oogenesis, since they have been retained throughout evolution and occur in animals whose most recent common ancestor was probably an extremely primitive bilateral worm of an early coelomate grade of organization.

In Table IX are also summarized a few scattered data regarding the length of the lampbrush chromosome stage of the diplotene. The observations cited, tentative though they are, are consistent with the conclusion that the lampbrush stage is always a protracted affair. We are left with the impression that a prolonged accumulation of the products assembled as a result of the activity of lampbrush chromosomes is needed in order for oogenesis to be successfully completed.

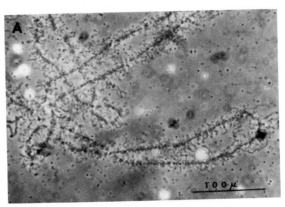

FIGURE 62A.

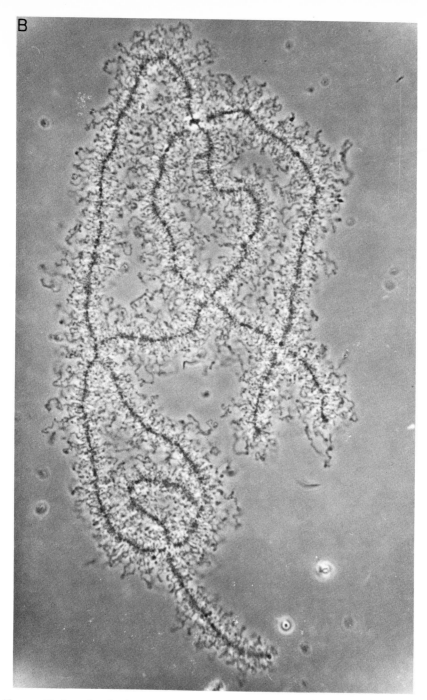

FIGURE 62. Lampbrush chromosomes of *Triturus viridescens* unfixed. (A) Low power view showing homologs joined at chiasmata. (B) Higher magnification showing the loops projecting laterally from the main chromosomal axis.

TABLE IX. Occurrence of Lampbrush Chromosomes in Animal Oocytes and the Duration of the Lampbrush Stage

Species and affiiation of animals in which lampbrush chromosomes have been reported	Ref.	Estimated duration of lampbrush stage where available	Ref.
Deuterostome			
Chaetognath			
Arrow worm	310		
Echinoderm			
Sea urchin	332, 333		
Chordate			
Cyclostome	317	Several months in lamprey	318
Shark	341, 342		
Teleost	341, 342		
Amphibian	315, numerous earlier references are reviewed in Ref. 343		
Urodele		Seven months in *Triturus*	344
Anuran		Four to eight months in *Xenopus*	316
		Two months in *Engystomops*	321
Reptile	322	Some months in lizards	322, 345
Bird	323, 324	Three weeks in chick	324
Mammal	327a	Perhaps years in man	327a, b
Protostome			
Mollusk			
Gastropod	See Fig. 61		
Cephalopod	343		
Insect			
Orthopteran	338, 339, 346	Three months in cricket	346

synopsis: temporal aspects of female germ-line differentiation

The differentiation of the female germ line, like that of certain other cell lineages, may begin as early as the first few cleavages. Following the initial determination of the primordial germ cells a number of oogonial divisions typically occur, and for many species this number is important in determining the limits of fecundity. Selected oogonia later proceed into the meiotic prophase, where they tend to remain for a prolonged period, as measured in terms of the life cycle of the animal. During this period the chromosomes remain tetraploid in DNA content, and their progression through the classically defined stages of meiosis may be interrupted by lengthy resting periods or oocyte storage stages which intervene in various organisms at several points in the prophase process.

While leptotene, zygotene, pachytene, and diplotene can be regarded as mechanically essential steps in the preparation of the first reduction division, this is not so of the mid-diplotene lampbrush structures. Nor can the extended duration of the mid-diplotene lampbrush stage be explained in this way. In oocytes other than those developing in the meroistic manner the meiotic processes are temporally arrested at the diplotene stage, and it is during this period, which is characterized by intensive activity on the part of the oocyte genome, that much of the oocyte cytoplasm is created, and the oocyte enters on the final definitive course of maturation. Thus in the pattern of events general to female germ-line differentiation several elements can be discerned which suggest that a period of extensive genomic function is an essential aspect of oogenesis. These features include the protracted mid-diplotene pause in the meiotic process; the presence of the 4C amount of DNA in the oocyte genome; the intense activity of the mid-diplotene genome (see below); and related to the latter, the widespread incidence of lampbrush chromosomes at this stage of oogenesis. The example of meroistic oogenesis provides a further indication in showing that in insects the lengthy period of lampbrush chromosome function can be *replaced* by a brief period of cooperative function on the part of the intercommunicating, polytene nurse cells. We proceed now to evidence from another source, viz., the pattern of chromosome loss and retention in organisms which eliminate a portion of their genomic material in the course of germ-line differentiation.

2

Clues to oocyte genome function from organisms displaying chromosome elimination

In certain organisms chromosome elimination is associated with some phase of germ line differentiation. At the point of initial germ-line specification, for example, the germ-line stem cell alone may retain the total chromosome heritage while all other blastomeres suffer the early elimination of a particular portion of their chromosome set. We have already considered the most illustrious instance of this phenomenon, that of chromosome diminution in the specification of the *Ascaris* germ-line stem cells. The analysis of this case, which it will be recalled is owing to Boveri (239) and his student Hogue (240), shows that a certain portion of the egg cytoplasm endows the germ-line stem cell with the property of avoiding chromosome elimination. Its significance in the present context is the suggestion that certain elements of genomic information are utilized only in gametogenesis, or in the postoogenesis, precleavage period, or both. It will be recalled that in *Ascaris* the male pronucleus carries out an active synthesis of both ribosomal and informational RNA destined for later use by the embryo [(142a); see Section I]. This synthesis takes place during an intrauterine period lasting several days, and as Kaulenas and Fairbairn have suggested (142a), the chromosomal material which is eliminated soon thereafter in all but the germ-cell stem line may be needed precisely in order to carry out this precleavage transcription. The newly fertilized egg already contains some stored template RNA, according to the data of these authors, and thus it is also possible that the special genomic complement of the germ cells contains genes which are required during oogenesis. In either case the *Ascaris* diminution phenomenon serves to focus our attention on the special role of prior gene transcription in preparing the eggs for development.

It is of interest to consider briefly certain other cases of chromosome diminution in germ line differentiation in order to ascertain whether an interpretation of this nature might be applied generally. Diminution of the chromosome complement is known in various beetles, flies, butterflies, grass-hoppers, midges, and mites, as well as in nematodes (347, 350). An impor-tant group of examples concerns the diminutions occurring in the formation of the meroistic ovarioles of certain beetles, particularly *Dysticus* (347). Here the final four oogonial divisions result in the appearance of 15 nurse cells and one oocyte, of which the oocyte is the only cell to retain the total chromatin complement. As each nurse cell is formed, a ring of chromosomal material is excluded from its nucleus. In this system the excluded chromatin could have been utilized either prior to nurse cell-germ cell differentiation in the oogonial stem line or during the subsequent stages of oogenesis by the oocyte per se. The latter would seem less likely since, as pointed out above, in polytropic meroistic ovaries oocyte nuclear function is minimal, and since the special chromatin appears to remain in clumped, inactive-looking masses throughout the remainder of oogenesis (347). In *Sciara* just as in *Ascaris*, chromosomes are also eliminated early in cleavage from somatic cells but not from germ cells. However, chromosome elimination occurs in the germ line of *Sciara* at a later point as well, after the oogonial divisions have been completed and the germ cells have assumed an ovarian location, but before they actually enter on meiotic prophase (352). Thus if the last eliminated chromatin is utilized at all in *Sciara*, it must be in the course of the premeiotic development of the germ line.

A somewhat different but not unrelated phenomenon is responsible for sex determination in coccid insects (350, 353), and among the variety of curious mechanisms for sex determination known in this group are several of particular interest to us. Sex determination in certain species depends upon the hetrochromatization of half the chromosomes, in some cases the paternal half. Organisms bearing a heterochromatized chromosome set be-come males, and those with a normal diploid set become females. Other species can develop parthenogenically, constructing a diploid karyotype at the onset of development by means of the fusion of the first two haploid cleavage nuclei. In a certain number of these synthetically diploid eggs half of the chromosomes become heterochromatized, and the individuals develop-ing from these eggs again become males. According to Brown and Nur, who have recently reviewed these interesting systems (353), heterochromatization is reversible. What is of particular interest here is the fact that in coccids showing sex determination by heterochromatization, parthenogenic or other-wise, and irrespective of whether chromosome loss occurs at some stage of the process, it is *always the female germ line which retains the full diploid complement of active chromosomes.*

Processes of germ line specification involving chromosome elimination have also been reported in midges. Various genera of gall midges (cecidomyi-dae) are known in which an *Ascaris*-like chromosome diminution occurs early in cleavage. As a result of this diminution the somatic cells retain only 6–12 chromosomes, this number being a fuction of the sex of the organisms and of the species, while the germ line cells retain the full complement of over 40 chromosomes. The function of the normally discarded chromatin has now been studied experimentally in one species, *Wachtliella persicariae,* by Geyer-Duszynska (354), and the results confirm the proposition that the germ cells retain extra chromatin which is utilized in germ cell differentiation. Germ-line stem cells which have undergone diminution in the same way as somatic cells can be produced in *Wachtliella* by ligaturing the embryo at the binucleate stage in such a way as to prevent the descent of the nuclei into the germ cell determinant cytoplasm. If the ligature is removed after chromosome elimination has taken place in the fourth cleavage, one of the resulting nuclei, now containing 8 rather than 40 chromosomes, subsequently moves into the presumptive germ-cell-forming region, is walled off, and gives rise to a germ line. Geyer-Duszynska has found that females developing from ligatured eggs, while normal in other aspects, are *unable to carry out oogenesis.* The fault appears to lie early in the processes of oogenesis, where the eggs arrest, and/or in the prior development of the definitive meroistic ovarian structures, since the ovaries of ligatured females are rudimentary and morphologically abnormal. Males developing from ligatured eggs are normal in all respects, including the structure of the reproductive system, and such males even produce sperm. During pupation, however, the larval sperm in these males degenerates. These experiments indicate directly the significance of the chromatin not required by the somatic cells: It contains genetic information transcribed in oogenesis, and in organisms where diminution occurs the genetic elements bearing this information are packaged together, rather than being scattered throughout the genome. The special characteristics of oogenesis point, as we have seen, to a requirement for extensive gene activity in oocyte development, and the chromosome diminution cases provide from an unexpected quarter an interesting corroboration of this interpretation.

3

Accessory cell functions
in oogenesis

In any discussion of synthetic activity during oogenesis it is essential to bear in mind the possible role of the ovarian accessory cells. Accessory cells participate in virtually all forms of oogenesis, and from both a cytological and a physiological standpoint it is clear that accessory cell function is closely linked to oocyte metabolism and is involved in the accretion of oocyte substances. The remainder of this section is concerned primarily with the synthetic activities of the oocyte genome per se, and it is appropriate to preface the discussion of that subject with a brief glance at several of the various types of accessory cell-oocyte interrelations.

the origin and physiological role of nurse cells

The most spectacular accessory cell-oocyte relationships in the metazoan world are perhaps the nurse cell-oocyte complexes which attain their most elaborate form in the meroistic insect ovary; we are already somewhat familiar with the functional nature of these complexes from the foregoing discussion of meroistic and panoistic oogenesis (cf. Fig. 58). Nurse cells, originating from the same germinal oogonium (by definition) as does the oocyte, are characteristically joined directly to the oocyte; at least in the early stages of oogenesis, they are often larger than the oocyte itself. If true nurse cells exist at all in deuterostomes it is only in the most primitive forms, such as in *Sagitta* [the "inner and outer accessory cells" of Burfield (355)] and in the lamprey (318), but they are common among the protostomes. The role of nurse cells in feeding the oocyte has long been remarked upon [see Wilson (347) for early references]. Early workers claimed to have observed whole mitochondria passing from nurse cells to oocyte in several species. An instructive variation exists in turbellarian flatworms, where the nurse cells, filled with yolk, are encapsulated in a cocoon along with the oocytes *after* oogenesis is completed, and the nurse cell contents are used to sustain the

193

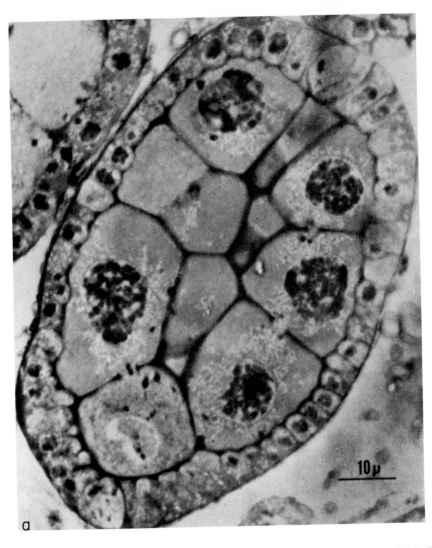

FIGURE 63. (a) A photomicrograph of a 2-μ section (stained by the periodic acid-Schiff procedure) through a stage-6 *Drosophila* egg chamber. At this stage a single layer of cuboidal follicle cells surrounds the oocyte, which occupies a position at the lower left corner of the chamber, and the 15 nurse cells, 9 of which are evident in this section. Three ring canals are evident, one connecting the oocyte with a nurse cell and two interconnecting three nurse cells. Note the particulate material which appears to have been fixed during its passage through the ring canals. Koch, E. A., Smith, P. A., and King, R. C., *J. Morphol.* **121**, 55 (1967). (b) An electron micrograph of a section through a ring canal connecting a nurse cell (N₂) to the oocyte (O). Two

194

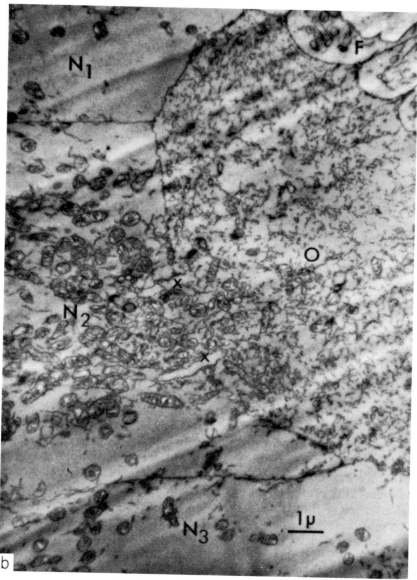

other nurse cells (N_1 and N_3) and portions of several follicle cells (F) are evident. An electron-pale material (X) is evident. Mitochondria which seem to have been fixed while entering the oocyte are evident within the ring canal. The higher concentration of particulate material in the oocyte suggests that materials contributed by the nurse cells are accumulating in the oocyte. ($KMnO_4$-OsO_4 fixation, embedded in epon.) Brown, E. H., King, R. C., *Growth* **28**, 41 (1964).

growth of the embryos just as is *intracellular* yolk in other eggs [see Raven (356) for a general survey of accessory cell-oocyte arrangements in invertebrates]. This unusual pattern of events draws attention to the essential nature of nurse cell function, that of providing the oocyte with preformed materials it will require for development. Recent studies on meroistic insect ovaries have yielded pertinent new information regarding the intimacy of the connections linking nurse cells to each other and to the oocyte.

Figure 63a depicts nurse cell-oocyte and nurse cell-nurse cell junctions in the *Drosophila* germarium as they appear in the light microscope, and in Fig. 63b an electron micrograph of such an interconnection is reproduced (357). These figures derive from recent investigations by Brown and King (357) and by Koch, Smith, and King (358) into the formation of the compound egg chamber in *Drosophila*. A parallel study of the formation of the polytropic egg chamber in the moth *Hyalophora cecropia* has also been published by King and Aggarwal (359). These workers have shown that in both cases the oocyte-nurse cell complex, which in *Hyalophora* includes 7 nurse cells and in *Drosophila* 15 nurse cells, is constructed in the terminal three and four oogonial divisions, respectively. With the first of these divisions the future oocyte is clearly segregated from the nurse cell. Each nurse cell is connected to other nurse cells and/or to the oocyte by the open cytoplasmic bridges, termed "ring canals" (357) or "fusomes" (351) photographed in Fig. 63. The ring canals are retained as remnants of the formative divisions through which the cells are initially separated, and they evidently result from an incomplete walling off of the daughter cells after each mitosis. The disposition of the ring canals therefore provides a key to the order of appearance of the nurse cells and the sequence of steps by which the egg chamber is constructed. Reconstructions of this process as it occurs in *Drosophila* and in *Cecropia* are shown in Figs. 64a (358) and 64b (359), respectively. It can be seen that except for that nurse cell which is formed first, the oocyte is the cell with the largest number of intercellular ring canals, and it is significant that both the first nurse cell and the oocyte initially form synaptinemial chromosomal structures. The synaptinemial complexes developing in the nurse cell nucleus later disappear, whereas in the oocyte the usual meiotic prophase movements continue.

In Fig. 63b mitochondria are to be observed densely packed in the ring canal, thus justifying the earlier claims to this effect based on light microscopy [e.g., see Wilson (347)]. If mitochondria can pass between nurse cell and oocyte obviously anything smaller, including all cellular macromolecules, can do so as well. We have already cited the work of Bier indicating that RNA synthesized in the nurse cells is fed into the oocyte, and both Bier and Koch *et al.* (358) have found that endogenous RNA synthesis in

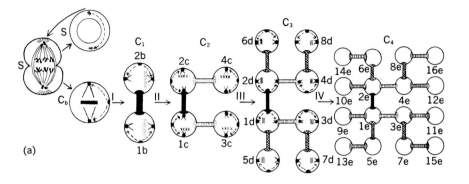

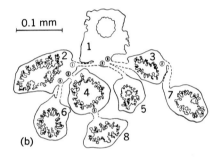

FIGURE 64. (a) Diagrammatic model showing steps in the production of a cluster of 16 interconnected cystocytes in *Drosophila*. In this drawing the cells are represented by circles lying in a single plane, and the ring canals have been lengthened for clarity. The area of each circle is proportional to the volume of the cell. The stem cell (S) divides into two daughters, one of which behaves like its parent. The other differentiates into a cystoblast (C_b) which by a series of four divisions (I–IV) produces 16 interconnected cystocytes: C_1, first; C_2, second; C_3, third; and C_4, fourth generation cystocyte. The original stem cell is shown at early anaphase. Each parent-daughter pair of centrioles is attached to the plasma membrane by astral rays. The daughter stem cell receives one pair of centrioles. One remains in place while the other moves to the opposite pole. This movement is represented by a broken arrow. In the daughter cystoblast and all cystocytes the initial position of the original centriole pair is represented by a solid half circle, whereas their final positions are represented by solid circles. The position of the future cleavage furrow is drawn as a strip of defined texture. The canal derived from the furrow is treated in a similar fashion. Koch, E. A., Smith, P. A., and King, R. C., *J. Morphol.* **121**, 55 (1967). (b) A diagram showing the way in which the 8 cells of a stage-3 egg chamber of *Hyalophora cecropia* are interconnected by 7 canals. Each cell is traced from a magnified image of a section passing through its center, and its nucleus is outlined. Since the cells are represented as lying in one plane, the canals have been lengthened. Note the large, deeply crenelated polytene nuclei of the nurse cells. King, R. C., and Aggarwal, S. K., *Growth* **29**, 17 (1965).

meroistic oocytes is repressed. Bier's radioautographic demonstration that RNA is synthesized in the nurse cell nuclei for transport into the oocyte is presented in Fig. 65 (351). Newly synthesized RNA localized over the polytene nurse cell nuclei (Fig. 65a) after a 30-minute labeling period can be seen 5 hours later (Fig. 65b) distributed in the nurse cell cytoplasm and apparently pouring through a ring canal visible in this section into the cytoplasm of the oocyte. The possibility is not formally excluded in these experiments (335, 351), that the labeled moieties seen in the oocyte at 5 hours represent reutilized precursor transported to the oocyte in low molecular weight form and subsequently incorporated into RNA by the oocyte, but a priori this would seem unlikely in view of the relatively low level of endogenous oocyte RNA synthesis in this form (Fig. 59). Ribonucleic acid transport from nurse cell to oocyte is consistent both with expectations based on comparisons with oogenesis in panoistic insects (see above) and with

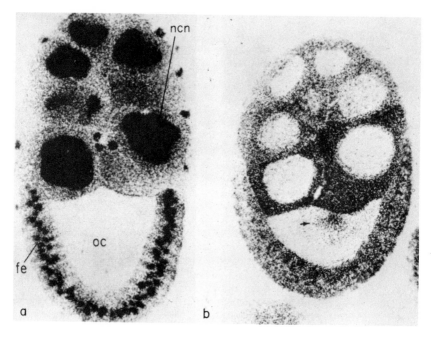

FIGURE 65. (a) Radioautograph of an oocyte (OC), its nurse cells, and follicular epithelium (fe) of *Musca domestica* incubated for 30 minutes with cytidine-³H. (b) The same, 5 hours later. Labeled RNA can be seen entering the oocyte from an adjacent nurse cell (arrow). The densely labeled RNA present in the nurse cell nuclei (ncn) in (a) is now mainly localized in the nurse cell cytoplasm. Bier, K., *J. Cell Biol.* **16**, 436 (1963).

direct cytological studies of transport through the ring canals, e.g., those in Fig. 63. It seems clear that cooperative genomic function of the multiple egg chamber unit in the preparation of the oocyte enables the organism to dispense with a prolonged meiotic prophase and a lampbrush chromosome stage, but the underlying significance of the fact that the nurse cell nuclei are themselves descendants of the same primary oogonium as is the oocyte remains an obscure though fascinating problem. The simplest interpretation would seem to be that some part of the pattern of gene activity required for oogenesis must be elicited by factors active during the prior course of oogonial differentiation.

Wherever nurse cells are observed the intimate nature of the oocyte-nurse cell interaction is evident. In certain annelids, for example, one or two nurse cells with large, convoluted polytene nuclei are applied to each oocyte, and the oocyte-nurse cell complex is released into the lumen of the ovary relatively early in oogenesis. Oocyte growth occurs at the expense of the nurse cells, which shrink progressively until they become small compared to the now enormous oocytes (356). In insects possessing the telotropic meroistic form of oogenesis, however, the nurse cells are not directly applied to the oocyte but communicate with it via a "nutritive cord" which forms an open channel directly into the oocyte (Fig. 58). The histochemical studies of Bonhag (360) show that in the milkweed bug *Oncopeltus fasciatus*, proteins, RNA, and even DNA from degenerating tropic cells are transported into the oocyte by means of these nutritive cords.

The evident nature of nurse cell function serves to remind the student of oogenesis that the *de novo* appearance of gene products in a growing oocyte does not necessarily imply activity on the part of the oocyte genome. Ribonucleic acid, as well as other molecules, ribosomes, and even whole cell organelles, can be synthesized within these accessory cells and transported into the oocyte from them, to the extent that in extreme cases the synthetic activity of the nurse cells appears to substitute for that of the recipient oocyte.

follicle cells

Almost all oocytes develop within a covering layer of follicle cells, which may be of origin other than the germ line. The role played by follicular structures in feeding various substances into the oocyte is not as dramatically clear as that of the nurse cell complexes, where the latter exist, but there is ample evidence that protein molecules of external origin may be transported by the follicle cells into the oocyte. For example, *Calliphora* ovaries have been transplanted by Bier into host females previously incubated with labeled amino acids in order to study the entrance of labeled proteins synthesized earlier by the tissues of the host into the oocyte (361). According to Bier's radioautographs the follicular epithelium surrounding the oocyte is continuously engaged in the transport of yolk proteins into the oocyte (Fig. 58). In such widely separated groups as insects (361, 362, 362a), amphibians (363, 363a), and birds (364) it has been shown that specific egg yolk proteins are synthesized outside of the ovary altogether, and it is clear that these proteins must be transported into the ovary via the follicular epithelium surrounding the growing oocyte. Furthermore, it is unlikely that the follicle cells serve solely a transport function, for protein and RNA synthesis are carried on at a high rate in follicle cells. Radioautographic studies have shown this to be true in the panoistic cricket ovariole (365), in amphibian ovaries (366), and in sea urchin ovaries, (366, 367) among many others.

In the higher chordates follicular layers of great complexity surround the young oocyte, and the fine structural specializations manifest in electron micrographs of the follicle-oocyte junction suggest that important molecular traffic is maintained between follicle cell and oocyte. This interesting region has been examined in the rat by Sotelo and Porter (368), one of whose micrographs is reproduced in Fig. 66. Cytoplasmic projections originating from both follicle cell and oocyte can be observed in the intervening noncellular zona pellucida. The latter contains a high concentration of acid mucopolysaccharides and probably functions as a transport highway for the appropriately selected molecules and a barrier to others (369).

Numerous cases have been discovered elsewhere in the animal world in which follicle cells are unequivocally involved in the provisioning of the oocyte with their own substance. For instance, in the gastropod *Helix*, as in some other gastropods and some coelenterates, the oocyte eventually phagocytizes and absorbs its follicle cells, nucleus and all (347). In certain arthropods, e.g., the louse, the follicle cells literally open into the adjacent oocyte cytoplasm and extrude their contents into the latter (370). These examples could be multiplied extensively [many useful references have been collected by Raven (356)]. To summarize, it is evident that *the maturation of the oocyte always requires the synthetic products of cells other than itself*. Where nurse cells are present RNA's synthesized in the nurse cell genomes are included in the oocyte, and all oocytes probably contain proteins synthesized externally. The extent to which the genetic information ultimately stored in the oocyte RNA is the result of transcription by the oocyte genome as opposed to the follicle or nurse cell genomes is in most cases unknown, and this is evidently a variable which depends on the species.

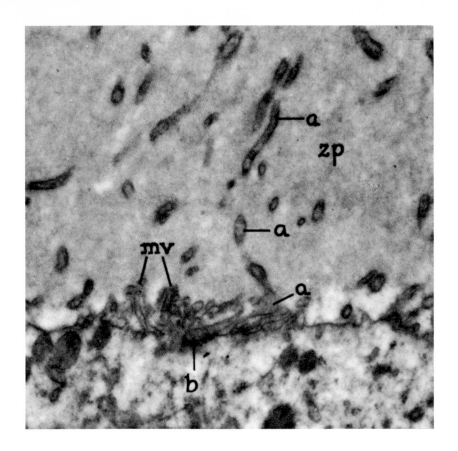

FIGURE 66. Micrograph of cortex and zona pellucida (zp) of full grown rat oocyte. The gelatinous material of the zona appears essentially homogeneous. Projections of the corona cells are evident at various points in the zona as they are caught in the section. Profiles interpreted as segments of a pseudopodium are shown in four places at (a) with the last segment in contact with the egg surface at (b). Microvilli (mv) are distributed unevenly over the egg surface. Patches of low density in the zona are presumed to be artifacts. × 20,000. Sotelo, J. R., and Porter, K., *J. Biophys. Biochem. Cytol.* **5,** 327 (1959).

4

Gene activity in the oocyte nucleus: ribosomal RNA synthesis

nucleolar function in the oocyte

We turn now to the available experimental information regarding the biochemical activity of the oocyte genome, with the foregoing discussion and that in Sections I and II serving to indicate the likely significance of this activity. An initial subject is the synthesis of ribosomal RNA, which in quantitative terms represents the major molecular product of the oocyte genomic apparatus.

The nuclei of many growing oocytes are characterized by a comparatively enormous quantity of nucleolar material. This may be present either as a single giant, lobular or compound nucleolus, as in many invertebrates (Fig. 67) and some vertebrates; as hundreds of individual nucleoli floating free in the nuclear sap, the case in amphibians; or as some combination of these two extremes. In the latter situation there may exist one or more "master" nucleoli and a small number of peripheral nucleoli. In another variant, changes in the nucleolar material occur during oogenesis such that the large oocyte nucleoli eventually fragment into many smaller ones, sometimes of irregular form [for examples, see Loyez (322) and Wilson (347)]. Oocyte nucleoli, like other nucleoli, contain high concentrations of RNA, as was first shown by Brachet (371), and this basic fact has been verified numerous times by many observers [references are collected in Raven (372)]. The ribosomal nature of the nucleolar RNA in oocytes has been directly demonstrated by Edstrom and Gall, who measured the base composition of the RNA extracted from hand-isolated *Triturus* oocyte nucleoli (349). Their data show that the oocyte nucleolar RNA is characterized by a typically ribosomal, high G-C base composition indistinguishable from that measured with the same procedures for the bulk cytoplasmic RNA of this oocyte. Similar analyses were published by Vincent for the nucleolar RNA

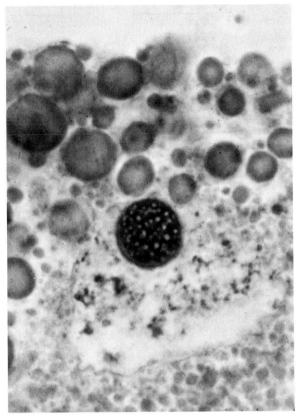

FIGURE 67. Growing oocyte of *Ilyanassa obsoleta;* note giant multilobular nucleolus.

of starfish oocytes (373), and the RNA of various other oocyte nucleoli has been studied with parallel results. The connection between the oocyte nucleoli and the nucleolar organizer region of the oocyte chromosomes is in some animals obscure, but in the cases of the axolotl and certain newts the relation of the large excess of nucleolar material to the organizer region is well established. In these amphibians the particular lampbrush chromosome loop pairs which contain the nucleolar organizers are known (374–376); and in some species, though not others, free nucleoli similar to those already present in the oocyte nucleoplasm can be observed deriving from the lampbrush region (374, 376–378). On grounds of appearance (e.g., refractility), the fact that they contain ribosomal RNA, their origin where known at the nucleolar organizer, and their fine structure, which displays a typical nucleolar core and cortex in electron micrographs (377, 379), the free-floating oocyte nucleoli must be regarded as homologous with the nucleoli of somatic cells. It is now clear that the oocyte nucleoli are the sites of ribosomal RNA synthesis during oogenesis, and the enlarged or multiplicate nucleolar apparatus of the oocyte can be regarded a priori as the likely site for the immense accumulation of ribosomal RNA which must take place during oogenesis.

Nucleolar ribosomal RNA synthesis is quantitatively the dominant aspect of gene activity during oogenesis. This can be stated with certainty for amphibian oogenesis, and it would seem prima facie to be true in general, judging from the relatively enormous quantities of ribosomal RNA present in the mature egg when it is shed (see Table V for the bulk or ribosomal RNA content of unfertilized eggs in various animals). Unfortunately, very little biochemical work directed at the nature of gene activity in oogenesis has been carried out on nonamphibian forms; exceptions are the studies of RNA synthesis during oogenesis in the sea urchin recently published by Gross, Malkin, and Hubbard (330) and by Piatagorsky, Ozaki, and Tyler (367). An initial question to consider is when in oogenesis the large ribosomal RNA stockpile present in the mature egg is synthesized. This problem has been examined directly in *Xenopus,* an amphibian in which all stages of oocyte can be found maturing simultaneously in the ovary at any one time [in what follows the oocyte staging system employed is that of Duryee (315), which is illustrated above in Fig. 55]. According to results obtained in the writer's laboratory (380) the stage-3 *Xenopus* oocyte (early lampbrush stage) possesses less than 20% of the total RNA contained in the mature stage-6 oocyte. By the end of the maximum lampbrush stage (stage 4), however, the total RNA content has increased to essentially the final or stage-6 value. In *Xenopus* oocytes of either stage 4 or stage 6 at least 95% of the total RNA is ribosomal RNA (25, 380, 381); therefore, measurement of total RNA content amounts essentially to measurement of ribosomal RNA content. When the relative rates of total RNA synthesis are considered for the various stages of oogenesis in *Xenopus* a picture consistent with the data on accumulation of RNA is obtained: The highest rate of synthesis exists at the maximum lampbrush stage. Both earlier and later than maximum lampbrush the rate of total RNA synthesis is lower, and in the resting stage-6 ovarian oocytes RNA synthesis is practically quiescent. These data add up to the fact that most of the ribosomal RNA in the oocyte is synthesized during stage 4, the maximum lampbrush stage.

Most of the RNA synthesized in the oocyte nucleus in *Xenopus* is ribosomal in nature, and this appears to be true even for the shortest labeling periods it is possible to use. Thus in experiments in which isolated lampbrush-stage oocytes are exposed to labeled precursor for only 30 minutes the base composition and sedimentation characteristics of the labeled RNA are ribosomal, just as they are after labeling periods several hundred times longer (e.g., 4–7 days). The lampbrush-stage oocyte differs from Hela or liver cells, for example, in that a large proportion of the high molecular weight RNA synthesized per unit time in the latter cell types is nonribosomal. Because synthesis and turnover rates of some of these nonribosomal RNA species are relatively high they can be studied in many somatic cell types by taking advantage of the nonribosomal labeling patterns characteristically obtained in short pulse, or pulse-chase experiments (see Section IV). Since in the lampbrush-stage oocyte virtually all the precursor is incorporated

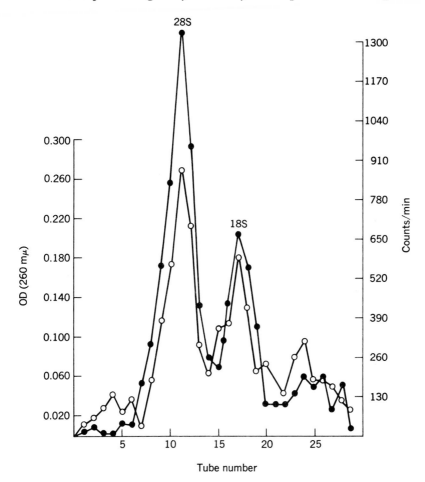

FIGURE 68. Sucrose gradient sedimentation pattern and base composition of uridine-^{3}H-labeled stage-4 oocyte RNA. From the base composition and sedimentation profile it is clear that this RNA is ribosomal in nature. (Open circles) OD at 260 mμ (filled circles); (U) 18.9%; (G) 39.5% (C) 25.6%; (A) 15.9%; G + C/A + U = 1.87. Davidson, E. H., Allfrey, V. G., and Mirsky, A. E., *Proc. Natl. Acad. Sci. U.S.* **52,** 501 (1964).

into ribosomal RNA even at short labeling times, it has not been possible to demonstrate the synthesis of a nonribosomal RNA fraction with the pulse labeling methods of use with other cells.

In Fig. 68 the sedimentation pattern and base composition (21, 380) of a typical lampbrush-stage oocyte RNA preparation is displayed, and the almost complete correspondence between the radioactivity trace and the sedimentation pattern representing the preexistent ribosomal RNA of the oocyte can be observed. This correspondence is obtained irrespective of the duration of labeling because almost all the RNA synthesized in the oocyte per unit time is in fact ribosomal. The difference between this result and those typically obtained in studies of RNA synthesis in most other cells is not due to the absence of nonribosomal, informational RNA synthesis in the oocyte, however, but rather to two other factors: (*a*) the *relative* amount of ribosomal RNA synthesis is vastly greater in the oocyte nucleus than in other nuclei; and (*b*) evidence which is reviewed in detail below indicates that neither appreciable rapid turnover nor differentially fast labeling of nonribosomal RNA appears to exist in the oocyte nucleus. The kinetics of accumulation of informational RNA are therefore similar to those describing the accumulation of ribosomal RNA. The empirical consequence of this situation is that experimental differentiation of informational and ribosomal RNA in the oocyte on the basis of difference in labeling and turnover rates is not at present possible.

the retention of ribosomal RNA synthesized in the amphibian oocyte

In the *Xenopus* lampbrush-stage oocyte over 95% of the RNA molecules synthesized per unit time are ribosomal RNA molecules (381). These molecules are retained in the oocyte for at least a number of months. An experiment demonstrating retention of ribosomal RNA synthesized at the lampbrush stage is presented in Table X (380), which describes the changes in RNA specific activity in various stages of *Xenopus* oocyte at various times following the *in vivo* administration of uridine-³H. The counts initially incorporated at the lampbrush stage in the experiment of Table X are observed subsequently to be distributed among stage-4, stage-5, and stage-6 oocytes. At first the specific activity of the total RNA of the stage-4 oocytes is highest, since they synthesize RNA at the highest rate, but after 6–10 weeks the stage-5 and stage-6 oocyte populations become more highly labeled. This cannot result from a delayed new synthesis of RNA in the older oocytes at the expense of the original precursor, since the precursor label included in the total acid soluble pool of the stage-4 and stage-5 oocytes

TABLE X. RNA Synthesis in *Xenopus* Oocytes[a]

Stage	State of nuclear apparatus	Pooled data:[b] Relative specific activity of RNA 3–7 days after labeling	Average specific activity (counts/min/µg RNA) of RNA after labeling with 1 mCi uridine-³H in one representative experiment				
			1 day	3 days	14 days	42 days	75 days
6	Lampbrush retracted	16	14	10	30	53	60
5	Late lampbrush	77	40	65	100	38	57
4	Lampbrush maximal	100	37	81	108	32	34
Total counts/min in the RNA of an average stage 4– plus an average stage 5– plus an average stage-6 oocyte			226	417	441	382	392

[a] The animals were labeled with three 0.33-mCi injections of uridine-³H given on the third, fourth, and fifth days following hormonal stimulation. The animals were caused to ovulate again at 30 days, to remove previously ripened stage-6 oocytes and thus decrease dilution of the newly maturing stage-6 oocyte population. From Ref. 380.

[b] Each lot of toads tends to label at a different overall rate, in our experience, and it is consequently difficult to pool absolute specific activity data. However, relative synthetic activities of the different stages of oocyte agree well in different experiments. Value for stage 4 set at 100.

drops to less than 5% of the starting values within 10 days of labeling and to essentially nothing by 40 days (380). The experiment therefore indicates that (under conditions of external gonadotropin stimulation) the minimum time separating the oldest stage-4 oocyte and the youngest stage-6 oocyte is in the range of 1½–2½ months in *Xenopus*, though 2½ months is shorter than the duration of stage 4 alone. The most significant aspect of the data in Table X, however, is the retention of essentially all of the RNA counts incorporated during the lampbrush phase for the whole period covered by the experiment in the face of the rapid decline and eventually the near disappearance of all precursor pool label: this is shown in the last line of Table X in which is tabulated the total RNA counts in an average stage-4, stage-5, and stage-6 oocyte at various times after labeling. Almost all the RNA synthesized at the lampbrush stage, most of which we know to be ribosomal RNA, is thus conserved throughout the remainder of oogenesis. In itself this is a remarkable fact since it constitutes an unprecedented example of long-term storage of a direct gene product, ribosomal RNA. Brown and Littna, in an experiment in which *Xenopus* females were labeled with ³H-orotic acid and 8 months later induced to shed their mature oocytes, have arrived at a similar conclusion. These workers have found that ribosomal RNA which must have been synthesized (in stage-4 or stage-5 oocytes) not long after the introduction of the labeled precursor is present in the mature oocytes after 8 months, the labeled molecules apparently having been conserved throughout much of this extended experimental period (382). In the *Xenopus* female already mature oocytes, if not shed, can be held in the ovary for many months before resorption and replacement occurs (316); and for the whole of this final resting period, plus the period required for the stage-4 (lampbrush-stage) oocyte to arrive at maturity (stage 6), the ribosomal RNA molecules synthesized during the lampbrush stage are evidently conserved. By way of comparison it is of interest to note that in adult rat liver parenchymal cells which, like the oocyte, are an active but essentially nondividing cell type, ribosomal RNA turnover continues incessantly, and the liver-ribosomal RNA population present at any one time decays exponentially with a half-life of only 5 days (384). Assuming that in other amphibians most of the oocyte ribosomal RNA originates at the lampbrush stage as demonstrated here in *Xenopus*, the duration of ribosomal RNA storage must be even more remarkable in those temperate zone frogs in which at least a year elapses between the lampbrush stage and ovulation. It is clear that the pattern of intensive synthesis and accretion without noticeable turnover provides the means by which the vast stores of ribosomal RNA needed for cleavage and blastulation can be accumulated in the egg. Stockpiling of ribosomal gene products is not a phenomenon peculiar to this species of RNA, for, as will become apparent below, the same synthesis and accretion model is useful in dealing with oocyte-synthesized informational RNA.

evidence that the free nucleoli of amphibian oocytes are the major sites of ribosomal RNA synthesis

Radioautographic evidence regarding the location of RNA-synthesizing sites in the amphibian lampbrush-stage oocyte nucleus shows that RNA synthesis takes place in the several hundred free-floating nucleoli as well as in the chromosomal apparatus (379, 385, 386). Most such experiments have failed to provide a quantitative comparison between the rate of RNA synthesis in the nucleoli and that in the chromosomes, however, for the simple reason that the nucleoli usually appear black with superimposed grains by the time the chromosomal label is heavy enough to quantitate. The relative rate of nucleolar RNA synthesis is of significance because a nucleolar rate of synthesis which is high compared to that in the chromosomes, in combination with the large number of individual nucleoli, would constitute an explanation for the apparent preponderance of ribosomal RNA synthesis during the lampbrush stage, according to the biochemical evidence. Radio-autographic experiments intended specifically to yield an approximate comparison between the RNA synthesis rate in nucleoli and in the lampbrush chromosomes of the same nucleus have been performed with *Xenopus* oocytes (316, 381), and they indicate that nucleolar label accumulates at least 60 times faster than does label in the lampbrush chromosomes themselves (381). Despite the active RNA synthesis in the lampbrush chromosomes (385, 386), the even more intense RNA synthesis occurring in the free-floating nucleoli, and the large number of these nucleoli [over 1400 per nucleus in *Xenopus* (387)], result in the complete domination of the overall oocyte RNA synthesis pattern by the nucleolar RNA synthesis products. The nucleoli are therefore necessarily the sites of synthesis of the ribosomal RNA stockpile which is conserved throughout the subsequent stage of oogenesis and ultimately bequeathed to the embryo. This is not to say that the chromosomal ribosomal RNA genes are quiescent, for the nucleolar organizer loops of these chromosomes are in fact also active in RNA synthesis, but that by far the major burden of this synthesis is borne by the nucleoli. This conclusion corroborates various earlier radioautographic investigations which appear to indicate that the nucleoli of the oocyte are the most rapidly labeling of the RNA-synthesizing components. Such studies exist for echinoderm (388) and insect oocytes (338), among others.

Electron microscope observations have now documented thoroughly the role of the oocyte nucleoli in synthesizing ribosome precursors. Miller and Beatty (383) have shown that the granular cortex of the oocyte nucleolus is packed with particles, each containing what appears to be a single newly synthesized ribosomal RNA precursor molecule. Furthermore, the recent investigation of Rogers (388a) has now demonstrated that newt and axolotl oocyte nuclei contain 50–55S ribosomal precursor particles, in which both protein and ribosomal RNA components are newly synthesized. Smaller ribosomal precursor particles (30S) bearing newly synthesized RNA are also found, but 78S ribosomes appear to be absent from the oocyte nucleus.

nucleolar DNA and the selective replication of genes for ribosomal RNA

Since the main part of the massive RNA stockpile accumulated by the oocyte appears to stem from nucleolar synthesis, it is of particular interest that the free-floating nucleoli of the oocyte have recently been proved to contain DNA, notwithstanding earlier assertions to the contrary. Unequivocal evidence for this comes from three independent directions: (*a*) the demonstrations of Izawa, Allfrey, and Mirsky (385) that oocyte nucleolar

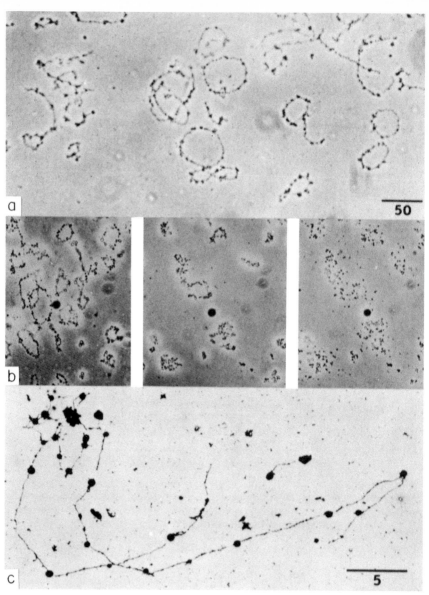

FIGURE 69. (a) Nucleolar cores in circular form derived from cluster nucleoli during late stages of oogenesis by isolation in low molarity saline. Largest circles are approximately 165 μ in circumference. Linear cores presumably result from opening of the circles by mechanical breakage during isolation. Phase contrast. $\times$ 240. (b) Same as (a) except cores isolated into medium containing deoxyribonuclease. $\times$ 255. (c) Electron micrograph of circular nucleolar core isolated in low molarity saline. A portion of the core was broken away in the preparation for microscopy. $\times$ 3400. Miller, O. L., *Natl. Cancel Inst. Monograph* **23**, 53 (1966).

210

RNA synthesis is DNA dependent since it is completely blocked by actinomycin, (b) observations leading to the conclusion that amphibian oocyte nucleoli contain a ringlike DNA structure (see below), and (c) the recent RNA-DNA hybridization studies of Brown (389), Brown and David (389a), and Gall (395), which prove directly that the nucleoli contain DNA complementary to ribosomal RNA.

In the last few years the investigations alluded to in (b) above have established without a doubt that the free-floating nucleoli of urodele oocytes contain DNA. Miller (377) has shown that *Triturus* oocyte nucleoli isolated in low molarity saline solutions dissolve into circular structures resembling bead necklaces. Examples can be seen in Fig. 69a, and in Fig. 69b the fragmentation of these necklaces by DNase is shown. Ultrastructural studies of the low-saline nucleolar structures reveal the presence of a single deoxyribonucleoprotein fiber, as in Fig. 69c. In some urodeles the nucleoli apparently fragment into necklacelike structures spontaneously. These have been observed by ourselves in newt oocytes and have been described in detail by Callan (374) as a normal stage traversed by nucleoli in the development of the axolotl oocyte. A similar conclusion has been drawn by Lane from studies with maturing *Triturus* oocyte nucleoli (390a). A diagrammatic description of nucleolar maturation in the axolotl (*Ambystoma mexicanum*), as prepared by Callan, is presented in Fig. 70. According to the radioautographic studies of Lane (390a), RNA synthesis occurs throughout the series of stages portrayed in Fig. 70. Initially the nucleoli are spherical (Fig. 70) and RNA synthesis is confined to a restricted, eccentric region, reflecting a localized concentration of nucleolar DNA at this stage. In the extended ring forms, however, RNA synthesis is distributed throughout the nucleolar structures, as is the DNA (390a).

In salamanders of the genus *Plethodon* nucleolar ring necklaces held together by DNase-sensitive strands also form naturally. Peacock (390), who has studied this system, is able to locate a portion of the lampbrush chromosomes on which the characteristic nucleolar rings can be observed still attached to the chromosomes; the looplike structures formed by these rings are *unpaired*, unlike the other chromosome loops, and they exactly resemble the free nucleolar rings in the same nuclei. Photographs of the latter, as they occur in two *Plethodon* species, are presented in Figs. 71a and b, and the chromosomal region where the rings appear to originate (evidently the nucleolar organizer) is shown in Fig. 71c.

Earlier assertions that DNA is present in the free-floating nucleoli of amphibian oocytes had been based on the presence of Feulgen-positive nucleolar spots, but in many forms no evidence for nucleolar DNA could be obtained with classical histochemical methods (344). It is to be noted, nonetheless, that as far back as 1940 both Brachet (391) and Painter and

Nuclear membrane

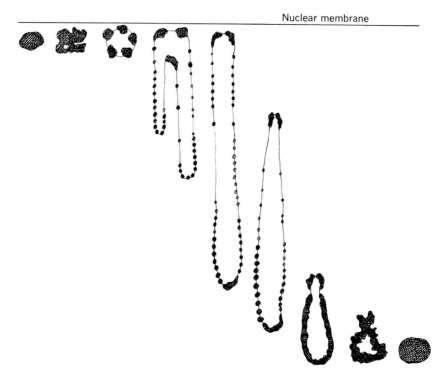

FIGURE 70. A sketch to show the transformations of axolotl nucleoli in oocytes developing from about 1 mm (extreme left) to 1.9 mm (extreme right) diameter. Callan, H. G., *J. Cell Sci.* **1**, 85 (1966).

Taylor (392), on the basis of Feulgen staining, claimed that the free nucleoli of anuran oocytes contain DNA. Painter and Taylor had in fact already concluded (1942) "that the germinal vesicle of the toad is highly polyploid in nucleolar organizers but otherwise lampbrush chromosomes are normal meiotic structures" (392). In the oocytes of most organisms the nucleoli do not become separated from the chromosomes as they do in amphibian oocytes, and demonstrations of oocyte nucleolar DNA by the Feulgen reaction exist for mollusks, insects, nematodes, crustaceans, and mammals (393).

The DNA contained in the nucleoli of amphibian oocytes must include genes for ribosomal RNA, since, as shown above, ribosomal RNA is definitely synthesized in these nucleoli, and since this synthesis is DNA dependent (385). The nucleoli each contain far less than the haploid amount of DNA, however, or the amphibian oocyte nucleus would contain hundreds of times the 4C value of DNA, which it does not (387, 394), and the dimensions of the nucleolar rings would be enormously greater than they are. Therefore

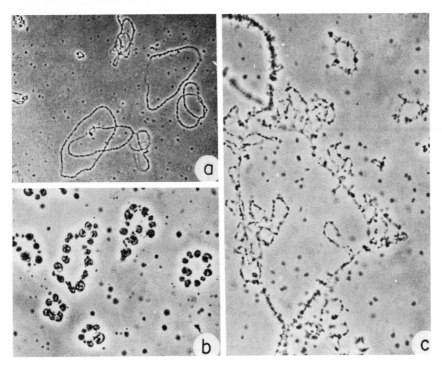

FIGURE 71. (a) Ring nucleoli of *Plethodon vehiculum,* free in the nucleus. Circumference of the larger ones approximates 200 μ. (b) Nucleolar rings of *Plethodon cinereus* at the "beaded necklace" stage. (c) Portion of the "nucleolar ring" bivalent of *Plethodon cinereus* showing detail of the region of "nucleolar loops." In many places it can be seen that the "nucleolar ring loops" are not paired. Peacock, W. J., *Natl. Cancer Inst. Monograph* **18,** 101 (1965).

it is evident a priori that at some point in oogenesis a *partial genomic replication* has taken place, resulting in the *differential multiplication of the ribosomal RNA cistrons* (and perhaps of other genetic material as well). This too has now been demonstrated directly by the use of RNA-DNA hybridization methods. Brown (389) and Brown and David (389a) have compared the germinal vesicle and somatic cell DNA of several amphibians with respect to that DNA fraction which is complementary to ribosomal RNA. The latter can easily be separated from the remainder of the DNA since the ribosomal RNA-DNA hybrids display a greater density in CsCl sedimentation. The total germinal vesicle DNA turns out to contain several hundred times as much DNA complementary to ribosomal RNA as is present in the somatic cell DNA, according to these experiments (389, 389a). Since the number of nucleoli in the germinal vesicle is of a similar order, each nucleolus would appear to contain a single copy of the replicate ribosomal RNA gene cluster normally present in each nucleolar organizer. In the urodeles studied by Miller (377) each nucleolus also is found to contain one DNA ring, though in *Xenopus,* according to Perkowska, Macgregor, and Birnsteil (387), each nucleolus contains five DNA rings.

Selective replication of the ribosomal RNA cistrons occurs early in oogenesis, long before the lampbrush stage. Recent experiments of Gall (395) demonstrate that in *Xenopus* and *Bufo* oocytes incorporation of thymidine-^{3}H into nonchromosomal DNA-containing granules occurs at an early point in the meiotic prophase sequence (pachytene). Deoxyribonucleic acid labeled at this stage can be separated from chromosomal (somatic) DNA in a CsCl gradient by virtue of its high G-C content; as expected, this DNA is rich in ribosomal cistrons and it hybridizes preferentially with ribosomal RNA. Increase in the total mass of nuclear DNA beyond the 4C amount present at the onset of oogenesis was years ago shown by Painter (396) to occur during the pachytene in *Bufo* oocytes. In *Xenopus* a similar DNA accumulation can be detected. Thus the spectrophotometric measurements of Perkowska *et al.* (387) indicate that a mass of 42 $\mu\mu$g of DNA is present in the postzygotene *Xenopus* oocyte, and of this only 12 $\mu\mu$g (the 4C content, is chromosomal. The remaining 30 $\mu\mu$g would thus be nucleolar. Brown and David (389a), using CsCl centrifugation, have quantitatively separated and measured the ribosomal DNA of the *Xenopus* germinal vesicle, and they estimate 25 $\mu\mu$g of nucleolar DNA per nucleus.

In *Xenopus* the amount of the genome which is ribosomal is about 0.11%, assuming that only one strand of the DNA duplex is used as template for the synthesis of the ribosomal RNA's, since 0.057% of the DNA by weight is complementary to the 28S and 18S ribosomal RNA components (99). This amounts to about 0.0033 $\mu\mu$g of ribosomal DNA per haploid set. Taking 1.5×10^3 as the average number of nucleoli in the oocyte nucleus (387), and 25 $\mu\mu$g as their aggregate DNA content (389a), the DNA content per nucleolus is about 5 times the DNA content of one haploid set of ribosomal RNA cistrons (25 $\mu\mu$g/1.5×10^3/0.0033 $\mu\mu$g). Similar calculations can be made for other amphibian species, though the absolute magnitude of the RNA values are very different. Directly testing this proposition, Brown and David (389a) report 2.4 times more nucleolar DNA than is contained in a single ribosomal gene cluster in *Siredon,* 5.6 times as much in *Necturus,* and 4.7 times as much in *Xenopus.* According to the hybridization studies (see above), each nucleolus contains on the average only one set of ribosomal cistrons, however, and it is therefore to be presumed that the nucleolar DNA includes some closely linked genetic material other than that coding specifically for 28S and 18S ribosomal RNA's. Jeanteur, Amaldi, and Attardi (397) have in fact provided direct evidence that ribosomal precursor molecules contain extensive sequences which are not present in the final 18S and 28S RNA products, accounting for as much as 50% of the total precursor sequence. Furthermore, according to the recent studies of Brown and Weber (397a), the DNA sequences coding for 18S and 28S ribosomal RNA are arranged in alternate fashion and are totally contained in a single replicate cluster: While these facts might render a twofold excess of total nucleolar DNA as compared to ribosomal nucleolar DNA interpretable, the presence of greater than fivefold excesses remains mysterious.

It is clear that the partial genomic replication of the (already redundant) ribosomal RNA locus results, in amphibian oocytes, in a very significant multiplication of the sites at which ribosomal RNA can be synthesized. The *Xenopus* oocyte at maturity contains some 1.1×10^{12} ribosomal RNA molecules (387). At the rate of ribosome generation occurring in rapidly dividing somatic tissues the synthesis of the oocyte ribosomal RNA would require 1.7×10^5 days were no replication of the ribosomal cistrons to have occurred, according to the calculations of Perkowska *et al.* (387). Reduction of this time period by a factor of $1-1.5 \times 10^3$, the number of nucleoli per nucleus, brings the required synthesis period down to 3–6 months, the duration actually estimated on other grounds for the lampbrush stage in *Xenopus* (we assume here that, as Brown's hybridization studies indicate, each nucleolus contains one set of ribosomal cistrons).

Selective replication of the ribosomal genes is thus the specialized mechanism underlying the massive synthesis and accretion during oogenesis of all the ribosomal RNA actually needed to support development far into embryonic life. It will be recalled that in *Xenopus*, homozygous 0-nu embryos which are unable to synthesize their own ribosomal RNA arrest and die only after progressing through gastrulation and tubulation to the swimming tadpole stage (96), and this gives evidence of the extent to which maternal ribosomal RNA is used in embryogenesis. Brown has also shown that selective replication of the ribosomal RNA cistrons occurs during oogenesis in a protostome, the echiuroid worm *Urechis* (389a), and it is likely that this phenomenon is as universal as is reliance on maternal ribosomal RNA in early development. Thus, like the prolonged diplotene, the presence of a 4C chromosomal DNA complement, and the existence of lampbrush chromosomes, selective replication of the ribosomal cistrons should probably be considered a basic characteristic of oocyte differentiation.

In *Xenopus* ribosomal RNA synthesis does not take place in the resting stage-6 oocyte, though nucleoli remain visible until germinal vesicle breakdown, but it can be stimulated to occur at a rate about 15% of that in the lampbrush-stage oocyte by treating the mother with gonadotropic hormones. Similarly, a certain amount of ribosomal RNA synthesis appears to be carried out in a minority fraction of terminal sea urchin oocytes under conditions stimulating final oocyte maturation (330). In resting mature sea urchin oocytes, on the other hand, synthesis of all classes of RNA is essentially halted (398). Histochemical studies of late oogenesis in a variety of organisms have demonstrated a marked loss of (ribosomal) RNA from the nucleoli as oogenesis draws to a close and the egg enters its last resting period preparatory to ovulation.

5

Gene activity in the oocyte
nucleus: synthesis
of informational RNA

the temporal location of informational
RNA synthesis in oogenesis

Though most of the RNA synthesized during oogenesis and stored in the
mature oocyte is ribosomal, it is obvious that ribosomal RNA itself cannot
account for the known properties of the RNA stockpile carried in the egg
cytoplasm. The conclusion that informational as well as ribosomal components are present in the store of preformed egg RNA's as development
begins is at present unavoidable (see Sections I and II for evidence and
references). It is clear that the stored informational RNA's are synthesized
during oogenesis, but in which phases of the long process of oocyte development has been unknown until recently. Gross *et al.* (330), in their study
of RNA synthesis in sea urchin oogenesis, have obtained evidence that
informational RNA's inherited by the embryo are synthesized during the
terminal period of oogenesis. Their experiments concern oocytes completing
vitellogenesis, a period of late oogenesis which may occur long after the
lampbrush stage (refer to Fig. 55 and the accompanying discussion for a
summary of the chromosomal transformations occurring during oogenesis in
echinoderms). Ribonucleic acid labeled during this time includes sequences
complementary to DNA well beyond the level expected of ribosomal RNA,
and informational RNA synthesis thus appears to be taking place at this
stage. Furthermore, since the period between administration of labeled
precursor to the oocytes and harvest of the mature eggs amounts to 1–2 weeks
in the experiments of Gross *et al.*, at least some portion of the labeled informational RNA in the mature eggs is over a week old. Recently, Piatagorsky and Tyler have published further studies relevant to the question of
when in oogenesis there occurs the synthesis of informational RNA's inherited by the echinoderm embryo (398). Female sea urchins were labeled

217

in this work as long as 3 months prior to ovulation, and the labeled RNA still present in the mature eggs at various times after labeling was extracted and subjected to conventional analytical procedures. Most of the label incorporated in the egg RNA sediments as ribosomal RNA after more than a month of labeling, but evidence exists for incorporation into a class of nonribosomal, heterogeneously sedimenting RNA as well. Informational RNA synthesis in the sea urchin oocyte would thus appear to be taking place at least a month prior to maturation of the eggs (398), and to continue, at least under stimulatory conditions, right up to the last week before shedding (330). As noted above, however, very young oocytes, which are likely to be significantly more than a month away from maturation, label most heavily of all in radioautographic studies of RNA synthesis during sea urchin oogenesis [(330); see Section I]. Thus to date investigation may not have extended sufficiently far back into early stages to permit a conclusion as to when in sea urchin oogenesis the main part of the maternal informational RNA is actually synthesized.

Amphibian embryos, according to Brown and Littna (91, 102) contain sizable quantities of informational RNA which is synthesized during the very last hours of oogenesis. The experiments of these workers demonstrate the occurrence of a burst of informational RNA synthesis during the terminal 8–12 hours of oogenesis in *Xenopus*. These RNA's are synthesized following the hormonal stimulation which induces ovulation. During the ovulation period the eggs traverse the oviducts, where they are exposed to further hormonal stimulations and where they are encased in their membranes. Brown and Littna have estimated that the unfertilized ovulated *Xenopus* egg contains at least 1 mμg of newly synthesized informational RNA, characterized according to its DNA-like base composition. According to Brown and Littna (102) the total newly synthesized informational RNA in the early *Xenopus* gastrula, which contains many thousands of active nuclei, amounts to only about 10 mμg. Thus the synthesis of 1 mμg (or more) of informational RNA within the 12 hours of the ovulation period by one nucleus would seem to indicate a remarkable burst of synthetic activity. The length in hours of the ovulation period is not very different from the time required for the embryo to develop to stage 10. Given the circumstances, the synthesis of informational RNA is probably to be regarded as a response on the part of the mature oocyte genome to the sudden increase in the level of pituitary and other hormones which accompanies ovulation.

The complex hormone-mediated events of ovulation include a number of essential intracellular changes, and in amphibian eggs these all appear to depend on oocyte genome function. Dettlaff (399) and Brachet (399a) have shown that germinal vesicle breakdown itself, and the distribution of the germinal vesicle constituents into the cytoplasm, are blocked in ovulated amphibian eggs by exposure to actinomycin or puromycin. These findings are interpreted as an indication that the ovulation process is normally directed by oocyte informational RNA's newly synthesized in response to hormonal stimulation. In this connection we recall the studies of Graham (297) and Gurdon (298) which demonstrate that the capacity to evoke DNA synthesis appears in oocyte cytoplasm during ovulation (see Section II). Preovulation oocytes fail to stimulate nuclei transfered into them to make DNA in these experiments, and only after pituitary hormone injection and germinal vesicle breakdown does this inductive capacity appear. According to Gurdon this cytoplasmic potentiality, which is of course critical for the onset of development, "arises as an effect of pituitary hormone on mature oocytes" (298). Hormonal response is thus an important aspect of the vital last-minute functions in which the oocyte nucleus is engaged in the ovulating amphibian egg. Actually this pattern of events may be very general: Brachet and Steinert have shown that actinomycin also prevents meiotic metaphase from taking place in starfish oocytes (399b). It is known, furthermore, that in the starfish germinal vesicle breakdown and the meiotic metaphase processes are regulated by the action of a hormonelike "radial nerve factor" acting on the ovarian tissue (399c). The intense burst of informational RNA synthesis detected by Brown and Littna in ovulation-stage *Xenopus* eggs during this period is to be regarded as associated with ovulation functions and included, no doubt, is the synthesis of template molecules which for some reason must be assembled directly prior to their utilization. In what follows, however, it becomes clear that the template-active RNA synthesized during the ovulation period and inherited by the embryo can constitute no more than a small fraction of the total template-active informational RNA stockpile with which the egg is supplied when it enters ovulation.

In order to investigate the template-active RNA content of the *preovulation oocyte* a method is required with which it is possible to measure quantitatively the template activity of a small fraction of the oocyte RNA in the presence of a comparatively huge amount of ribosomal RNA. A low background cell-free protein synthesis system which can be depended on to respond quantitatively to the addition of exogenous template-active RNA provides such a method, and in the writer's laboratory an attempt to detect stored template RNA in the *preovulation* oocytes of *Xenopus* has recently been made. In these experiments (25) an *E. coli* ribosome system is used, and a sharp stimulation of protein synthesis is found to result from the addition of total RNA from *ovarian* stage-6 oocytes. This can be seen in Fig. 72, which also portrays the response of the cell-free system to added F-2 coliphage RNA. The linear increase in protein synthesis rate with increasing total exogenous RNA concentrations shows that the rate of in-

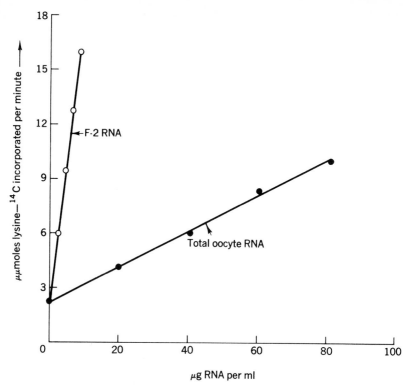

FIGURE 72. Response of the cell-free protein synthesis system to exogenous template-active RNA. Reaction mixture (200 μl) containing 1.11 mg of S-30 protein was present in each reaction tube. At 2-minute intervals, 20-μl samples were adsorbed on Whatman 3 MM filter pads and assayed for hot TCA-insoluble lysine-^{14}C counts. The rate of synthesis obtained directly from the time course of incorporation is a linear function of the RNA concentration. Davidson, E. H., Crippa, M., Kramer, F. R., and Mirsky, A. E., *Proc. Natl. Acad. Sci. U.S.* **56,** 856 (1966).

corporation is proportional to the amount of template RNA present, irrespective in the case of the oocyte preparations of the presence of an enormous excess of ribosomal RNA, itself inactive as a template. Figure 73, from further studies of Kramer (400), provides added evidence that the proteins synthesized in response to additions of *Xenopus* oocyte RNA are not simply the result of some artifactual stimulation of endogenous bacterial RNA translation. Thus, Fig. 73 shows that the amino acid compositions of the proteins synthesized from *Xenopus* RNA, from endogenous *E. coli*, and from *F-2* coliphage RNA are clearly distinct. Comparing the amount of template activity in RNA preparations extracted from different stages of oocyte, we have found that *there is no further addition of template activity after the lampbrush stage* (25). The template-active RNA stockpile of the quiescent stage-6 ovarian oocyte is therefore synthesized as far back as the lampbrush stage of oogenesis and is held in the oocyte throughout vitellogenesis (stages 5 and 6). The same pattern of storage of lampbrush-stage gene products, which we have previously verified for maternal ribosomal

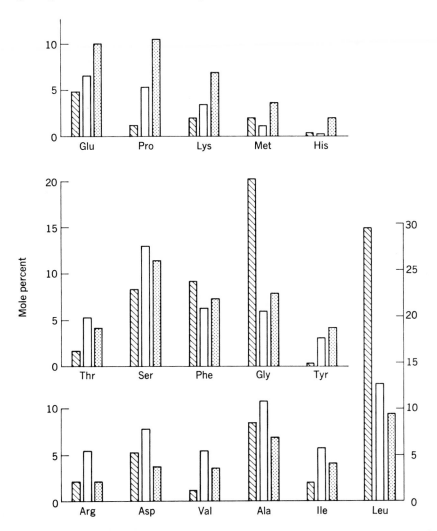

FIGURE 73. Mole percent amino acid compositions of proteins synthesized *in vitro* by an S-30 ribosome system of *E. coli* stimulated with exogenous RNA from *Xenopus* oocytes and from F-2 coliphage, or operating with its own endogenous template RNA. (Crosshatched) *E. coli,* (clear) F-2 coliphage, (stippled) *Xenopus.* Kramer, F. R., In preparation (1968).

RNA, thus appears to hold for maternal template RNA, according to these data.

By reference to the template activity of the F-2 coliphage RNA standard operating in the same system it is possible to arrive at an estimate of the actual mass of template-active RNA through direct comparison of the slopes shown in Fig. 72. Such an estimate, however, depends on the equality of translation rate for both template sets, the coliphage and the *Xenopus*, and since the F-2 coliphage is evolutionarily adapted to the E. *coli* protein synthesis machinery, the template-active RNA values calculated on the basis of this comparison are possibly to be regarded as minimum estimates. Kramer has recently shown, however, that the cell-free protein synthesis system used in these experiments translates polio virus RNA at a rate close to that with which F-2 coliphage RNA is translated, and polio is of course adapted to a chordate host. Both Slater and Spiegelman, working with unfertilized sea urchin egg RNA (180), and ourselves have sought to assay template-RNA content by comparison with a viral standard (Section I), and with similar results: About 4.5% of the unfertilized sea urchin egg RNA and about 2.5% of the *Xenopus* mature oocyte RNA appear to be template active. In the case of the *Xenopus* oocyte this means that the amount of template-active RNA stored from before ovulation is almost two orders of magnitude greater than the amount synthesized during ovulation, according to Brown and Littna [the values obtained from the ovarian stage-6 oocyte are of the order of 0.5–1×10^2 mμg of template-active RNA per oocyte (25, 400)]. These experiments thus leave us with two significant conclusions: (*a*) the template RNA stockpile present in the mature ovarian oocyte appears to have been synthesized much earlier in oogenesis, *at the lampbrush stage*; and (*b*) this template RNA constitutes by far the largest part of that inherited by the embryo as maternal messenger, provided that it survives ovulation and fertilization. That in fact it does so is demonstrated presently, our more immediate problem being the particulars of informational RNA synthesis at the lampbrush stage.

lampbrush chromosome structure and DNA content

Lampbrush chromosome structure has long been considered suggestive of intense and widespread gene activity. As diagramed in Fig. 55 the chromosomes attain their maximum degree of extension at the mid-lampbrush stage (stage 4), and the linear, alternating, loop-chromomere arrangement suggests the linear arrangement of genetic sites in the genome. It is known (401, 402) that each loop contains one DNA duplex, and each pair of loops and each chromosome two such duplexes. Chiasmata connect the chromatids periodically (see, for example, those apparent in Fig. 62), as expected in diplotene bivalents. The continuity of the enormously long DNA fibers between loop and chromomeres has been verified by Callan and Lloyd in an experiment in which the chromosome structure is unraveled into two very long fibrous threads by direct application of opposing physical tensions with dissecting needles [for detailed discussion of lampbrush chromosome structure see the monograph by Callan and Lloyd (376) and the review by Callan (343)]. There are about 20,000 loops in the whole chromosome set of *Triturus*, some of which are very large, over 50 μ in axial length (343); there are about 5000 loops per haploid set. Although it has been supposed that each loop represents a gene, 5000 might seem far too small a number of genes, and the arithmetic of DNA content/loop renders this hypothesis very unlikely in any case. Thus a loop which actually contained a linear DNA fiber long enough to constitute the cistron coding for the hemoglobin β chain could possess an axis no more than 0.2 μ long. While some organisms, e.g., *Xenopus*, do indeed possess exceedingly small loops, consider the dimensions of the *Triturus* lampbrush chromosome loops (Fig. 62), some of which are several hundred times this length. An alternative suggestion owing to Callan and Lloyd (376) and Callan (403), and one which also provides an interpretation of the enormous differences in genomic DNA content existing even among related organisms (e.g., *Xenopus* and *Triturus*, both amphibians), is that *each loop represents the linear replicates of a single gene*. According to this idea, the differences in DNA content among species and particularly among related species [see references in Callan (403) for some striking examples] is a function of the amount of redundancy in all or some of the organism's genetic sites. Deoxyribonucleic acid content per genome is generally to be correlated with cell size, a significant fact deriving from the extensive investigations of genomic DNA content in organisms ranging from sponges to chordates carried out by Mirsky and Ris in 1951 (404). In order to service a more extensive cytoplasm an increase in "gene power" would thus appear to be required, in the form of repetitive genetic sites (rather than an increase in the number of diverse genes). Three possibilities here exist:

(1) In redundant areas of the genome only one or a few of the genes in each replicate gene family are functional. In this way it is possible to escape from the dilemma which arises in attempting to explain the occurrence of change in phenotype resulting from mutation if all the many replicates of a given gene are expressed.

(2) All genetic sites are replicated but only one cistron out of each set of replicates, the "master copy" need be affected by mutation, and the master copy would then "correct" the sequence in the replicates. This idea has been put forth by Callan in a recent article (403), in which it was

proposed that the lampbrush chromosome is in fact the site of this "correction" process. Callan's interpretation rests pivotally on the premise that 100% of the genetic material which is redundant moves through the chromosome loops synthesizing RNA and, as is pointed out below, this position may be untenable. In Callan's model the "correction" of each replicate would be accomplished through some mechanism which begins with base pairing between each replicate copy and the master copy of the gene; deviations in nucleotide sequence between a replicate and the master copy, whether because of mutation or error occurring in premeiotic DNA synthesis, would result in mismatching. One difficulty with this ingenious conception is that the redundant areas of the genome are actually not perfectly replicate, except for a few minor fractions, but rather are *near* replicate [(108); see discussion in Section I]. One would thus be faced with the added difficulty of explaining discrimination between mismatching which is the result of error or mutation and that which results from the basic construction of the genome.

(3) The lampbrush chromosome loops contain replicate genes which are all expressed, but which code for indispensable housekeeping functions only. Mutations of a qualitative sort (other than total deletions, that is) might not be easily observed in such redundant loci, and deleterious mutations would be completely intolerable in any case. The redundant gene families coding for ribosomal and transfer RNA are cases in point with which we are already familiar. As far as lampbrush chromosome structure itself is concerned, no reliable evidence exists in any case with respect to whether each loop produces more than one species of gene product. Until this basic question can be answered it would seem difficult to develop an unequivocal interpretation of lampbrush chromosome structure in terms of genomic redundancy.

Total oocyte nuclear DNA has been measured spectrophotometrically with the Feulgen reaction in a number of organisms in which the nucleus is small enough to provide the necessary DNA concentrations. Organisms as diverse as mammals (328, 405), insects (406), and various worms (407, 408) turn out to contain either the 4C nuclear DNA content expected for a meiotic prophase nucleus, or an amount slightly greater than this, probably because of the excess nucleolar DNA. In organisms whose oocytes contain much larger nuclei, however, the stainability of the chromosomal apparatus tends to disappear as the oocyte enters its maximum growth stage and the chromosomes become diffuse. The significance of this was discussed as long ago as 1907 by Maréchal (342), and the apparent disappearance during oogenesis of those chromatin elements usually staining with basic dyes, while the chromosomal structures themselves persist morphologically, was for years regarded as a potent argument against the idea that DNA could be the genetic material in the chromosomes [see, for example, Wilson's 1925 discussion of this problem (409)]. Lampbrush chromosomes are a case in point, for though the chromosomes and certain other granules are in fact Feulgen-positive (410), the chromosome loops do not contain high enough DNA concentrations to react to the usual Feulgen procedure. If the chromatin of the lampbrush-stage amphibian oocyte nucleus is deliberately concentrated at one pole of the nucleus by centrifugation, however, a Feulgen-positive reaction can be easily demonstrated, as was shown by Brachet (410). The DNA content of mid-lampbrush *Triturus* chromosomes and of the nonchromosomal nuclear material has recently been measured by Izawa, Allfrey, and Mirsky (394), using a sensitive microprocedure for the analysis. Measurements of DNA content were made on samples of 100 hand-isolated *Triturus* lampbrush chromosomes or on whole lampbrush-stage oocyte nuclei, and only DNase-solubilized material was regarded as DNA in this study. In Table XI some comparisons based on the results of Izawa *et al.* are presented.

It can be seen that the lampbrush chromosomes of the *Triturus* oocyte appear to contain over four times as much DNA as expected on the basis of the 4C DNA values required of the meiotic prophase chromosomes. It is also clear, however, that the meiotic chromatids actually contain no more than the anticipated pair of DNA duplexes, one duplex in each loop and two in the interloop chromomeres. The most direct evidence for this comes from the electron micrographs of Miller (401), though a few years earlier Gall had derived the correct structure of the chromosomes from a kinetic study of lampbrush chromosome breakage in DNase (402). The nature of the excess chromosomal DNA of Izawa *et al.* (Table XI) thus remains obscure, since it cannot easily be accounted for in terms of the general structure of the lampbrush chromosomes. The chromosomal preparations studied by these workers contained little or no obvious nucleolar material, though the excess DNA measured by them cannot be easily explained other than as the result of nucleolar contamination. One possibility is that the DNA contained in the various large Feulgen-positive granules present at

Table XI. DNA Contents ($\mu\mu$g) of *Triturus* Lampbrush Chromosomes and Nuclei[a]

Diploid (2C) value: 89
Theoretical meiotic prophase (4C) value: 178
Measured chromosome content: 780
Whole nuclear DNA content: 1600
Nuclear sap and nucleolar DNA content: 820

[a] From Ref. 394.

several locations in the chromosomes (344, 410) contributes significantly to the overall chromosomal DNA values. If so, the functional role of these localized DNA concentrations could be of great interest, particularly if they were to represent other selective replications of the genome, similar to that responsible for the replication of the ribosomal RNA cistrons.

Table XI shows that the nuclear sap in the lampbrush-stage newt oocyte contains about the same amount of DNA as the chromosomal apparatus itself. In view of the selective replication of ribosomal cistrons known to occur in amphibian oogenesis, some of this DNA is to be attributed to the nucleoli (see above).

RNA synthesis in lampbrush chromosomes

The most striking attribute of the lampbrush structures is the intensity of the RNA synthesis carried out in them. According to Gall (411) and Callan (344) only about 5% of the total calculated length of genomic DNA in *Triturus* is actually included in the loops in any one nucleus, the remainder being present in the Feulgen-positive interloop chromomeres. Radioautographic studies of RNA synthesis in the chromosomes by Gall (412), Gall and Callan, and others (385, 386, 413) shows that the loops are the main site of labeling, though RNA of the chromosomal axis (i.e., the chromomeres) may label as well. Most of the loops incorporate precursors into RNA in all regions, as does the loop pair shown in Fig. 74. Protein synthesis also occurs all over the chromosome loops (386). The loops, however, are polarized in the sense that the matrix constituting the body of the loop material and surrounding the single DNA fiber traversing the loop is thicker at one end of the loop than at the other (344, 376). There are under normal conditions in *Triturus* oocytes at least two particular pairs of giant loops (out of the hundreds sufficiently prominent to be observable) which display an interesting deviation from the uniform pattern of RNA synthesis portrayed in Fig. 74, in that these loops *label* in a polarized fashion as well (344, 386). In loops showing polarized synthesis of RNA only the areas at the thinner insertion of the loop appear to serve as sites of synthesis, and in radioautographic experiments only this region of the loop shows uptake into RNA after 1 day's exposure to labeled precursor. At 2 days a larger area is labeled, at 4 days half of the loop is labeled, at 7 days two-thirds is labeled, and at 14 days labeled RNA is present all over the loop. Gall and Callan (386) observe that this phenomenon can be interpreted either as movement of the RNA gene product alone or as movement of the RNA gene product together with movement of the DNA template. Opting for the latter, Gall and Callan (386) and Callan (403) have developed an interpretation according to which the DNA present in the chromomeres at any one time is spun out into the loops at a later time, and at a still later time, having traversed the whole loop structure, it is returned to the next chromomere. The RNA gene products are postulated to move along with the DNA. Thus, though only 5% of the DNA may be present in the loops at

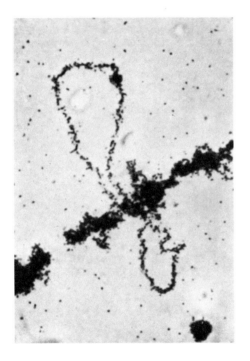

FIGURE 74. Radioautograph of a single *Triturus* lampbrush chromosome loop pair exposed to uridine-³H. Labeling along the chromosome axis could result from smaller, heavily labeled loops which have collapsed against the axis during fixation. × 1000. Gall, J., reproduced in O. Hess, "Probleme der biologischen Reduplikation. 3. "*Wiss. Konf. Ges. Deut. Naturforsch. Arzte Semmering, Vienna, 1965* p. 29 (1966).

any one time, an amount many times this would transiently be spun out into the loops if the whole lampbrush phase is taken into consideration. Since no area of the loops is observed to be quiescent in RNA synthesis a direct and significant consequence would be the expression, in the course of oogenesis, of a far larger proportion of the genomic information than is present in the loops at any one time, perhaps 100%. The alternative proposition is that the loops are static with respect to the DNA which they contain, and that the DNA within the interloop chromomeres and the other large Feulgen-positive chromosome granules is also statically assigned. In this case the occasional polarity of labeling observed by Callan and Gall in the *Triturus* lampbrush chromosomes should be attributed to a prolonged process of accumulation of the newly synthesized RNA gene products at the thick end of the loop rather than to transit of the gene per se. A consequence which is the reverse of that deriving from the moving template theory then follows, viz., that no more than about 5% of the total genomic information in the chromosomes is expressed throughout the lampbrush stage if the loops at any one time contain only about 5% of the genomic DNA.

the RNA and protein content of lampbrush chromosomes

The matrix containing the labeled RNA of the lampbrush loops is composed of RNA and protein, according to experiments with stains and enzymes [reviewed by Callan and Lloyd (376) and Callan (344)]. Quantitative estimates of the RNA and protein contents in *Triturus* lampbrush chromosomes have been published by Izawa, Allfrey, and Mirsky (394), and their data show that the complete chromosomal set contains about 0.4 μg of protein and about 0.007 μg of RNA, compared with about 0.0008 μg of DNA. The ratio of RNA/DNA in the lampbrush chromosomes, about 9, is almost 145 times higher than the RNA/DNA ratio in liver chromatin, which is here taken as an example of chromatin from a representative somatic cell (394). This clearly suggests *accretion of gene products on the chromosome*. A similar pattern obtains for the ratio protein/DNA in lampbrush chromosomes, which is over 550, a value about 195 times higher than the protein/DNA ratio in liver chromatin. Information also exists regarding the *nature* of the relatively enormous amount of RNA in these chromosomes: Microanalyses of RNA extracted from hand-dissected *Triturus* lampbrush chromosomes by Edstrom and Gall (349) have demonstrated that the chromosomal RNA closely resembles the genomic DNA in nucleotide base composition. Data from this study are reproduced in Table XII.

TABLE XII. The Base Composition of Lampbrush Chromosome and Nucleolar RNA and the Genomic DNA of *Triturus cristatus carnifex*[a]

	A (%)	C (%)	G (%)	U(T) (%)	G + C (%)
Chromosomal RNA	26.0	25.2	20.6	28.3	45.8
Nucleolar RNA	18.1	28.7	31.7	21.7	60.4
DNA (calculated from A/G ratio)	27.8	22.2	22.2	27.8	44.4

[a] From Ref. 349.

Ribonucleic acid of a base composition indicative of informational nature is present in large quantities in lampbrush chromosomes, according to Table XII. This important result is consistent with the impression of enormous diversity in RNA synthesis sites left by the radioautographic studies cited above.

informational RNA synthesis in the lampbrush-stage oocyte

Direct evidence for the synthesis of informational RNA's during the lampbrush chromosome stage of oogenesis comes from recent investigations into the species of RNA synthesized in stage 4 (lampbrush-stage) *Xenopus* oocytes. These studies were carried out by the writer, in collaboration with Crippa and Mirsky (25), and by Crippa *et al.* (115). As pointed out above, the usual gradient and base composition procedures are not useful for the detection of informational RNA synthesis in amphibian oocytes because of the avalanche of rapidly synthesized ribosomal RNA stemming from the oocyte nucleoli, and recourse was therefore had to the RNA-DNA hybridization method. The hybridization technique not only permits the study of informational RNA in the face of overwhelming ribosomal RNA synthesis but it also provides an opportunity to estimate the level of genomic function at the lampbrush stage. This level can be calculated from the level at which DNA is saturated with newly synthesized lampbrush-stage RNA, under hybridizing conditions, if the actual specific activity of the hybridizing RNA is known so that the amount of RNA hybridized per unit weight of genomic DNA can be obtained. We are dealing here with RNA preparations extracted from several thousand asynchronous lampbrush-stage oocytes belonging to a *Xenopus* female which has been labeled for 3 days with an isotopic RNA precursor, and for this case the specific activity of the informational RNA in synthesis is essentially that of the bulk ribosomal RNA of the preparations. This follows from the fact that (a) both classes of RNA are in the main accumulated [rather than being turned over (25, 115)]. Ribonucleic acid accumulation continues for many days in the lampbrush chromosomes themselves (386) and is in accordance with the general accretion logistics obtaining during the oocyte growth phase. Furthermore, (b) both ribosomal and informational RNA are synthesized from the same precursor pool; (c) all substages of the lampbrush stage are represented in the preparation; and (d) the preceding stage of oogenesis, stage 3 (cf. Fig. 55) appears to be a resting or oocyte storage stage, and accumulation of an informational RNA stockpile prior to stage 4 is therefore unlikely.

The general validity of these arguments has been verified directly by reextracting the lampbrush-stage RNA from the RNA-DNA hybrids formed at saturating ratios of RNA after destroying nonhybridized RNA with RNase and comparing the specific activity of the hybridizing RNA with that of the bulk (ribosomal) RNA of the starting preparation. It is found that the specific activity of the hybridizing informational RNA synthesized in the stage-4 oocyte nucleus is in fact almost exactly that of the ribosomal RNA extracted with it, if correction is made for the small amount of ribosomal RNA already present when stage 4 begins.

Figure 75 (115) describes the hybridization saturation curves obtained by exposing denatured ^{3}H-DNA to increasing amounts of Xenopus lampbrush-stage oocyte ^{32}P-RNA under moderate annealing conditions, and then assaying the yield of RNase-resistant ^{32}P-RNA–^{3}H-DNA hybrids. At saturation an average value of about 1.6% by weight of the DNA is hybridized. The results are not very different from preparation to preparation, each preparation representing 1500–3000 manually defollicled oocytes from one individual Xenopus female. Quantitatively the same result is obtained whether the hybrids are assayed by trapping the DNA and DNA-RNA hybrids on filters or by isolation of the DNA and hybridized RNA by gel filtration (25). Since stage-4 oocytes of every gradation in maturity have contributed to each RNA preparation it is clear that the 1.6% value is not peculiar to particular animals or particular substages of lampbrush development. Only one strand of DNA is expected to be active in RNA synthesis in vivo. These data therefore show that at the maximal lampbrush stage about 3% of the internally redundant fraction of this organism's total genome is functional, excluding that part of the genome expected to code for ribosomal RNA. The latter in Xenopus is about 0.1% of the genome [0.057% of the DNA by weight is complementary to ribosomal RNA, according to Brown and Weber (99)]. Since over 30 times more redundant genetic material appears to be active at the lampbrush stage than codes for ribosomal RNA, it is clear that informational RNA synthesis takes place during the lampbrush phase of oogenesis. Three percent of the genome in transcription during the lamp-

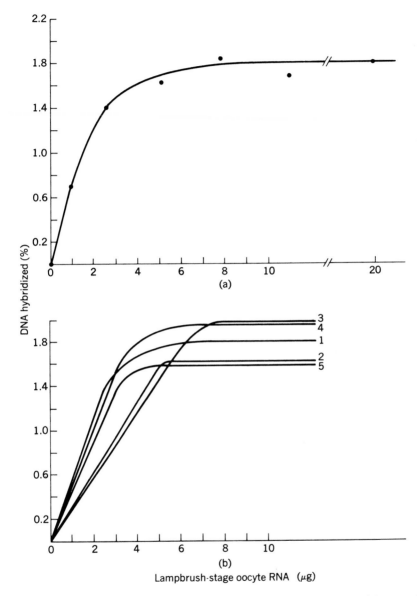

FIGURE 75. Saturation of DNA with lampbrush-stage oocyte ^{32}P-RNA: (a) a single representative saturation curve; (b) superimposed saturation curves for five separate ^{32}P-RNA preparations, each obtained from the lampbrush-stage oocytes of one animal. Each sample contained 5 μg of ^{3}H-DNA and the amounts of ^{32}P-RNA shown on the abscissa, in a total volume of 200 μl. Crippa, M., Davidson, E. H., and Mirsky, A. E., *Proc. Natl. Acad. Sci. U.S.* **57**, 885 (1967).

brush stage could constitute an enormous quantity of genetic information, for recent studies in this laboratory have shown that at least as 45% of the *Xenopus* genome contains internally redundant sequences. It is this fraction which is saturated in the hybridization experiments of Fig. 75 (see Section I for a discussion of the effects of genomic redundancy on the hybridization technique). If only 3% of 45% of the total genome is active, this means that greater than 90% of the internally redundant fraction remains repressed during the lampbrush stages. The value is a minimum one because the active fraction could be somewhat overestimated if near-redundant genomic areas are transcribed during the lampbrush stage, and a certain amount of "cross hybridization" takes place between gene products of one site and similar, but distinct, genes belonging to the same internally redundant gene family but not actually functioning during the lampbrush stage. In any case it is clear that redundant genomic material is included in the active lampbrush loops, but the extent to which the single-copy fraction of the genome is also expressed at the lampbrush stage (if at all) is still unknown.

A striking aspect of the value for the amount of the genome active in the lampbrush stage obtained in this study is the close correspondence between this value, though it refers only to about one-half of the total genome, and the 5% of the genomic DNA estimated (in *Triturus*) to be present in the loops of the lampbrush chromosomes. The haploid quantity of DNA in *Xenopus* is only about one-fifteenth that in *Triturus,* and the lampbrush chromosomes of *Xenopus* are barely visible in the light microscope, while those of *Triturus* are enormous; it is remarkable that these estimates agree so closely. If this comparison is other than fortuitous then the correlation between the percentage of the DNA present in the lampbrush chromosome and the size of that internally redundant genomic fraction active during the lampbrush stage provides a basis for interpretation of radioautographs which demonstrate RNA synthesis in all loops of the lampbrush structures. Thus a possibility consistent with both values is that the visible areas of chromosomes, mainly the loops, contain the functional DNA, and that this is the only DNA destined to be functional during the lampbrush stage. This would exclude the hypothesis that the DNA fibers of the loops are constantly being spun out of the preceding chromomere, into the loop, and into the next chromomere for, as we have noted, that hypothesis necessitates that between the beginning and the end of the lampbrush stage a fraction of the genome must be active far beyond that actually present in the loops at any one time. Pending further evidence, the lampbrush chromosome loops are at present probably best regarded as qualitatively static for the duration of their existence, with respect both to the genetic material they contain and to the species of RNA synthesized in them.

the fate of lampbrush-synthesized informational RNA in later oogenesis

Various lines of evidence indicate that much of the informational RNA synthesized at the lampbrush stage is retained throughout oogenesis and is still present in the egg at the time of fertilization. The model posed by the synthesis of ribosomal RNA during mid-oogenesis, its prolonged storage, and its ultimate inheritance by the embryo would appear applicable to informational gene products as well. Some of the relevant evidence we have already discussed: (a) the large amounts of template-active RNA present in the mature oocyte which are already stockpiled as early as the lampbrush stage; (b) the radioautographic studies which show that labeled RNA in the chromosomes remains present for over 2 weeks in the very chromosome loops where it has been synthesized rather than being rapidly transported to the cytoplasm, used, and degraded; and (c) the comparatively enormous accumulation of chromosomal RNA always present in the chromosome loops. In *Triturus* DNA-like chromosomal RNA amounts to some nine times the total DNA of the chromosomal apparatus, chromomeres included, 36 times the total 4C DNA value, or over 780 times the mass of DNA estimated to be present in the loops per se (344, 349, 394, 411). Furthermore, (d) RNA synthesis level after the lampbrush stage drops to a small fraction of what it had been during the lampbrush stage, and since the chromosomal loops have by then retracted it is likely that little or no informational RNA synthesis takes places in these later stages (5 and 6). These items of evidence all point to accretion and storage of the informational RNA synthesized on the lampbrush chromosome rather than its immediate utilization.

A comparison between the informational content of the gene transcription occurring during the lampbrush stage and the informational content of the RNA stockpiled in the mature stage-6 ovarian oocyte is displayed in Fig. 76. In this experiment unlabeled stage-6 oocyte RNA is used to compete with ^{32}P-labeled stage-4 RNA for DNA binding sites. The experiment shows that about 65% of the species of RNA in synthesis at mid-lampbrush stage are also present in the quiescent mature oocytes. Other experiments have yielded up to 74% homology between the gene products present in stage 6 and the gene products in synthesis at stage 4. The remaining 25–35% of the genes active at the lampbrush stage but not represented in the population of RNA molecules stockpiled in the mature oocyte may constitute that part of the genetic complement required to direct the protein synthesis taking place during oogenesis itself. In any case it is clear that *at least 65% of the genetic information transcribed from redundant fractions of the genome during the lampbrush stage is still present in the stored RNA's of the terminal oocyte.*

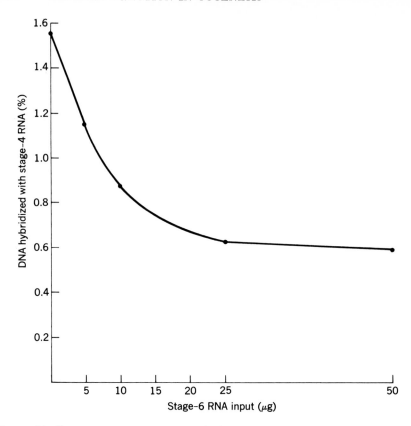

FIGURE 76. Competition experiment in which DNA-binding sites complementary to ^{32}P stage-4 RNA are competed for by unlabeled RNA from mature stage 6 oocytes. Each tube contained 5 μg of DNA, 5 μg of stage-4 RNA, and the amounts of stage-6 RNA shown on the abscissa. Davidson, E. H., Crippa, M., Kramer, F. R., and Mirsky, A. E., *Proc. Natl. Acad. Sci. U.S.* **56**, 856 (1966).

It will be recalled that in *Xenopus* the period separating the end of the lamp-brush stage from stage 6 is at minimum a matter of a month or more, not including the probable 4–8-month duration of the lampbrush stage itself, or the amount of time the mature ovarian oocyte may remain in a viable state. The experiment of Fig. 76, taken in conjunction with the preceding data, demonstrates the survival and storage of informational RNA for these very long periods, the most extensive so far known for animal cell informational RNA's.

The lampbrush chromosome is thus the site of elaboration of enormous quantities of very long-lived informational gene products, and its unusual structure may be related to this specialized role. The newly synthesized RNA could be packaged *in situ,* on the loops themselves, within newly synthesized protector proteins. This might explain the presence of the astonishingly high protein and RNA contents of the chromosomes (349, 394), and of the intense protein synthesis occurring continuously and ubiquitously on the lampbrush loops (386). The sequential labeling patterns, and the accumulation of labeled RNA at one end of some loops reported by Gall and Callan (386), can without difficulty be interpreted in terms of a polarized RNA packaging phenomenon occurring on those giant loops where this phenomenon has been observed. An interesting light is thrown on the subject of lampbrush function in oogenesis by the studies of Hess dealing with lampbrush chromosomes in *Drosophila* spermatocytes (414). Hess has shown that five pairs of large lateral loops exist in the primary spermatocytes of this genus, organized by specific chromosomal loci. These loops are the sites of active RNA synthesis, and their presence is essential to the production of viable sperm. Since after meiosis only one-half of the spermatids possess a Y-chromosome, genetic information from the Y-chromosome must be released in the preceding spermatocyte stage and then be stored for later use in spermatid maturation. Protein synthesis occurs in spermatids but RNA synthesis does not, indicating directly the presence of preformed templates; on these completely independent grounds, Hess has also suggested that the loops of lampbrush chromosomes constitute a special set of structures for the *synthesis and packaging of large quantities of precociously synthesized gene products.*

the fate of lampbrush-synthesized informational RNA in embryogenesis

Returning to the fate of the informational RNA synthesized in the *Xenopus* stage-4 oocyte, further studies along the lines of the experiment illustrated in Fig. 76 have revealed the important fact that the informational RNA stored in the mature ovarian oocyte survives ovulation without attrition, in terms of its qualitative information content, and persists far into embryogenesis. Experiments demonstrating this are presented in Figs. 77a and b (115). In Fig. 77a unlabeled 2-cell and early blastula RNA's compete with saturating amounts of ^{32}P-labeled lampbrush-stage RNA for *Xenopus* DNA-binding sites. The experiment shows that there is no detectable decrease in the informational content of the RNA inherited by the embryo between the beginning of cleavage and the midblastula stage, when there are 500–2000 cells in this embryo (415). Furthermore, there is evidently as much homology between newly synthesized lampbrush-stage oocyte RNA and early cleavage-stage embryo RNA as between mature ovarian oocyte RNA and

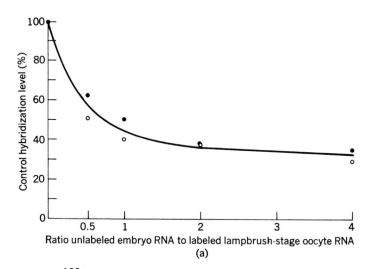

(a)

Ratio unlabeled embryo RNA to labeled lampbrush-stage oocyte RNA

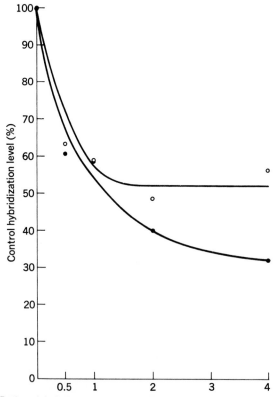

(b)

Ratio unlabeled embryo RNA to labeled lampbrush-stage oocyte RNA

lampbrush-stage RNA. Thus stage-7 embryos (early blastula) contain RNA homologous with an average of 64% of that synthesized at the lampbrush stage, and this is precisely the value obtained in similar experiments with stage-6 oocyte RNA, as seen above in Fig. 76. In Fig. 77b the same type of analysis is extended to an even later stage of embryogenesis, the late blastular period. The results now become somewhat different, and experiments such as those in Fig. 77b show clearly that between mid- and late blastula a definite amount of lampbrush-transcribed genetic information disappears from the store of embryonic RNA's. Ribonucleic acids complementary to an average of 18% of the DNA sites hybridized by newly synthesized lampbrush-stage RNA appear to have been lost during this period. It is again stressed that the hybridized DNA sites in these experiments are primarily redundant; whether the total lampbrush-synthesized RNA population includes single copy gene products as well, and if so, whether their subsequent history is different from that described here remains to be seen. Ribonucleic acid complementary to only about 65% of the DNA sites monitored as functional in the lampbrush stage is present at the termination of oogenesis, and since this RNA is what is transmitted to the early embryo, we conclude that over 28% (18%/65%) of the genetic information in the RNA's inherited by the embryo from the lampbrush stage of oogenesis is utilized and degraded, or otherwise caused to disappear, between mid- and late blastulation.

The mid-to-late blastular period, as we have seen, is a critical time in development. This is the period immediately preceding the first widespread appearance of differentiated cells, and at least in deuterostomes, from echinoderms to frogs, it is during this period that gene transcription in preparation for gastrulation occurs (the evidence on which this statement is based is summarized in Section I). In *Xenopus* radioautographic and biochemical studies (also reviewed in Section I) have revealed that a dramatic, near embryo-wide stimulation of nuclear RNA synthesis occurs during the mid-to-late blastular period. It will be recalled that in both presumptive ectoderm and endoderm rates of informational RNA synthesis increase over 20-fold within little more than an hour at this stage, so that by early gastrulation the embryo has already attained per cell RNA synthesis rates close to those

FIGURE 77. (a) A representative competition experiment in which increasing amounts of (filled circles) stage-2 and (open circles) stage-7 embryo RNA are added to lampbrush-stage oocyte ^{32}P-RNA and ^{3}H-DNA under hybridizing conditions. (b) A representative competition experiment in which increasing amounts of (filled circles) stage-7 and (open circles) stage-9 embryo RNA are added to constant quantities of ^{3}H-DNA and lampbrush-stage oocyte ^{32}P-RNA under hybridizing conditions. Crippa, M., Davidson, E. H., and Mirsky, A. E., *Proc. Natl. Acad. Sci. U.S.* **57**, 885 (1967).

which are to persist throughout subsequent differentiation. This correlation lends an added significance to the fact that midblastular RNA competes with newly synthesized oocyte RNA significantly better than does late blastular RNA (Fig. 77b). Thus the disappearance of a large body of stored genetic information at this point in embryogenesis indicates that utilization of these RNA's must have been completed within the critical mid-to-late blastular period; and an obvious speculation suggests that informational RNA's, stored ever since the lampbrush chromosome stage of oogenesis, are in some way involved in the embryo-wide increase in the level of gene activity. Figure 77b also shows that most of the RNA-borne genetic information the embryo has inherited from oogenesis is still present in the embryo beyond the late blastula stage.

A possible objection to this interpretation of the experiments portrayed in Figs. 77a and b is that part of the competition registered in these experiments results from newly synthesized embryo RNA's rather than from stored lampbrush-stage oocyte RNA. However, it is extremely unlikely that this is the case, since the amount of informational RNA synthesized between fertilization and the early blastula is almost negligible compared to the amount of informational RNA already in the egg at fertilization. Up to the early blastula stage the vast majority of the RNA molecules bearing this information are necessarily those synthesized at the lampbrush stage of oogenesis. Furthermore, we now know that the same molecules are responsible for all the residual competition obtained with late blastulae, since direct tests for homology between newly synthesized late blastular RNA (stage 9) and oocyte RNA yield a negative answer in *Xenopus* (117).

the nature of the informational RNA inherited by the embryo

As far as any direct experimental evidence is concerned, we remain essentially ignorant of the molecular functions entrusted to the impressive informational RNA stockpile inherited by the embryo. It is noted above that part of the informational RNA whose synthesis we have monitored during the lampbrush stage of oogenesis, perhaps one-third in terms of genetic information, is probably used to program protein synthesis during the remaining months of oocyte development. Another fraction is no doubt destined to serve as maternal messenger after embryogenesis begins. The quantity of stored genetic information may be so vast, however, that simple interpretation of the informational RNA inherited by the embryo as maternal messenger presents certain conceptual difficulties. Maternal messengers for cleavage and blastular processes are by definition to be thought of as providing for a finite number of relatively ubiquitous cellular "housekeeping" proteins, e.g., mitotic spindle proteins and glycolytic enzymes (see discussion of this concept in Section I).

Now it is evident, as we have pointed out, that the genetic information transcribed at the lampbrush stage is at least in part redundant, and therefore the actual degree of diversity in the stored genetic information of the oocyte is difficult to estimate at present. Evidence in fact exists that a minority of RNA species may constitute the bulk of the informational RNA in synthesis at the lampbrush stage, these being present in a disproportionately large number of copies. This evidence comes from an experiment (25) in which a single sample of total lampbrush-stage RNA is subjected to three successive cycles of hybridization, each time with previously unhybridized DNA. In the first cycle of hybridization RNA complementary to 32% of the DNA which initially hybridizes with newly synthesized lampbrush-stage RNA is removed from the preparation as RNA-DNA hybrid. During the second cycle of exposure to DNA a smaller group of gene products is exhausted. However, the third cycle of exposure fails to result in further decrease in the hybridization frequency, i.e., in the qualitative range of genetic information represented in the newly synthesized RNA. At this point RNA is still present in the preparation which is capable of hybridizing with about 0.76% of the DNA (compared to 1.6% initially). The rarest newly synthesized RNA species are in this experiment removed at once, with the first exposure to DNA, whle those RNA species present in greater copy number persist until they are presented with a quantity of homologous DNA large enough to bind and remove them from the RNA population.

Since RNA's homologous with about 0.76% of the total DNA remains present in the RNA population, even after three cycles of exposure to DNA, the experiment indicates the existence of disproportionately large quantities of certain gene products representing about 0.70% of the total DNA beyond that complementary to the bulk ribosomal RNA of the preparation. In a related study a direct effort was made to measure the proportion of the genome active at the lampbrush stage which might be concerned with ubiquitous housekeeping cellular machinery. This can be done with the hybridization technique by obtaining a measure of the competition for DNA-binding sites between RNA from various tissues and newly synthesized lampbrush-stage RNA. The storage of ubiquitous housekeeping messenger RNA's for the maintenance of the high metabolic activity and rapid cell division characteristic of the cleavage stage embryo could constitute a major function of the lampbrush-stage nucleus. Were this so it might be expected that a competition experiment in which newly synthesized lampbrush-stage oocyte RNA is challenged with unlabeled total RNA from any metabolically active adult tissue would reveal significant homology between RNA's in the oocyte and tissue preparations.

Contrary to such expectation, however, it is found that neither total RNA from heart nor total RNA from hormone-stimulated testis is able to compete noticeably with lampbrush-stage RNA. In the case of the testis RNA, it is certain that some DNA synthesis and cell division were taking place when the RNA was extracted, while the adult heart RNA preparations themselves contain newly synthesized RNA which hybridizes with *Xenopus* DNA. The data do not exclude a low level of competition (of the order of that expected from ribosomal RNA), but it would seem that the major fraction of the genes operating during the lampbrush stage are not concerned with the production of any housekeeping proteins also possessed by the adult, unless the RNA messengers for these proteins are present at extremely low concentrations (relative to ribosomal RNA) in adult toad tissues.

We conclude tentatively that either the housekeeping information carried in lampbrush-synthesized RNA constitutes a very small part of the total genetic information transcribed during oogenesis or that most of the housekeeping enzymes of the early embryo are simply different from those of adult tissues. Denis has shown that adult tissue RNA's can compete with late gastrular RNA in *Xenopus* (104), and if the earliest embryonic housekeeping RNA's are indeed inherited from oogenesis and are different from adult housekeeping RNA messages, the switchover to adult form must occur very early in development. In any case it is not unlikely that the housekeeping information encoded in the informational RNA bequeathed to the embryo constitutes only a minor fraction of the total genetic information store, though the housekeeping category may well include a large fraction of the *mass* of informational RNA molecules present in the maternal RNA stockpile.

This discussion of informational RNA synthesis during the lampbrush stage of oogenesis can be summarized, at least with reference to amphibian oogenesis, as follows: Gene transcription in the lampbrush chromosomes involves about 3% (or possibly less) of the total redundant genomic information possessed by the organism. The main sites of synthesis and the initial sites of accretion and possibly packaging of the lampbrush chromosome gene products are the chromosome loops. The latter are provisionally to be regarded as static, with respect to the qualitative nature of the genetic information transcribed in them, and with respect to the identity of the genomic DNA which they contain. *At least two-thirds of the informational RNA synthesized in the lampbrush chromosomes is stored in the oocyte for the duration of oogenesis and is inherited by the embryo as the major component of an enormous stockpile of maternal informational RNA.* The latter includes the bona fide maternal messenger discussed in Section I. Virtually all of the genetic information encoded in the RNA inherited by the embryo remains present up to the midblastula. Between mid- and late blastula, however, the utilization of about 28% of this information is completed. During the same period most of the nuclei in the embryo display a dramatic increase in genomic activity in preparation for gastrular differentiation, but the connection between these two significant events, if any, remains unknown.

It is clear that this last gap in our sketchy understanding of the relation between genomic function in oogenesis and the events of embryogenesis lies squarely at the most significant conceptual juncture. We may now be face to face with the problem of defining and understanding the accretion during oogenesis of gene products which in a specific manner will interact with the embryonic cell nuclei, either directly or indirectly. Is this fundamental phenomenon in fact mediated via RNA's synthesized at the lampbrush stage and later inherited by the embryo? Are these RNA's used as templates for proteins which in turn affect the embryonic nuclei? In the solution to these presently obscure questions may lie the answers (in principle at least) to the problem of the *specification* of the initial patterns of cell differentiation.

Relevant to this area of consideration is an interesting recent report of Briggs and Cassens (416) who have investigated a recessive mutation in the axolotl discovered by Humphrey (417). Females homozygous for this mutation ("o") produce eggs which are unable to complete gastrulation. Briggs and Cassens have demonstrated that the *cytoplasm* of eggs from o/o females is deficient in some unknown gene products required by the developing embryo in order for gastrulation to occur. However, cytoplasm from mature +/o or +/+ eggs, injected into fertilized eggs of o/o females, restores to them the ability to carry out gastrulation. Nucleoplasm obtained from stage-6 *ovarian oocytes* is shown to contain materials of exactly similar corrective power when injected into the fertilized o/o eggs, and, strikingly, the responsible agents are far more concentrated in the stage-6 nucleoplasm than in ovulated egg cytoplasm. The active agents are believed by the authors to be of high molecular weight, and are apparently of protein nature, according to a recent study of Briggs and Justus (417a). This case constitutes an empirical demonstration of the relations between gene action in oogenesis and the storage of substances needed for early differentiation in embryogenesis.

It is appropriate at this juncture to return for a moment to the possible role of ovarian accessory cells. Adequate evidence now exists to indicate that in amphibians the informational RNA stockpile of the mature oocyte almost certainly derives from the lampbrush chromosomes rather than from accessory cells, while the opposite appears to be true of meroistic insect develop-

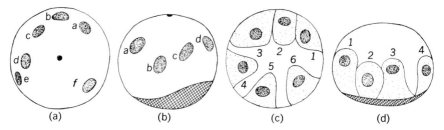

(a)   (b)   (c)   (d)

FIGURE 78. (a) and (b) Diagrams of *Limnaea* egg immediately after oviposition: (a) from the animal pole and (b) from the side. Black dots indicate animal end of first maturation spindle and stippling surface area of vegetal pole plasm. (*a–f*) Subcortical "patches" of different staining. (c) and (d) Diagram of arrangement of the inner follicle cells around oocyte: (c) from inner pole of oocyte and (d) from the side. Crosshatching indicates area of contact with gonad wall; 1–6: inner follicle cells. Raven, C. P., *Develop. Biol.* **7**, 130 (1963).

ment. An interesting series of observations by Raven (418, 419) is relevant in this connection. This author has studied localized patches of subcortical cytoplasm in the egg of the snail *Limmaea stagnalis;* these patches display a particular fine structure and stainability. The location of these six patches, which represent an empirical case of a cytoplasmic mosaic, is shown in Figs. 78a and b. Raven has noticed a striking parallel between the patch location diagramed in the figure and the characteristic location of the six follicle cells surrounding the oocyte during oogenesis: these are shown in Figs. 78c and d.

In cleavage the cortical patches form a regular dorsoventral pattern and are distributed in certain ways among the early blastomeres. Raven's study thus suggests that ovarian accessory cells may play a critical role in determining the specific topology of cytoplasmic localication patterns, particularly if considered in conjunction with the wealth of older observations demonstrating that egg polarity and even the dorsoventral orientation of the future embryo can often be related to the orientation of the egg vis-à-vis its ovarian accessory cells. The function of accessory cells in examples such as this may be merely to demarcate in some way the locale for future deposition of gene products (or *their* products) deriving originally from the oocyte nucleus. However, it also may be that accessory cell nuclei, which after all contain the same genomic information as the oocyte, contribute directly to the informational RNA store of the oocyte, at least in some organisms, as well as to its ultimate patterns of deposition. The division of genomic enterprise in oogenesis represents another still obscure but obviously important question.

In dealing with the nature of genomic information storage in egg cytoplasm we have so far confined ourselves to RNA gene products. Large quantities of DNA are also present in the cytoplasm of eggs and oocytes, however, and it has been pointed out by Brachet (420) that extranuclear DNA could also serve as a vehicle for the transfer and storage of developmental information in the egg cytoplasm. Before leaving the topic of oogenesis it is therefore of importance to examine the existing evidence regarding the fate and function of the large DNA reserves generally present in egg cytoplasm as development begins.

6

DNA of the oocyte cytoplasm

The eggs of many species, both deuterostome and protostome, contain quantities of DNA far in excess of the nuclear DNA content. Several representative measurements are collected in Table XIII. It is common for eggs to contain hundreds of times the 4C value of DNA, according to these data, though a word of caution is here in order in that the methods used for DNA determination in eggs can often be criticized as incompletely specific, given the reported existence in egg cytoplasm of a range of chromogenic and presumably DNA-like components. Thus, some of the diphenylamine-reactive material in the egg is clearly not DNA. According to Dawid, for example, about twice as much diphenylamine-reactive, ethanol-insoluble material is present in the *Xenopus* egg as there is true DNA (348). There is, however, no direct evidence for low molecular weight oligodeoxyribonucleotides (i.e., "acid soluble DNA's") in egg cytoplasm, and even if such DNA did exist, it would remain necessary to account for the large amounts of bona fide high molecular weight cytoplasmic DNA listed in Table XIII (421–425). The values quoted in Table XIII appear to be among the more reliable estimations in the literature, and those cited from the work of Dawid and Piko, Tyler, and Vinograd (421) are not in any sense subject to doubts

TABLE XIII. DNA Contents of Various Mature Oocytes

Animal	Diploid value ($\mu\mu g$)	Egg value ($\mu\mu g$)	Egg value/ 4C value	Ref.
Sea urchin (*Lytechinus*)	1.6	8.3	2.6	421
Amphibian (*Rana*)	15	3600	120	348
(*Xenopus*)	6	3100	258	348
Bird (*chick*)	1.4	179×10^6	6.5×10^7	422
Nematode (*Ascaris*)	5	290	29	423
Insect (*Gryllus*)	11.4	83×10^3	3700	424
Mollusk (*Illyanassa*)	6.6	428	33	425

[a] Piko, L., Tyler, A., and Vinograd, J., *Biol. Bull.* **132**, 68 (1967).
[b] Dawid, I. B., *J. Mol. Biol.* **12**, 581 (1965).
[c] Solomon, J., *Biochim. Biophys. Acta* **24**, 584 (1957).
[d] Nigon, V., and Bovet, P., *Compt. Rend. Soc. Biol.* **149**, 129 (1955).
[e] Durand, M., *Bull. Biol. France Belg.* **95**, 28 (1961).
[f] Collier, J. R., and McCann-Collier, *Exptl. Cell Res.* **27**, 553 (1962).

regarding assay specificity since in these studies the DNA was extracted in high molecular weight form and thereafter characterized with respect to absolute specific density in CsCl, thermal denaturation, and ability to serve as a template in RNA synthesis [see also the experiments of Bibring et al. (301) and of Carden et al. (426)]. The presence of cytoplasmic DNA amounting to many times the expected 4C chromosomal DNA content, or the total nuclear DNA content (nucleoli included), thus stands at present on a firm footing, and from this as well as from direct determinations of DNA in enucleated eggs it is evident that the excess DNA is mainly cytoplasmic. Deoxyribonucleic acid determinations were first performed with enucleated eggs of several *Rana* species by Hoff-Jörgensen and Zeuthen, who were pioneers in this field (427), and have since been carried out with centrifugally enucleated sea urchin eggs (393).

What is the nature of this cytoplasmic DNA? Dawid has demonstrated that the bona fide cytoplasmic DNA of the amphibian egg may have a different specific density (base composition) from that of somatic cell nuclear DNA, and that it is complementary to only 0.1–5.0% of the somatic cell nuclear DNA. In other words, it contains sequences different from almost all of the nuclear DNA. It is thus a highly specialized form of DNA, which could not be used as a precursor for nuclear DNA without complete breakdown to the nucleotide level. Convincing evidence, owing mainly to Dawid (348, 428) and to Piko et al. (421) now exists to the effect that egg cytoplasmic DNA is essentially mitochondrial DNA. This evidence can be summarized as follows:

(1) Cytoplasmic DNA follows the distribution of mitochondria in cell fractionation studies in amphibian eggs (428) and according to Bibring et al. (301) and to Piko et al. (421) this is true for sea urchin eggs as well. Thus enucleate and nucleate halves of sea urchin eggs, each of which is expected to contain an approximately equal amount of mitochondria, have about the same DNA content (301).

(2) In the amphibian over two-thirds of the total cytoplasmic DNA can actually be extracted from the purified mitochondria of eggs (428). According to Piko et al. (421) the yolk spherules of sea urchin eggs as well as the mitochondria contain DNA. These spherules are about one-third as numerous as mitochondria, and they contain one-third as much DNA as do the purified mitochondria. Yolk spherules, as is now well known, originate as mitochondria. Together the yolk spherule and mitochondrial DNA of the sea urchin egg account for up to 89% of the cytoplasmic DNA in the sea urchin egg.

(3) The specific density and sequence complementary of the egg DNA are compatible with a mitochondrial origin (348).

(4) Calculations (421, 428) based on the mitochondrial DNA content and the cellular content of mitochondria account perfectly for the amount of cytoplasmic DNA in the egg.

(5) In addition, Piko *et al.* have shown that sea urchin egg mitochondria contain circular DNA rings of the same size as those reported for mitochondria of other cells.

At present, therefore, there remains little evidence for cytoplasmic DNA other than mitochondrial DNA, with one possible exception. This is a recent study of Brachet (428a) in which labeled actinomycin is used as a localizing agent to detect the whereabouts of the cytoplasmic DNA. A somewhat surprising result is obtained in view of the foregoing, for the actinomycin is bound to a variety of cytoplasmic elements, e.g., cortical granules, as well as to certain yolk particles. Although it is perfectly clear from the elaborate researches of Dawid, Piko *et al.,* and others that most of the large reserve of cytoplasmic DNA present in egg cytoplasm is indeed mitochondrial, and that the size of the DNA stockpile is simply the consequence of the large amount of cytoplasm in the egg as compared to other cells, the question must remain open as to whether other small DNA-containing cytoplasmic particles might exist, and if so, whether their DNA could be functional in the transfer of information from oocyte nucleus to egg cytoplasm, as Brachet has suggested (420).

Moreover, the possibility that the mitochondrial genomes themselves play a role in the organization of the egg cytoplasm is difficult to exclude. Tyler (189) has recently shown that sea urchin egg mitochondria synthesize protein which in part is transported out of the mitochondria and into the egg cytoplasm. In the present state of knowledge we have no way of assaying the significance of this finding for the larger problems of development.

CONCLUSIONS

In this section we have carried our discussion of genomic information flow in development back to its primary source, the oocyte genome. We know that the genomes of ovarian accessory cells, and perhaps even those of the egg mitochondria may be important as well. Classical biologists long ago observed that embryogenesis begins in oogenesis, and from the contemporary vantage point we are in a position to appreciate the validity of this insight as never before. Thus the evidence reviewed here shows that informational RNA is synthesized in mid-oogenesis for utilization long afterward, in the course of embryogenesis. A more literal demonstration of the elegant classical conception of the relation between oogenesis and embryonic development could hardly be proposed.

IV

✱ immediacy of gene control and the regulation of gene activity

The lengthy interval separating gene transcription in mid-oogenesis and embryonic utilization of the oocyte gene products months or years later is paralleled in few situations elsewhere in the biological world. As one surveys various biological systems a wide distribution of temporal relationships between gene action and utilization of the gene products becomes apparent, with the oocyte case and a few allied examples representing one extreme of this distribution. Examples of extremely short-lived messenger RNA's constitute the other extreme. In discussing the temporal parameters of genetic control systems we shall find it useful to refer to the "immediacy" of gene control, a term applied by us a few years ago (429) to denote the closeness of the temporal link between gene action, meaning readout or transcription of genetic information, and translation of the gene product into some phenotypic character which is ultimately dependent on gene action for its manifestation. Immediacy of gene control varies in a revealing and characteristic way in the course of embryogenesis, and this variation provides interesting insights into the nature of the regulative process which governs development. Before considering the parameter of immediacy in embryogenesis per se, however, it is useful to survey briefly some of the temporal relationships existing in various other genetic control systems. For the purposes of such a survey gene products can be conveniently classified according to their temporal fate as (a) gene products which are very long lived, (b) gene products which are moderately long lived, or (c) gene products which decay with first-order kinetics beginning immediately after their synthesis. Only the latter class was considered in the original definitions of the messenger RNA (mRNA) theory (430). In what follows we confine our attention to informational gene products.

247

1
Very long-lived gene products

The most striking examples in this category, those concerning informational RNA's synthesized during oogenesis, we have already discussed in detail. A remarkable parallel to the oogenesis case appears to exist in the seeds of various plants; Marcus and Feeley (431, 432) and Dure and Watters (433), in an interesting series of investigations on cotton, wheat, and peanut seeds, have shown that preformed template-active RNA is stored in the dormant seed as it is stored in the dormant mature oocyte. In wheat seeds protein synthesis equivalent in rate to 28% of the eventual maximum capacity is detected within 1 hour after seed activation, which is accomplished by soaking the seeds in water. By 3–5 hours the synthetic rate is 65% of the eventual maximum. Ribosomes extracted from seeds previous to imbibition are inactive in protein synthesis but are capable of responding perfectly well to exogenous template (431, 432, 434). As in the sea urchin egg, the phenomenon underlying the increase in protein synthesis after fertilization or parthenogenic activation is the appearance of new polysomes (431, 433, 435), and this is shown in Fig. 79 (431). Experiments with actinomycin demonstrate that these polysomes are formed from presynthesized components already stockpiled in the seed tissues and that their assembly does not depend on the *de novo* synthesis of template RNA's (431, 433). Thus, in the presence of sufficient actinomycin to severely inhibit RNA synthesis, the polysomal profile remains the same as in the controls, as is illustrated in Fig. 80 (433); the rate of protein synthesis in the newly activated seeds remains totally unaffected. Furthermore, electron microscope observations show that the densely packed ribosomes of dry pea seeds are converted during imbibition into polysomal structures, and in this species no synthesis of RNA can be detected during the germination period (433, 435). Now seeds may remain dormant for extremely long periods, and all of these experiments suggest that however long the dormancy period may be, usable informational RNA remains present. In the case of the seeds used in the studies cited, dormancy periods of a year or more are normal. As an extreme example, however, consider the germination of ancient lotus seeds: Seeds of this species (*Nelumbo lucifera*) collected from deposits unequivocally

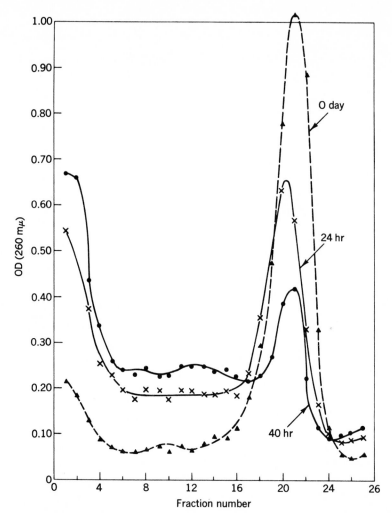

FIGURE 79. Sucrose density-gradient profile of ribosomes from dry and imbibed peanut cotyledons. 4.4 ml of 5–20% sucrose gradient were layered over 0.4 ml of 50% sucrose. The quantities of ribosomal RNA layered over the gradient were 0.34, 0.48, and 0.54 mg for the 0-day (dashed line with triangles), 24-hour (solid line with crosses), and 40-hour (solid line with circles) samples, respectively. Marcus, A., and Feeley, J., *J. Biol. Chem.* **240**, 1675 (1965).

dated at greater than 1700 years of age have been shown to be viable (436). Since the informational RNA stored in seeds is quantitatively responsible for their early postgermination protein synthesis, it is clear that it is essential to germination. It can be concluded that the life length for informational

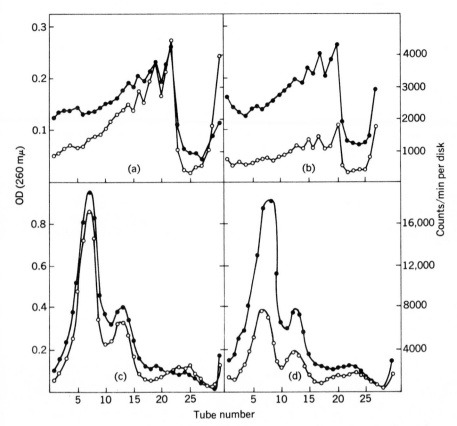

FIGURE 80. Sucrose density-gradient profiles of absorbancy and radioactivity from wheat
embryos incubated with ^{32}P for 30 minutes. (Open circles) counts/minute per
sample; (filled circles) OD. (a) Ribosomes from untreated embryos. (b) Ribosomes from embryos treated with actinomycin D (20 μg/ml). (c) Nuclear
RNA from untreated embryos. (d) Nuclear RNA from embryos treated
with actinomycin D (20 μg/ml). Dure, L., and Watters, L., *Science* **147**,
410 (1965). Copyright © 1965 by the American Association for the Advancement of Science.

RNA molecules is under certain conditions almost unlimited; that is to say,
it is limited only by the onset of those environmental changes leading to
activation and utilization, as in germination. Decay in these very long-lived
informational RNA populations is thus evidently confined to the postactiva-
tion period.

2

Moderately long-lived
informational RNA

There exist a growing number of examples of moderately long-lived template RNA's which are known to be stored for periods ranging from several hours to several days. The key point here is the interposition between synthesis and utilization of an apparently decay-free storage period; frequently the storage takes place in polyribosomes whose temporary inactivity is associated with unusual resistance to ribonuclease. We have already considered several such situations in Section I. Recall, for instance, the well-studied example of the inactive polyribosomes containing informational RNA synthesized in the early sea urchin embryo, or the temporarily inactive template-bearing polyribosomes of the *Ascaris* embryo. In this category we also include informational RNA's protected from cellular nucleases by structures other than polyribosomes, e.g., the informosomes of Spirin (for detail and references the reader is referred to Section I). Spirin divides the various mechanisms through which the life of informational RNA's can be extended into several categories (171): the RNA may be stored in postribosomal informosome-like particles; it may be stored in repressed polyribosomes; it may be stored in heavy complexes containing informosomes and numbers of ribosomes. In addition it may be protected from degradation for prolonged periods in functioning, nonrepressed polyribosomes, perhaps by virtue of association with other stable structures, e.g., membranes (see below). Our present interest in this area, however, does not include the particulars of the mechanisms of protection, and in the examples which follow these are emphasized only insofar as they are germane to the evidence by which the extended life of the moderately long-lived template RNA is demonstrated.

specific moderately long-lived template RNA's
in the polysomes of differentiating tissues

One of the cases initially influential in focusing attention on long-lived template RNA is that of feather keratin synthesis in the developing chick, studied by Humphreys, Penman, and Bell (437). Feather keratin synthesis occurs intensively in 15-day chick embryos, and cell-free preparations from skin tissue at this stage of development reveal an active polyribosomal protein synthesis, a major component of which is feather keratin synthesis. This is shown in Fig. 81c. The synthesis of keratins occurs only after a certain developmental stage is reached, and in the 13-day embryo this function has just begun to be carried out (Fig. 81a). All protein synthesis in the 13-day embryo skin stops within 24 hours of treatment with actinomycin (Fig. 81b), but, in contrast, in the 15-day embryo (Fig. 81d) polysomal protein synthesis,

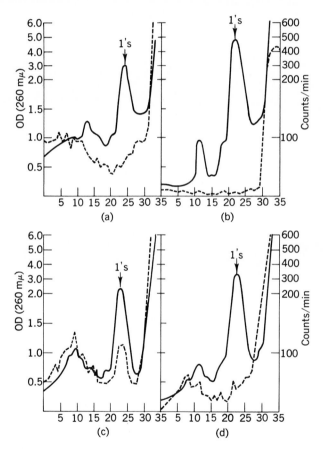

FIGURE 81. Polysome profiles of cytoplasmic extracts labeled with radioactive amino acids and centrifuged at 24,000 rpm for 3 hours on a 15–30% sucrose gradient. (Solid line) OD; (broken line) TCA precipitable counts/minute. (a) and (b) Extracts from 13-day feathers. (c) and (d) Extracts from 15-day feathers. (a) and (c) Freshly isolated tissue. (b) and (d) Tissue treated with actinomycin D for 24 hours. Humphreys, T., Penman, S., and Bell, E., *Biochem. Biophys. Res. Commun.* **17**, 618 (1964).

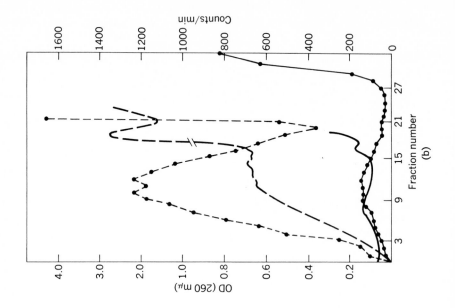

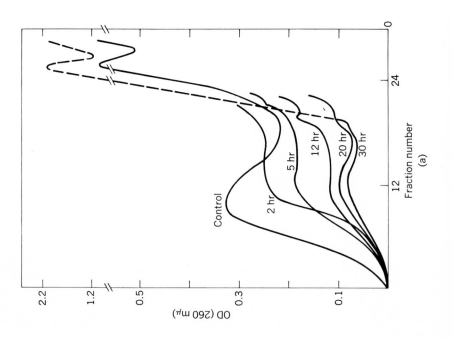

including feather keratin synthesis, continues after 24 hours of actinomycin, which is employed here at a concentration sufficient to obliterate 99% of all RNA synthesis in the embryo. These results indicate that the template RNA for feather keratin synthesis has been presynthesized and is stored in the skin cells. Thus it would appear that by 15 days of development histospecific protein synthesis in these cells depends largely on previously synthesized, stable template, while 2 days earlier this is not the case.

Another example of temporal separation between template synthesis and utilization is that of lens protein synthesis in the embryonic chick. This case, which is owing to Reeder and Bell (438a), and to Scott and Bell (439, 440), similarly involves the temporary storage of template RNA in inactive polyribosomes. Figure 82 portrays the polysomal profiles obtained by Scott and Bell (440) from control and actinomycin-treated 14-day embryonic lens, and, for contrast, from control and actinomycin-treated 10-day chick embryo lens. It is clear that previously synthesized template RNA is functional in the lens cells of the 14-day chick, but that active polysomes bearing pre-formed template are totally absent at the earlier stage. Reeder and Bell have shown that the lens cells undergo a change as differentiation progresses in that long-lived templates for only two histospecific lens proteins eventually supplant the earlier more complex pattern of protein synthesis (438a).

A similar phenomenon appears to exist in bovine lens cells. These cells continue to differentiate throughout the life of the animal (441). In adult bovine lens differentiation the change from reliance of specific lens protein (crystallin) synthesis on newly synthesized templates to reliance of lens crystallin synthesis on preformed or old templates can be followed directly. Studies of this nature have been carried out by Papaconstantinou and his

FIGURE 82. (a) The effect of actinomycin D on polyribosomes of 14-day embryonic lenses. Curves are numbered according to the number of hours that the lenses were incubated in nutrient medium containing actinomycin (40 μg/ml). The rate of disappearance of polyribosomes is taken as a measure of the disappearance of messenger RNA with which ribosomes are complexed. Protein synthesis on polyribosomes, as measured by incorporation of radioactive amino acid into nascent protein, occurred in lenses at all time intervals shown. (b) The effect of actinomycin D (40 mg/ml) on polyribosomal protein synthesis in 10-day embryonic chick lenses. The protein was labeled with ^{14}C-algal hydrolyzate for 2 minutes after 20 hours in actinomycin. The reaction was stopped by washing the tissue in ice-cold saline. (Dashed lines) controls, (solid lines) actinomycin; (lines with filled circles) counts per minute, (lines without circles) OD at 260 mμ. Scott, R. B., and Bell, E., Science 147, 405 (1965). Copyright © 1965 by the American Association for the Advancement of Science.

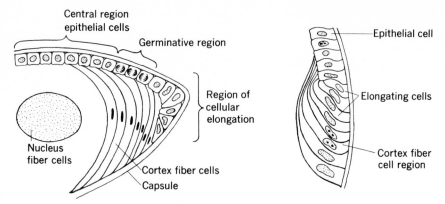

FIGURE 83. (a) Diagram of the lens of the adult vertebrate. The lens is surrounded by an external noncellular capsule. Beneath the capsule are the lens epithelial cells. The region of cellular elongation is in the peripheral area. This is the region of transition where the epithelial cells begin to elongate into fiber cells. The fiber cells that are newly laid down constitute the cortex region; the fiber cells laid down during the early growth period of the lens compose the nucleus region of the adult lens. (b) Diagram of the region of cellular elongation in the vertebrate lens. Papaconstantinou, J., *Science* **156**, 338 (1967).

associates (441, 442), and the process of lens fiber cell differentiation, as described by these workers, is represented in Fig. 83. For us the key observation is the progression from actinomycin-sensitive to actinomycin-insensitive crystallin synthesis which accompanies the complex course of differentiation diagramed in Fig. 83. Papaconstantinou *et al.* have shown that this change affects all the species of lens crystallins synthesized, viz., a, β, and γ (442). Ultimately the lens fiber cells appear to transform into masses of pure crystallin, a process associated with disappearance of nuclei and gross loss of DNA. The last DNA synthesis occurs no later than the epithelial cell stage, according to Papaconstantinou (441). The occurrence of virtual enucleation in a differentiated cell type which has accumulated a moderately long-lived store of histospecific template RNA's is not unique to the lens cell case, and various other examples of this association are now well known. Differentiating feather keratin cells (Fig. 81) in fact provide another example, for the nuclei of these cells eventually "keratinize" along with the cytoplasm (438), presumably after all the templates they are to need have been synthesized and stored. The best known case in this category is, of course, that of the enucleate mammalian red blood cell, which is known unequivocally to contain moderately long-lived template RNA for hemoglobin.

a well-studied example: moderately long-lived template in hemoglobin-synthesizing cells

Direct evidence for long-lived hemoglobin template comes from the persistence of hemoglobin synthesis after spontaneous enucleation in mammalian reticulocyte maturation (443), and stable hemoglobin template exists in the nucleated reticulocytes of lower chordates as well. The course of RNA and protein synthesis in the differentiating nucleated reticulocyte series of the chicken has been assayed radioautographically by Cameron and Prescott, and their results are reproduced in Fig. 84 (444). Over 90% of reticulocyte protein synthesis is hemoglobin synthesis (445). Since RNA synthesis is practically null at the reticulocyte stage, the active protein synthesis carried on in the reticulocyte must be based on template molecules

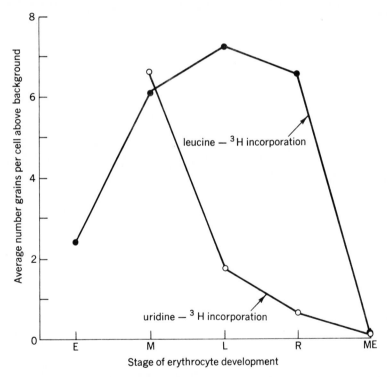

FIGURE 84. A plot of the average grain count in each stage of the erythrocyte series 45 minutes after injection of either uridine-³H or leucine-³H. Erythrocyte series: (E) early polychromatic, (M) midpolychromatic, (L) late polychromatic, (R) reticulocyte, (ME) mature erythrocyte. Cameron, I. L., and Prescott, D. M., *Exptl. Cell Res.* **30**, 609 (1963).

synthesized during the earlier periods (Fig. 84). Cytological changes oc-curing in the course of erythrocyte differentiation in fetal mammalian liver are also suggestive in this direction (446). Thus after the early hematoblast stage the chromatin of the cell nucleus becomes clumped and electron dense, and the nucleoli disappear, events which denote the cessation of RNA syn-thesis and which anticipate the actual extrusion of the nucleus from the cell. The length of time previous to the maturation (release) of circulating retic-ulocytes at which synthesis of the reticulocyte RNA actually occurred has been measured by DeBellis, Gluck, and Marks (447) in anemic rabbits, and their data show that it is not until 40–42 hours after administration of an isotopic RNA precursor that circulating reticulocytes become maximally labeled. This, then, is the probable *minimum* period of survival of the gene products needed for hemoglobin synthesis in the rabbit.

The rabbit reticulocyte, when released, definitely contains previously synthesized informational RNA for hemoglobin synthesis; this has been made certain by experiments on hemoglobin synthesis in cell-free reticulocyte ribo-some systems. Arnstein, Cox, and Hunt (448), for example, have chromato-graphed bona fide hemoglobin together with the labeled soluble proteins synthesized on reticulocyte polysomes *in vitro* and have shown thereby that the latter is indeed hemoglobin, or at least is very similar to hemoglobin. This is illustrated in Fig. 85c. Figures 85a, b demonstrate an even more important point, namely, that reticulocyte monosomes ("light ribosomes") respond to purified high molecular weight reticulocyte RNA by synthesizing hemoglobin. These and similar experiments have established beyond doubt that hemo-globin template remains present and active in the polysomes of the enucleate reticulocyte. The kinetics of the subsequent gradual disappearance of this template RNA population are not well known, though its eventual complete decay is indicated by the fact that the mature erythrocyte carries out no protein synthesis. By maturity the erythrocyte, however, has also suffered a heavy loss of ribosomes. A study by Scott and Malt (449) which is also relevant here shows that both chicken and turtle reticulocytes continue to synthesize protein *in vitro* for at least 24 hours in the presence of large amounts of actinomycin. A gradual linear decay of synthesis rate with time is evident in their experiments, with 50% of control level attained at 7–9 hours after the initiation of actinomycin treatment.

Another system, but one which is essentially to be classed with the mammalian hemoglobin synthesis system, is that of contractile protein syn-thesis in human blood platelets. Like mammalian erythrocytes, platelets are naturally enucleated cells, and Booyse and Rafelson (450) have recently shown that contractile protein synthesis (contractile proteins amount to about 15% of the dry weight of the cell) continues unabated *in vitro* for long periods either in the presence or the absence of actinomycin. Their study

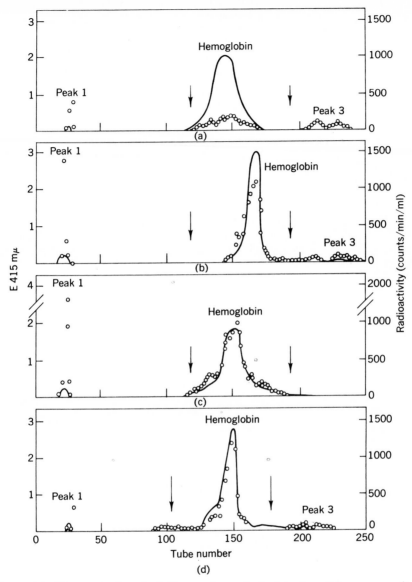

FIGURE 85. Chromatography of soluble protein synthesized in the cell-free system after the addition of high molecular weight RNA. Hemoglobin was converted into the cyanmet form and chromatographed. The arrows indicate change of buffer. (Open circles) radioactivity of the protein; (solid line) extinction of fractions at 415 mμ. The soluble protein was derived from a cell-free system containing (a) light ribosomes, (b) light ribosomes and high molecular weight reticulocyte RNA, or (c) heavy ribosomes (no added RNA). (d) The chromatography of soluble protein synthesized by intact reticulocytes. Arnstein, H. R. V., Cox, R. A., and Hunt, J. A., *Biochem. J.* **92,** 648 (1964).

indicates that the store of template RNA for this protein lasts for at least 72 hours without visible attrition.

It is interesting that moderately long-lived template RNA is involved in hemoglobin biosynthesis from the very first appearance of this histospecific function. Wilt (451) has used actinomycin to ascertain the point at which transcription for the first hemoglobin synthesis in the blood islands of the chick embryo is terminated. Hemoglobin synthesis in this tissue is detectable no earlier than the 7–8 somite stage, according to a variety of very sensitive techniques, but Wilt has found that inhibition of RNA synthesis with actinomycin prevents the initiation of hemoglobin synthesis only if the actinomycin is employed prior to the head-fold stage. Exposure to actinomycin as early as the midprimitive streak stage completely precludes the subsequent synthesis of hemoglobin. Actinomycin treatment later than the head-fold stage permits hemoglobin synthesis to be carried out even in the continuous presence of actinomycin for 24 hours at levels sufficient to block all high molecular weight RNA synthesis. Templates for hemoglobin synthesis are thus formed before the first somite pair becomes visible, even before the head-fold stage, many hours prior to the onset of their translation in the blood islands.

the presence of moderately long-lived template RNA and the repression of nuclear activity

It has been frequently emphasized that in all of the cases we have so far reviewed the presence of a long-lived histospecific template is associated with a course of differentiation ultimately involving effective inactivation of the nuclei. The existence of template RNA which is capable *in vivo* of programming protein synthesis over long time periods can in such cases be regarded as a compensatory device enabling the cell to function beyond the moment of nuclear inactivation. Moderately long-lived template RNA's, however, are far more extensively distributed than are cases in which the nuclei become quiescent as differentiation proceeds to an end point. Consider, for example, the studies of Grobstein, Wessells, and their associates, which concern the *in vitro* differentiation of mouse pancreas rudiments (452–455). Fully differentiated pancreas cell nuclei remain active in RNA synthesis (452), and therefore can in no sense be regarded as quiescent or moribund. The experimental system used by Wessells and his co-workers is diagramed in Fig. 86 (453). Transfilter induction of the presumptive pancreatic acinar cells by salivary mesenchyme cells results in the appearance, at 2 days of culture, of polysomal rosettes in the cell cytoplasm and of increased expanses of rough-surfaced endoplasmic reticulum; at 3 days prozymogen granules

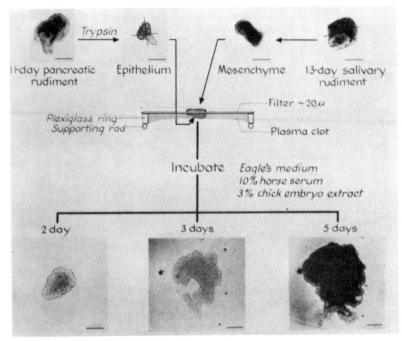

FIGURE 86. Schematic representation of experimental procedure for pancreatic morphogenesis *in vitro*. The experimental procedure involves: (1) dissection and separation of embryonic tissues (first line of photographs); (2) appropriate placement of tissues on filter assembly: pieces of pancreatic epithelium on underside of the filter in a plasm clot, the mesenchyme stranded on upper side of the filter, and (3) incubation of filter assemblies under defined nutritional conditions. Black appearance of 5-day explant is due to accumulation of zymogen granules. The line in lower right-hand corner of each photo is 150 μ. Rutter, W. J., Wessells, N. K., and Grobstein, C., *Natl. Cancer Inst. Monograph* **13**, 51 (1964).

appear; and after 5 days zymogen granules are present in some cells (454). These events are associated with the establishment of a nondividing cell population which from 72 hours on has ceased to synthesize DNA (455), this being the population undergoing differentiation into zymogen-secreting pancreas cells. Experiments with actinomycin (452) show that pancreatic differentiation, assayed as the appearance of zymogen granules and of amylase activity, can be abolished with low concentrations of actinomycin if the latter is applied to the explants at 48–53 hours after the initiation of the culture or earlier. Actinomycin treatment as late as 72 hours, however, fails to prevent subsequent acinar cell differentiation. The actinomycin levels used block the synthesis of 72% of rapidly labeled high molecular weight RNA and 97% of stable high molecular weight RNA (the latter category of course, includes ribosomal RNA). At the low concentrations of actinomycin required to prevent differentiation here (0.014 μg/ml) the cells of the explant are so little damaged that mitotic figures may be observed. It is evident from these experiments that precocious synthesis of template RNA's for pancreatic differentiation takes place many hours before differentiated structures and activities actually materialize. By the onset of histospecific differentiation, at 72 hours, the essential templates have already been completely formed and some of them are at least 19 hours old. Differentiated activity continues for at least the succeeding 48 hours (Fig. 86), and it is likely that the maximum length of life of these templates is to be measured in terms of days.

Though the long-lived templates active in pancreatic differentiation are clearly not the product of nuclei which are destined to become moribund, the onset of this differentiation does appear to involve the repression of DNA synthesis and mitosis. Other examples exist in which a course of differentiation involving repression of division potential also appears to require the early synthesis of long-lived histospecific template RNA molecules. Among these is the differentiating myotube system studied by Yaffe and Feldman (456), who found that actinomycin treatment sufficient to block 95% of RNA synthesis and to kill undifferentiated fibroblasts fails to destroy differentiated multinucleate myotubules or significantly decrease their rate of protein synthesis after 24 hours. Puromycin, however, kills differentiated and undifferentiated muscle cells with equal ease, so it is clear that protein synthesis remains vital to the multinucleate muscle fibers. The quality of being differentiated rather than being multinucleate per se is what is significant with respect to actinomycin insensitivity, since differentiated (beating) mononucleate cardiac fibroblasts also survive actinomycin, according to this study. Histospecific informational readout in differentiating muscle cells thus appears to occur at some point prior to the development of their characteristic form and contractile function.

It is to be emphasized that cells which normally cease to divide after a certain stage of differentiation is attained are not the only cells in which long-lived template is encountered. The generality of long-lived template can only be guessed at present. Consider the 11–13 somite chick embryo, a rapidly growing system in which, as Klein and Pierro have demonstrated (457), morphogenesis depends in part on long-lived informational RNA's synthesized earlier; the period of transcription for anterior mesodermal structures appears to occur prior even to somitic segmentation. Thus notochord, somites, and anterior neural structures all complete their differentiation in the presence of levels of actinomycin inhibitory to other morphogenesis in the same embryos. It is scarcely necessary to point out that the embryonic cells participating in this early actinomycin-insensitive morphogenesis are mitotically active. Another example of long-lived histospecific template associated with mitotically active differentiating cells is to be found in the work of Jainchill, Saxen, and Vainio on induction of metanephrogenic mesenchyme in the mouse (458). In the *Xenopus* embryo certain informational RNA's produced after neurulation possess a life of at least 45 hours, according to the studies of Denis (104) and Brown and Gurdon [(95); these studies were reviewed in Section I], and during this period of development the embryo increases in cell number from about 60,000 to 600,000 cells. A similar relationship holds in teleost and sea urchin embryos; in both cases newly synthesized informational RNA's are stored or otherwise protected for prolonged periods while differentiation and active cell division are under way (cf. Section I).

While it may remain formally possible that the long-lived informational RNA populations present in early embryos are confined to cell types which have already terminated their reproductive life, there are numerous reasons for considering this possibility highly unlikely, prima facie. Among these are the facts that informational RNA synthesis appears to take place in all the embryo nuclei and at least the main part of the early informational RNA is stored in actinomycin-insensitive polysomes or informosomes; that cell division and DNA accumulation continue for a long time after the appearance of the first differentiated cells; that mitotic figures are present in differentiated, functional embryonic tissues which normally lack them in adult life; that the reproductive life of a cell can never actually be considered terminated unless the nuclear DNA is physically missing in any case. In the latter connection we recall the striking demonstrations of Harris (299) and Gurdon (298) which show that in the appropriate cytoplasmic context DNA synthesis can be induced to recur even in erythrocyte and brain cell nuclei. A well-known case is that of liver parenchymal cells, in which a constant low rate of cellular turnover normally persists throughout life, and which can be stimulated to divide en masse by partial hepatectomy. Revel and Hiatt have shown that cytoplasmic template RNA in liver cells exists which may possess a life of at least 40 hours (459), and Cozzone and Marchis-Mouren have corroborated this finding (460). Immediacy of genomic control in this tissue is discussed at more length below, and at this point we refer to the example of liver only for the purpose of demonstrating the presence of long-lived template RNA's in a differentiated cell type which is known unequivocally to retain its mitotic potentialities.

We conclude that moderately long-lived template RNA exists in cells which remain mitotically active, particularly in embryogenesis, as well as in many cells containing functional, but reproductively quiescent nuclei.

Moderately long-lived template is thus of widespread occurrence, and it is not confined to cell types which suffer loss or total inactivation of their nuclei.

moderately long-lived template RNA in microorganisms

Moderately long-lived informational RNA's have been found in certain microorganisms as well. One interesting example is offered in the studies of Sussman and Sussman (461), which indicate the precocious synthesis of template RNA's not used until many hours later at certain stages of morphogenesis in slime molds. In bacteria the most spectacular (though by no means the only) cases are those involving sporulation. Figure 87a, from a study of Aronson (113), describes the growth and sporulation of a culture of *Bacillus cereus* grown in a medium which induces 98–100% of the cells to sporulate. Sporulation occurs synchronously in response to limitation of various medium components, and involves striking, large-scale shifts in structural components, enzyme content, and various other cellular characteristics (113, 462). Figure 87b (463) describes the shift from actinomycin sensitivity to actinomycin insensitivity which occurs as the population ceases to multiply, at about 9 hours, this being the period called "transition point" in Fig. 85a. The experiment shows that the informational RNA needed for sporulation has been synthesized by 9–10 hours after the culture is begun. Since sporulation remains sensitive to interference with protein synthesis by chloramphenicol (Fig. 85b) during the 9–16-hour period of spore preparation, templates for sporulation must persist in active form for 6 hours or more.

The RNA-DNA hybridization experiments of Aronson (113) and similar experiments carried out by Doi and Igarashi with sporulating B. *subtilis* (464) indicate that *qualitatively diverse groups of genes* are active during early log growth, at the time of transcription for spore formation, and during the late stationary phase. In these experiments labeled RNA from one stage is hybridized with DNA in the presence of excess quantities of RNA from other stages, and the amount of overlap in the distributions of genomic information present at the various stages is calculated from the amount of competition observed. The changes in template RNA population diagramed in Fig. 85c are deduced from these experiments. Three partially overlapping populations of template RNA are figured: (*a*) an early short-lived messenger RNA associated with the reproductive growth phases; (*b*) the long-lived spore-forming RNA synthesized at around 9 hours; and (*c*) a new short-lived RNA population associated with stasis in cell number after 9 hours.

A further interesting and significant fact is shown in Fig. 85d, also from the investigation of Aronson (113). Figure 85d represents a saturation

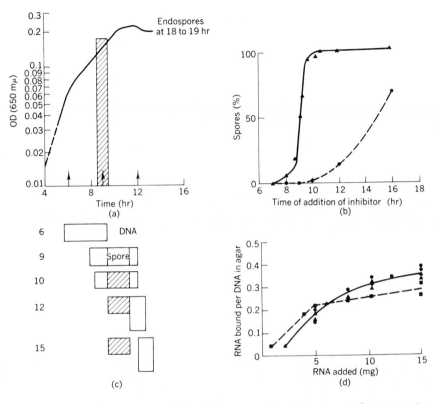

FIGURE 87. (a) Growth curve of *Bacillus cereus*. Crosshatched area designates time of transition (see text). Arrows along abscissa show times of pulse labeling for experiments summarized in (c) and (d). (b) Effect of the time of addition of actinomycin D (10 µg/ml) (solid line with triangles) or chloramphenicol (50 µg/ml) (dashed line with circles) on spore formation. Antibiotics added at indicated times and cells incubated a total of 30 hours. (c) Schematic diagram of overlap of messenger RNA populations synthesized at different stages of growth and sporulation. Area of rectangles represent size of messenger RNA populations (approximately the same at all times). The length represents the extent of heterogeneity of the populations studied in the competition experiments. The clear areas represent messenger RNA synthesized during pulse labeling, and the crosshatched areas are the messages which presumably persist. (d) Saturation curves for messenger RNA from *Bacillus cereus* at different stages of growth and sporulation. Deoxyribonucleic acid values on ordinate are input values and are not corrected for losses during incubation. (Solid line with circles) 5-hour RNA; (solid line with triangles) 9-hour RNA; (dashed line with squares) 12-hour RNA. (a), (c), and (d) From Aronson, A. I., *J. Mol. Biol.* **11,** 576 (1965) (b) is from Aronson, A. I., and Rosas del Valle, M., *Biochim. Biophys. Acta* **87,** 267 (1964).

hybridization experiment in which the amount of genomic information actually in transcription at 9 hours is measured by assaying the ratio of RNA to DNA in the hybrids at saturation. At the highest inputs of 9-hour RNA some 35% of the DNA is apparently hybridized. When corrections for the efficiency of hybrid assay are made according to internal controls, the actual amount of the DNA involved in hybrid formation is found to be close to 50%. Since only one strand of the DNA is functional in transcription, this experiment shows that approximately 100% of the genomic information is in transcription in the 9-hour culture. A similar value was obtained in hybridization experiments by McCarthy and Bolton, carried out with exponentially growing *E. coli* RNA (114). Some of the gene products in synthesis at 9 hours, as Fig. 85c shows, are destined for immediate use, while other fractions will persist for several hours longer, serving as templates for the synthesis of new proteins associated with sporulation.

Moderately long-lived template RNA's appear to exist in bacteria independently of sporulation as well. Some cases of this are discussed below. Among the examples available are the templates for penicillinase in *B. subtilis* (465), for flagellins in *Hemophilus* (466), and for ribosomal proteins in *E. coli* (467).

3

Rapidly decaying template RNA

rapidly decaying template RNA in bacteria

Like moderately long-lived informational RNA, template RNA populations which decay exponentially from the moment of their synthesis are also known in all sectors of the biological world. Woese, Naono, Sofer, and Gros (468) showed that when further RNA synthesis in *E. coli* is blocked by the addition of proflavin and DNP the total informational RNA population decays at once following first-order kinetics. The half-life for the RNA population is 8 minutes under the conditions of these experiments. In *B. subtilis* similar kinetics obtain, and Levinthal, Keynan, and Higa have estimated a mean life of about 2 minutes for the messenger RNA of this organism (469). Zimmerman and Levinthal, however, have recently suggested that this and other similar values obtained with actinomycin may actually underestimate messenger RNA half-life by taking into account the decay not only of mature messenger molecules but of rapidly degrading unfinished polynucleotide chains as well (469a). These authors present data obtained in other ways which suggests that the half-life of the template RNA population in *B. subtilis* is actually closer to 4.8 minutes. Mangiarotti and Schlessinger (469b) have demonstrated a slightly slower exponential decay rate for the total polyribosomal template RNA of *E. coli* also. Their data, which provide several independent half-life estimates, show that the chemical half-life for functioning *E. coli* messenger is actually 11–12.5 minutes. The half-life for the specific β-galactosidase messenger in *E. coli* is only 2–5 minutes, according to Nakada and Magasanik (470). In other bacteria half-lives for messenger RNA of the order of 2 minutes have also been measured (471–473). Template half-lives are not immutable, but depend on the stage of cellular metabolism. Thus anerobiosis and various other treatments result in prolonged template life in *E. coli,* according to Fan (471) and Fan, Higa, and Levinthal (472), and interference with protein synthesis in mammalian cells also causes changes in template life length (460).

    An interesting study of the dynamics of the whole macromolecular synthetic system of *E. coli* is that of Dresden and Hoagland (474, 475). In

267

their experiments no inhibitors are used, advantage being taken of the reversible response of *E. coli* grown in minimal medium to sudden glucose starvation. On withdrawal of glucose protein synthesis rates fall sharply, as shown in Fig. 88a (474). The curve is initially log-linear, with a half-life of 1.4 minutes for total protein synthesis. Figure 88b presents semilog plots describing the exponential polysome to monosome transformation which underlies this decrease in protein synthesis rate, and which is directly owing to degradation of the messenger RNA in the polysomes at the onset of starvation. On readdition of glucose to the starved cells, the polyribosomes are immediately reassembled as new messenger RNA is synthesized; this is shown in Fig. 88c (475). Resynthesis of messenger sets in with almost no

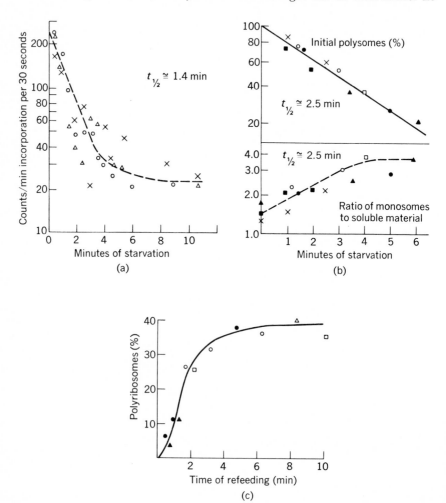

lag and is complete by 2½ minutes. The resulting increase in polysome content is paralleled closely by the increase in protein synthesis rate. It is thus apparent that the protein synthesis rate in E. *coli* is very closely linked to the decay and synthesis rates of template RNA; in other words, the E. *coli* genome controls the synthesis of most of its proteins with a very high degree of immediacy.

Most of the cases of immediate template decay we have so far cited refer to populations composed of many species of RNA. It is reassuring, therefore, to find that individual species of messenger RNA such as the β-galactosidase messenger also decay with the expected kinetics. As noted above the half-life of this messenger is 2½ minutes. Another example is that of histidase messenger decay in B. *subtilis,* studied by Hartwell and Magasanik (476). This inductive enzyme decays exponentially when the inducer is withdrawn from the culture, and disappearance of enzyme activity is directly owing to decay of the histidase messenger RNA. Under these (repression) conditions the half-life of the overall system for histidase synthesis is only 2–4 minutes.

rapidly decaying template RNA in differentiated cells

Given an important difference in time constants, examples of rapidly decaying template RNA are known in differentiated cells which in their kinetics are basically similar to those studied in bacteria. A case in point is the study

FIGURE 88. (a) Rate of protein synthesis during glucose starvation in E. *coli*. Exponentially growing cells were rapidly harvested and resuspended in glucose-free medium containing leucine-^{14}C. Aliquots (1 ml) of the culture were pipetted into 4 ml of 5% trichloroacetic acid at 30-second intervals after the initiation of starvation. Hot acid-insoluble material was deposited on Millipore filters and counted. The radioactivity incorporated during the 30-second intervals is plotted as a function of starvation time. Three separate experiments are presented as indicated. (b) Breakdown of polysomes during glucose starvation. Cells growing exponentially were rapidly harvested. The cell pellet was resuspended in 5–10 ml of cold glucose-free medium at 37°. Aliquots (3 ml each) were removed and chilled after various times of starvation. Extracts were prepared and examined by sucrose gradient centrifugation (six separate experiments are represented here). The percentage of polysomes was determined in each case by summation of the relative areas under the polysome and monosome regions of the gradient, and calculated as a function of the initial polysome content, setting this equal to 100% at zero time. (a) and (b) From Dresden, M. H., and Hoagland, M. B., *J. Biol. Chem.* **242**, 1065 (1967). (c) Kinetics of polysome appearance during refeeding. Cell cultures starved of glucose for 1–1½ hour were refed with glucose for various time periods. Dresden, M. H., and Hoagland, M. B., *J. Biol. Chem.* **242**, 1069 (1967).

of Tschudy, Marver, and Collins (477) regarding δ-aminolevulinic acid (ALA) synthetase induction in rat liver. This enzyme, an initial component of the porphyrin synthesis system, is inducible *in vivo* by injection of various substrates (here allylisopropyl acetamide is used). Once induced, the turnover rate of the enzyme may be measured by assaying the rate of enzyme disappearance in puromycin-treated cultures. Figure 89 describes the result of actinomycin treatment at two different points in the induction sequence. δ-Aminolevulinic acid synthetase activity disappears exponentially, and calculations based on both the rate of enzyme protein turnover and the rate of enzyme disappearance following treatment with actinomycin indicate that the half-life of the ALA synthetase template is in the range of only 40–70 minutes. This value lies among the shortest exponential decay constants recorded for any metazoan template RNA. Villa-Trevino, Farber, Staehelin, Wettstein, and Noll (478) have published another study relevant to the dynamics of template turnover in rat liver, but one which is concerned with the overall template RNA population rather than the message for one enzyme. These workers found that the protein synthesis inhibitor ethionine causes a rapid breakdown of free polysomes. Ethionine is incorporated as S-adenosylethionine, and its primary action is apparently to block template

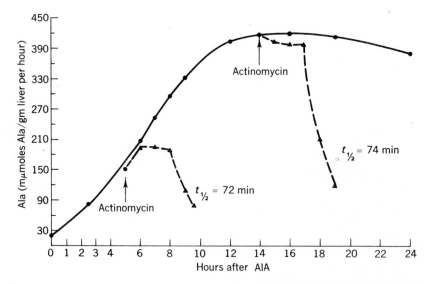

FIGURE 89. The effect of actinomycin D given at two different times during the induction of S-aminolevulinic acid (ALA) synthetase. The solid line represents the course of induction of ALA synthetase after allylisopropylacetamide (AIA) administration, and the dotted lines represent the curves of ALA synthetase when actinomycin D was given 5 or 14 hours after the inducer (AIA). Tschudy, D. P., Marver, H. S., and Collins, A., *Biochem. Biophys. Res. Commun.* **21**, 480 (1965).

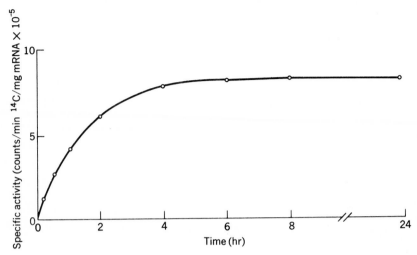

FIGURE 90. Specific activities of liver messenger RNA plotted against pulse-labeling time. Trakatellis, A. C., Axelrod, A. E., and Montjar, M., *J. Biol. Chem.* **239,** 4237 (1964).

RNA synthesis by reducing the amount of ATP available. The inhibition can be relieved by addition of methionine plus adenine, and in ethionine-inhibited liver cells the polysomes re-form and normal protein synthesis rates are quickly restored upon addition of these compounds. By measuring the rates of polysome breakdown and reformation following the imposition and relief of ethionine poisoning a half-life is calculated for the total free polysomal template RNA of about 48 minutes, the same as that characterizing liver ALA synthetase messenger RNA. A slightly longer half-life has been estimated by Trakatellis, Axelrod, and Montjar for the free polysomal template RNA of mouse liver (479). In these experiments use of inhibitors of any kind is avoided, and the estimate is based directly on the rate at which optimum levels of labeling are attained following the administration of a single pulse of labeled orotic acid. The data obtained are plotted in Fig. 90, which shows that the messenger RNA of the entire polysome population must be renewed every 4 hours; i.e., that the half-life for this RNA population is about 2 hours.

Mammalian liver cells also contain long-lived polysomal template (i.e., messenger) RNA. Revel and Hiatt have provided strong evidence for this in an investigation into the effects of actinomycin on protein synthesis in rat liver (459). As long as 40 hours after complete inhibition of RNA synthesis by actinomycin no decrease in total protein synthesis is observed *in vivo.* Relative template activities in cytoplasmic and nuclear RNA fractions isolated after long exposures to actinomycin were also assayed by Revel and Hiatt, with the aid of a cell-free *E. coli* ribosome system. Their experiments show that for at least 17 hours in the total absence of new RNA synthesis the cytoplasmic RNA preparations remain fully active, as compared to normal controls, and only 50% of the nuclear template activity is lost within this period. Cozzone and Marchis-Mouren (460) have also demonstrated long-lived informational RNA in liver. After actinomycin the total extractable DNA-like RNA of liver decays very slowly, according to these workers, so that by 6 hours only about 20% of the counts initially present in this class of RNA have disappeared. Evidence of this kind may appear contradictory to that showing that liver polysomal messenger decays exponentially and immediately, but actually it is not. The rapidly decaying liver template RNA's described in the studies we have just reviewed belong explicitly to the polysomes extracted from the cell sap, while the intracellular source of the stable templates of Revel and Hiatt is not confined in this way. Blobel and Potter (480, 482) and Howell, Loeb, and Tomkins (481) have demonstrated that about 75% of the total ribosomal RNA of liver is bound to heavy intracellular structures and hence is excluded from the postmitochondrial supernatant fraction used to prepare free polysomes. The bound ribosomes are fully active, being responsible for most of the protein synthesis carried out in the liver cell (481), and they are present mainly as polysomes (482). High molecular weight, heterogeneously sized RNA of a nonribosomal nature has been extracted directly from liver endoplasmic reticulum fractions (483), and it is proposed explicitly by Pitot (484) that the membrane-bound informational RNA is the stable template RNA of the liver cell. It is clear in any case that *template RNA populations of widely different half-lives may coexist in the same cell.* Furthermore, this parameter is a characteristic of particular states of differentiation, and various cell types differ in their average template lives. Pancreas, in contrast to liver, for instance, has a total average DNA-like RNA turnover rate of only 4 hours (460).

In rapidly dividing mammalian cells relatively short-lived, exponentially decaying template RNA can also be identified, even under conditions of continuous growth and replication. The best studied cell types in this class are long-term mammalian tissue culture cells, particularly HeLa cells. Penman, Scherrer, Becker, and Darnell have measured the decay rate for the bona fide messenger RNA of HeLa cell cytoplasm (485), as defined by its location in functioning polysomes, and it is of interest to compare their results with the values obtained for liver polysomal template RNA. In the HeLa cell most of the nucleotides incorporated into RNA per unit time are incorporated into high molecular weight ribosomal RNA precursors (486), which are rapidly transformed into smaller ribosomal components and transported to the cytoplasm (487, 488). In addition a considerable amount of labeled precursor is incorporated into a rapidly degrading species of nuclear RNA, and a small fraction of newly synthesized RNA can be identified as true cytoplasmic

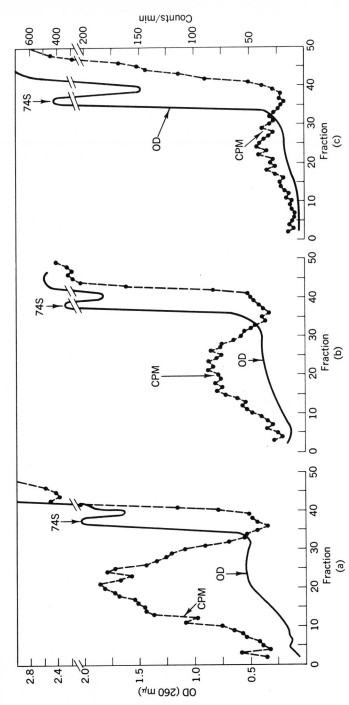

FIGURE 91. Fate of cytoplasmic polyribosomes after treatment of HeLa cells with actinomycin D. Actinomycin D (5 μg/ml) was added to a 200-ml culture of HeLa cells, and (b) 3 hours and (c) 7 hours afterward the cytoplasm of the cells was examined for polysomes. The cells were provided with eight labeled 8 amino acids (valine, isoleucine, leucine, arginine, proline, tyrosine, histidine, and lysine). A culture not treated with actinomycin served as control (a). The sedimentation analysis was at 24,000 rpm for 60 minutes. Penman, S., Sherrer, K., Becker, Y., and Darnell, J. E., Proc. Natl. Acad. Sci. U.S. **49**, 654 (1963).

template or messenger RNA (486–490). Within a few hours after actino-mycin treatment polysomal protein synthesis declines as shown in Fig. 91 (485), and the monosome to polysome ratio in this experiment can be seen from the OD (260 mμ) traces to have increased. The half-life for the total cytoplasmic messenger RNA population in actinomycin-treated HeLa cells is about 3–4 hours, according to Penman *et al.* (485). That one is indeed dealing with template RNA in these experiments has been made clear in a variety of other studies. Thus the molecular size of the nonribosomal, labeled RNA's extracted from HeLa cell polysomes has been shown to relate directly to the length of the polysome fractions from which they are derived (490), and these RNA's possess a DNA-like base composition (485). Latham and Darnell (490) have found that new messenger RNA molecules cease becom-ing incorporated into the cytoplasmic polysome population in as short a time as 7 minutes after the shutoff of all RNA synthesis by actinomycin, an interesting fact which suggests the absence of more than a few minutes advance supply of cytoplasmic messenger in the growing HeLa cell.

the use of actinomycin in studies of template life

In the studies we have just considered, as in many of the others relevant to this area of intracellular dynamics, interpretation of the experimental results depends at least partly on the extent to which actinomycin inhibition is confined to DNA-dependent RNA synthesis. If actinomycin, for example, were to interfere with breakdown of RNA as well as interfering with its synthesis on the DNA template, there would obviously be grounds for serious doubt as to the value of RNA turnover data obtained through the use of actinomycin. Various suggestions have in fact been made to the effect that actinomycin interferes with metabolic processes vital to RNA *usage* as well as to RNA synthesis, and each investigator who has employed this potent agent has been forced to consider the problem of possible side effects on its own merits and in the context of his particular application. The burden of the evidence at present lies in favor of the position that actinomycin is not likely to give rise to side effects of such gravity as would tend to alter the basic interpretation of RNA turnover studies, however. This statement is based on several varieties of evidence:

(1) The high degree of specificity of actinomycin-DNA binding, and the preferential effect of actinomycin on RNA synthesis compared even to such closely related processes as DNA synthesis.

(2) The fact, which we have seen demonstrated again and again in tissues ranging from sea urchin eggs to rabbit reticulocytes, that protein synthesis may proceed normally in the presence of actinomycin provided

only that stable templates are present. The lack of interference by actinomycin with either qualitative or quantitative aspects of protein synthesis implies that events on the ribosome are in general impervious to actinomycin, and also that the underlying precursor uptake machinery and bioenergetic mechanisms can function normally in actinomycin-treated cells. Other evidence of the same genre comes from observations that cell division may continue in actinomycin-treated cells [e.g., see Wessells (455)] as it does in actinomycin-treated embryos. In order for mitosis to take place a great many cellular processes must be in functional order, ranging from protein synthesis to membrane assembly.

(3) A third line of evidence supporting a straightforward interpretation of actinomycin experiments is the correspondence, where such comparisons are possible, between results obtained through the use of actinomycin and those obtained by other means. In the data reviewed here the most direct illustration of this is in the studies of free polysome template life in mammalian liver. Thus, use of inhibitors whose mode of action is completely different, e.g., ethionine (478), or of no inhibitors at all (479), has yielded approximately the same values as obtained through the use of actinomycin (478). Furthermore, a direct comparison of template lives as established by measurement of RNA decay rates and by change in rate of incorporation of amino acids into protein after actinomycin treatment has been carried out by Cozzone and Marchis-Mouren (460), and no difference in results is obtained by these two methods.

It is evident from this preliminary survey that the temporal parameters of intracellular genomic control vary widely. In bacteria the time separating cessation of gene action and unavailability of the template gene products is characteristically a matter of several minutes. The longest temporal separation known between bacterial gene transcription and template utilization is in the cases of sporogenesis, where the sporulation templates must resist decay for a number of hours. In seeds and oocytes, however, template RNA lives are in principle unlimited in that the template molecules are stored in a protected state until such time as environmental circumstances permit and activation occurs, typically months or even years after their synthesis. In most cell types some template RNA populations begin to decay exponentially from the earliest point at which their existence can be detected, but moderately long-lived template RNA's occur as well in cells ranging from sporulating bacteria to the differentiating tissues of higher vertebrates. The temporal distance separating the synthesis of informational RNA molecules from their time of utilization is a measure of the closeness of simple control by the genome over the functions which it directs, and it is evident from these examples that there exists an enormous range of variation in the temporal aspects of gene control.

multiple levels of immediacy in gene control

Even within the same cell different degrees of immediacy seem to pertain to different cell functions or sets of cell function. We have already encountered this phenomenon in reviewing the evidence for both long- and short-lived template RNA's in liver and in sporulating *B. cereus.* Similarly, in their studies of long-lived templates in embryonic chick tissues, Scott and Bell (440) and Humphreys *et al.* (437) found that most of the protein synthesis in these tissues is carried out on short-lived templates though long-lived templates are present at the same time. The coexistence of diverse degrees of immediacy in gene control within the same cell became apparent in a study of differentiated tissue culture cells carried out in the writer's laboratory, in which the histospecific synthesis of acid mucopolysaccharides was compared to a mitochondrial respiratory enzyme activity with respect to their rates of decay after blockade of nuclear activity with actinomycin (429). Though mitochondria contain their own genetic systems the presence of mitochondrial enzyme components ultimately requires nuclear genomic factors, but as might be expected, the activity of such an enzyme (in this case succinic dehydrogenase) does not decline for periods as long as 24 hours in the absence of RNA synthesis. In these same cells, however, acid mucopolysaccharide synthesis begins to decline within a few minutes if RNA synthesis is blocked with actinomycin, apparently as a consequence of starvation for short-lived templates on which the polysaccharide-synthesizing enzymes are themselves continuously being synthesized.

A striking instance of diverse template lives within the same cell is presented in Table XIV, from a study of Pitot, Peraino, Lamar, and Kennan (491). The table shows that *individual template stability actually depends on template species* and on other factors as well. Note the difference in the stability of the template for the same enzyme in normal liver and in two different hepatomas.

Protein synthesis in actinomycin-treated pancreas declines rapidly, but as in the liver decay rates vary according to the protein in question. Marchis-

TABLE XIV. Template Half-Lives for Rat Liver Enzymes[a]

Enzyme	Template half-life
Serine dehydrase	6–8 hours
Ornithine transaminase	18–24 hours
Tyrosine transaminase	3 hours
Rauber hepatoma serine dehydrase	2 hours
Morris hepatoma serine dehydrase	2 weeks

[a] From Ref. 491.

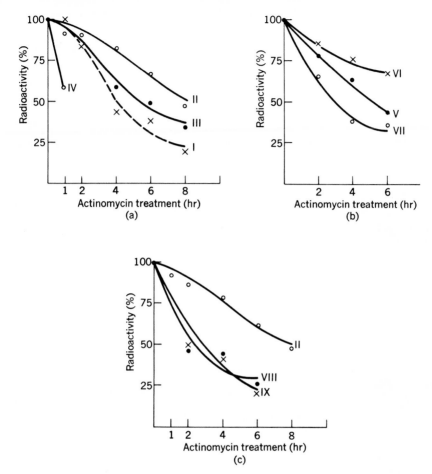

FIGURE 92. (a) Effect of actinomycin on valine incorporation into: I, total proteins (dashed line with crosses); II, amylase (solid line with open circles); III, RNase (solid line with filled circles); IV, nuclear proteins (solid line with open circles). (b) Effect of actinomycin on valine incorporation into: V, soluble proteins (solid line with filled circles); VI, basic proteins (solid line with crosses); VII, acidic proteins (solid line with open circles). (c) Effect of actinomycin on valine incorporation into: II, amylase (solid line with open crcles); VIII, chymotrypsinogen (solid line with filled circles) IX, trypsinogen 2 (solid line with crosses). Marchis-Mouren, G., and Cozzone, A., *Biochemistry* **5,** 3684 (1966).

Mouren and Cozzone have studied valine incorporation into purified histo-specific enzyme proteins of pancreas after actinomycin, and some of their experiments are shown in Fig. 92 (492). Each enzyme or class of protein investigated displays a certain characteristic decay rate, and these decay rates are shown to be related directly to decay of the template RNA's responsible for their synthesis (460, 492).

Almost all the cells which have been examined closely appear to display certain simultaneous variations in the rapidity with which their template RNA's decay, and hence in the immediacy with which the cellular genome controls their diverse functions. This is true of growing bacteria as well as of liver and pancreas cells. A hint that a longer lived template population exists in *E. coli* can be observed in the experiment of Dresden and Hoagland portrayed in Fig. 88a, and Forchhammer and Kjeldgaard (493) have demonstrated this directly. Uracil starvation in an *E. coli* mutant auxotropic for uracil results in abrupt cessation of RNA synthesis and these authors have shown that the template activity of the RNA extractable at various times after the withdrawal of uracil decreases in a biphasic manner. Approximately one-half of the template-active RNA's disappear with a half-life of about 5 minutes while the half-life calculated for the remaining template RNA population is about 42 minutes.

These examples, which are not in the slightest degree unique, demonstrate that differential degrees of immediacy in gene control coexist for different cell functions. It is clear that the relative variation in the temporal parameters of genomic controls, as one compares cells of diverse tissues or even of organisms from diverse phyla, is scarcely greater than the variation encountered within any one cell type. In two respects bacterial control systems differ in absolute terms from metazoan systems, however: (*a*) the rates of degradation of the most short-lived exponentially decaying template RNA's in bacteria are 1–2 orders of magnitude higher than the decay rates of the most rapidly degrading metazoan *template* RNA's known; and (*b*) no parallel so far exists in bacteria for the essentially unlimited template lives verified for the stored informational RNA's of seeds and eggs.

significance of immediacy of gene control in the cellular genomic response system

It is clear from the above that gene control over cellular function includes a complex temporal dimension extending beyond the primary selection of active as opposed to repressed genes. It is obvious that the higher the decay rate of a population of gene products the more quickly can repression of transcription affect the function of a cell. The rapidity with which alterations in the spectrum of active genes is registered at the functional level will therefore be affected by the dynamics of informational RNA decay; this parameter, as we have seen, is itself a highly variable one, depending clearly on the species of RNA, the state of the cell, etc. Now variation in gene activity is a fundamental mode of environmental response on the part of all types of cell, and many examples are known in which particular alterations in gene function follow as a direct consequence of changing external signals. In this category of phenomenon we might include the response of various cells to hormones which have been shown to act at the nuclear level [reviewed by the writer (494)]; the response of kidney cells to explantation (495); the response of competent embryonic tissues to inductive agents [see reviews in Tiedemann (247) and Yamada (248); also Denis (85)]; or the response of dark-adapted plant leaves to light (496, 496a, 496b). Dozens of other cases, equally striking, exist. From this point of view it is evident that *the immediacy with which cell behavior is controlled by the genome will directly affect the reactivity of the cell to environmental changes*, and immediacy is therefore a parameter of key importance. The systems which are most rapidly reactive to simple control at the genome level would thus be those for which the templates decay immediately and exponentially so that the rate at which the system operates is linked closely to the continuation of template synthesis. Among the other factors which must contribute to the kinetic characteristics of environmental reactivity and control on the part of the cell nucleus are the size of the preformed template pool and the activities of the intracellular nucleases and proteases. In that they affect the immediacy of gene control these factors all constitute significant aspects of the metabolic plasticity which enables cells to deal with environmental change. The cell types in which the extremes of template longevity are observed therefore appear to be those which for one reason or another are not challenged to display major environmental reactivity, e.g., cells which are highly insulated from the environment, such as seeds and impermeable eggs surrounded by membranes, capsules, or shells. Expendable, dead-end, fully committed cell types such as mature reticulocytes and lens cells provide other examples of cells which have attained a stage where they have no further apparent need of the full range of environmental reactivity, and only long-lived preformed templates are ultimately retained in such cells.

changes of immediacy in embryonic development

In the course of embryogenesis the whole range of temporal regulations of which the metazoan genome is capable is utilized. The initial morphogenetic events in the highly protected, closed embryonic system are independent of immediate control by the zygote genome, being preprogrammed in the long-lived informational RNA stockpiled during oogenesis. During early embryogenesis, transcription from the zygote genome results in the appearance of a population of moderately long-lived informational RNA's which is retained for a number of hours, until utilized during gastrulation or later. *Apparently the genome is not entrusted with high immediacy of control until the onset of differentiation.* From this point on a pattern appears to be established in which moderately long-lived templates for certain processes such as featherogenesis, lens proteins synthesis, and hemoglobin synthesis coexist with more rapidly decaying templates. The latter are to be associated with processes subject to continuous modulation from the nuclear level of control and with the institution of new processes. In some embryos the development of maximum immediacy of control coincides with the onset of the period when for the first time the cells *must* respond to environmental changes, in particular the advent of new tissue types adjacent to them. Thus the first embryonic inductions are among the earliest morphogenetic events which are subject to rapid arrest by appropriate treatment with actinomycin. Additional evidence comes from the RNA-DNA hybridization experiments reviewed in Section I which show that in both sea urchin and amphibian embryos newly synthesized late blastular and gastrular gene products disappear in the succeeding stage of development, and that a new group of gene products is produced at each stage thereafter. This pattern of events clearly indicates that a close temporal link connects genome function with the resulting program of developmental changes. Thus protein synthesis, from gastrulation onward, has been shown to depend on immediate gene action. With the onset of visible differentiation (and tissue-level induction) it is apparent from these demonstrations that embryo genome control is now being exercised with a high degree of immediacy, in contrast to the situation during cleavage.

Consider in this light the mammalian egg, which in certain respects is so different from molluskan, insect, fish, amphibian, or echinoderm eggs. The mammalian egg, unlike these, ceases to develop when treated with actinomycin as early as the 2- or 4-cell stage (see Section I for references). Eggs of eutherian mammals possess little yolk, and ribosomal RNA synthesis, as judged by the precocious appearance of active nucleoli, probably sets in during early cleavage. It is significant that the mammalian egg is vitally dependent on a constant external supply of metabolic substrates even as it descends the fallopian tubes during the initial hours or days of its development. Thus it has been demonstrated by Whittingham and Biggers that from the beginning cleaving mouse eggs require an external source of energy substrates such as pyruvate and lactate, normally supplied by the secretions of the fallopian tube (138, 497). Between the 2- and 8-cell stage, furthermore, new patterns of substrate utilization are imposed as the egg becomes further removed from the influence of the follicle cells and more completely dependent on the fallopian environment (497, 498, 498a). Thus Daniel, in an analysis of the ability of rabbit embryos to utilize some twenty-five different substrates, has shown that the repertoire of acceptable bioenergetic metabolites begins to change as early as the second day of development. Two-day eggs can deal with at least three diverse metabolites as sole energy intermediate, and 5-day eggs with at least fifteen metabolites, according to this study (498a). In order to exploit most effectively the (environmental) fallopian conditions, it is likely that embryo genome regulation of embryo metabolism must operate, and perhaps it is a requirement of this nature which explains the precocious onset of high immediacy in genome control characteristic of mammalian embryos.

4

The rapidity of variations
in gene activity
in differentiated cells

A temporal aspect of gene control over cellular function which we have not so far discussed is the rapidity of response in metazoan cells to *activation* (or derepression) signals of external origin. It is now well known that inducible bacterial systems react almost at once to the appropriate inductive stimulus. In the case of histidase induction in B. *subtilis,* for instance, the synthesis of histidase messenger RNA begins within less than 2 minutes of histidine introduction. Following the addition of inducer, messenger RNA for β-galactosidase is synthesized within 2–2½ minutes in E. *coli* (499), and similar time factors characterize various other inductive enzyme systems in bacteria. These lag times amount simply to the time required for synthesis of the complete RNA messenger molecule, according to recent estimates (469a, 469b). Evidence exists showing that rapid genomic response to appropriate environmental stimuli also occurs in metazoan cells. Some of the best demonstrations of this are available in the literature describing hormonal effects on gene activity in various mammalian cells. An example is presented in Fig. 93, in which is reproduced a countercurrent separation of liver RNA's extracted within minutes of cortisol injection. The spectrum of RNA's present changes markedly within as little as 5 minutes from the time of hormone addition in this experiment, which is taken from an investigation of Kidson and Kirby (500). A certain fraction of these 5 minutes is undoubtedly required merely for the penetration of the hormone to the genomic site of RNA synthesis. In the same study parallel results are obtained with various other hormones as well, viz., testosterone (to which male and female liver react differently) and the nonsteroids thyroxin and insulin. Means and Hamilton report that *within 2 minutes* of estrogen treatment the nuclear RNA of uterine cells increases in specific activity as much as 40% (501). Cortisone derivatives repress rather than activate lymph cells, and Kidson (502) has found that the kinetics of this genomic response are similar to the

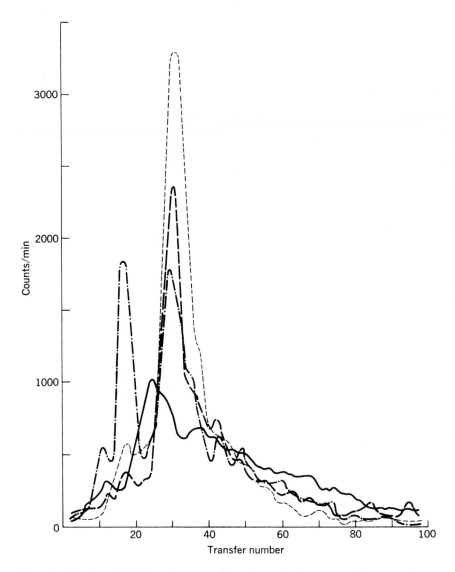

FIGURE 93. Effects of hydrocortisone succinate (5 mg/rat) on mRNA patterns in rat liver in 100 transfer countercurrent distribution procedure. (solid line) control (mRNA from rat liver); (dashes and dots) mRNA from livers of rats receiving intraperitoneal hydrocortisone 5 minutes before pulsing with ³H-orotic acid; (heavy dashed line) mRNA from livers of rats receiving hydrocortisone 15 minutes before pulsing with ³H-orotic acid; (fine dashed line) mRNA from livers of rats receiving hydrocortisone 30 minutes before pulsing with ³H-orotic acid. Kidson, C., and Kirby, K. S., *Nature* **203,** 599 (1964).

kinetics of gene activation by the same hormone in liver. Thus the effect is near-instantaneous, as shown in Fig. 94, and when the values obtained from the experiment of Fig. 94 are corrected for the measured time required for the hormone to penetrate into the cell, the initial response at the genomic level can be seen to have occurred in a matter of seconds.

Rapid genomic response rates probably exist in plant cells as well: thus, Roychoudhury, Datta,and Sens (503) have reported that significant increases in RNA synthesis in isolated coconut endosperm nuclei take place within a few minutes of exposure to giberellin, auxin, or kinetin. Johri and Varner have also demonstrated a rapid response to giberellin in pea nuclei: the new RNA's produced as a result of exposure to giberellin are qualitatively novel (503a). Clark, Matthews, and Ralph (496), investigating the effect of sunlight on dark-adapted cabbage leaves, have uncovered another case of rapid genome-level response to change in environmental conditions. After prolonged darkness the leaf contains mainly monosomes, according to these workers, and relatively little protein synthesis is being carried out. Within

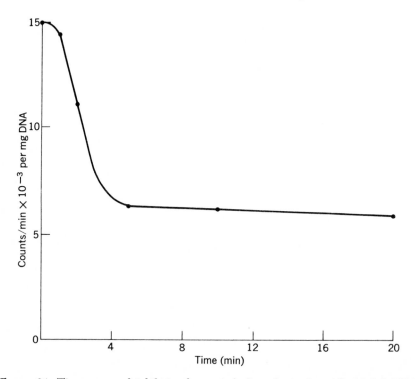

FIGURE 94. Time course of inhibition by cortisol of synthesis of rapidly labeled RNA. Cortisol (5 μg/ml) given for varying times prior to a 5-minute pulse with uridine-³H. Kidson, C., *Biochem. Biophys. Res. Commun.* **21,** 283 (1965).

as little as 4 *minutes of exposure to bright light*, however, new template RNA's have been assembled, and as they become available, the polysome population of the leaves increases sharply. Similar reactions have now been described for other plant species, but at least in some cases the response time is considerably longer (see, e.g., 496a).

According to these examples the metazoan cell genome is capable of responding to the appropriate environmental stimuli with the same rapidity as the bacterial genome, i.e., within a brief period of time ranging from seconds to 1 or 2 minutes. A *temporal asymmetry* thus exists in the metazoan genomic control system in the sense that change in the patterns of cell function resulting from gene *activation* can be effected with far greater temporal sharpness (*vide* Fig. 93) than can control by gene *repression,* even though the genome-level response may be equally rapid in cases of external signals causing gene repression (e.g., Fig. 94). The asymmetry follows from the fact that metazoan template RNA populations decay and disappear much more slowly than new template RNA's *appear* after the activation of new genes. This is not to say that the cells of higher organisms are unable to alter their patterns of activity with great rapidity, for they possess a range of elegant mechanisms which permit them to do precisely that; the point is made simply that *direct genomic control* over these patterns of function can be exercised far more rapidly in the case where previously repressed genes become activated than where previously active genes become repressed. Bacteria offer a striking contrast to this in that here repression and activation can be temporally symmetrical because of the very high rates of template degradation which are characteristic of bacteria. Thus it is found that in many bacterial systems induction and repression occur with exactly the same speed (e.g., 499).

5

Characteristics of bacterial
repression-derepression systems

By an oblique route we are approaching in this discussion a speculative confrontation with the basic unsolved problem in this field, viz., the actual nature of the genomic regulation machinery operating in differentiated cells. Frequent attempts have been made to apply to this problem the bacterial repression-derepression models of gene regulation originally suggested by Jacob and Monod (430, 504) and subsequently modified by various other writers [see, for example, discussions of differentiation by Moore (505) and Jacob and Monod (504)]. It is desirable for us to consider at this point the salient characteristics of these models with their potential applicability to metazoan differentiation in mind. Figure 95, reproduced from Jacob and Monod (430, 504), describes induction and repression variants of the operon model and by combining two such operons shows how more complex effects might be obtained with these systems. In the combined system of Fig. 95b, for example, the structural genes SG_1, SG_2, and SG_3 can be activated by transient exposure to an inducer which by the same token would activate RG_2, and thereby shut off the supply of the repressor controlling these structural genes. Conversely, transient exposure to the inducer I_2 would block the activity of the structural genes indefinitely, or until I_1 again entered the system. A stable pattern of gene activity thus follows from a transient induction phenomenon. Note that at least one of the two regulator genes must be firing at any one time in this system. Other models proposed by Jacob and Monod (504) envision the direct products of structural genes as enzymes which in turn mediate the synthesis of inducers or repressors for these genes. In principle, at least, it would appear that diverse mechanisms along these lines could account for the variations in the patterns of gene action which lie at the root of the differentiation phenomenon, as Jacob and Monod have suggested (504).

286

MODEL I

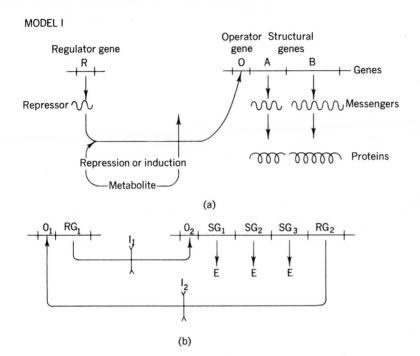

(a)

(b)

FIGURE 95. (a) Operon model. Jacob, F., and Monod, J., *J. Mol. Biol.* **3**, 318 (1961). (b) Compound operon system: The regulatory gene RG_1 controls the activity of an operon containing three structural genes (SG_1, SG_2, and SG_3) and another regulatory gene RG_2. The regulatory gene RG_1 itself belongs to another operon sensitive to the repressor synthesized by RG_2. The action of RG_1 can be antagonized by an inducer I_1, which activates SG_1, SG_2, SG_3, and RG_2 (and therefore inactivates RG_1. The action of RG_2 can be antagonized by an inducer I_2 which activates RG_1, (and therefore inactivates the systems SG_1, SG_2, SG_3, and RG_2). (O) operator. Jacob, F., and Monod, J., *Symp. Soc. Study Develop. Growth* **21**, 30 (1963).

the genetic basis for coordinate control and the generality of coordinate systems

The models of Fig. 95 possess certain general characteristics. One of these is the presence of contiguous, coordinately controlled genes. Linked structural genes for metabolically linked processes have been known for some years in bacteria (506, 507). The most intensively studied systems are the *E. coli* lactose system, containing three such structural genes which are repressed and activated coordinately: the 5-gene tryptophan synthesis system of *E. coli* which also operates under coordinate control, and the coordinately controlled 10-gene histidine synthesis system of *Salmonella*. A number of other coordinate control systems are also known, including four structural genes for the pyrimidine biosynthesis pathway, genes for certain citric acid cycle enzymes, genes for valine and isoleucine synthesis, and genes for arabinose synthesis—all in *E. coli*. The model of Fig. 95a essentially represents a scheme by which the phenomenon of coordinate control over the activity of linked genes can be explained, and in the absence of such compound gene systems this model per se is not directly applicable.

Thus, to quote Jacob and Monod on this subject (430): "It is clear that when an operator controls the expression of only a single structural cistron the concept of the operon does not apply, and in fact there are no conceivable genetic-biochemical tests which could identify the operator-controlling genetic segment as distinct from the cistron itself." In considering the general relevance of the operon concept an initial problem is therefore to discover how widely distributed are coordinately controlled, linked genes. Unfortunately the genetics of few organisms are known with sufficient thoroughness to permit this question to be answered in any real sense, and this is particularly true of metazoan organisms in which differentiation can be studied. There exists some evidence, nonetheless, which suggests that coordinate control of metabolically linked sequences is not confined to bacteria. Measurements of the relative activities of various Embden-Meyerhof pathway enzymes, in sources ranging from yeasts to mammalian and insect tissues, demonstrate that these enzymes are always present in constant proportions even though their absolute activities vary by orders of magnitude (508). It has been calculated by Meir and Cotton (509) that the activity ratios characteristic of the constant proportion group of enzymes are in fact the very ratios to be expected if the enzymes are present in *equimolar quantities,* and this correspondence provides a very strong indication for their coordinate synthesis, as from a single polycistronic template.

Genetic mapping experiments have also uncovered several cases in multicellular organisms in which functionally related steps in intermediary metabolism are shown to be controlled by extremely closely linked genes, and a table listing these cases has been assembled by Pontecorvo (510). In *Neurospora* a cluster of 5 genes controlling the coordinate synthesis of aromatic amino acid synthesizing enzymes has recently been identified (511). Similarly, in both yeast (*Saccharomyces*) and *Neurospora,* three of the genes for the histidine-synthesizing enzymes (those governing reactions 2, 3, and 10 in the synthesis sequence) appear to be tightly clustered, and the combined unit is reported to show many of the genetic features of the bacterial operons. These cases, however, appear to be exceptional, and most of the functionally related loci of eukaryotic organisms are scattered throughout the genome. A germane example is immediately at hand in the remainder of the loci governing the histidine-synthesizing enzymes of yeast, for these are widely distributed in the genome (512) as they are also in *Neurospora* (513). The 10-enzyme cluster of histidine genes known in *Salmonella* has thus been replaced in the ascomycetes by a very different arrangement in which individual loci are distributed among different chromosomes, except for the one 3-gene cluster. In *E. coli*, to take another example, the 8 genes governing the arginine synthesis pathway are scattered in five separate regions of the genome, and overall *coordinate* control is absent in this pathway even though the whole synthesis sequence is repressible by arginine (514). Though we are not yet in a position to appreciate the actual distribution of coordinately controlled, linked gene systems, it is clear that these are limited in occurrence. That limitation sets a primary boundary on the applicability of the operon model per se, in bacteria as well as in eukaryotic organisms.

polycistronic messenger RNA, the molecular basis of coordinate control

Where coordinate control exists it is based on the synthesis of polycistronic messenger RNA. Polycistronic template RNA products of the lac operon in *E. coli* have been demonstrated by Kiho and Rich (515), who utilized various deletion mutants lacking certain regions of the operon. Sedimentation analyses of the polysomal populations in induced cells show that β-galactosidase is synthesized on polysomes and that these polysomes are of larger size in wild-type *E. coli* than in mutants synthesizing galactosidase but bearing deletions in the transacetylase region. Templates for both the transacetylase and the galactosidase must therefore be included in the same messenger RNA molecule, since polysome size is a function of messenger length, and the messenger is thus by definition polycistronic. The relatively giant polysomes containing this polycistronic template RNA have now been visualized in the electron microscope (515a). They contain as many as 50 ribosomes. Such enormous polysomes are rare in *E. coli*, according to the recent investigations of Mangiarotti and Schlessinger (469b). These authors conclude that most of the template RNA in *E. coli* polysomes is monocistronic, an observation consistent with the view that polygene operon systems are the exception rather than the rule in this organism.

Ribonucleic acid and protein synthesis are both linear sequential processes beginning at one end of the polynucleotide strand and ending at the other, and a direct consequence of the mediation of operon action by a polycistronic message is that a *temporal polarity* will be characteristic of operon action. Thus, the product of one gene will appear in advance of the product of the next, etc.; Lieve and Kollin have shown that after new RNA synthesis is blocked with actinomycin, the appearance of β-galactosidase is affected at 2½ minutes, while transacetylase synthesis does not become actinomycin sensitive until 4 minutes have elapsed (516). Polycistronic messenger has also been identified by Imamoto *et al.* in the tryptophan operon (517, 518) and its polarity determined in an analysis of the effects of numerous amber and ocher mutants (518–520). For the histidine operon of *Salmonella* there is also a variety of evidence indicating the existence of a polycistronic RNA product of the operon. This evidence derives from the analysis of polar mutant effects (e.g., 521), the direct biochemical observation of what is probably the polycistronic template produced by this operon (522), and studies of the temporal sequence with which the various enzymes produced by the operon disappear under repression conditions (523). The temporal order of disappearance of the respective enzyme proteins is found to be the same as the order in which the genes for these enzymes are arranged in the his region of the genome, a result which is again most directly interpreted as a consequence of the sequential translation of a polycistronic message.

the operator gene concept

In the original operon model (Fig. 95a) the properties attributed to the operator gene itself were based on observations of two classes of lac system mutants, the "operator-constitutive" (O^c) and the "operator-negative" (O^0) mutants; O^c mutants fail to display proper sensitivity to the repressor and hence are always to some extent derepressed, irrespective of external conditions. The operator locus is thus defined as the site of repressor action in the operon, a site which affects only structural genes linked directly to it. The O^0 class of mutants appear permanently repressed, i.e., they fail to display control levels of activity on the part of any of the structural genes of the operon even though these genes actually remain present in the genome of the mutant organism. The properties of O^0 mutants suggested that the operator gene is also the site of initiation of transcription for the operon so that a critical lesion at this site would preclude the expression of the whole operon. Mutants of this variety have been found in several operon systems to map within the first structural gene of the series (519, 524, 525). In the lac operon, furthermore, it was shown by Jacob and Monod that a revertant of an O^0 mutant which had recovered the ability to synthesize β-galactosidase produces an altered variant of this protein, one which is abnormally temperature sensitive (524). From this and the mapping data it was concluded that the operator locus actually constitutes the starting sequences of the first structural gene of the operon.

The site of initiation of transcription, the site of repressor action, and the nucleotide sequence bearing genetic information for a part of the first protein of the series were thus regarded as synonymous, and together they constituted the definition of the operator locus as conceived in the model of Fig. 95a. The synonymity of these functional sites has broken down under the intensive investigations to which the bacterial operon systems have been subject since the presentation of the operon model, however, and it is now clear that the operator locus as originally defined does not exist. For one thing, mutants behaving exactly like O^0 mutants have been located in other than the initial gene of the series in several operon systems. To take one example, a result of this kind has been reported by Lee and Engelsberg with reference to the arabinase linkage group in the E. coli genome (526). Here mutants of the O^0 type are found to lie within the third structural gene of a 4-gene operon-like series. Numerous other observations could also be cited in this connection. Thus, Yanofsky and Ito have shown that in the tryptophan synthesis operon a number of mutations mapping within the structural genes of the system also behave in a manner similar to O^0 mutants (519). It is in fact clear at this point that O^0 mutations are simply extreme (i.e., extremely proximal) cases of polar mutations such as may occur throughout the operon, interfering with the expression of genetic information situated distally to them. [For discussion of this point, see the reviews of Stent (527) and Beckwith (528).]

Polar mutations of various kinds have now been intensively investigated (e.g., 519, 521, 527, 529) and their modes of action can be divided into several categories. Among the best known are the amber mutations, which, if situated within the structural genes of an operon, behave as polar mutations in that they block translation of the polycistronic messenger RNA distally to themselves simply by causing premature chain termination (518, 519, 530). Since such polar mutations, whether located near the beginning of the operon as are the O^0 mutations or elsewhere, have nothing to do with genetic control of the operon, the term "operator-negative" is a misnomer, as Beckwith has explicitly pointed out (528). By analyzing a series of deletion mutants in the lac operon it has been shown, furthermore, that O^0 mutations are physically separated from the repressor-sensitive site (531), which actually lies outside the first structural gene of the series. It is the repressor-sensitive site which is affected by the O^c mutations and these are probably all deletions (528). Strong evidence for the fact that effective mutations at this site are deletions has come from studies with mutagens: O^c mutations can be produced by X-irradiation, which causes deletions, but not by chemical mutagens which cause base substitutions (532). Mutations at the *repressor-sensitive site* of the lac operon affect in no way whatsover the molecular constitution of the β-galactosidase protein, according to data obtained with immunological methods, by peptide analysis, and by various physical procedures (533). The repressor-sensitive region (operator locus) probably synthesizes no proteins at all, since mutations in this region are never suppressible by suppressors of chain-terminating mutants (534), and the repressor-sensitive region is clearly not a part of the lead structural gene of the operon. The repressor-sensitive region is also to be distinguished from the initiation site for transcription of the polycistronic message. Thus Jacob *et al.* (532) and Beckwith (528, 528a) have provided evidence that the latter function belongs to a closely linked but distinct site, the "promoter" locus. In the tryptophan operon of *E. coli*, according to two recent reports (534a, 534b), the rate of initiation of transcription in fact depends on a repressor-insensitive, specific chromosomal site located at the operator end of the operon. In the 5-gene tryptophan operon of *Salmonella* two sites for initiation of transcription evidently exist (534c), one of which is situated distantly from the operator locus, between the second and third genes of the operon. The existence of such a site clearly establishes that the distinction between the repressor-sensitive operator locus and the transcription-controlling initiator or promoter locus (or loci) is real.

regulatory genes in coordinate and other systems

Another essential characteristic of the repression-derepression model illustrated in Fig. 95a is the functional role postulated for the noncontiguous regulatory genes. The products of this type of gene are envisioned as affecting the operator locus; more generally, *regulatory gene products affect the activity of other genes*. Of course, viewed in the latter terms, the general idea of regulatory genes long antedates the operon model, dating back more than 50 years to the discovery of position effects in the *Drosophila* genome. Many apparent examples of intergenic effects are known in higher organisms. Particularly relevant are the investigations of McClintock in maize (535) which have documented the existence of complex intergenic regulatory relationships apparently similar to those associated with regulatory genes in bacteria. In yeast and bacteria noncontiguous regulatory genes affecting the function of other genes have also been known for some years. Regulatory genes appear to be more widely distributed than are coordinately controlled polycistronic operon systems, and it is clear that the regulator gene concept, which stands independently of the operon model, is also the more general concept. The proposal that regulatory gene products can recognize and specifically affect other genes has recently received direct experimental support in the studies of Gilbert and Müller-Hill (536, 536a), Ptashne (537, 538), and others. These workers have succeeded in partially purifying the regulatory gene products which specifically control the operation of the lac operon in E. coli and of the λ-phage genome, respectively.

In the case of the lac operon the repressor protein has been shown to possess the ability to bind the lac system inducer molecule against a concentration gradient. The repressor protein is not present in strains which lack functional regulator genes while retaining the lac operon structural genes, nor can it be demonstrated in strains requiring enormous amounts of inducer, i.e., in strains which produce repressor proteins of low affinity for the inducer. The protein binds to that DNA which constitutes the operator gene for the lac operon, furthermore, and this binding is subject to interference by the inducer molecule. The lac repressor protein has been further purified by Riggs et al (538a, 538b). Its molecular weight is approximately 150,000, and it appears to be composed of subunits of 40,000–50,000 in molecular weight. The phage repressor studied by Ptashne (537) is a product of the "C" gene of the phage genome and confers immunity to the phage. By irradiating E. coli hosts with ultraviolet light, thereby destroying host protein synthesis, and then infecting with the phage in the presence of ^{14}C-amino acids a labeled protein preparation is obtained which is highly enriched in proteins coded for by the phage genome, including the C protein. This protein binds specifically to λ-phage DNA. The repressor molecule appears to be an acid protein of about 30,000 in molecular weight, and it is capable of binding only to native DNA (538). These recent findings, taken together with the accumulated earlier evidence, show that genes coding for proteins which specifically affect other areas of the genome are a reality. Regulator genes mapping noncontiguously with the structural genes whose activity they govern are known in many induction-repression systems in bacteria, including those belonging to the operon systems discussed above.

More than a single regulatory gene may be relevant to each system, however. In the lac operon, for example, a second distantly located regulatory gene besides the "i" gene has been discovered by Loomis and Magasanik (539). Similarly, a second, noncontiguous regulatory gene for the tryptophan operon is now known (540). At least two regulatory genes govern the operation of the arginine synthesis gene system in E. coli, which is composed in part of scattered loci controlled in a noncoordinate manner (541), and no less than 5 noncontiguous regulatory genes are now known to affect the operation of the histidine operon in Salmonella (542, 542a). In some of the best studied of the compound bacterial gene systems, in other words, it would appear that the number of genes with specific regulatory effects is of the same order as the number of structural genes responsive to them!

In certain respects the patterns of gene regulation operating in the coordinate induction-repression systems of bacteria have thus turned out to be somewhat different from those postulated in the diagrams of Fig. 95a, while other aspects of the operon model have received very strong support from direct biochemical observations. As far as it goes, the basic design of the model is clearly correct; viz., that linked structural genes undergo coordinate activation and repression mediated by the products of other genes possessing specific regulatory functions. The observations of Gilbert and Müller-Hill (536) and of Riggs *et al* (538b) show that as predicted the regulator gene product is able to react specifically with external inducer molecules. The concept of operator gene function originally proposed has undergone much change. However, the suggested function of these genes resolves into the functions of the repressor-sensitive site and the transcription-initiating site, which are apparently distinct entities. The applicability of the operon model per se is in any case limited to operons, i.e., to coordinately regulated polygenic systems, which in eukaryotic genomes appear to be relatively rare, and even in bacteria are not particularly common.

For animal cell biologists, therefore, the most general and significant result devolving from these investigations is probably the added insight into the function of regulatory genes, which now stand on a very firm footing. Biochemically, the operon is a contiguous polycistronic system producing a polycistronic messenger, and its characteristic properties of coordinate control and polarity follow directly from this fact. It is also to be noted that all the bacterial repression-derepression systems so far studied in this context consist of relatively small numbers of structural genes (2–10). The functional efficacy of all known operon systems depends directly on the extremely rapid rates of template (and enzyme) decay in bacteria, so that repression of polycistronic messenger synthesis within a few minutes results in disappearance of both the RNA and protein products of the operon.

6

Characteristics of gene
regulation systems in
differentiated cells

Gene regulation in differentiated cells is a process of diverse attributes, and there is now available a great variety of data relevant to the nature of this process. Having glanced briefly at the characteristics of regulation in the coordinate control systems of bacteria we consider now the regulation systems operating in higher cells, an area of interest central to developmental biology. Our immediate purpose is to review some of the general characteristics of gene regulation in metazoan cells, i.e., to consider phenomenologically the properties of genomic function in differentiated cell types. We begin with a question of long-standing interest, and one on which there is now available a certain amount of experimental data, viz., the approximate proportion of the genome which is actually functional in the typical differentiated cell.

the proportion of the genome active in differentiated cells

Estimates of the proportion of the genome active in thymus and in bone marrow cells have been published by Paul and Gilmour (27, 29, 29a). In their experiments chromatin from these tissues is made to serve as a primer for exogenous RNA polymerase, and the complementary RNA formed is then extracted and hybridized with DNA. By extrapolating to saturation (with excess RNA), and comparing the hybridization levels obtained with those recorded when instead of native chromatin deproteinized DNA is utilized as the primer for complementary RNA synthesis, the authors have arrived at the conclusion that about 5% and 7.5% of the genomic sites in the DNA are available for transcription (i.e., potentially functional) in thymus and marrow, respectively. These values are not subject to the objection that the chromatin isolation procedure could have altered the normal level of repression existing *in vivo* (29a), and, as we shall see, they fall close to the

295

values reported for other tissues and obtained in other ways. A very similar procedure was employed by Georgiev, Ananieva, and Kozlov (28) in studying the accessibility to transcription of the ascites cell genome under normal conditions and after stepwise removal of the chromatin proteins (see below). The hybridization experiments of these authors show that only about 4% of the DNA can be hybridized by complementary RNA synthesized from the native ascites cell chromatin template. The template activity of the native chromatin is also only 4% or 5% of that obtained with totally deproteinized ascites cell DNA. Other estimates of the percent of the genome active depend on measurement of the hybridized fraction of DNA at the saturation plateau level obtaining when a sufficient excess of newly synthesized RNA is hybridized with homologous DNA. (The reader is referred to the detailed discussion of this procedure in Section I.) In this laboratory such studies have been carried out with the RNA synthesized in lampbrush-stage amphibian oocytes (see Section III), and it has been estimated that only about 3% of the redundant fraction of the genome is functional in this cell type throughout the whole of the lampbrush stage (25, 115). In fact all of the hybridization data cited here should be considered as relevant only to the degree of activity of the internally redundant gene families in the genome. Denis' saturation hybridization experiments (104) measuring the percent of the genome which appears to be active at various stages of embryogenesis in *Xenopus* have also been discussed previously (the results of this study are summarized in Table IV). Under Denis' conditions, by the late-gastrula stage only about 2.4% of the DNA can be hybridized with newly synthesized RNA; i.e., about 4.8% of the genomic information is observed to be active up to this stage. By the tail-bud stage some 10% of the genomic information is monitored in the total embryo RNA, with about 6% present in the RNA synthesized during the tail-bud stage itself (Table IV). A similar comparison shows that at the swimming tadpole stage about 17% of the total genomic information is detected in the tadpole RNA, and about 3.6% is observed in the RNA's transcribed during that stage itself. It is to be stressed that these values refer to the RNA synthesized *in the whole embryo* with its many diverse cell types, rather than in any single cell type. Much less of the genome will of course be functional in any one type of differentiated cell. Another investigation in which the amount of the functional genome is measured by the hybridization procedure is that of Shearer and McCarthy (26). Here the cell type under study is the L cell, a mouse connective tissue derivative adapted to permanent culture. Saturation experiments in which a set amount of L-cell DNA is exposed to increasing amounts to total labeled L-cell RNA yield at saturation the ratio $RNA/DNA = 0.04$. In other words, in this experiment about 8% of the total genomic information is monitored as being present in the L-cell RNA's. Since the labeling period is 2 days (about twice the mean generation time for these cells) and the cells were not synchronized, the value obtained is a cumulative approximation which includes genes expressed at all phases of the cell cycle. Stevenin, Samec, Jacob, and Mandel have used the same general methods to estimate the amount of the genome active in rat brain (543a). Only 1.2% of the DNA can be hybridized with the RNA's in synthesis in this tissue, according to this report.

These studies suggest that less than one-tenth of the total genomic information is functional in any particular cell type. It is to be noted in this connection that both the L cell and the Ehrlich ascites cell are hypotetraploid in karyotype and both display the capability of malignant growth. On either score it could be concluded that the regulation system limiting genomic activity in these cell types has become hereditarily deranged, and, hence, that estimates of the level of genomic function based on this material should be taken as an upper extreme in comparisons with differentiated cells in general. However, the values reported are similar to those obtained with other differentiated cell types. Though the hybridization procedures used in these experiments suffice to detect hybridization mainly (or exclusively) with the internally redundant fractions of the genome, the overall fraction of single-copy genes active may well be similar to that in the internally redundant fraction. Annealing between the gene products of one gene and other partially homologous members of the same redundant gene family could, in such experiments, result in an overestimate of the proportion of the genome actually functional. Nonetheless, despite the large uncertainties in each of the investigations cited, there is general agreement in the results, whether obtained from saturation hybridization experiments, from hybridization experiments based on complementary RNA synthesized *in vitro* on whole chromatin templates, or from direct assays of template activity in whole chromatin as opposed to deproteinized DNA. The latter procedure has been applied with similar results to relatively nondividing cell types, e.g., liver cells (e.g., 543), and a collection of such measurements is presented in Table XV, which is reproduced from Bonner (544). Template activity of the native chromatin preparations listed in Table XV is of the order of 10–20% of the template activities recorded with purified DNA. Furthermore, *in vitro* measurements of template activity carried out in this manner may be regarded as representative of the actual state of the chromatin *in vivo since the RNA synthesized in vitro from an isolated chromatin template is homologous only with RNA extracted from the donor cell type.* This has been demonstrated in a number of similar studies (e.g., 28, 29, 29a, 542, 542b). The low template activity of isolated chromatin thus constitutes the strongest and most direct evidence for the general state of repression characteristic of the animal cell genome.

TABLE XV. Chemical Compositions of Varied Chromatins[a]

Source of chromatin	DNA	Histone	Nonhistone protein	RNA	Template activity (% of DNA)
Pea embryonic axis	1.00	1.03	0.29	0.26	12
Pea vegetative bud	1.00	1.30	0.10	0.11	6
Pea growing cotyledon	1.00	0.76	0.36	0.13	32
Rat liver	1.00	1.00	0.67	0.043	20
Rat ascites tumor	1.00	1.16	1.00	0.13	10
Human HeLa cells	1.00	1.02	0.71	0.09	10
Cow thymus	1.00	1.14	0.33	0.007	15
Sea urchin blastula	1.00	1.04	0.48	0.039	10
Sea urchin pluteus	1.00	0.86	1.04	0.078	20

[a] From Ref. 544.

A striking distinction between differentiated animal cells and bacterial cells follows from the conclusion that 80% or 90% of the genome in any given differentiated cell type is not transcribed. Consider the case which is perhaps closest to differentiation in bacteria, that of sporulation. As in metazoan differentiation sporulation requires the activity of large numbers of genes (113). In the sporulating bacterium, however, as emphasized above (Fig. 87c), these large numbers of genes at one point in the process constitute close to 100% of the total genomic information possessed by the organism, rather than something less than 10% or 20% as in the differentiated animal cell. Even in log-phase nonsporulating cultures as much as 60% of the total genome appears to be operative in *B. cereus*, and close to 100% may be utilized during log growth in *E. coli* (114). Though bacteria also display repression of the genome, at least under certain conditions, the degree of this repression is quantitatively of a different order of magnitude, and this is true whether the comparison is made with normal differentiated animal cells, irrespective of cell type or organism, or with cancerous cells.

relative change in gene function associated with change in state of differentiation

A question closely related to the absolute proportion of the genome active is the *relative* amount of genomic information involved in changes in the pattern of gene activity which are associated with changes in the state of differentiation. An example is tissue-specific hormone response. A glance at Fig. 93, which is reproduced from the studies of Kidson and Kirby cited above (500), suffices to demonstrate that the effect of cortisone on the pattern of RNA synthesis in the liver nucleus is an extremely diverse one. Thousands of individual species of informational RNA are undoubtedly present in the liver cell, and each of the peaks observable in the countercurrent distribution tracing portrayed in Fig. 93 must therefore represent a large number of individual molecular species (these peaks, of course, do not necessarily all represent informational as opposed to other classes of RNA). Cortisone treatment appears to result in a quantitatively enormous change in the spectrum of RNA molecules in synthesis, a change which clearly affects a significant proportion of the activity taking place in the liver cell genome.

Figure 96 illustrates another experiment which suggests that a very large fraction of the gene activity in a given cell type may undergo change in the course of differentiation. This experiment forms part of a study by Church and McCarthy (112, 545) regarding changes in gene function associated with liver regeneration and liver neogenesis in the mouse. In this figure are displayed the competition curves obtained when unlabeled RNA extracted from embryonic livers of mice at 14, 15, and 17 days of gestation, from mice at term, and from adult mice is added to a hybridizing mixture of mouse DNA and pulse-labeled RNA extracted from 14-, 15-, or 17-day embryonic liver or from adult liver. The experiments are carried out with excess DNA, and the competition recorded is a function of the degree of overall homology between the competing populations of molecules. The experiment demonstrates that remarkably large-scale alterations in the pattern of gene activity accompany liver differentiation. Thus within only 1 day of development, as shown in the upper-left-hand graph, some 70% of the apparent homology in the liver RNA populations has disappeared. Changes of this magnitude also distinguish embryonic from adult liver RNA. A further experiment is presented in Fig. 97, which concerns liver regeneration (112). Here it is shown that the patterns of gene activity in regenerating liver remain constant for no more than 3 hours after hepatectomy, though as early as 1 hour after the operation the RNA in the surviving lobe appears to be many times more effective as a competitor to labeled 1-hour RNA than is RNA from the livers of sham-operated animals. By 6 hours a significant portion of the informational RNA's synthesized during the first 3 hours as a result of hepatectomy have already disappeared. As regeneration continues the distribution of RNA molecules in the liver continues to alter, just as it does in the developing embryonic liver. Some of the genes active in regeneration in fact appear to be the same as those which function in liver neogenesis (545).

In a general sense it is of course clear even without these explicit and quantitative demonstrations that very large numbers of genes must be involved in differentiation. The range of metabolic and cytological changes

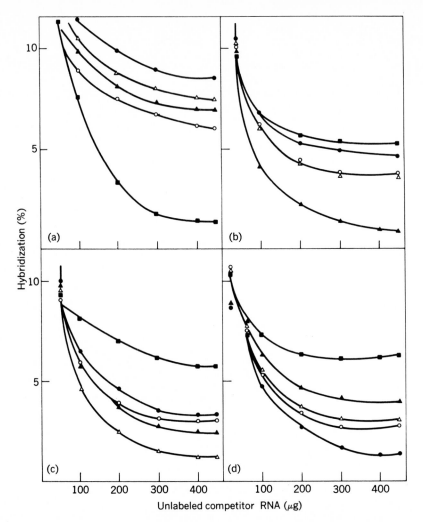

FIGURE 96. Competition by unlabeled RNA from various stages of embryonic liver in the reaction of 10 μg of ³²P pulse-labeled RNA from embryonic and adult livers with 30 μg of DNA. (a) The competition by unlabeled RNA in the hybridization reaction of ³²P pulse-labeled RNA prepared from 14-day embryonic liver. (b) The competition by unlabeled RNA in the hybridization reaction of pulse-labeled RNA isolated from 15-day embryonic liver. (c) Similar competition in the hybridization reaction of pulse-labeled 17-day embryonic liver RNA. (d) The competition by unlabeled RNA in the hybridization reaction of ³²P pulse-labeled adult liver RNA. The specific radioactivities of the various labeled RNA preparations were in the range of 300–700 counts/min/μg. As shown in the figure, the percentage of RNA hybridized at low levels of RNA is much higher. Embryonic livers isolated at 14 days (filled squares); 15 days (filled triangles); 17 days (open circles); term (filled circles); adult liver RNA (filled circles). Church, R. B., and McCarthy, B. J., *J. Mol. Biol.* **23**, 477 (1966).

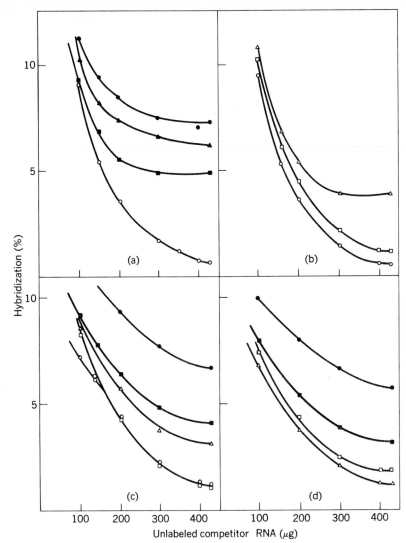

FIGURE 97. Competition by unlabeled RNA from various stages of regeneration of liver in the reaction with RNA pulse-labeled with ^{32}P from early regeneration stages. (a) and (b) Competition of unlabeled RNA in the hybridization reaction of RNA pulse labeled with ^{32}P from 1-hour regenerating liver. (c) and (d) Competition of unlabeled RNA in the hybridization reaction of RNA pulse labeled with ^{32}P from 3- and 6-hour postoperative regenerating liver, respectively. The unlabeled RNA preparations used as competitors are symbolized as follows: (closed circles) sham-operated liver; (open circles) 1-hour postoperative; (open squares) 3-hour postoperative; (open triangles) 6-hour postoperative; (closed squares) 12-hour postoperative; (closed triangles) 48-hour postoperative. The specific radioactivities of the various labeled RNA preparations employed were in the range of 300–600 counts/ min/μg. Church, R. B., and McCarthy, B. J., *J. Mol. Biol.* **23,** 459 (1967).

underlying morphogenetic processes such as gastrulation or embryonic induction is so great that no other supposition is likely. Direct comparisons of the patterns of gene activity at successive stages of embryogenesis have demonstrated this to be the case, and it is no longer a matter of speculation that developmental morphogenesis is accompanied by truly massive alterations in the patterns of genome function [see Section I, where relevant hybridization experiments (104, 116, 117, 130, 131) are reviewed]. Experiments such as those presented in Figs. 93, 96, and 97 dramatize in an elegant way the quantitative magnitude of the variations in genomic function which underlie typical differentiation phenomena within a single cell. It is clear that any model proposing to explain genomic regulation in differentiated cells must include a reasonable interpretation for this very large-scale switching on and off of genes. Massive as it is, we have seen that the switching phenomenon may in some cases occur with extreme rapidity, within minutes, a period of the same order of magnitude as that required for bacterial repression-depression systems to change their state of operation.

the nature of the repressive agents functioning in the differentiated cell genome

It is desirable at this point to consider briefly the probable molecular nature of the repressive agents responsible for the functional inactivity of most of the differentiated cell genome. It is clear that these agents are proteins, since removal of chromatin proteins from chromatin results experimentally in apparent derepression of the genome; we have already cited several experiments of this genre (27–29, 543). The evidence that chromatin deproteinization actually results in genomic derepression (rather than some specious stimulation of polymerase activity) is incontrovertible, since the qualitative range of genomic information released by the deproteinized genome has been shown to increase with deproteinization some 5- to 20-fold. In Fig. 98 the previously cited experiment of Georgiev et al. is portrayed (28). Here the proteins are removed stepwise from ascites tumor cell chromatin with increasingly concentrated salt solutions, and at each step a sample of the partially deproteinized chromatin is assayed for its ability to serve as a template for RNA synthesis. It can be seen that the increase in template function parallels the increase in the hybridization of the complementary RNA as deproteinization proceeds. Ribonucleic acid synthesized in the ascites cells in vivo competes for ascites cell DNA to the extent of 60–80% with RNA synthesized in vitro from the starting chromatin preparations, according to Georgiev et al. Thus, any damage done to the chromatin in the course of its original isolation is not such as to result in a

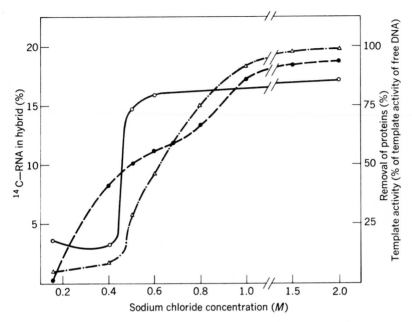

FIGURE 98. Influence of removal of protein from the DNA-protein complex on its template activity and on the hybridization properties of RNA synthesized on the DNA-protein template: (dashed line with filled circles) protein removed; (dashes and dots with open triangles) template activity; (solid line with open circles) hybridizability. Georgiev, G. P., Ananieva, L. N., and Kozlov, J. V., *J. Mol. Biol.* **22**, 365 (1966).

large amount of derepression. With deproteinization, however, the amount of genomic information transcribed increases, and it is found that the *normal* ascites cell RNA's become less efficient in competing for the DNA sites represented in the derepression populations of complementary RNA. The quantitative extent of the increase in template activity which occurs when chromatin is deproteinized is given for a variety of other cell types in Table XV, which is reproduced from a recent article of Bonner *et al.* (544). Also provided there are relative data regarding the amount of histone and nonhistone protein present in the chromatins studied. *Since template restriction is cell-type specific, these chromatin proteins are clearly the agents which impose directly on the genome its differentiated patterns of gene repression.*

Which chromatin proteins are responsible and how they function is another question, however. In the experiment of Fig. 98, some of the proteins removed as the salt concentration is increased are nonhistone proteins. Paul and Gilmour (29a) have also shown that the qualitative range of genomic information available for transcription increases with removal of nonhistone proteins from chromatin. Nonhistone chromatin proteins were extracted from isolated cell nuclei in 1946 by Mirsky and Pollister (546), and they have since been the subject of a number of interesting investigations. Their likely implication in the mechanisms of genomic control is suggested by many items of evidence:

(1) Nonhistone nucleoproteins appear to exist *in situ* in some form of chemical binding to the chromatin DNA and to form complexes with DNA *in vitro* (547–551). Thus, for example, it has been shown that DNA melts at a higher temperature in the presence of acidic nuclear proteins (552).

(2) Nonhistone chromatin proteins constitute a significant fraction of the deoxyribonucleoprotein in the nucleus. For example, in the calf thymus nucleus acidic chromatin proteins constitute 21–25% of the total chromatin protein according to Wang (548). They are thus present in an amount which is of the same order of magnitude as the amount of DNA and the amount of histone in the nucleus (see also Table XV).

(3) Nonhistone chromatin nucleoproteins show a high metabolic activity, at least in some nuclei, being synthesized rapidly, and also turning over rapidly (548, 549, 553–556). Furthermore, it is known that in liver their rate of synthesis is correlated with the state of activity of the cells, and more specifically, with the extent to which the cells are engaged in informational RNA synthesis (556a).

(4) Acidic chromatin nucleoproteins also form complexes with histones (548, 549).

(5) Some evidence exists that the biosynthesis of some nonhistone proteins, including the acidic chromatin nucleoproteins, is a DNA-dependent process (548, 555, 557).

Despite these suggestive data, however, no clear conception as to their possible function in gene regulation as yet exists.

The nucleohistones, however, are more firmly implicated in the process of genomic control in animal cells, and the problem here is to determine what aspect(s) of the control machinery they are responsible for [the reader is here referred to reviews summarizing the intensive investigations to which histone function has recently been subjected (558–560)]. Histones constitute a portion of the deoxyribonucleoprotein mass which is equal to or greater than the mass of the nuclear DNA, with which they are in close association, being linked to the phosphoric acid groups of the DNA double helix. Histones, particularly lysine-rich histones, are clearly important in the physical organization of chromatin. Thus chromatin structure in the interphase nucleus is reversibly affected by the removal of lysine-rich histones (561), and recent X-ray diffraction studies suggest that histones are responsible for the ordered alignment of the DNA helices in chromatin (562). Histones drastically alter the structure of isolated lampbrush chromosomes, resulting in the rapid collapse of the loops (385). *In vitro* they behave as inhibitors for a variety of metabolic reactions, including the synthesis of ATP in isolated nuclei (563), nuclear protein synthesis (560), and even the function of mitochondrial enzyme systems (564). Allfrey, Littau, and Mirsky have demonstrated that histones are also potent inhibitors of DNA-dependent RNA synthesis *in vivo*, by adding them directly to isolated nuclei engaged in RNA synthesis (565). That the primary site of histone inhibition of RNA synthesis is in fact the polymerase reaction has been certified in several laboratories, in studies assaying the effects of histones on *in vitro* RNA synthesis systems [a review of these particular experiments is given by Bonner and Huang (566), who have been prominent contributors in this field.]

A key experiment of Allfrey *et al* (565) demonstrating that histones function as inhibitors of gene activity *in situ* as well as in subnuclear polymerase systems is portrayed in Fig. 99. By treating isolated calf thymus nuclei with trypsin the histones can be selectively hydrolyzed and leached out of the nucleus. In this manner over 80% of the nuclear histone may be removed, and the high specificity of the procedure is attested to by the fact that less than 5% of the nonhistone chromatin proteins are lost (566) and that RNA polymerase activity remains unimpared. The experiment shows that when the histones are removed from the living nuclei a three- to four-fold increase in RNA synthesis may occur. The trypsin inhibitor control shows that this cannot result from some unexpected primary effect of trypsin in the polymerase system per se, and readdition of histones results in the immediate resuppression of RNA synthesis. Removal of the histones alone, as opposed to the other chromatin proteins, may result in the near total derepression of chromatin DNA. Thus, Marushige and Bonner have shown that the template activity of liver chromatin extracted with 0.2 N HCl is almost as high as that of pure DNA at a point where 97% of the histones have been extracted, but 86% of the nonhistone proteins remain (543). On the other hand Paul and Gilmour report that less than half the genomic information monitored in totally deproteinized DNA is available for transcription in DNA from which the histones alone have been extracted (29a).

These experiments add up to the conclusion that histones act *in situ* as the biological inhibitors of genomic RNA synthesis. Their suggested role as regulators of genomic function implies something more than the ability to inhibit polymerase-mediated RNA synthesis, however. In order to regulate gene activity not only must the DNA-primed assembly of RNA

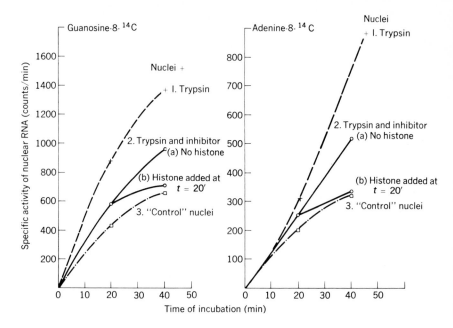

FIGURE 99. The effect of removing histones on nuclear RNA synthesis. The incorporation of guanosine-8-¹⁴C and adenine-8-¹⁴C is plotted as a function of the
time of incubation at 37°C. The lower curve (curve 3) shows the time
course of ¹⁴C uptake in control nuclei. The upper curve (curve 1) shows
the uptake in nuclei which were treated with trypsin to remove 70% of the
total histones. Curve 2 is for nuclei treated with trypsin plus soybean inhibitor to moderate the enzyme action. Curve 2b shows that the addition of
4 mg of histone at 20′ again suppresses nuclear RNA synhtesis. Allfrey,
V. G., Littau, V. C., and Mirsky, A. E., *Proc. Natl. Acad. Sci. U.S.* **49,**
414 (1963).

be prevented but also the distribution of repressed as opposed to active genes
must be correctly specified. We postpone for the moment further considerations as to what role in the genomic regulation process the histones are
most likely to play, pending the completion of this short summary of the
general characteristics of the regulatory systems operating in differentiated
cells. So far we have considered the temporal parameters of these systems;
we have touched on the level of gene activity and of repression in differentiated cells and the relative amount of change in the pattern of gene
function associated with alteration in the state of differentiation. We turn
now to the nature of the gene products synthesized at those sites of the
differentiated cell genome which are active.

gene products of the differentiated cell nucleus

Until recently it was considered that the population of RNA's synthesized in the animal cell nucleus consists of (*a*) 18S, 28S, and 5S ribosomal RNA's or their higher molecular weight precursors; (*b*) template or messenger RNA's such as can be isolated in protein-synthesizing polysomes; and (*c*) the transfer RNA's. At present, however, the simplicity of this scheme no longer appears justified. Thus new low molecular weight species of RNA have been reported, including one which seems to be associated particularly with intracellular membranes and is probably of mitochondrial origin [e.g., see Attardi and Attardi (567)]. Furthermore, a whole new class of informational nuclear RNA's has been discovered to exist in a variety of mammalian cell types. This development was actually foreshadowed by observations which have been available in the literature for some time. There has existed a curious, seeming contradiction between the data demonstrating a 1–3-hour half-life for the most rapidly decaying polysomal messenger RNA's in animal cells on the one hand, and a series of observations suggesting much more rapid turnover of newly synthesized RNA in these same cell types on the other. Decay studies carried out in actinomycin led to the biochemical detection of a rapidly turning over fraction of newly synthesized nonribosomal RNA's in HeLa cells by Scherrer et al. (486), and Girard et al. (487), for example. On the basis of radioautographic data, Harris also claimed that the HeLa cell nucleus synthesizes a very quickly degrading class of RNA's (568, 569). These observations can not be easily explained if the only types of high molecular weight RNA produced in the genome are the known polysomal messenger and ribosomal RNA's. Very recently, however, a novel category of giant-size, rapidly labeled nuclear RNA has been characterized by Attardi, Parnas, Hwang, and Attardi (570), and these authors have provided evidence that this RNA is definitely to be regarded as distinct from cytoplasmic messenger RNA. This short-lived RNA is extracted directly from the nuclei of immature duck erythrocytes labeled for brief periods *in vitro*. Sedimentation, specific activity, and base composition analyses demonstrate the existence in these nuclei of an actively synthesized fraction of RNA's sedimenting more rapidly than any other informational RNA's known outside of some giant viral RNA's. These RNA molecules are calculated to range from 2×10^6 to 10^7 in molecular weight units, with sedimentation coefficients up to 90S. In contrast the total cytoplasmic polysomal messenger RNA of the same cells sediments at 6–30S [it is to be noted that prior reports of extremely large nonribosomal RNA's have also existed in the literature for several years (571, 572)]. The turnover of these very large gene products is illustrated in the actinomycin experiments of Fig. 100. During the period of this

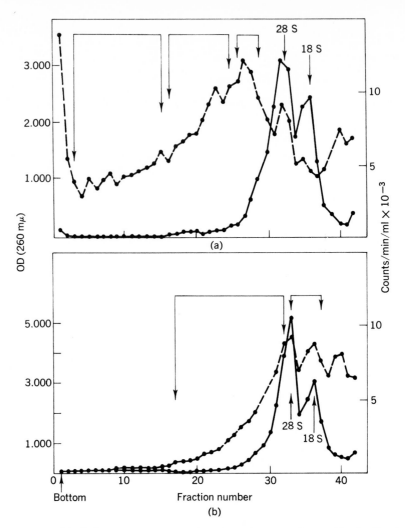

FIGURE 100. (a) Sedimentation pattern of total RNA extracted from blood cells of an
anemic duck exposed for 30 minutes to ^{32}P orthophosphate, as compared
to that of (b) RNA from cells labeled with ^{32}P for the same time and
subsequently treated for 3 hours with actinomycin D. Blood cells from a
phenylhydrazine-treated duck were incubated in a phosphate-free medium
in the presence of ^{32}P carrier-free orthophosphate. After a 30-minute incubation, one-half of the suspension was removed and the cells were harvested; to the other half actinomycin D was added at a concentration of
50 gm/ml, and incubation was continued for an additional 3 hours. Total
RNA was extracted from both samples and analyzed in a sucrose gradient.
The components corresponding to the portions of the sucrose gradient
patterns indicated by arrows were used for base composition analysis.
(Solid line) OD; (dashed line) acid-insoluble radioactive material. Attardi,
G., Parnas, H., Hwang, M-I. H., and Attardi, B., *J. Mol. Biol.* **20**, 145
(1966).

experiment the actinomycin-treated cells continue to convert ribosomal RNA precursors into mature ribosomal RNA subunits, and the cytoplasmic polysomal template remains completely stable (as expected for reticulocytes; see above). For the heaviest RNA's a half-life of only 30 minutes is estimated. Figure 101 illustrates an experiment demonstrating that the characteristically high sedimentation values of the nuclear RNA cannot result from adsorption of the RNA by traces of DNA in the preparation. Nor can aggregation, chelation, or presence of protein contaminants be implicated in accounting for the large size of these molecules (570). The rapidly decaying RNA is strictly confined to the nucleus, moreover, and on this ground it would appear impossible to regard it as a precursor of the cytoplasmic polysomal template RNA. Furthermore, its base composition is not strictly DNA-like, while the base composition of the cytoplasmic messenger RNA is similar to that of the DNA, particularly in its symmetry. For example, in the experiment of Fig. 100 the composition of the RNA greater than 75S in size (first set of arrows) is A-25.1, C-19.7, U-31.1, and G-24.1, while that of the cytoplasmic messenger extracted from 8–13S polysomes is A-26.6, C-25.6, U-26.0, and G-22.7. The decay kinetics of the rapidly labeled nuclear RNA also clearly precludes a precursor relationship with the cytoplasmic template RNA. What appear to be essentially similar species of RNA were reported at about the same time to be present in rapidly dividing HeLa cells as well (573–575). Here again RNA molecules are identified which are characterized by sedimentation constants ranging up to 80S, extremely high turnover rates, physical confinement to a nuclear location, and the same high-U nucleotide base composition observed in the duck reticulocytes. Since the cytoplasmic polysomal messenger of the HeLa cell displays a moderately high decay rate (see above) in contrast to that of the reticulocyte, it is more difficult in this cell type to exclude on kinetic grounds the possibility that the unstable heavy nuclear RNA is a precursor to the cytoplasmic template RNA. However, the difference in base composition between the two is again striking and would seem to argue against a precursor relationship; according to Houssais and Attardi (575) the base composition of > 75S HeLa cell nuclear RNA is A-21.3, C-26.4, U-31.0, and G-21.1, which is to be compared with A-28.0, C-24.3, U-28.1, and G-19.5 for the bona fide cytoplasmic messenger. Edstrom and Daneholt (575a) have identified a class of enormous RNA's in the polytene nuclei of Chironomus salivary gland cells. By isolating individual labeled chromosomes and extracting the RNA from them, these authors have shown that the RNA's, which sediment at values as high as 90S, are synthesized in all of the chromosomes. This, plus their evident polydispersity in gradients, indicates a high degree of molecular heterogeneity.

Recent experiments of Shearer and McCarthy (26) have proved with independent methods that rapidly turning-over informational RNA's exist

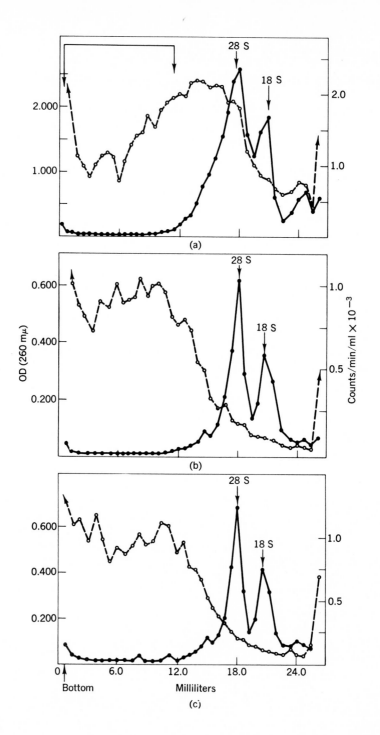

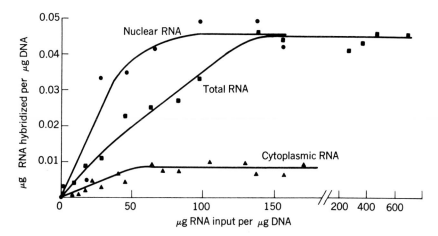

FIGURE 102. Saturation of complementary sites on DNA by randomly labeled, total nuclear, and cytoplasmic RNA. Various amounts of ^{32}P labeled L-cell RNA were incubated with filters containing 12μg of mouse DNA. Shearer, R. W., and McCarthy, B. J., *Biochemistry* **6**, 283 (1967).

which are confined to the cell nucleus and under normal circumstances are never present in the cytoplasm. These workers have studied the sequence complementarity existing between short-lived nuclear RNA and cytoplasmic messenger RNA populations in L cells by using RNA-DNA hybridization procedures. Their critical saturation experiment is reproduced in Fig. 102. The experiment shows that nuclear RNA hybridizes with five times more DNA than does cytoplasmic RNA under saturation conditions, which is to say that *far more genomic information is present in the rapidly synthesized nuclear RNA than in the cytoplasmic RNA.* Competition studies reported in the same paper show that all sequences represented in the cytoplasmic

FIGURE 101. Sedimentation pattern of the heavy components of fast-labeled RNA rerun on a sucrose gradient after a second DNase treatment. Total RNA was extracted from blood cells of an anemic duck exposed *in vitro* for 60 minutes to uridine-^{3}H and analyzed in a sucrose gradient. (a) The components corresponding to the portion of the pattern indicated by arrows were precipated with 2 volumes of ethanol in the presence of carrier duck rRNA, centrifuged down, dissolved in buffer, and divided into two equal portions: (b) one-half was left as a control; (c) one-half was treated with RNase-free DNase (10 μg/ml, 25°C, 20 minutes). Each of the two samples was then run on a 5–20% sucrose gradient. (Solid line with filled circles) OD; (dashed line with open circles) acid-insoluble radioactive material. Attardi, G., Parnas, H., Hwang, M-I. H., and Attardi, B., *J. Mol. Biol.* **20**, 145 (1966).

RNA are also present in the nuclear RNA but that much of the genomic information in the nuclear RNA is not present in the cytoplasmic RNA. Similar information exists for rabbit kidney cells (26) and for both normal and regenerating liver cells (111). Furthermore, Church and McCarthy have shown that a fraction of the new genes activated as a result of hepatectomy produce RNA's confined strictly to the nucleus (111). These results suggest that a basic revision of the usual ideas regarding the nature of gene activity may be in order. Thus, the animal cell nucleus appears to be engaged in large part in the transcription of genomic information which may or may not be utilized as template for nuclear protein synthesis, but it is normally not used as template for any of the protein synthesis carried out in the cytoplasm. In the L cell it is clear that, qualitatively, only a minority fraction of the readout is concerned with actual cytoplasmic template function. The high turnover rate, exclusive nuclear localization, unique base composition, and enormous molecular size of these RNA's mark them apart from any known previously, and it may be necessary to face the fact that the larger part of the information present in the total informational RNA pool of a cell is confined exclusively to nuclear RNA's of this class.

7

Some hypotheses regarding
the nature of genomic regulation
in differentiated cells

possible relevance of the operon concept

Given the properties observed, what mechanisms seem likely to operate in controlling the animal cell genome? Various hypotheses have been proposed in recent years in answer to this question, and even though it is impossible at present to proceed much beyond speculation in such a discussion it is of some interest to consider these ideas in terms of the actual observed characteristics of genomic regulation in animal cells. The most clearly defined candidate (504), and therefore the easiest to discuss, is the operon theory of Jacob and Monod (Fig. 95). From our earlier considerations regarding the nature of those bacterial repression-derepression systems to which the operon model has been successfully applied, however, it seems clear that this model possesses too narrow an applicability to serve as a general base for the understanding of genomic regulation in higher cells. The operon represents a system for the coordinate control of polycistronic loci, and even in bacteria these are scarcely ubiquitous. As we have seen, in eukaryotic organisms, even those as relatively simple as ascomycetes, certain of the same enzyme systems which are controlled coordinately in bacteria are genetically scattered and are controlled in noncoordinate fashion. In higher organisms no polycistronic messengers have so far been clearly validated, though Brown and Gurdon have proposed that size shifts occurring during postgastrular development from larger to smaller informational RNA molecules indicate the breakdown of polycistronic to monocistronic messengers (96). On the other hand, polysomes of a size appropriate for monocistronic messenger have been observed with the electron microscope in hemoglobin-synthesizing reticulocytes (576), and in other differentiated cell types as well (e.g., 438); in the hemoglobin case the template has been isolated and shown to be of exactly the predicted size for the *mono*cistronic messenger, about 150,000 in molecular weight (577). Furthermore, the 6–20S size of the total polysomal template RNA of HeLa cells (485, 490) and liver cells (481) would seem to preclude the presence of at least very large polycistronic messengers, unless they break down as soon as they are formed, prior to their incorporation in polysomes. Pretranslation breakdown, however, does not happen in the authenticated cases of operon polycistronic messenger (see above). Indications of coordinate control in a few enzyme systems of higher organisms probably implies the mediation of synthesis of these enzymes by polycistronic messenger [e.g., in the case of the glycolytic enzymes analyzed by Pette *et al.* (508) and Meir and Cotten (509)], but the burden of the evidence at present leans toward this being more an exception than the rule.

As we have already emphasized, operon regulation depends on a very rapid turnover of the structural gene messenger RNA, and also on the continuous firing of regulatory genes manufacturing rapidly turning over repressor proteins. These features are perfectly compatible with the extremely high turnover rates characteristic of informational RNA in bacteria, but they do not mesh well with the known characteristics of many induction and repression systems encountered in the differentiation of higher cell types. Consider embryonic or hormonal induction, for example, where an initial brief exposure to an inducing agent may result in a long-lasting, massive, chain reaction response at the genome level. During most of the response period the inducing agents are no longer required, even in dividing tissues. Though such a pattern is in principle obtainable from compound operon systems (Fig. 95b), these systems all involve continuous firing of negative regulatory genes, and new difficulties accrue from this characteristic in attempting to apply the operon models to the problem of animal cell regulation. Consider, for example, the state of near-complete repression which obtains in the late ovarian oocyte or the nucleated erythrocyte: Many repressive regulatory genes cannot be firing continuously in these quiescent cells, and one would be forced to argue that the regulatory gene products once formed must be stable in order to account for the general state of repression by mechanisms of the type portrayed in Fig. 95. In this way the regulatory genes could be repressed as well in almost totally repressed cells. But, then, what represses them? To postulate intermittent regulatory gene activity, this being the corollary of the idea of long-lived repressor, results simply in multiplying the control problem, since we now would have regulatory genes which must be derepressed at the appropriate times as well as structural genes which must be derepressed at the appropriate times. These difficulties stem from an incompatibility between a high immediacy control system depending for repression on continuous gene action, as it depends for most of its other metabolic processes on continuous gene action, and a system which in contrast tends mainly to be repressed, and which frequently separates the time when genomic control is organized (transcription) from the resulting cellular event. A way out of this problem would follow only if the animal cell genome is constituted mainly of giant, polycistronic, operon-like control units, each with a certain genomic regulatory machinery, if the latter amounts to a very small percentage of the total genome so that continuous firing of the regulatory genes could actually be taking place even in apparently repressed cells. Here we encounter other problems, however, such as the fact that given the number of cell types, the diversity of patterns of gene activity in higher organisms, and the existence of cells producing mainly one product (e.g., reticulocytes), giant, obligatorily linked control units seem a priori unlikely. Even in the known bacterial operons, furthermore, the number of genes with regulator effects per operon are of the same order as the number of structural genes in the operon (for example, two regulators for the 3-gene lac system, and at least five for the 10-gene his system), and regulation in the metazoan genome can scarcely be expected to require less machinery on a relative basis than it does in the bacterial genome. It is worth noting that regulatory genes are not to be regarded as tiny fractions of the usual structural genes in size, for the studies of Ptashne (538) and of Riggs *et al* (538a, 538b) have shown that at least two regulator gene products are proteins of appreciable dimensions, respectively two and three times as large as that of a hemoglobin subunit.

Though bacterial repression-derepression systems of the operon type probably represent an unlikely model for the *general* interpretation of genomic regulation in higher cells, polycistronic, operon-like control systems may indeed exist in the genomes of these cells. A possible candidate, for example, is the complex ribosomal RNA polycistron which appears to be composed of hundreds of alternating, contiguous 18S and 28S ribosomal RNA genes (389, 389a). In the cytoplasm of unfertilized amphibian eggs, to continue the analogy, there is present an inhibitor of RNA synthesis (296, 578) which specifically blocks ribosomal but not informational or transfer RNA synthesis.

the nature of gene regulation in differentiated cells

The molecular agents which modulate, interfere with, or inhibit genomic RNA synthesis are often termed "repressors" in both bacterial and animal cell systems. General use of the germ "repressor" may result in a costly error, however, for as employed with reference to bacterial repression-derepression systems the term "repressor" carries denotations which cannot be applied to the metazoan case without tacitly accepting certain basic and unproved assumptions regarding the nature of repression. In the bacterial repression-derepression models (whether or not of the polycistronic operon type) the protein repressors of gene action clearly bear specific structural information which permits them to bind specifically to the DNA loci which are to be repressed, thereby preventing RNA synthesis or the initiation of RNA synthesis. As long as they remain present the genes for which they have affinity remain inactive, and, as we have seen, direct biochemical evidence for repressor proteins with specific affinities for certain sites of the DNA genome now exists (536–538). Bacteria, however, contain no histones. In considering higher cells it is necessary a priori to distinguish two separate problems in accounting for the quiescence of most of the genome: (a) the molecular nature of the actual *inhibitors of DNA-dependent RNA synthesis* in the chromatin, and (b) the molecular nature of the process by which the correct genes are *selected* to be inhibited (and/or activated).

Use of the term "repressor" conceals the possible dual nature of the overall process beneath the assumption that the selective function depends simply on the specificity of binding characteristic of the molecules also fulfilling the inhibitory function (a). Now it is very likely, as we have seen, that histones are the molecules responsible for the *inhibition* of RNA synthesis in most of the genome of higher cells, but serious difficulties arise in attempting to assign to histones the *selective* role of chemically specifying the genes they are to inhibit. Histones bind to any DNA (or to any other acid polyanion) and there is no evidence that histones possess the ability to recognize and selectively bind to any particular polydeoxyribonucleotide sequences (579). Furthermore, histones appear to include something less than 30 diverse components [see Murray (580) for references], obviously several orders of magnitude less than there are particular genes to be repressed. Studies of the histone fractions present in diverse tissues fail to reveal any significant histospecific differences. For example, it has been reported by Hnilica (581) that N- and C-terminal amino acids of histone fraction F2b from rat spleen, calf thymus, rat thymus, Walker-256 rat sarcoma, and chicken red blood cells are perfectly identical, as are the complete F2b amino acid compositions in the case of Walker rat sarcoma and calf thymus. Similarly, histone fractions F1, F2a, F2b, and F3 are completely identical in normal and in regenerating rat liver and in rat hepatoma, spleen, and testis (582). Nor are differences detectable in the total acrylamide gel electrophoresis patterns for the histones of rat liver, kidney, brain, heart, and lung (582a). The total histone to DNA ratios also remain constant as various tissues are compared, irrespective of their relative states of activity (583).

At the level of chromatin fine structure certain fractions of histones do display a kind of selectivity in binding, however. This has been shown by Littau, Burdick, Allfrey, and Mirsky (561) in their study of the role played by histones in the maintenance of the structural states assumed by chromatin in the interphase nucleus. At least the major part of that fraction of the genome which at any one time is active is located, in such a nucleus, in structurally diffuse chromatin [(24); see, e.g., Fig. 2]. The inactive (majority) fraction of the genome is mainly present, on the other hand, in condensed chromatin masses, and the experiments of Littau *et al.* indicate that in such masses dense packing of the individual nucleoprotein fibers results from fiber cross-linking by lysine-rich histones. In the calf thymus nucleus the lysine-rich histones amount to only 20% of the total histone content. If the lysine-rich histones are selectively extracted from the nucleus the condensed chromatin unravels and its characteristic, heavily clumped form opens up; by adding back to such extracted nuclei exogenous, lysine-rich histones the condensed form can be experimentally reestablished. Readdition of arginine-rich histones is ineffective. Thus at the level of gross chromatin structure, i.e., at the level of spatial separation of active from inactive chromatin fractions, at least the lysine-rich histones appear to play a specific selective role, since they are bound in such a manner as to cross-link those particular areas of chromatin which are to be maintained in a condensed state. This function emphasizes the role of histones as the *agents of inhibition of gene activity,* but it leaves unanswered the nature of histone function in the *selective specification of the individual genes* which are to be inhibited. Nonetheless, it is to be observed that in dealing with the role of lysine-rich histones, we face, although on a different scale, a very similar problem: It is not known how to account for the special disposition of the lysine-rich histones in condensed chromatin, as opposed to their disposition in diffuse, active chromatin where they are present in the same relative concentration but are not engaged in interfiber cross-linking.

Three classes of alternative follow from this point, with reference to the inhibitory function of histones at the molecular level of specific gene recognition:

(1) Histones serve as the direct inhibitors of RNA synthesis, at least in a majority of the repressed sites, while other molecules mediate the selection of which genomic sites are to be inhibited and which activated.

(2) Only a small number of histones is actually required for gene control because the genes are linked together in a small number of gigantic control groups activated or repressed in concert. A model of this kind was recently proposed by Goodwin (584). This model rests on certain very problematical assumptions, however. One of these is that the animal cell genome possesses some 10^4 structural genes (only 2–3 times the number

estimated for *E. coli*) and that the remainder of the genetic material need not be included in the regulation scheme. In animal cells, however, the amount of DNA is so enormous that 10^4 structural genes would constitute only a small fraction of the total. Whether the excess DNA is replicate or near replicate in information content (108), it is clearly as subject to repression control as is the single-copy fraction of the genome, since 80% or 90% of the *total* animal cell genome is empirically observed to be repressed. As Bonner has pointed out, even if the excess DNA is per se control machinery, in higher cells selective regulation of this fraction of the genome is also of critical importance (585). The Goodwin model seeks to explain how 10^2 histone species could constitute the animal cell control machinery by postulating that specificity of each histone is sufficiently limited so that 10^2 genes could be recognized by it (these genes constituting a control group), but so far no histone has been shown to be able to "recognize" any particular sequence of DNA (585).

(3) A third alternative is that chemical modification of histone, in particular acetylation, could somehow confer enough diversity on the histone populations to permit chemical recognition by them of the required number of individual genetic sites. Histone acetylation takes place after the histone molecule is assembled, and it occurs in the chromatin, rather than elsewhere in the nucleus (586). Allfrey *et al.* have shown that acetylated arginine-rich histone *in vitro* is a less effective inhibitor of the RNA polymerase reaction than is nonacetylated histone. In subsequent studies Allfrey and his associates have accumulated evidence indicating that change in the state of histone acetylation is correlated with change in the state of gene activation in a number of *in vivo* systems (reviewed in 587). Thus, in the diffuse, active chromatin of the thymus nucleus, histone acetylation is far more intense than in inactive condensed chromatin. Histone acetylation is inactive in the quiescent nuclei of mature duck erythrocytes, however. A particularly interesting comparison concerns the effect of phytohemagglutinin on histone acetylation in two reticuloendothelial cell types which are known to respond oppositely to this agent. In human lymphocytes a sharp increase in the rate of RNA synthesis occurs within a few minutes of exposure to phytohemagglutinin. In this cell type an immediate increase in the rate of acetylation follows the addition of phytohemagglutinin, preceding the change in RNA synthesis rate, but in equine granulocytes, a cell type in which RNA synthesis is depressed rather than activated by phytohemagglutinin, histone acetylation is also depressed. In regenerating liver the turnover rate of histone acetyl groups declines from the control level during the period of intense RNA synthesis which follows hepatectomy. Histone acetylation in liver also responds to hydrocortisone treatment which, as we

have seen (Fig. 93), causes immediate changes in the spectrum of RNA molecules synthesized in the liver nuclei. Within 30 minutes of hydrocortisone injection into adrenolectomized rats, histone acetylation is stepped up in this tissue. By contrast, in lymphocytes, where RNA synthesis is rapidly repressed by hydrocortisone treatment (Fig. 94) the latter also represses histone acetylation. These findings demonstrate a tight correlation between histone acetylation and genomic activation, but the nature of the connection between these events is still unknown. The acetyl groups are present mainly as N-terminal derivatives and possibly as O-seryl acetyl as well (588). The amount of possible increase in histone diversity resulting from histone acetylation thus seems too limited to permit the hypothesis of selective gene recognition by a population of specific histones. Alternatively, since the disposition of histones in chromatin is known to be of significance in the maintenance of active, as opposed to inactive chromatin structures (561), and since acetylation is correlated with the active chromatin state both structurally and physiologically, histone acetylation may be required in order for the structural change associated with alteration in gene activity to take place without acetylation being involved directly in the primary selection of the active sites. Thus, Allfrey et al. conclude from their studies that "a change in the structure of the chromatin brought about by or coincident with acetylation of the histones is a necessary prerequisite to the synthesis of new RNA's at previously repressed gene loci" (587).

If it is tentatively concluded that histones in their various forms function as inhibitors of RNA synthesis, as essential structural elements of chromatin, and as facilitators of genomic activation, but not as the cistron-specifying selective agents in genomic regulation, then another class of molecule must be implicated in order to account for the latter aspect of regulation in higher cells. In this case, furthermore, the repressors operating in the known bacterial repressor-derepressor systems cannot serve as literal models for the regulative elements of active animal cells since the bacterial repressors apparently perform both the selective and inhibitory functions at one and the same time. If they are indeed distinct in molecular terms, the separation of these functions in higher cells perhaps follows from the evolutionary substitution of a greater diversity in the degree of immediacy in gene control over cell function for the instantaneous, continuous action control systems characteristic in bacteria, except for unusual cases. It would seem advantageous, for example, to be able to specify at some particular moment a genomic site which is to remain repressed for hours or days or months to come without requiring continuous repetition of the selective (specifying) action. Obviously other simplifications in the control problem also will accrue if, in the face of an increased range of genomic information requiring regulation, a very small range of genomic *inhibitors* can be utilized, with specificity of regulation confined to those moments when the pattern of gene activity is to undergo change.

Turning to the possible nature of these specifying elements, an area of discussion which is almost purely speculative, there exist several alternatives which cannot at present be excluded. The molecues responsible for *recognition* of the genomic sites to be activated or repressed could be nonhistone chromatin proteins, or other proteins, or they could be nonprotein macromolecules, the most likely of which is probably RNA. The nonhistone chromatin proteins, as noted above, bind to DNA and histone, turn over rapidly and may (or may not) be present in great diversity. Paul and Gilmour (29a) have recently presented experimental data which suggest that the qualitative specification of that portion of the genome which is inhibited from transcription by the histones actually depends on the nonhistone proteins present in the chromatin. Thus, according to hybridization experiments, a normal spectrum of RNA molecules is synthesized in reconstituted chromatin formed by adding the nonhistone proteins of calf thymus nuclei plus calf thymus histones to DNA, while DNA plus histones alone results in a totally inhibited preparation. Some nucleoproteins are actively phosphorylated, and like acetylation this phenomenon appears to be closely correlated with the processes leading to gene activation (589, 590). Nonhistone nuclear phosphoprotein binds to histone (591) and tends to be concentrated in active chromatin fractions (592). At present, however, it appears most likely that nuclear phosphoprotein metabolism is also involved with alterations in chromatin structure associated with genomic activation.

The molecular species which must selectively recognize a particular genetic site must possess the property of binding (reversibly) with given sequences of genetic DNA and under normal conditions not with other DNA sequences. Various precedents exist for specific molecular recognition between proteins and polynucleotide sequences. These include: (a) the specific recognition of and reversible binding to the appropriate transfer RNA's on the part of amino acid activating enzymes; (b) the binding of DNA glucosylating enzymes which operate on particular viral DNA's; (c) the binding of other enzymes which alter certain nucleic acids but not others, e.g., the methylating enzymes affecting ribosomal RNA; (d) the repressor proteins for the *E. coli* lac operon and the λ phage (see above). These examples, particularly the last, prove that specific polynucleotide-protein recognition and binding are possible, and therefore that a theory of selective gene recognition mediated by specific proteins is feasible. It is obvious that RNA gene products, by virtue of their intrinsic structure, also contain the information necessary for selective gene recognition and binding. Thus, any RNA molecule could recognize specifically and bind to that portion of the genome homologous to the template on which it was originally synthesized.

At this point it is necessary to consider the question of whether genetic regulation in animal cells operates by way of repression of an otherwise totally active genome or activation of an otherwise totally repressed genome. The former is an underlying assumption in any repression-derepression scheme based on selective recognition of genomic sites by *repressor* products of regulatory genes, as, for example, in the operon model. In bacteria a tremendous proportion of the genome is normally operative, as we have emphasized, and genomic repression in bacteria can be (rather crudely) viewed as a maneuver occasionally required by certain changes in the environmental situation. The opposite condition is manifest in higher cells, however, judging from the minor fraction of the genome which is normally found to be active in these cells. In animal cells life begins with near-total repression, and in the history of each cell line transient periods of enlarged gene activity occur, frequently succeeded by return to a state of general repression. Proportionately the major changes in the state of gene activity during development and growth are in the level of activation. Thus, a priori it might be assumed to be simpler for the selective machinery to *specify* 2–10% of the genes in a cell for activation than for it to *specify* 90–98% for repression.

A strong argument to the effect that regulation in animal cells should be carried out by means of activation of an otherwise repressed genome rather than the converse can also be derived from the temporal asymmetry of activation and repression in higher cells. Thus immediate *activation* is available within seconds or minutes in animal cells, but in every known mammalian system, in contrast, a lag of at least several hours duration separates shutoff of structural gene transcription and disappearance of the template molecules from the cytoplasmic polysomes. The study of immediacy relations in higher cell types thus leads to the interesting conclusion that *at the genomic level rapid cellular response to environmental signals* can come in higher cells only via the activation of previously repressed genes, and it cannot be obtained by repression of previously activated genes.

A further argument concerns the nature of egg cytoplasm effects on the embryonic cell genomes. Here we have a simple test: If selective repressors are stored in the egg cytoplasm, extirpation of a portion of the cytoplasm in an animal with asymmetric patterns of cytoplasmic localization should result in abnormal gene activation in the embryo. However, if selective gene activators are stored in the egg cytoplasm the removal of a morphogenetically significant cytoplasmic region should result in failure of activation. As detailed in Section II, the latter is always the result of such operations.

The animal cell genome would thus appear to be regulated though the specification of active loci in an otherwise repressed genome, by means of macromolecules possessing the specific capability of recognizing the DNA sites to be activated. These regulatory molecules, furthermore, must stem originally from other regions of the genome, and this much animal cell regulation systems must share with bacterial repression-derepression systems whether of the operon type or otherwise. The relatively stable functional state of both repressed and activated genomic regions in animal cells appears, however, to depend on histones and possibly on nonhistone chromatin proteins as well. Now if a bacterium finds it necessary to have five regulatory genes affecting the operation of one simple, substrate-sensitive amino acid synthesis pathway (the histidine pathway in *Salmonella*) the amount of selective regulatory machinery required for the functional integration of the animal cell genome in a complex process such as development must be very large indeed. The ratio of regulatory to structural genes therefore must be extremely high in animal cells, a position which may help to explain the enormous amount of DNA in these cells compared to that in the bacterium. Vogel (593) has estimated that the amount of genetic material in the human, for example, may be as high as 100 times the amount estimated to be contained in a reasonable number of structural genes, and a number of authors have suggested that the regulatory machinery of the genome might account for some of this large amount of DNA (e.g., 26, 570, 585, 593): As the complexity of an organism increases the relative amount of regulative genomic machinery must increase much faster.

If much of the genome in a higher cell is indeed regulative machinery concerned with the selection and specification of the genes which are to be activated, and with the integration of this activity, then much of the activity occurring in the genome at any one time might be expected to be regulative gene activity. In the L cell, as Shearer and McCarthy have shown [(26); Fig. 102] most of the gene activity (qualitatively speaking, in terms of apparent diversity of genetic information) is in fact the synthesis of RNA's confined to the cell nucleus. Evidence for this is available for other cell types as well, judging from the relatively rapid synthesis and location of this class of RNA molecules in HeLa cells, reticulocytes, etc. (references are given above). It can be postulated that the nuclear RNA's are the regulatory gene products of the animal cell, and both Shearer and McCarthy (26) and Attardi et al. (570) have suggested that these RNA's serve a regulatory function. The rapid turnover rates characteristic of these RNA's lend direct support to this suggestion. Thus the regulation machinery, if it is to be responsive to change, cannot afford the long delays in response time tolerable in the cytoplasmic messenger population: Regulatory gene products should decay very rapidly and be replaced rapidly. (From this point of view the nucleus of the eukaryotic cell could be considered a device for isolating the very rapidly turning-over regulatory RNA population from the rest of the cellular machinery.) If the nuclear RNA's do serve a regulatory function, their high turnover rate can be interpreted in terms of the responsiveness of the interaction between the outside environment and the regulatory machinery. A potentially responsive animal cell regula- tion system would be one in which the spectrum of genes *active* depends on a dynamic, continuous process of regulatory gene activity, though the nature of the relations between environment and regulatory genomic ele- ments is at present a most obscure matter. Equally obscure are the mechan- isms by which the products of regulatory genes might function.

We do not even know, for example, whether the RNA's confined to the cell nucleus are used *in vivo* as templates for protein synthesis. A curious speculation suggests itself in this connection, viz., that the presence in higher cell genomes (though not in bacterial genomes) of a large amount of genetic material which is internally redundant is related to the putative regulatory function of much of the animal cell genome. Thus the genome could be organized as a series of overlapping and interlocking groups of genes with partial complementarity among them serving as the primitive structural base for selective recognition among the regulative and structural elements, or among the various regulative elements. Other hypotheses as to the sig- nificance of the internally redundant sequences of higher cell genomes in- clude the possibility that these sequences represent amplifications of the genetic potential to synthesize certain much needed RNA's (variants of this idea are discussed in Section III). Alternatively, it is possible that most of the copies in a given gene family are inactive and remain present only as vestigial holdovers from the prior evolutionary history of the species. The latter interpretation, however, would seem inconsistent with the observa- tion of Mirsky and Ris that for a given cell type (erythrocytes) cell size is correlated with nuclear DNA content, at least in comparisons among diverse chordate species (404). In some organisms the genome is almost entirely composed of redundant gene families (108), and genome size has probably to do largely with the degree of redundancy. Thus, if the relation between DNA content and cell size is general, it is hard to see why degree of redundancy would be correlated with cell size if the redundant gene copies are vestigial and inactive. Irrespective of whether or not there is any fundamental link between the presence of near-homologous gene families and the putative regulatory functions we have attributed to the animal cell genome, it seems clear that both features exist and that both must deeply affect the basic structure of the genome.

* conclusion

This rather speculative discussion has perhaps led too far afield from the problems of development. The little understood genomic regulation systems we have been considering lie at the base of the phenomenon of development, however, and it is obvious that until we are able to comprehend the functional outlines of these systems, no truly satisfactory interpretation of the onset of differentiation will be possible.

From the foregoing discussion we might tentatively conclude that the animal cell regulation system has the following general properties:

(1) Most of the genome is inactive in any one cell at any one time.

(2) Regulation occurs by activation of otherwise inactive genomic sites rather than the reverse.

(3) Change from inactivity to activity (and vice versa) is mediated by changes in the chromatin proteins.

(4) Structural gene products are used as template for protein synthesis, and these gene products possess varying lengths of life. Template life is inversely proportional to the immediacy with which synthesis of the respective proteins can be controlled simply through cessation of template synthesis in the nucleus.

(5) Much of the genome is regulatory, and a large portion of the genome is redundant in informational content.

(6) Some regulatory gene products must decay with significantly greater rapidity than do the cytoplasmic messenger RNA's of structural genes if the genomic system is to be optimally reactive to external signals.

(7) Regulatory elements must be able to affect other regulatory elements as well as structural genes in order to account for the flexible integration of large groups of genes in processes of differentiation. A certain amount of redundancy in control patterns probably also exists [i.e., the same structural gene being subject to several types of control (584)]. These requirements would both necessitate a proportionately large amount of regulative as compared to structural genomic machinery.

It is also possible that structural genes serve as regulatory elements, and that there is no real distinction; but in view of the recent finding of nucleus-confined RNA's not homologous with cytoplasmic RNA's, and of the authenticated existence of bacterial regulatory genes, this would seem less likely.

As we have seen, there are certain situations where rapid reaction to changing external conditions on the part of the genomic control mechanism is not a requirement, e.g., in the storage of genomic information in the oocyte. The evidence reviewed in Section II regarding the localization phenomenon suggests that the *information stored in the egg cytoplasm includes the products of genomic regulatory elements,* as well as gene products (of structural genes) which are used directly as maternal messenger for the synthesis of useful cytoplasmic proteins. If regulation of the differentiated cell genome is, in fact, mediated by the gene products of regulatory genes, then localization of these gene products in egg cytoplasm would explain the phenomenon of specification of blastomere lineage fate by constituents of egg cytoplasm. The initial patterns of differentiation appearing in the early embryo must result from the imposition of certain patterns of gene activity in the embryo nuclei. The initial *self-differentiations* on the part of the blastomere lineages, then, could be regarded as the effect of the regulatory gene products present in the cytoplasm of the early blastomeres. The earliest program for embryo genome activity in this case would be that resident in the regulatory gene products synthesized long previously, in oogenesis, and stored in the egg cytoplasm until the latter is partitioned among the blastomeres by cleavage. If the regulatory gene products function as *selective activators* of the embryo genomes, they would possess all the characteristics which the factors active in localization must have in order to account for the localization phenomenon (see Section II). In addition, an explanation for the apparently large informational content of the gene products stored during oogenesis would be at hand (cf. Section III). From the point of view of this hypothesis the main difference between the oocyte-embryo system and other differentiated cell systems has to do with the *dynamics* of the regulation process: In cells such as the early reticulocyte or tissue culture cells the regulation system itself has a high rate of renewal and thus short time constants, while the equivalent gene products in the oocyte-embryo are sequestered and stored until use. We can perhaps go one step further and relate the extreme temporal stability of the oocyte informational RNA stockpile to the lack of need for feedback regulation in the early embryogenesis of lower animals. This is the same argument we used previously in discussing lack of immediacy in gene control over maternal template use, i.e., over utilization of the first *structural* gene products needed in early development. In other words, we can hypothesize the existence of varying degrees of immediately in *regulatory* gene product utilization just as such variation exists in *structural* gene product utilization. Thus still another level of control can be imagined. Perhaps in this we are offered an insight into the elegance and the complexity of the regulation system, the understanding of which is now a major objective in the experimental study of gene action in development.

Bibliography

1. Driesch, H., Entwicklungsmechanik. *Anat. Anz.* **7**, 584 (1892).
2. Morgan, T. H., ed., *Experimental Embryology.* New York: Columbia University Press, 1927, pp. 468–492.
3. Wilson, E. B., *The Cell in Development and Heredity.* New York: Macmillan, 1925, pp. 1059–1062.
4. Bridges, C. B., "The Bar 'gene' a duplication." *Science* **83**, 210 (1936).
5. Stone, L. S., "Neural retina degeneration followed by regeneration from surviving retinal pigment cells in grafted adult salamander eyes." *Anat. Record* **106**, 89 (1950).
6. Maximow, A., "Cultures of blood leucocytes from lymphocyte and monocyte to connective tissue." *Arch. Exptl. Zellforsch. Gewebezucht.* **5**, 169 (1927).
7. Petrakis, N. L., Davis, M., and Lucia, S. P., "The *in vivo* differentiation of human leukocytes into histiocytes, fibroblasts and fat cells in subcutaneous diffusion chambers." *Blood* **17**, 109 (1961).
8. Mirsky, A. E., and Ris, H., "Variable and constant components of chromosomes." *Nature* **163**, 666 (1949).
9. Boivin, A., Vendrely, R., and Vendrely, C., "Biochimie de l'herédite.—L'acide désoxyribonucléique du noyau cellulaire, dépositaire des caractères heréditaires; arguments d'ordre analytique." *Compt. Rend.* **226**, 1061 (1948).
10. Gurdon, J. B., "Adult frogs derived from the nuclei of single somatic cells." *Develop. Biol.* **4**, 256 (1962).
11. Gurdon, J. B., and Uehlinger V., " 'Fertile' intestine nuclei." *Nature* **210**, 1240 (1966).
12. Berendes, H. D., and Keyl, H. G., "Distribution of DNA in heterochromatin and euchromatin of polytene nuclei of *Drosophila hydei.*" *Genetics* **57**, 1 (1967).
13. Breuer, M. E., and Pavan, C., "Behavior of polytene chromosomes of *Rhynchosciara angelae* at different stages of larval development." *Chromosoma* **7**, 371 (1955).
14. Ritossa, F. M., Atwood, K. C., Lindsley, D. L., and Spiegelman, S., "On the chromosomal distribution of DNA complementary to ribosomal and soluble RNA." *Nat. Cancer Inst. Monograph* **23**, 449 (1966).
15. McCarthy, B. J., and Hoyer, B. H., "Identity of DNA and diversity of messenger RNA molecules in normal mouse." *Proc. Natl. Acad. Sci. U.S.* **52**, 915 (1964).
16. Morgan, T. H., *Embryology and Genetics.* New York: Columbia University Press, 1934.
17. Mirsky, A. E., "The chemistry of heredity." *Sci. Am.* **188**, No. 27, 47 (1953).
18. Mirsky, A. E., "Some chemical aspects of the cell nucleus." *In* L. C. Dunn, ed., *Genetics in the Twentieth Century.* New York: Macmillan, 1951, pp. 127–153.
19. Stedman, E., and Stedman, E., "Cell specificity of histones." *Nature* **166**, 780 (1950).
20. Sonneborn, T. M., "The cytoplasm in heredity." *Heredity* **4**, 11 (1950).
21. Allfrey, V. G., and Mirsky, A. E., "Some effects of substituting the deoxyribonucleic acid of isolated nuclei with other polyelectrolytes." *Proc. Natl. Acad. Sci. U.S.* **44**, 981 (1958).

22. Allfrey, V. G., and Mirsky, A. E., "Evidence for the complete DNA-dependence of RNA synthesis in isolated thymus nuclei." *Proc. Natl. Acad. Sci. U.S.* **48**, 1590 (1962).

23. Frenster, J. H. Allfrey, V. G., and Mirsky, A. E., "Repressed and active chromatin isolated from interphase lymphocytes." *Proc. Natl. Acad. Sci. U.S.* **50**, 1026 (1963).

24. Littau, V. C., Allfrey, V. G., Frenster, J. H., and Mirsky, A. E., "Active and inactive regions of nuclear chromatin as revealed by electron miscroscope autoradiography." *Proc. Natl. Acad. Sci. U.S.* **52**, 93 (1964).

25. Davidson, E. H., Crippa, M., Kramer, F. R., and Mirsky, A. E., "Genomic function during the lampbrush chromosome stage of amphibian oogenesis." *Proc. Natl. Acad. Sci. U.S.* **56**, 856 (1966).

26. Shearer, R. W., and McCarthy, B. J., "Evidence for ribonucleic acid molecules restricted to the cell nucleus." *Biochemistry* **6**, 283 (1967).

27. Paul, J., and Gilmour, R. S., "Template activity of DNA is restricted in chromatin." *J. Mol. Biol.* **16**, 242 (1966).

28. Georgiev, G. P., Ananieva, L. N., and Kozlov, J. V., "Stepwise removal of a protein from a deoxyribonucleoprotein complex and de-repression of the genome." *J. Mol. Biol.* **22**, 365 (1966).

29. Paul, J., and Gilmour, R. S., "Restriction of deoxyribonucleic acid template activity in chromatin is organ-specific." *Nature* **210**, 992 (1966).

29a. Paul, J., and Gilmour, R. S., "Organ-specific restriction of transcription in mammalian chromatin." *J. Mol. Biol.* **34**, 305 (1968).

30. Miyagi, M., Kohl, D., and Flickinger, R. A., "Detection of qualitative differences between the RNA of livers and kidneys of adult chickens and a temporal and regional study of liver RNA in chick embryos." *J. Exptl. Zool.* **165**, 147 (1967).

30a. Thaler, M. M., and Villee, C. A., "Template activities in normal, regenerating, and developing rat liver chromatin." *Proc. Natl. Acad. Sci. U.S.* **58**, 2055 (1967).

30b. O'Malley, B., McGuire, W. L., and Middleton, P. A., "Altered gene expression during differentiation: Population changes in hybridizable RNA after stimulation of the chick oviduct with oestrogen." *Nature* **218**, 1249 (1968).

31. Boveri, T., "An organism produced sexually without characteristics of the mother." *Am. Naturalist* **27**, 222 (1893).

32. Boveri, T., "Zwei Fehlerquellen bei Merogonieversuchen und die Entwicklungsfä higheit merogonischer und partiellmerogonischer Seeigelbastarde." *Arch. Entwicklungsmech. Organ.* **44**, 417 (1918).

33. von Ubisch, L., "Ueber Seeigelmerogone." *Pubbl. Staz. Zool. Napoli* **25**, 246 (1954).

34. Hörstadius, S., "Studien über heterosperme Seeigelmerogone nebst Bemerkungen über einige Keimblattchimaeren." *Mem. Musee Hist. Nat. Belg.* [2] **3**, 801 (1936).

35. Kölreuter, J. G., "Preliminary report of experiments and observations concerning some aspects of the sexuality of plants." (Translated) *In* B. R. Voeller, ed., *Classic Papers in Development and Heredity: The Chromosome Theory of Inheritance.* New York: Appleton, 1968.

36. Fol., H., "Recherches sur la fécondation et le commencement de l'héogénie chez divers animaux." *Mem. Soc. Phys. Geneve* **26**, 12 (1878).

37. Zamboni, L., Mishell, D. R., Jr., Bell, J. H., and Baca, M., "Fine structure of the human ovum in the pronuclear stage." *J. Cell Biol.* **30**, 579 (1966).

38. Van Beneden, E., "Recherches sur la maturation de l'ouef et la fécondation et la division cellulaire." *Arch. Biol.* **4**, 265 (1883).

39. Baltzer, F., "Uber die Beziehung zwischen dem Chromatin und der Entwickelung und Vererbungsrichtung bei Echinodermenbastarden." *Arch. Zellforsch.* **5**, 497 (1910).

40. Morgan, T. H., *Experimental Embryology.* New York: Columbia University Press, 1927, pp. 608–656.

41. Whiteley, A. H., and Baltzer, F., "Development respiratory rate and content of desoxyribonucleic acid in the hybrid *Paracentrotus* ♀ × *Arbacia* ♂." *Pubbl. Staz. Zool. Napoli* **30**, 402 (1958).

42. Chen, P. S., "Biochemistry of nucleo-cytoplasmic interactions in morphogenesis." *In* R. Weber, ed., *The Biochemistry of Animal Development.* New York: Academic Press, 1967, Vol. 2, pp. 115–191.

43. Fankhauser, G., "The role of nucleus and cytoplasm." *In* B. H. Willier, P. A. Weiss, and V. Hamburger, eds., *Analysis of Development.* Philadelphia: Saunders, 1956, pp. 126–150.

44. Tennent, D. H., "The early influence of the spermatozoan upon the characters of echinoid larvae." *Carnegie Inst. Wash. Publ.* **182**, 129 (1914).

45. Driesch, H., "Uber rein-mütterliche Charaktere an Bastardlarven von Echiniden." *Arch. Entwicklungsmech. Organ.* **7**, 65 (1898).

46. Moore, J. A., "Developmental rate of hybrid frogs." *J. Exptl. Zool.* **86**, 405 (1941).

47. Hennen, S., "Chromosomal and embryological analyses of nuclear changes occurring in embryos derived from transfers of nuclei between *Rana pipiens* and *Rana sylvatica.*" *Develop. Biol.* **6**, 133 (1963).

48. Schönmann, W., "Der diploide bastard *Triton palmatus* ♀ × *Salamandra* ♂." *Arch. Entwicklungsmech. Organ.* **138**, 345 (1938).

49. Chen, P. S., "The rate of oxygen consumption in the lethal hybrid between Triton ♀ and Salamandra ♂." *Exptl. Cell Res.* **5**, 275 (1953).

50. Gregg, J. R., and Lovtrup, S., "A reinvestigation of DNA synthesis in lethal amphibian hybrids." *Exptl. Cell Res.* **19**, 621 (1960).

51. Newman, H. H., "Modes of inheritance in teleost hybrids." *J. Exptl. Zool.* **16**, 447 (1914).

52. Newman, H. H., "Development and heredity in heterogenic teleost hybrids." *J. Exptl. Zool.* **18**, 511 (1915).

53. Minganti, A., "Lo sviluppo embrionale e il comportamento dei cromosomi in ibridi tra 5 specie di ascidie." *Acta Embryol. Morphol. Exptl.* **2**, 269 (1959).

54. Minganti, A., "Androgenetic hybrids in ascidians. I. *Ascidia malaca* (♀) × *Phallusia mamillata* ♂." *Acta Embryol. Morphol. Exptl.* **2**, 244 (1959).

55. Hyman, L. H., *The Invertebrates: Echinodermata.* New York: McGraw-Hill, 1955, Vol. IV.

56. Harvey, E. B., "Parthenogenetic merogony or cleavage without nuclei in *Arbacia punctulata.*" *Biol. Bull.* **71**, 101 (1936).

57. Harvey, E. B., "A comparison of the development of nucleate and non-nucleate eggs of *Arbacia punctulata.*" *Biol. Bull.* **79**, 166 (1940).

58. Fankhauser, G., "Cytological studies on egg fragments of the salamander *Triton.* IV. The cleavage of egg fragments without the egg nucleus." *J. Exptl. Zool.* **67**, 349 (1934).

59. Briggs, R., Green, E. U., and King, T. J., "An investigation of the capacity for cleavage and differentiation in *Rana pipiens* eggs lacking 'functional' chromosomes." *J. Exptl. Zool.* **116**, 455 (1951).

60. Gross, P. R., and Cousineau, G. H., "Effects of actinomycin D on macromolecule synthesis and early development in sea urchin eggs." *Biochem. Biophys. Res. Commun.* **10,** 321 (1963).

61. Gross, P. R., and Cousineau, G. H., "Macromolecule synthesis and the influence of actinomycin on early development." *Exptl. Cell Res.* **33,** 368 (1964).

62. Gross, P. R., Malkin, L. I., and Moyer, W. A., "Templates for the first proteins of embryonic development." *Proc. Natl. Acad. Sci. U.S.* **51,** 407 (1964).

63. Collier, J. R., "The transcription of genetic information in the spiralian embryo." *Current Topics Develop. Biol.* **1,** 39 (1966).

63a. Feigenbaum, L., and Goldberg, E., "Effect of Actinomycin D on morphogenesis in *Ilyanassa.*" *Am. Zoologist* **5,** 198 (1965).

64. Lockshin, R. A., "Insect embryogenesis: Macromolecular syntheses during early development." *Science* **154,** 775 (1966).

65. Brachet, J., and Denis, H., "Effects of actinomycin D on morphogenesis." *Nature* **198,** 205 (1963).

66. Brachet, J., Denis, H., and de Vitry, F., "The effects of actinomycin D and puromycin on morphogenesis in amphibian eggs and *Acetabularia mediterranea.*" *Develop. Biol.* **9,** 398 (1964).

67. Wallace, H., and Elsdale, T. R., "Effects of actinomycin D on amphibian development." *Acta Embryol. Morphol. Exptl.* **6,** 275 (1963).

68. Reverberi, G., Personal communication (1967).

69. Smith, K. D., "Genetic control of macromolecular synthesis during development of an ascidian: *Ascidia nigra.*" *J. Exptl. Zool.* **164,** 393 (1967).

70. Lentz, T. L., and Trinkhaus, J. P., "A fine structural study of cytodifferentiation during cleavage, blastula and gastrula stages of *Fundulus heteroclitus.*" *J. Cell Biol.* **32,** 121 (1967).

71. Wilde, C. E., Jr., and Crawford, R. B., "Cellular differentiation in the anamniota. III. Effects of actinomycin D and cyanide on the morphogenesis of *Fundulus.*" *Exptl. Cell Res.* **44,** 471 (1966).

72. Crawford, R. B., and Wilde, C. E., Jr., "Cellular differentiation in the anamniota. IV. Relationship between RNA synthesis and aerobic in *Fundulus heteroclitus* embryos." *Exptl. Cell Res.* **44,** 489 (1966).

73. Hultin, T., "The effect of puromycin on protein metabolism and cell division in fertilized sea urchin eggs." *Experientia* **17,** 410 (1961).

74. Karnofsky, D. A., and Simmel, E. B., "Effects of growth-inhibiting chemicals on the sand-dollar embryo, *Echinarachnius parma.*" *Progr. Exptl. Tumor Res.* **3,** 254 (1963).

75. Brachet, J., Decroly, M., Ficq., A., and Quertier, J., "Ribonucleic acid metabolism in unfertilized and fertilized sea-urchin eggs." *Biochim. Biophys. Acta* **72,** 660 (1963).

76. Denis, H., "Effets de l'actinomycine sur le développement embryonnaire. III. Etude biochimique: influence de l'actinomycine sur la synthèse des proteines." *Develop. Biol.* **9,** 473 (1964).

77. Barros, C., Hand, G. S., Jr., and Monroy, A., "Control of gastrulation in the starfish, *Asterias forbesii.*" *Exptl. Cell Res.* **43,** 167 (1966).

78. Giudice, G., Mutolo, V., and Donatuti, G., "Gene expression in sea urchin development." *Arch. Entwicklungsmech. organ.* (1968) (in press).

79. Gilchrist, F. G., "The time relations of determination in early amphibian development." *J. Exptl. Zool.* **66,** 15 (1933).

80. Neyfakh, A. A., "Radiation investigation of nucleo-cytoplasmic interrelations in morphogenesis and biochemical differentiation." *Nature* **201,** 880 (1964).
81. Terman, S. A., and Gross P. R., "Translation level control of protein synthesis during early development." *Biochem. Biophys. Res. Commun.* **21,** 595 (1965).
82. Gross, P. R., "The control of protein synthesis in embryonic development and differentiation." *Current Topics Develop. Biol.* **2,** 1 (1967).
82a. Ellis, C. H., Jr., "The genetic control of sea urchin development, a chromatographic study of protein synthesis in the *Arbacia punctulata* embryo." *J. Exptl. Zool.* **163,** 1 (1966).
83. Spiegel, M., Ozaki, H., and Tyler, A., "Electrophoretic examination of soluble proteins synthesized in early sea urchin development." *Biochem. Biophys. Res. Commun.* **21,** 135 (1965).
83a. Westin, M., Perlmann, H., and Perlmann, P., "Immunological studies of protein synthesis during sea urchin development." *J. Exptl. Zool.* **166,** 331 (1967).
84. Wilde, C. E., Jr., "The differentiation of vertebrate pigment cells." Advan. *Morphogenesis* **1,** 267 (1961).
85. Denis, H., "Effets de l'actinomycine sur le dévéloppement embryonnaire. I. Etude morphologique: Suppression par l'actinomycine de la compétence de l'ectoderme et du pouvoir inducteur de la lèvre blastoporale." *Develop. Biol.* **9,** 435 (1964).
86. Okazaki, K., "Skeleton formation of sea urchin larvae. V. Continuous observation of the process of matrix formation." *Exptl. Cell Res.* **40,** 585 (1965).
87. Morrill, J. B., and Norris, E., "Electrophoretic analysis of hydrolytic enzymes in the *Ilyanassa* embryo." *Acta Embryol. Morphol. Exptl.* **8,** 232 (1965).
88. Tocco, G., Orengo, A., and Scarano, E., "Ribonucleic acids in the early embryonic development of the sea urchin. I. Quantitative variations and ^{32}P orthophosphate incorporation studies of the RNA of subcellular fractions." *Exptl. Cell Res.* **31,** 52 (1963).
89. Bristow, D. A., and Deuchar, E. M., "Changes in nucleic acid concentration during the development of *Xenopus laevis* embryos." *Exptl. Cell Res.* **35,** 580 (1964).
90. Kutsky, P. B., "Phosphate metabolism in the early development of *Rana pipiens.*" *J. Exptl. Zool.* **115,** 429 (1950).
91. Brown, D. D., and Littna, E., "RNA synthesis during the development of *Xenopus laevis,* the South African clawed toad." *J. Mol. Biol.* **8,** 669 (1964).
92. Decroly, M., Cape, M., and Brachet, J., "Studies on the synthesis of ribonucleic acids in embryonic stages of *Xenopus laevis.*" *Biochim. Biophys. Acta* **87,** 34 (1964).
93. Bachvarova, R., Davidson, E. H. Allfrey, V. G., and Mirsky, A. E., "Activation of RNA synthesis associated with gastrulation." *Proc. Natl. Acad. Sci. U.S.* **55,** 358 (1966).
94. Gurdon, J. B., Personal communication (1967); Woodland, H. R., and Gurdon, J. B., "The relative rates of transfer RNA, ribosomal RNA, and DNA synthesis in different regions of developing *Xenopus laevis* embryos." *J. Embryol. Exptl. Morphol.* (1968) (in press).
95. Brown, D. D., and Gurdon, J. B., "Size distribution and stability of DNA-like RNA synthesized during development of anulceolate embryos of *Xenopus laevis.*" *J. Mol. Biol.* **19,** 399 (1966).
96. Brown, D. D., and Gurdon, J. B., "Absence of ribosomal RNA synthesis in the anucleolate mutant of *Xenopus laevis.*" *Proc. Natl. Acad. Sci. U.S.* **51,** 139 (1964).

97. Elsdale, T. R., Fischberg, M., and Smith, S., "A mutation that reduces nucleolar number in *Xenopus laevis.*" *Exptl. Cell Res.* **14**, 642 (1958).

98. Kahn, J., "The nucleolar organizer in the mitotic chromosome complement of *Xenopus laevis.*" *Quart. J. Microscop. Sci.* **103**, 407 (1962).

99. Brown, D. D., and Weber, C. S., "Gene linkage by RNA-DNA hybridization: I. Unique DNA sequences homologous to 4 s RNA, 5 s RNA and ribosomal RNA." *J. Mol. Biol.* **32**, 661 (1968).

99a. Hay, E. D., and Gurdon, J. B., "Fine structure of the nucleolus in normal and mutant *Xenopus* embryos." *J. Cell. Sci.* **2**, 151 (1967).

100. Karasaki, S., "Electron microscopic examination of the sites of nuclear RNA synthesis during amphibian embryogenesis." *J. Cell Biol.* **26**, 937 (1965).

101. Brown, D. D., and Littna, E., "Synthesis and accumulation of low molecular weight RNA during embryogenesis of *Xenopus laevis.*" *J. Mol. Biol.* **20**, 95 (1966).

102. Brown, D. D., and Littna, E., "Synthesis and accumulation of DNA-like RNA during embryogenesis of *Xenopus laevis.*" *J. Mol. Biol.* **20**, 81 (1966).

103. Bachvarova, R., and Davidson, E. H., "Nuclear activation at the onset of amphibian gastrulation." *J. Exptl. Zool.* **163**, 285 (1966).

104. Denis, H., "Gene expression in amphibian development. II. Release of the genetic information in growing embryos." *J. Mol. Biol.* **22**, 285 (1966).

105. Guild, W. R., and Robinson, M., "Evidence for message reading from a unique strand of pneumococcal DNA." *Proc. Natl. Acad. Sci. U.S.* **50**, 106 (1963).

106. Bautz, E. K. F., "Physical properties of messenger RNA of bacteriophage T₄." *Proc. Natl. Acad. Sci. U.S.* **49**, 68 (1963).

107. Hayashi, M., Hayashi, M. N., and Spiegelman, S., "Restriction of *in vivo* genetic transcription to one of the complementary strands of DNA." *Proc. Natl. Acad. Sci. U.S.* **50**, 664 (1963).

107a. Denis, H., "Gene expression in amphibian development. I. Validity of the method used." *J. Mol. Biol.* **22**, 269 (1966).

108. Britten, R. J., and Kohne, D. E., "Nucleotide sequence repetition in DNA." *Carnegie Inst. Wash. Yearbook* **65**, 78 (1965–1966).

108a. Britten, R. J., and Kohne, D., "Repeated nucleotide sequences." *Carnegie Inst. Wash. Yearbook,* **66**, 73 (1967).

108b. Britten, R. J., Kohne, D., and Rake, A., *Carnegie Inst. Wash. Yearbook* **67**. (in press).

109. Walker, P. M. B., and McLaren, A., "Specific duplex formation *in vitro* of mammalian DNA." *J. Mol. Biol.* **12**, 394 (1965).

110. Martin, M. A., and Hoyer, B. H., "Thermal stabilities and species specificities of reannealed animal deoxyribonucleic acids." *Biochemistry* **5**, 2706 (1966).

111. Church, R., and McCarthy, B. J., "Changes in nuclear and cytoplasmic RNA in regenerating mouse liver." *Proc. Natl. Acad. Sci. U.S.* **58**, 1548 (1967).

112. Church, R. B., and McCarthy, B. J, "Ribonucleic acid synthesis in regenerating and embryonic liver I. The synthesis of new species of RNA during regeneration of mouse liver after partial hepatectomy." *J. Mol. Biol.* **23**, 459 (1967).

113. Aronson, A. I., "Characterization of messenger RNA in sporulating *Bacillus cereus.*" *J. Mol. Biol.* **11**, 576 (1965).

114. McCarthy, B. J., and Bolton, E. T., "Interaction of complementary RNA and DNA." *J. Mol. Biol.* **8**, 184 (1964).

115. Crippa, M., Davidson, E. H., and Mirsky, A. E., "Persistence in early amphibian embryos of informational RNA's from the lampbrush chromosome stage of oogenesis." *Proc. Natl. Acad. Sci. U.S.* **57**, 885 (1967).

116. Flickinger, R.A., Greene, R., Kohl, D. M., and Miyagi, M., "Patterns of synthesis of DNA-like RNA in parts of developing frog embryos." *Proc. Natl. Acad. Sci. U.S.* **56**, 1712 (1966).

117. Davidson, E. H., Crippa, M., and Mirsky, A. E., "Evidence for the appearance of novel gene products during amphibian blastulation." *Proc. Natl. Acad. Sci. U.S.* **60**, 152 (1968).

118. Comb, D. G., and Brown, R., "Preliminary studies on the degradation and synthesis of RNA components during sea urchin development." *Exptl. Cell Res.* **34**, 360 (1964).

119. Comb, D. G., Katz, S., Branda, R., and Pinzino, C. J., "Characterization of RNA species synthesized during early development of sea urchins." *J. Mol. Biol.* **14**, 195 (1965).

120. Nemer, M., and Infante, A. A., "Ribosomal ribonucleic acid of the sea urchin egg and its fate during embryogenesis." *J. Mol. Biol.* **27**, 73 (1967).

121. Wilt, F. H., "The synthesis of ribonucleic acid in sea urchin embryos." *Biochem. Biophys. Res. Commun.* **11**, 447 (1963).

122. Wilt, F. H., "Ribonucleic acid synthesis during sea urchin embryogenesis." *Develop. Biol.* **9**, 299 (1964).

123. Nemer, M., "Old and new RNA in the embryogenesis of the purple sea urchin." *Proc. Natl. Acad. Sci. U.S.* **50**, 230 (1963).

124. Nemer, M., and Infante, A. A., "Messenger RNA in early sea urchin embryos: size classes." *Science* **150**, 217 (1965).

125. Siekevitz, P., Maggio, R., and Catalano, C., "Some properties of a rapidly labelled ribonucleic acid species in *Sphaerechinus granularis.*" *Biochim. Biophys. Acta* **129**, 145 (1966).

126. Gross, P. R., Kraemer, K., and Malkin, L. I., "Base composition of RNA synthesized during cleavage of the sea urchin embryo." *Biochem. Biophys. Res. Commun.* **18**, 569 (1965).

127. Comb. D. G., "Methylation of nucleic acids during sea urchin embryo development." *J. Mol. Biol.* **11**, 851 (1965).

127a. Giudice, G., and Mutolo, V., "Synthesis of ribosomal RNA during sea urchin development." *Biochim. Biophys. Acta* **138**, 276 (1967).

128. Cowden, R. R., and Lehman, H. E., "A cytochemical study of differentiation in early echinoid development." *Growth* **27**, 185 (1963).

129. Millonig, G., "The structural changes of the nucleolus during oogenenis and embryogenesis of *Arbacia lixula.*" *J. Cell Biol.* **35**, 177a (1967).

130. Glisin, V. R., Glisin, M. V., and Doty, P., "The nature of messenger RNA in the early stages of sea urchin development." *Proc. Natl. Acad. Sci. U.S.* **56**, 285 (1966).

131. Whiteley, A. H., McCarthy, B. J., and Whiteley, H. R., "Changing populations of messenger RNA during sea urchin development." *Proc. Natl. Acad. Sci. U.S.* **55**, 519 (1966).

132. Ozaki, H., Piatagorsky, J., and Tyler, A., "Electrophoretic patterns of soluble proteins synthesized during oogenesis and early development of sea urchin." *Biol. Ann. Rept. Calif. Inst. Technol., Pasadena* pp. 44–45 (1966).

132a. Marushige, K., and Ozaki, H., "Properties of isolated chromatin from sea urchin embryo." *Develop. Biol.* **16**, 474 (1967).

133. Belitsina, N. V., Aitkhozhin, M. A., Gavrilova, L. P., and Spirin, A. S., "Messenger RNA of differentiating animal cells." *Biochemistry* (USSR) (English Transl.) **29**, 315 (1964).

134. Aitkhozhin, M. A., Belitsina, N. V., and Spirin, A. S., "Nucleic acids during early development of fish embryos." *Biochemistry (USSR) (English Transl.)* **29**, 145 (1964).

135. Pankova, N. B., "The changes in cell nucleus at early stages of development of the loach, *Misgurnus fossilis*." *Tsitologiya* **5**, 36 (1963).

136. Lerner, A. M., Bell, E., and Darnell, J. E., Jr., "Ribosomal RNA in the developing chick embryo." *Science* **141**, 1187 (1963).

137. Brinster, R. L., "Studies of the development of mouse embryos *in vitro:* Energy metabolism." *Ciba Found. Symp., Preimplantation Stages Pregnancy* pp. 60–81 (1965).

138. Whittingham, D. G., and Biggers, J. D., "Fallopian tube and early cleavage in the mouse." *Nature* **213**, 942 (1967).

139. Mintz, B., "Synthetic processes and early development in the mammalian egg." *J. Exptl. Zool.* **157**, 85 (1964).

140. Silagi, S., "Some aspects of the relationship of RNA metabolism to development in normal and mutant mouse embryos cultivated *in vitro*." *Exptl. Cell Res.* **32**, 149 (1963).

141. Perry, R. P., "The cellular sites of synthesis of ribosomal and 4S RNA." *Proc. Natl. Acad. Sci. U.S.* **48**, 2179 (1962).

142. Skalko, R. G., Personal communication (1967).

142a. Kaulenas, M. S., and Fairbairn, D., "RNA metabolism of fertilized *Ascaris lumbricoides* eggs during uterine development." *Exptl. Cell Res.* (in press).

143. Dunn, L. C., and Gluecksohn-Waelsch, S., "Genetic analysis of seven newly discovered mutant alleles at locus T in the house mouse." *Genetics* **38**, 261 (1953).

144. Smith, L. J., "A morphological and histochemical investigation of a preimplantation lethal (t^{12}) in the house mouse." *J. Exptl. Zool.* **132**, 51 (1956).

145. Mintz, B., "Formation of genetically mosaic mouse embryos, and early development of 'lethal (t^{12}/t^{12})–normal' mosaics." *J. Exptl. Zool.* **157**, 273 (1964).

146. Brown, D. D., "The nucleolus and synthesis of ribosomal RNA during oogenesis and embryogenesis of *Xenopus laevis*. *Nat. Cancer Inst. Monograph* **23**, 297 (1966).

147. Cowden, R. R., and Markert, C. L., "A cytochemical study of the development of *Ascidia nigra*." *Acta Embryol. Morphol. Exptl.* **4**, 142 (1961).

148. Raven, C. P., *Morphogenesis: The Analysis of Molluscan Development*. Oxford: Pergamon Press, 1958, p. 76.

149. Kiknadze, I. I., "On the existence of nucleoli at early stages of cleavage." *Tsitologiya* **5**, 319 (1963).

150. Haslett, G. W., and Davidson, E. H., Unpublished observations (1967).

151. Dauwalder, M., "Initiation of RNA synthesis and nucleolar modification during cleavage in *Helix aspersa*." *J. Cell Biol.* **19**, 19A (1963).

152. Das, C. C., Kaufmann, B. P., and Gay, H., "Histone protein transition in *Drosophila melanogaster*. II. Changes during early embryonic development." *J. Cell Biol.* **23**, 423 (1964).

153. Kaulenas, M. S., and Fairbairn, D., "Ribonuclease-stable polysomes in the egg of *Ascaris lumbricoides*." *Develop. Biol.* **14**, 481 (1966).

154. Harris, S. E., and Forrest, H. S., "RNA and DNA synthesis in developing eggs of the milkweed bug, *Oncopeltus fasciatus* (Dallas)." *Science* **156**, 1613 (1967).

155. Davidson, E. H., Haslett, G. W., Finney, R. J., Allfrey, V. G., and Mirsky, A. E., "Evidence for prelocalization of cytoplasmic factors affecting gene activation in early embryogenesis." *Proc. Natl. Acad. Sci. U.S.* **54**, 696 (1965).

156. Campbell, A., Haslett, G. W., and Davidson, E. H. Unpublished experiments (1967).

157. Collier, J. R., "Nucleic acid and protein metabolism of the *Ilyanassa* embryo." *Exptl. Cell Res.* **24**, 320 (1961).

158. Collier, J. R., "Ribonucleic acids of the *Ilyanassa* embryo." *Science* **147**, 150 (1965).

159. Hastings, J. R. B., and Kirby, K. S., "The nucleic acids of *Drosophila melanogaster*. I. Constitution and amount of the ribonucleic acids in the unfertilized egg." *Biochem. J.* **100**, 532 (1966).

160. Levenbook, L., Travaglini, E. C., and Schultz, J., "Nucleic acids and their components as affected by the Y chromosome of *Drosophila melanogaster*." *Exptl. Cell Res.* **15**, 43 (1958).

161. Edström, J. E., and Beermann, W., "The base composition of nucleic acids in chromosomes, puffs, nucleoli and cytoplasm of *Chironomus* salivary gland cells." *J. Cell Biol.* **14**, 371 (1962).

162. Reamer, G. R., "The quantity and distribution of nucleic acids in the early stages of the mouse embryo." Ph.D. thesis, Boston University, 1963.

163. Collier, J. R., "The localization of ribonucleic acid in the egg of *Ilyanassa obsoleta*." *Exptl. Cell Res.* **21**, 126 (1960).

164. Silver, D. J., and Comb, D. G., "Acetic acid-soluble proteins in the developing sea urchin." *Develop. Biol.* **16**, 107 (1967).

165. Scarano, E., de Petrocellis, B., and Augusti-Tocco, G., "Studies on the control of enzyme synthesis during the early embryonic development of the sea urchins." *Biochim. Biophys. Acta* **87**, 174 (1964).

166. Gontcharoff, M., and Mazia, D., "Developmental consequences of introduction of bromouracil into the DNA of sea urchin embryos during early division stages." *Exptl. Cell Res.* **46**, 315 (1967).

167. Smith, L. D., and Ecker, R. E., "Protein synthesis in enucleated eggs of *Rana pipiens*." *Science* **150**, 777 (1965).

168. Spirin, A. S., and Nemer, M., "Messenger RNA in early sea-urchin embryos: Cytoplasmic particles." *Science* **150**, 214 (1965).

169. Infante, A. A., and Nemer, M., "Accumulation of newly synthesized RNA templates in a unique class of polyribosomes during embryogenesis." *Proc. Natl. Acad. Sci. U.S.* **58**, 681 (1967).

170. Malkin, L. I., Gross, P. R., and Romanoff, P., "Polyribosomal protein synthesis in fertilized sea urchin eggs: The effect of actinomycin treatment." *Develop. Biol.* **10**, 378 (1964).

171. Spirin, A. S., "On 'masked' forms of messenger RNA in early embryogenesis and in other differentiating systems." *Current Topics Develop. Biol.* **1**, 1 (1966).

172. Spirin, A. S., Belitsina, N. V., and Aitkhozhin, M. A., "Messenger RNA in early embryogenesis." *Zhu. Obshchei Biol.* **25**, Transl. Suppl., T907 (1965).

173. Monroy, A., "Fertilization." *In* M. Florkin and E. H. Stoty, eds., *Comprehensive Biochemistry*, No. 28, New York: American Elsevier, 1967, pp. 1–21.

174. Denny, P. C., and Tyler, A., "Activation of protein biosynthesis in non-nucleate fragments of sea urchin eggs." *Biochem. Biophys. Res. Commun.* **14**, 245 (1964).

175. Brachet, J., Ficq, A., and Tencer, R., "Amino acid incorporation into proteins of nucleate and anucleate fragments of sea urchin eggs: effect of parthenogenetic activation." *Exptl. Cell Res.* **32**, 168 (1963).

176. Tyler, A., "The biology and chemistry of fertilization." *Am. Naturalist* **99**, 309 (1965).

177. Monroy, A., and Tyler, A., "Formation of active ribosomal aggregates (polysomes) upon fertilization and development of sea urchin eggs." *Arch. Biochem. Biophys.* **103**, 431 (1963).

178. Gansen, P. van, "Etude au microscope electronique des structures ribosomales du cyptoplasme au cours de la segmentation de l'oeuf de *Xenopus laevis*." *Exptl. Cell Res.* **47**, 157 (1967).

179. Maggio, R., Vittorelli, M. L., Rinaldi, A. M., and Monroy, A., "In vitro incorporation of amino acids into proteins stimulated by RNA from unfertilized sea urchin eggs." *Biochem. Biophys. Res. Commun.* **15**, 436 (1964).

180. Slater, D. W., and Spiegelman, S., "An estimation of genetic messages in the unfertilized echinoid egg." *Proc. Natl. Acad. Sci. U.S.* **56**, 164 (1966).

181. Bibring, T., and Cousineau, G. H., "Percentage incorporation of leucine labeled with carbon-14 into isolated mitotic apparatus during early development of sea urchin eggs." *Nature* **204**, 805 (1964).

182. Gross, P. R., and Cousineau, G. H., "Synthesis of spindle-associated proteins in early cleavage." *J. Cell Biol.* **19**, 260 (1963).

183. Mangan, J., Miki-Noumura, T., and Gross, P. R., "Protein synthesis and the mitotic apparatus." *Science* **147**, 1575 (1965).

184. Stafford, D. W., and Iverson, R. M., "Radioautographic evidence for the incorporation of leucine-carbon-14 into the mitotic apparatus." *Science* **143**, 580 (1964).

184a. Wilt, F. H., Sakai, H., and Mazia, D., "Old and new protein in the formation of the mitotic apparatus in cleaving sea urchin eggs." *J. Mol. Biol.* **27**, 1 (1967).

185. Auclair, W., and Siegel, B. W., "Cilia regeneration in the sea urchin embryo: evidence for a pool of ciliary proteins." *Science* **154**, 913 (1966).

186. Runnstrom, J., and Manelli, H., "The stereocilia of the sea urchin embryo, the conditions of their formation and disappearance." *Atti Accad. Nazl. Lincei, Rend. Classe Sci. Fis., Mat. Nat.* [8] **42**, 1 (1967).

187. Auclair, W., and Meismer, D. M., "Cilia development and associated protein synthesis in the sea urchin embryo." *Biol. Bull.* **129**, 397 (1965).

188. Monroy, A., *Chemistry and Physiology of Fertilization*. New York: Holt, 1965.

189. Tyler, A., "Masked messenger RNA and cytoplasmic DNA in relation to protein synthesis and processes of fertilization and determination in embryonic development." *Develop. Biol.* (1968) (in press).

190. Bell, E., and Reeder, R., "The effect of fertilization on protein synthesis in the egg of the surf clam *Spisula solidissima*." *Biochim. Biophys. Acta* **142**, 500 (1967).

191. Bell, E., "The regulation of protein synthesis during cleavage and the effect of fertilization on synthetic processes." *A Symposium on "Fertilization," 1967*, Accad. Naz. Lincei, Rome (in press).

192. Epel, D., "Protein synthesis in sea urchin eggs: A "late" response to fertilization." *Proc. Natl. Acad. Sci. U.S.* **57**, 899 (1967).

193. Smith, L. D., Ecker, R. E., and Subtelny, S., "The initiation of protein synthesis in eggs of *Rana pipiens*." *Proc. Natl. Acad. Sci. U.S.* **56**, 1724 (1966).

194. Stafford, D. W., Sofer, W. H., and Iverson, R. M., "Demonstration of poly-ribosomes after fertilization of the sea urchin egg." *Proc. Natl. Acad. Sci. U.S.* **52**, 313 (1964).

194a. Cohen, G. H., and Iverson, R. M., "High-resolution density-gradient analysis of sea urchin polysomes." *Bioch. & Biophy. Res. Comm.* **29**, 349 (1967).

195. Hultin, T., "Activation of ribosomes in sea urchin eggs in response to fertilization." *Exptl. Cell Res.* **25**, 405 (1961).

196. Maggio, R., and Catalano, C., "Activation of amino acids during sea urchin development." *Arch. Biochem. Biophys.* **103**, 164 (1963).

197. Nemer, M., and Bard, S. G., "Polypeptide synthesis in sea urchin embryogenesis: An examination with synthetic polyribonucleotides." *Science* **140**, 664 (1963).

198. Wilt, F. H., and Hultin, T., "Stimulation of phenylalanine incorporation by polyuridylic acid in homogenates of sea urchin eggs." *Biochem. Biophys. Res. Commun.* **9**, 313 (1962).

199. Nemer, M., "Interrelation of messenger polyribonucleotides and ribosomes in the sea urchin egg during embryonic development." *Biochem. Biophys. Res. Commun.* **8**, 511 (1962).

200. Tyler, A., "The manipulations of macromolecular substances during fertilization and early development of animal eggs." *Am. Zoologist* **3**, 109 (1963).

201. Monroy, A., "Studies on the ribosomes of the unfertilized sea urchin egg." *A Symposium on "Fertilization,"* 1967, Accad. Naz. Lincei, Rome (in press).

202. Monroy, A., Maggio, R., and Rinaldi, A. M., "Experimentally induced activation of the ribosomes of the unfertilized sea urchin egg." *Proc. Natl. Acad. Sci. U.S.* **54**, 107 (1965).

203. Mano, Y., "Role of a trypsin-like protease in 'informosomes' in a trigger mechanism of activation of protein synthesis by fertilization in sea urchin eggs." *Biochem. Biophys. Res. Commun.* **25**, 216 (1966).

204. Lundblad, G., "Proteolytic activity in sea urchin gametes. IV. Further investigation of the proteolytic enzymes of the egg." *Arkiv Kemi* **7**, 127 (1955).

204a. Afzelius, B. A., "Electron microscopy on the basophilic structures of the sea urchin egg." *Z. Zellforsch.* **45**, 660 (1957).

205. Stavy, L., and Gross, P. R., "The protein-synthetic lesion in unfertilized eggs." *Proc. Natl. Acad. Sci. U.S.* **57**, 735 (1967).

205a. Harris, P., "Structural changes following fertilization in the sea urchin egg." *Exptl. Cell Res.* **48**, 569 (1967).

206. Piatagorsky, J., "Studies on the initiation of protein synthesis by sea urchin eggs at fertilization." *Bio. Ann. Rept. Calif. Inst. Technol., Pasadena* pp. 50–52 (1966).

207. Wilson, E. B., *The Cell in Development and Heredity.* New York: Macmillan, 1925, pp. 983–1034 and 1039–1121.

208. Conklin, E. G., "The organization and cell lineage of the ascidian egg." *J. Acad. Natl. Sci. (Philadelphia)* **13**, 1 (1905).

209. Hertwig, O., "Präformation oder Epigenese." *Z. Streitfragen Biol. (Jena)* (1894).

210. Bourne, G. C., "Epigenesis or evolution." *Sci. Progr. (London)* **1**, 105 (1894).

211. Whitman, C. O., "Evolution and epigenesis." *Biological Lectures delivered at the Marine Biological Laboratory of Woods Holl (10th lecture).* Boston: Ginn, 1895, p. 205.

212. Spencer, H., *in* C. O. Whitman, "Evolution and epigenesis." *Biological Lectures delivered at the Marine Biological Laboratory of Woods Holl (10th lecture).* Boston: Ginn, 1895, p. 210.

213. Huxley, T. H., "Evolution in biology." *In Encyclopedia Brittanica.* 1878, 9th ed., p. 187.

214. Bonnet, C., *Considerations sur les Corps Organisés.* 2 vols., p. 80 (1762) (reprinted 1768, revised 1779). Key passages from Bonnet's works are translated by C. O. Whitman (see references 211, 215, and 216).

215. Whitman, C. O., "The palingenesia and the germ doctrine of Bonnet." *Biological Lectures delivered at the Marine Biological Laboratory of Woods Holl (12th lecture).* Boston: Ginn, 1895, p. 241.

216. Whitman, C. O., "Bonnet's theory of evolution. A system of negations." *In Biological Lectures delivered at the Marine Biological Laboratory of Woods Holl (11th lecture).* Boston: Ginn, 1895, p. 225.

217. His, W., *Unsere Körperform und das physiologische Problem ihrer Entstehung.* Leipzig: F. C. W. Vogel, 1874.

218. Lankester, E. R., "Notes on the embryology and classification of the animal kingdom: Comprising a revision of speculations relative to the origin and significance of the germ-layers. 1. The planula theory." *Quart. J. Microscop. Sci.* **17**, 399 (1877).

219. Whitman, C. O., "The embryology of *Clepsine*." *Quart. J. Microscop.* Sci. **18**, 215 (1878).

220. Child, C. M., "The early development of *Arenicola* and *Sternapsis*." *Arch. Entwicklungsmech. Organ.* **9**, 587 (1900).

221. Penners, A., "Die Forchung von *Tubifex rivulorum*." *Zool. Jahrb. Anat.* **43**, 223 (1922).

222. Conklin, E. G., "The embryology of *Crepidula*." *J. Morphol.* **13**, 1 (1897).

223. Costello, D. P., "Cleavage, blastulation and gastrulation." *In* B. H. Willier, P. A. Weiss, and V. Hamburger, eds., *Analysis of Development.* Philadelphia: Saunders, 1956, pp. 213–229.

224. Van Beneden, E., "Recherches sur la maturation de l'oeuf et la fécondation et la division cellulaire." *Arch. Biol.* **4**, 265 (1884); translated in E. B. Wilson, *The Cell in Development and Heredity.* New York: Macmillan, 1925, p. 1042.

224a. Jazdowska-Zagrodzinska, B., "Experimental studies on the role of 'polar granules' in the segregation of pole cells in *Drosophila melanogaster*." *J. Embryol. Exptl. Morphol.* **16**, 391 (1966).

225. Wilson, E. B., "Experimental studies in germinal localization. II. Experiments on the cleavage-mosaic in *Patella* and *Dentalium*." *J. Exptl. Zool.* **1**, 197 (1904).

226. Penners, A., *in* T. H. Morgan, *Experimental Embryology.* New York: Columbia University Press, 1927, pp. 370–380.

227. Penners, A., "Experimentelle Untersuchungen zum Determinations-problem am Keim von *Tubifex*." *Z. Wiss. Zool.* **127**, 1 (1926).

228. Hegner, R. W., "Experiments with chrysomelid beetles. III. The effects of killing parts of the eggs of *Leptinotarsa decemlineata*." *Biol. Bull.* **20**, 237 (1911).

229. Crampton, H. E., "Experimental studies on gasteropod development." *Arch. Entwicklungsmech. Organ.* **3**, 1 (1896).

230. Clement, A. C., "Experimental studies on germinal localization in *Ilyanassa*. II. The development of isolated blastomeres." *J. Exptl. Zool.* **132**, 427 (1956).

231. Wilson, E. B., "Experimental studies on germinal localization. I. The germ-regions in the egg of *Dentalium*." *J. Exptl. Zool.* **1**, 1 (1904).

232. Stevens, N. M., "The effect of ultra-violet light upon the developing eggs of *Ascaris megalocephala.*" *Arch. Entwichlungsmech. Organ.* **27**, 622 (1909).

233. Costello, D. P., "Experimental studies of germinal localization in *Nereis*. I. The development of isolated blastomeres." *J. Exptl. Zool.* **100**, 19 (1945).

234. Hatt, P., "Essais experimentaux sur les localisations germinales dans l'oeuf d'un annelide (*Sabellaria alveolata* L.)." *Arch. Anat. Microscop. Morphol. Exptl.* **28**, 81 (1932).

235. Conklin, E. G., "Mosaic development in ascidian eggs." *J. Exptl. Zool.* **2**, 145 (1905).

236. Fischel, A., "Experimentelle Untersuchungen am Ctenophorenei. II. Von der Kunstlichen Erzeugung (halber) Doppel-und Missbildungen. III. Über Regulationen der Entwickelung. IV. Über den Entwickelungsgang und die Organizationsstufe des Ctenophoreneis." *Arch. Entwicklungsmech. Organ.* **7**, 557 (1898).

237. Morgan, T. H., *Experimental Embryology.* New York: Columbia University Press, 1927, pp. 501–504.

238. Hegner, R. W., *The Germ-Cell Cycle in Animals.* New York: Macmillan, 1914.

239. Boveri, T., *Die Entwicklung von Ascaris megalocephala mit besonderer Rücksicht auf die Kernverhältnisse.* Festchr. F. C. von Kupffer, Jena, 1899.

240. Hogue, M. J., "Über die Wirkung der Centrifugal Kraft auf die Eier von *Ascaris megalocephala.* "*Arch. Entwicklungsmech. Organ.* **29**, 109 (1910).

241. Clement, A. C., "Experimental studies on germinal localization in *Ilyanassa*. I. The role of the polar lobe in determination of the cleavage pattern and its influence in later development." *J. Exptl. Zool.* **121**, 593 (1952).

242. Clement, A. C., "Effects of micromere deletion on development in *Ilyanassa.*" *Biol. Bull.* **125**, 375 (1963).

243. Clement, A. C., "Development of *Ilyanassa* following removal of the D macromere at successive cleavage stages." *J. Exptl. Zool.* **149**, 193 (1962).

244. Clement, A. C., "The embryonic value of micromeres in *Ilyanassa obsoleta,* as determined by deletion experiments. I. The first quartet cells." *J. Exptl. Zool.* **166**, 77 (1967).

244a. Clement, A. C., "Development of the vegetal half of the *Ilyanassa* egg after removal of most of the yolk by centrifugal force, compared with the development of animal halves of similar visible composition." *Develop. Biol.* **17**, 165 (1968).

245. Hyman, L. H., *The Invertebrates: Platyhelminthes and Rhynchocoela. The Acoelomate Bilateria.* New York: McGraw-Hill, 1951, Vol. II, p. 18.

246. Cather, J. N., "Cellular interactions in the development of the shell gland of the gastropod, *Ilyanassa.*" *J. Exptl. Zool.* **166**, 205 (1967).

247. Tiedemann, H., "Biochemical aspects of primary induction and determination." *In* R., Weber, ed., *The Biochemistry of Animal Development.* New York: Academic Press, 1967, pp. 3–55.

248. Yamada, T., "Factors of embryonic induction." *Comp. Biochem.* **28**, 113–143 (1967).

249. Watterson, R. L., "Selected invertebrates." *In* B. H. Willier, P. A. Weiss, and V. Hamburger, eds., *Analysis of Development.* Philadelphia; Saunders, 1956, pp. 315–336.

250. Driesch, H., "Entwichelungsmechanische Studien. I–II." *Z. Wiss. Zool.* **53**, 160 (1891). Original references and an account of these experiments in English are provided in T. H. Morgan, *Experimental Embryology.* New York: Columbia University Press, 1927, pp. 307–313.

251. Zoja, R., "Sullo Sviluppo dei blastomeri isolati dalle uova di alcune meduse (e di altri organismi)." *Arch. Entwicklungsmech. Organ.* **2**, 1 (1896).
252. Wilson, E. B., "*Amphioxus*, and the mosaic theory of development." *J. Morphol.* **18**, 579 (1893).
253. Morgan, T. H., *Experimental Embryology*. New York: Columbia University Press, 1927, pp. 331–337.
254. Spemann, H., "Entwicklungsphysiologische Studien am *Triton*-Ei. II." *Arch. Entwicklungsmech. Organ.* **15**, 448 (1903).
255. Ruud, G., "Die Entwicklung isolierter Keimfragmente frühester Stadien von *Triton taeniatus*." *Arch. Entwicklungsmech. Organ.* **105**, 1 (1925).
256. McClendon, J. F., "The development of isolated blastomeres of the frog's egg." *Am. J. Anat.* **10**, 425 (1910).
257. Wilson, E. B., *The Cell in Development and Heredity*. New York: Macmillan, 1925, pp. 1072–1076.
258. Yatsu, N., "Experiments on the development of egg fragments in *Cerebratulus*." *Biol. Bull.* **6**, 123 (1903).
259. Hörstadius, S., "The mechanics of sea urchin development, studied by operative methods." *Biol. Rev. Camb. Phil. Soc.* **14**, 132 (1939).
260. Morgan, T. H., *Experimental Embryology*. New York: Columbia University Press, 1927, p. 290.
261. Hörstadius, S., "Experiments on determination in the early development of *Cerebratulus lacteus*." *Biol. Bull.* **73**, 317 (1937).
262. Novikoff, A. B., "Embryonic determination in the annelid, *Sabellaria vulgaris*. II. Transplantation of polar lobes and blastomeres as a test of their inducing capacities." *Biol. Bull.* **74**, 211 (1938).
263. Hatt, P., "La fusion experimentale d'oeufs de *Sabellaria alveolata* L. et leur développement." *Arch. Biol.* **42**, 303 (1931).
264. Penners, A., "Experimentelle Untersuchungen zum Determinations-problem am Keim von *Tubifex rivulorum Lam*. I. Die Duplicitas cruciata und organbildende Keimbezirke." *Arch. Mikroskop. Anat. Entwicklungsmech.* **102**, 51 (1924).
265. Novikoff, A. B., "Morphogenetic substances or organizers in annelid development." *J. Exptl. Zool.* **85**, 127 (1940).
266. Tyler, A., "Experimental production of double embryos in annelids and mollusks." *J. Exptl. Zool.* **57**, 347 (1930).
267. Reverberi, G., and Minganti, A., 'La distribuzione delle potenze nel germe di Ascidie allo stadio di otto blastomeri, analizzata mediante le combinazioni e i trapianti di blastomeri." *Pubbl. Staz. Zool. Napoli* **21**, 1 (1947).
268. Raven, C. P., *Morphogenesis: The Analysis of Molluscan Development*. Oxford, Pergamon Press, 1958, p. 198.
269. Reverberi, G., and Minganti, A., "Concerning the interpretation of the experimental analysis of the ascidian development." *Acta Biotheoret.* **9**, 197 (1951).
270. Mangold, O., "Fragen der Regulation und Determination an umgeordneten Furchungsstadien und verschmolzenen Keimen von *Triton*." *Arch. Entwicklungsmech. Organ.* **47**, 249 (1920).
271. Hörstadius, S., and Wolsky, A., "Studien über die Determination der Bilateralsymmetrie des Jungen Seeigelkeimes." *Arch. Entwicklungsmech. Organ.* **135**, 69 (1937).
271a. Giudice, G., Mutolo, V., and Moscona, A. A., "The role of interaction in the control of RNA synthesis." *Biochim. Biophys. Acta* **138**, 607 (1967).

272. Pfohl, R. J., and Giudice, G., "The role of cell interaction in the control of enzyme activity during embryogenesis." *Biochim. Biophys. Acta* **142**, 263 (1967).

273. Giudice, G., "Restitution of whole larvae from disaggregated cells of sea urchin embryos." *Develop. Biol.* **5**, 402 (1962).

274. Markman, B., *Studies of Nucleo-Cytoplasmic Interrelations in Early Sea Urchin Development.* Stockholm, Tryckeri Balder A. B., 1967.

275. Ancel, P., and Vintemberger, P., "Recherches sur le déterminisme de la symetrie bilatérale dans l'oeuf des amphibiens. *Bull. Biol. France Belg. Suppl.* 31, 1 (1948).

276. Child, C. M., "Lithium and echinoderm exogastrulation: With a review of the physiological-gradient concept." *Physiol. Zool.* **13**, 4 (1940).

277. Runnstrom, J., and Markman, B., "Gene dependency of vegetalization in sea urchin embryos treated with lithium." *Biol. Bull.* **130**, 402 (1966).

278. Seidel, F., "Die Determinierung der Keimanlage bei Insekten. I." *Biol. Zentr.* **46**, 321 (1926).

279. Boveri, T., "Die Polarität von Ovocyte, Ei und Larve des *Strongylocentrotus lividus.*" *Zool. Jahrb. Anat.* **14**, 630 (1901).

280. Hörstadius, S., "Uber die Determination des Keimes bei Echinodermen." *Acta Zool.* (Stockholm) **9**, 1 (1928).

281. Hörstadius, S., "Investigations as to the localization of the micromere, the skeleton, and the entoderm-forming material in the unfertilized egg of *Arbacia punctulata.*" *Biol. Bull.* **73**, 295 (1937).

282. Hörstadius, S., Josefsson, L., and Runnstrom, J., "Morphogenetic agents from unfertilized eggs of the sea urchin *Paracentrotus lividus.*" *Develop. Biol.* **16**, 189 (1967).

283. Runnstrom, J., "The mechanism of control of differentiation in early development of the sea urchin. A tentative discussion." *Exptl. Biol. Med.* **1**, 52 (1967).

284. Smith, L. D., "Role of a 'germinal plasm' in the formation of primordial germ cells in *Rana pipiens.*" *Develop. Biol.* **14**, 330 (1966).

285. Curtis, A. S. G., "Morphogenetic interactions before gastrulation in the amphibian *Xenopus laevis*—the cortical field." *J. Embryol. Exptl. Morphol.* **10**, 410 (1962).

286. Spemann, H., "Uber verzögerte Kernversorgung von Keimteilen." *Verhandl. Deut. Zool. Ges.* **24**, 216 (1914).

287. Holtfreter, J., and Hamburger, V., "Embryogenesis: Progressive differentiation. Amphibians." *In* B. H. Willier, P. A. Weiss, and V. Hamburger, eds., *Analysis of Development.* Philadelphia: Saunders, 1956, pp. 230–296.

288. Briggs, R., and King, T. J., "Nucleocytoplasmic interaction in eggs and embryos." *In* J. Brachet, and A. E. Mirsky, eds., *The Cell.* New York: Academic Press, 1959, Vol. 1, pp. 537–617.

289. Hebard, C. N., and Herold, R. C., "The ultrastructure of the cortical cytoplasm in the unfertilized egg and first cleavage zygote of *Xenopus laevis.*" *Exptl. Cell Res.* **46**, 553 (1967).

290. Harris, T. M., "Pregastrular mechanisms in the morphogenesis of the salamander *Ambystoma maculatum.*" *Develop. Biol.* **10**, 247 (1964).

291. Mulnard, J. G., "Studies of regulation of mouse ova *in vitro*, and Discussion." *Ciba Found. Symp., Preimplantation Stages Pregnancy* pp. 123–144 (1965).

292. Boveri, T., "Uber den Einfluss der Sämenzelle auf die Larvencharaktere der Echiniden." *Arch. Entwicklungsmech. Organ.* **16**, 340 (1903).

293. Wilson, E. B., "On cleavage and mosaic work." Appendix to H. E. Crampton, Jr. "Experimental studies on gastropod development." *Arch. Entwicklungsmech. Organ.* **8**, 19 (1896).

294. Wilson, E. B., *The Cell in Development and Heredity*. New York: Macmillan, 1925, p. 1112.

295. Clement, A. C., and Tyler, A., "Protein synthesizing activity of the enucleate polar lobe of the mud snail *Ilyanassa obsoleta*." *Science* **158**, 1457 (1967).

295a. Mahowald, A. P., 'Polar granules of *Drosophila* II. Ultrastructural changes during early embryogenesis." *J. Exptl. Zool.* **167**, 237 (1968).

296. Gurdon, J. B., and Brown, D. D., "Cytoplasmic regulation of RNA synthesis and nucleolus formation in developing embryos of *Xenopus laevis*." *J. Mol. Biol.* **12**, 27 (1965).

297. Graham, C. F., "The regulation of DNA synthesis and mitosis in multinucleate frog eggs." *J. Cell Sci.* **1**, 363 (1966).

298. Gurdon, J. B., "On the origin and persistence of a cytoplasmic state inducing nuclear DNA synthesis in frogs' eggs." *Proc. Natl. Acad. Sci. U.S.* **58**, 545 (1967).

299. Harris, H., "Behavior of differentiated nuclei in heterokaryons of animal cells from different species." *Nature* **206**, 583 (1965).

300. Thompson, L. R., and McCarthy, B. J., "Stimulation of nuclear DNA and RNA synthesis by cytoplasmic extracts *in vitro*." *Biochem. Biophys. Res. Commun.* **30**, 166 (1968).

301. Bibring, T., Brachet, J., Gaeta, F. S., and Graziosi, F., "Some physical properties of cytoplasmic deoxyribonucleic acid in unfertilized eggs of *Arbacia lixula*." *Biochim. Biophys. Acta* **108**, 644 (1965).

302. Franchi, L. L., Mandl, A. M., and Zuckerman, S., "The development of the ovary and the process of oogenesis." *In* S. Zuckerman, ed., *The Ovary*. New York: Academic Press, 1962, Vol. 1, pp. 1–88.

303. Buonoure, L. *L'Origine des Cellules Reproductrices et le Problème de la Lignee Germinale*. Paris: Gauthiers-Villars, 1939.

304. Geigy, R., "Action de l'ultra-violet sur le pole germinal dans l'oeuf de *Drosophila melanogaster* (castration et mutabilité)." *Rev. Suisse Zool.* **38**, 187 (1931).

305. Amma, K., "Uber die Differenzierung der Keimbahnzellen bei den Copepoden." *Arch. Zellforsch.* **6**, 497 (1911).

306. Raven, C. P., *Morphogenesis: The Analysis of Molluscan Development*. Oxford: Pergamon Press, 1958, pp. 254–262.

307. Hyman, L. H., *The Invertebrates: Smaller Coelomate Groups*. New York: McGraw-Hill, 1955, Vol. V, p. 32.

308. Swift, C. H., "Origin and early history of the primordial germ-cells in the chick." *Am. J. Anat.* **15**, 483 (1914).

309. Willier, B. H., "Experimentally produced sterile gonads and the problem of the origin of germ cells in the chick embryo." *Anat. Record,* **70**, 89 (1937).

310. Benoit, J., "Contribution à l'étude de la lignée germinale chez le poulet. Destruction précoce des genocytes primaires par les rayons ultra-violet." *Compt. Rend. Soc. Biol.* **2**, 1329 (1930).

311. Nieuwkoop, P. D., "The present state of the problem of the 'Keimbahn' in the vertebrates." *Experientia* **5**, 308 (1949).

312. Nelsen, O. E., *Comparative Embryology of the Vertebrates*. New York: McGraw-Hill (Blakiston), 1953, pp. 121–124.

313. Borum, K., "Oogenesis in the mouse: A study of the origin of the mature ova." *Exptl. Cell Res.* **45**, 39 (1967).

314. Waldeyer, W., *Eirstock und Ei*. Leipzig: Engelmann, 1870.

315. Duryee, W., "Chromosomal physiology in relation to nuclear structure." *Ann. N.Y. Acad. Sci.* **50**, Art. 8, 920 (1950).

342 BIBLIOGRAPHY

316. Davidson, E. H., Unpublished observations (1966).
317. Okkelberg, P., "The early history of the germ cells in the brook lamprey, *Entosphenus wilderi* (Gage), up to and including the period of sex differentiation." *J. Morphol.* **35**, 1 (1921).
318. Lewis, J. C., and McMillan, D. B., "The development of the ovary of the sea lamprey (*Petromyzon marinus.*)." *J. Morphol.* **117**, 425 (1965).
319. Hardisty, M. W., and Cosh, J., "Primordial germ cells and fecundity." *Nature* **210**, 1370 (1966).
320. Grant, P., "Phosphate metabolism during oogenesis in *Rana temporaria*." *J. Exptl. Zool.* **124**, 513 (1953).
321. Lizardi, P., and Davidson, E. H., Unpublished observations (1967).
322. Loyez, M., "Recherches sur le développement ovarien des oeufs méroblastiques." *Arch. Anat. Microscop. Morphol. Exptl.* **8**, 69 (1905).
323. Romanoff, A. L., *The Avian Embryo*. New York: Macmillan, 1960, pp. 13–18.
324. D'Hollander, F., "Recherches sur l'oogénèse et sur la structure et la signification du noyau vitellin de balbiani chez les oizeaux." *Arch. Anat. Microscop. Morphol. Exptl.* **7**, 117 (1904).
325. Slizynski, B. M., "Meiotic prophase in female mice." *Nature* **179**, 638 (1957).
326. Brambell, F. W. R., "The oogenesis of the fowl (*Gallus bankiva*)." *Phil. Trans. Roy. Soc. London* **B214**, 113 (1926).
326a. Franchi, L. L., and Mandl, A. M., "The ultrastructure of oogonia and oocytes in the foetal and neonatal rat." *Proc. Roy. Soc. B* **157**, 99 (1963).
327. Edwards, R. C., "Mammalian eggs in the laboratory." *Sci. Am.* **215**, 73 (1966).
327a. Baker, T. G., and Franchi, L. L., "Fine structure of the nucleus in the primordial oocyte of primates." *J. Anat.* **100**, 697 (1966).
327b. Baker, T. G., and Franchi, L. L., "The fine structure of oogonia and oocytes in human ovaries." *J. Cell Sci.* **2**, 213 (1967).
327c. Baker, T. G., "A quantitative and cytological study of germ cells in human ovaries." *Proc. Roy. Soc. London B* **158**, 417 (1963).
328. Alfert, M., "A cytochemical study of oogenesis and cleavage in the mouse." *J. Cellular Comp. Physiol.* **36**, 381 (1950).
329. Tennent, D. H., and Ito, T., "A study of the oogenesis of *Mespilia globulus* (Linné)." *J. Morphol.* **69**, 347 (1941).
330. Gross, P. R., Malkin, L. I., and Hubbard, M., "Synthesis of RNA during oogenesis in the sea urchin." *J. Mol. Biol.* **13**, 463 (1955).
331. Verhey, C. A., and Moyer, F. H., "Fine structural changes during sea urchin oogenesis." *J. Exptl. Zool.* **164**, 195 (1967).
332. Crippa, M., Lizardi, P., and Davidson, E. H., Unpublished observations (1967).
333. Jörgenssen, M., "Die Ei-und Nährzellen von *Piscicola.*" *Arch. Zellforsch.* **10**, 127 (1913).
334. Hyman, L. H., *The Invertebrates: Echinodermata*. New York: McGraw-Hill, 1955, Vol. IV, pp. 480–487.
335. Bier, K., "Oogenese, das Wachstum von Riesenzellen." *Naturwissenschaften* **54**, 189 (1967).
336. Bier, K., "Zur Funktion der Nährzellen im meroistischen Insektenovar unter besonderer Berücksichtigung der Oogenese adephager Coleopteren." *Zool. Jahrb. Physiol.* **71**, 371 (1965).
337. Grell, R. F., and Chandley, A. C., "Evidence bearing on the coincidence of exchange and DNA replication in the oocyte of *Drosophila melanogaster.*" *Proc. Natl. Acad. Sci. U.S.* **53**, 1340 (1965).

338. Kunz, W., "Funktionsstrukturen im Oocytenkern von *Locusta migratoria.*" *Chromosoma* **20**, 332 (1967).
339. Kunz, W., "Lampenbürstenchromosomen und multiple Nukleolen bei Orthopteren." *Chromosoma* **21**, 446 (1967).
339a. Zamboni, L., and Gondos, B., "Intercellular bridges and synchronization of germ cell differentiation during oogenesis in the rabbit." *J. Cell Biol.* **36**, 276 (1968).
340. Wilson, E. B., *The Cell in Development and Heredity.* New York: Macmillan, 1925, pp. 350–351.
341. Rückert, J., "Zur Entwicklungsgeschichte des Ovarialeies bei Selachiern." *Anat. Anz.* **7**, 107 (1892).
342. Maréchal, J., "Sur L'ovogénèse des selaciens et de quelques autres chordates. Premier memoire: Morphologie de l'élément chromosomique dans l'ovocyte. I chez les selaciens, les téléostéens, les tuniciers et l'amphioxus. *Cellule Rec. Cytol. Histol.* **24**, 1 (1907).
343. Callan, H. G., "The lampbrush chromosomes of *Sepia officinalis* L., *Anilocra physodes* L. and *Scyllium catulus* Cuv. and their structural relationship to the lampbrush chromosomes of amphibia." *Pubbl. Staz. Zool. Napoli* **29**, 329 (1957).
344. Callan, H. G., "The nature of lampbrush chromosomes." *Intern. Rev. Cytol.* **15**, 1 (1963).
345. Boyd, M. M. M., "The structure of the ovary and the formation of the corpus luteum in *Hoplodactylus maculatus,* Gray." *Quart. J. Microscop. Sci.* **82**, 337 (1941).
346. Bier, C. H., Personal communication (1967).
347. Wilson, E. B., *The Cell in Development and Heredity.* New York: Macmillan, 1925, pp. 256–393.
348. Dawid, I. B., "Deoxyribonucleic acid in amphibian eggs." *J. Mol. Biol.* **12**, 581 (1965).
349. Edstrom, J. E., and Gall, J. G., "The base composition of ribonucleic acid in lampbrush chromosomes, nucleoli, nuclear sap, and cytoplasm of *Triturus* oocytes." *J. Cell Biol.* **19**, 279 (1963).
350. Schrader, F., and Hughes-Schrader, S., "Haploidy in metazoa." *Quart. Rev. Biol.* **6**, 411 (1931).
351. Bier, K., "Synthese, interzellulärer Transport, und Abbua von Ribonukleinsäure im Ovar der Stubenfliege *Musca domestica.*" *J. Cell Biol.* **16**, 436 (1963).
352. Berry, R. O., "Chromosome behavior in the germ cells and development of the gonads in *Sciara ocellaris.*" *J. Morphol.* **68**, 547 (1941).
353. Brown, S. W., and Nur, U., "Heterochromatic chromosomes in the coccids." *Science* **145**, 130 (1964).
354. Geyer-Duszynska, I., "Genetic factors in oogenesis and spermatogenesis in *Cecidomyidae.*" *Chromosomes Today* **1**, 174 (1966).
355. Burfield, S. T., *Sagitta,* Liverpool Marine Biology Committee Memoire, No. 28. London: Hodder and Stoughton, 1927.
356. Raven, C. P., *Oogenesis: The Storage of Developmental Information.* Oxford: Pergamon Press, 1961, pp. 14–44 and 127–136.
357. Brown, E. H., and King, R. C., "Studies on the events resulting in the formation of an egg chamber in *Drosophila melanogaster.*" *Growth* **28**, 41 (1964).
358. Koch, E. A., Smith, P. A., and King, R. C., "The division and differentiation of *Drosophila* cystocytes." *J. Morphol.* **121**, 55 (1967).
359. King, R. C., and Aggarwal, S. K., "Oogenesis in *Hyalophora cecropia.*" *Growth* **29**, 17 (1965).

360. Bonhag, P. F., "Histochemical studies of the ovarian nurse tissues and oocytes of the milkweed bug, *Oncopeltus fasciatus* (Dallas)." *J. Morphol.* **96**, 381 (1955).

361. Bier, K., "Autoradiographische Untersuchungen über die Leistungen des Follikelepithels und der Nährzellen beider Dotterbildung und Eiweissynthese im Fliegenovar." *Arch. Entwicklungsmech. Organ.* **154**, 552 (1963).

362. Roth, T. F., and Porter, K. R., "Yolk protein uptake in the oocyte of the mosquito *Aedes aegypti* L." *J. Cell Biol.* **20**, 313 (1964).

362a. Telfer, W. H., "The mechanism and control of yolk formation." *Ann. Rev. Entomol.* **10**, 161 (1965).

363. Glass, L. E. "Immuno-histological localization of serum-like molecules in frog oocytes." *J. Exptl. Zool,* **141**, 257 (1959).

363a. Rudack, D., and Wallace, R. A., "On the site of phosvitin synthesis in *Xenopus laevis.*" *Biochim. Biophys. Acta* **155**, 299 (1968).

364. Clavert, J., "La biochimie de l'ovogénèse." *Arch. Neerl. Zool.* **10**, Suppl. 1 (1953).

365. Favard-Séréno, C. and Durand, M., "L'utilisation de nucléosides dans l'ovaire ᵈu Grillon et ses variations au cours de l'ovogénèse." *Develop. Biol.* **6**, 184 (1963).

366. Ficq, A., 1960. "Metabolisme de l'ovogénèse chez les amphibiens." *In Symposium on Germ Cells and Development.* Inst. Intern. d'Embryologie and Fondazione A. Baselli, 1960, pp. 121–140.

367. Piatagorsky, J., Ozaki, H., and Tyler, A., "RNA and protein synthesizing capacity of isolated oocytes of the sea urchin *Lytechinus pictus.*" *Exptl. Biol.* **15**, 1 (1967).

368. Sotelo, J. R., and Porter, K., "An electron microscope study of the rat ovum." *J. Biophys. Biochem. Cytol.* **5**, 327 (1959).

369. Harrison, R. J., "The structure of the ovary: Mammals." *In* S. Zuckerman, ed., *The Ovary.* New York: Academic Press, 1962, pp. 143–187.

370. Ries, E., "Die Prozesse der Eibildung und des Eiwachstums bei Pediculiden und Mallophagen." *Z. Zellforsch. Mikroskop. Anat.* **16**, 314 (1932).

371. Brachet, J., "La localisation des acides pentosenucléiques dans les tissus animaux et les oeufs d'amphibiens en voie de développement." *Arch. Biol.* **53**, 207 (1942).

372. Raven, C. P., *Oogenesis: The Storage of Developmental Information.*" Oxford: Pergamon Press, 1961, pp. 67–68.

373. Vincent, W. S., "The isolation and chemical properties of the nucleoli of starfish oocytes. *Proc. Natl. Acad. Sci. U.S.* **38**, 139 (1952).

374. Callan, H. G., "Chromosomes and nucleoli of the axolotl, *Ambystoma mexicanum.*" *J. Cell Sci.* **1**, 85 (1966).

375. Gall, J., "Lampbrush chromosomes from oocyte nuclei of the newt." *J. Morphol.* **94**, 283 (1954).

376. Callan, H. G., and Lloyd, L., "Lampbrush chromosomes of crested newts *Triturus cristatus* (Laurenti)." *Phil. Trans. Roy. Soc. London* **B243**, 135 (1960).

377. Miller, O. L., "Structure and composition of peripheral nucleoli of salamander oocytes." *Natl. Cancer Inst. Monograph* **23**, 53 (1966).

378. Macgregor, H. C., "The role of lampbrush chromosomes in the formation of nucleoli in amphibian oocytes." *Quart. J. Microscop. Sci.* **106**, 215 (1965).

379. Macgregor, H. C., "Pattern of incorporation of ³H-uridine into RNA of amphibian oocyte nucleoli." *J. Cell Sci.* **2**, 145 (1967).

380. Davidson, E. H., Allfrey, V. G., and Mirsky, A. E., "On the RNA synthesized during the lampbrush phase of amphibian oogenesis." *Proc. Natl. Acad. Sci. U.S.* **52**, 501 (1964).

381. Davidson, E. H., and Mirsky, A. E., "Gene activity in oogenesis." *Brookhaven Symp. Biol.* **18**, 77 (1965).

382. Brown, D. D., and Littna, E., "Variations in the synthesis of stable RNA's during oogenesis and development of *Xenopus laevis*." *J. Mol. Biol.* **8**, 688 (1964).

383. Miller, O. L., Jr., and Beatty, B. R., "Nucleolar structure and function." In *Handbook of Molecular Cytology*. North Holland Publishing Co. (in press).

384. Loeb, J. N., Howell, R. R., and Tomkins, T. M., "Turnover of ribosomal RNA in rat liver." *Science* **149**, 1093 (1965).

385. Izawa, M., Allfrey, V. G., and Mirsky, A. E., "The relationship between RNA synthesis and loop structure in lampbrush chromosomes." *Proc. Natl. Acad. Sci. U.S.* **49**, 544 (1963).

386. Gall, J. G., and Callan, H. G., "³H-uridine incorporation in lampbrush chromosomes." *Proc Natl. Acad. Sci. U.S.* **48**, 562 (1962).

387. Perkowska, E., Macgregor, H. C., and Birnstiel, M. L., "Gene amplification in the oocyte nucleus of mutant and wild-type *Xenopus laevis*." *Nature* **217**, 649 (1968).

388. Ficq, A., "Etude autoradiographique du métabolisme de l'oocyte d'*Asterias rubens* au cours de la croissance." *Arch. Biol.* **66**, 509 (1955).

388a. Rogers, E. M., "Ribonucleoprotein particles in the amphibian oocyte nucleus." *J. Cell Biol.* **36**, 421 (1968).

389. Brown, D. D., "The genes for ribosomal RNA and their transcription during amphibian development." *Current Topics Develop. Biol.* **2**, 47 (1967).

389a. Brown, D. D., and David, I. B., "Specific gene amplification in oocytes." *Science* **160**, 272 (1968).

390. Peacock, W. J., "Chromosome replication. *Natl. Cancer Inst. Monograph.* **18**, 101 (1965).

390a. Lane, N. J., "Spheroidal and ring nucleoli in amphibian oocytes. Patterns of uridine incorporation and fine structural features." *J. Cell Biol.* **35**, 421 (1967).

391. Brachet, J., "La localisation de l'acide thymonucléique pendant l'oogénèse et la maturation chez les amphibiens." *Arch. Biol.* **51**, 151 (1940).

392. Painter, T. S., and Taylor, A. N., "Nucleic acid storage in the toad's egg." *Proc. Natl. Acad. Sci. U.S.* **28**, 311 (1942).

393. Raven, C. P., *Oogenesis: The Storage of Developmental Information*. Oxford: Pergamon Press, 1961, p. 66.

394. Izawa, M., Allfrey, V. G., and Mirsky, A. E., "Composition of the nucleus and chromosomes in the lampbrush stage of the newt oocyte." *Proc. Natl. Acad. Sci. U.S.* **50**, 811 (1963).

395. Gall, J. G., "Differential synthesis of the genes for ribosomal RNA during amphibian oogenesis." *Proc. Natl. Acad. Sci. U.S.* **60**, 553 (1968).

396. Painter, T. S., "The elimination of DNA from soma cells" *Proc. Natl. Acad. Sci. U.S.* **45**, 897 (1959).

397. Jeanteur, P., Amaldi, F., and Attardi, G., "Partial sequence analysis of ribosomal RNA from HeLa cells. II. Evidence for sequences of non-ribosomal type in 45 and 32 s ribosomal RNA precursors." *J. Mol. Biol.* **33**, 757 (1968).

397a. Brown, D. D., and Weber, C. S., "Gene linkage by RNA-DNA hybridization, II. arrangement of the redundant gene sequences for 28 s and 18 s ribosomal RNA." *J. Mol. Biol.* **34**, 681 (1968).

398. Piatagorsky, P., and Tyler, A., "Radioactive labeling of RNA's of sea urchin eggs during oogenesis." *Biol. Bull.* **133**, 229 (1967).

399. Dettlaff, T. A., "Action of actinomycin and puromycin upon frog oocyte maturation," *J. Embryol. Exptl. Morphol.* **16**, 183 (1966).

399a. Brachet, J., "Effects of actinomycin, puromycin and cycloheximide upon the maturation of amphibian ovocytes." *Exptl. Cell Res.* **48**, 233 (1967).

399b. Brachet, J., and Steinert, G., "Synthesis of macromolecules and maturation of starfish ovocytes." *Nature* **216**, 1314 (1967).

399c. Schuetz, A. W., and Biggers, J. D., "Regulation of germinal vesicle breakdown in starfish oocytes." *Exptl. Cell Res.* **46**, 624 (1967).

400. Kramer, F. R., In preparation (1968).

401. Miller, O. L., "Fine structure of lampbrush chromosomes." *Natl. Cancer Inst. Monograph* **18**, 79 (1965).

402. Gall, J., "Kinetics of deoxyribonuclease action on chromosomes." *Nature* **198**, 36 (1963).

403. Callan, H. G., "The organization of genetic units in chromosomes." *J. Cell Sci.* **2**, 1 (1967).

404. Mirsky, A. E., and Ris, H., "The deoxyribonucleic acid content of animal cells and its evolutionary significance." *J. Gen. Physiol.* **34**, 451 (1951).

405. Van de Kerckhove, D., "Content of deoxyribonucleic acid of the germinal vesicle of the primary oocyte in the rabbit." *Nature* **183**, 329 (1959).

406. Swift, H., and Kleinfeld, R., "DNA in grasshopper spermatogenesis, oogenesis and cleavage." *Physiol. Zool.* **26**, 301 (1953).

407. Mulnard, J., "Etude morphologique et cytochimique de l'oogénèse chez *Acanthoscelides obtectus* Say (Bruchide-Coléoptère)." *Arch. Biol.* **65**, 261 (1954).

408. Govaert, J., "Etude quantitative de la teneur en acide désoxyribonucléique des noyaux des cellules somatiques et germinatives chez *Fasciola hepatica*." *Arch. Biol.* **68**, 165 (1957).

409. Wilson, E. B., *The Cell in Development and Heredity*. New York: Macmillan, 1925, pp. 351 and 653.

410. Brachet, J., *Chemical Embryology*. New York: Wiley (Interscience), 1950, p. 63.

411. Gall, J., "On the submicroscopic structure of chromosomes." *Brookhaven Symp. Biol.* **8**, 17 (1955).

412. Gall, J., "Chromosomal differentiation." *In* W. D. McElroy and B. Glass, eds., *A Symposium on the Chemical Basis of Development*. Baltimore: Johns Hopkins Press, 1958, p. 103.

413. Hess, O., "Funktionelle und structurelle Organization der Lampenbursten-Chromosomen. Probleme der biologischen Reduplikation. 3." *Wiss. Konf. Ges. Deut. Naturforsch. Arzte Semmering, Vienna 1965*, p. 29 (1966).

414. Hess, O., "Structural modifications of the Y-chromosome in *Drosophila hydei* and their relation to gene activity." *Chromosomes Today* **1**, 167 (1966).

415. Graham, C. F., and Morgan, R. W., "Changes in the cell cycle during early amphibian development." *Develop. Biol.* **14**, 439 (1966).

416. Briggs, R., and Cassens, G., "Accumulation in the oocyte nucleus of a gene product essential for embryonic development beyond gastrulation." *Proc. Natl. Acad. Sci. U.S.* **55**, 1103 (1966).

417. Humphrey, R. R., "A recessive factor (o, for ova deficient) determining a complex of abnoramalities in the Mexican axolotl (*Ambystoma mexicanum*)." *Develop. Biol.* **13**, 57 (1966).

417a. Briggs, R., and Justus, J. T., "Partial characterization of the component from normal eggs which corrects the maternal effect of gene O in the Mexican Axolotl (*Ambystoma mexicanum*)." *J. Exptl. Zool.* **167**, 105 (1968).

418. Raven, C. P., "The nature and origin of the cortical morphogenetic field in *Limnaea*." *Develop. Biol.* **7**, 130 (1963).

419. Raven, C. P., "The distribution of special cytoplasmic differentiations of the egg during early cleavage in *Limnaea stagnalis.*" *Develop. Biol.* **16**, 407 (1967).

420. Brachet, J., "Emission of Feulgen-positive particles during the *in vitro* maturation of toad ovocytes." *Nature* **208**, 596 (1965).

421. Piko, L., Tyler, A., and Vinograd, J., "Amount, location, priming capacity, circularity and other properties of cytoplasmic DNA in sea urchin eggs." *Biol. Bull.* **132**, 68 (1967).

422. Solomon, J., "Nucleic acid content of early chick embryos and the hen's egg." *Biochim. Biophy. Acta* **24**, 584 (1957).

423. Nigon, V., and Bovet, P., "La teneur des gamètes en acide desoxyribonucleique chez *Parascaris equorum* (Goeze)." *Compt. Rend. Soc. Biol.* **149**, 129 (1955).

424. Durand, M., "L'acide desoxyribonucleique (ADN) dans les gamètes et au cours des premiers stades de l'embryogénie des gryllides (Orth.)." *Bull. Biol. France Belg.* **95**, 28 (1961).

425. Collier, J. R., and McCann-Collier, M., "The deoxyribonucleic acid content of the egg and sperm of *Ilyanassa obsoleta.*" *Exptl. Cell Res.* **27**, 553 (1962).

426. Carden, G. A., Rosenkranz, S., and Rosenkranz, H. S., "Deoxyribonucleic acids of sperm, eggs, and somatic cells of the sea urchin *Arbacia punctulata.*" *Nature* **205**, 1338 (1965).

427. Hoff-Jörgensen, E., and Zeuthen, E., "Evidence of cytoplasmic deoxyribosides in the frog's egg." *Nature* **169**, 245 (1952).

428. Dawid, I. B., "Evidence for the mitochondrial origin of frog egg cytoplasmic DNA." *Proc. Natl. Acad. Sci. U.S.* **56**, 269 (1966).

428a. Brachet, J., and Ficq, A., "Binding sites of ^{14}C-actinomycin in amphibian ovocytes and an autoradiography technique for the detection of cytoplasmic DNA." *Exptl. Cell Res.* **38**, 153, (1965).

429. Davidson, E. H., Allfrey, V. G, and Mirsky, A E., "Gene expression in differentiated cells" *Proc. Natl. Acad. Sci. U.S.* **49**, 53 (1963).

430. Jacob, F., and Monod, J., "Genetic regulatory mechanisms in the synthesis of proteins." *J. Mol. Biol.* **3**, 318 (1961).

431. Marcus, A., and Feeley, J., "Protein synthesis in imbibed seeds." *J. Biol. Chem.* **240**, 1675 (1965).

432. Marcus, A., and Feeley, F., "Activation of protein synthesis in the imbibition phase of seed germination." *Proc. Natl. Acad. Sci. U.S.* **51**, 1075 (1964).

433. Dure, L., and Watters, L., "Long-lived messenger RNA: Evidence from cotton seed germination." *Science* **147**, 410 (1965).

434. Barker, G. R., and Rieber, M., "The development of polysomes in the seed of *Pisum arvense.*" *Biochem. J.* **105**, 1195 (1967).

435. Chapman, J. A., and Rieber, M., "Distribution of ribosomes in dormant and imbibed seeds of *Pisum arvense:* Electron-microsopic observations." *Biochem. J.* **105**, 1201 (1967).

436. Went, F. W., *The Plants.* New York: Time, Inc., 1963, pp. 94–95.

437. Humphreys, T., Penman, S., and Bell, E., "The appearance of stable polysomes during the development of chick down feathers." *Biochem. Biophys. Res. Commun.* **17**, 618 (1964).

438. Bell E., Humphreys, T., Slayter, H. S., and Hall, C. E., "Configuration of inactive and active polysomes of the developing down feather." *Science* **148**, 1739 (1965).

438a. Reeder, R., and Bell, E., "Protein synthesis in embryonic chick lens cells." *J. Mol. Biol.* **23**, 577 (1967).

439. Scott, R. B., and Bell, E., "Protein synthesis during development: control through messenger RNA." *Science* **145**, 711 (1964).
440. Scott, R. B., and Bell, E., "Messenger RNA utilization during development of chick embryo lens." *Science* **147**, 405 (1965).
441. Papaconstantinou, J., "Molecular aspects of lens cell differentiation." *Science* **156**, 338 (1967).
442. Stewart, J. A., and Papaconstantinou, J., "A stabilization of RNA templates in lens cell differentiation." *Proc. Natl. Acad. Sci. U.S.* **58**, 95 (1967).
443. Kruh, J., and Borsook, H., "Hemoglobin synthesis in rabbit reticulocytes *in vitro*." *J. Biol. Chem.* **220**, 905 (1956).
444. Cameron, I. L., and Prescott, D. M., "RNA and protein metabolism in the maturation of the nucleated chicken erythrocyte" *Exptl. Cell Res.* **30**, 609 (1963).
445. Dintzis, H. M., "Assembly of the peptide chains of hemoglobin." *Proc. Natl. Acad. Sci. U.S.* **47**, 247 (1961).
446. Grasso, J. A., Swift, H., and Ackerman, G. A., "Observations on the development of erythrocytes in mammalian fetal liver." *J. Cell Biol.* **14**, 235 (1962).
447. DeBellis, R. H., Gluck, N., and Marks, P. A., "Synthesis of ribonucleic acid in rabbit blood cells *in vivo*." *J. Clin. Invest.* **43**, 1329 (1964).
448. Arnstein, H. R. V., Cox, R. A., and Hunt, J. A., "The function of high molecular-weight ribonucleic acid from rabbit reticulocytes in haemoglobin biosynthesis." *Biochem. J.* **92**, 648 (1964).
449. Scott, R. B., and Malt, R. A., "Stable messenger RNA in nucleated erythrocytes." *Nature* **208**, 497 (1965).
450. Booyse, F. M., and Rafelson, M. E., "Stable messenger RNA in the synthesis of contractile protein in human platelets." *Biochim. Biophys. Acta* **145**, 188 (1967).
451. Wilt, F. H., "Regulation of the initiation of chick embryo hemoglobin synthesis." *J. Mol. Biol.* **12**, 331 (1965).
452. Wessells, N. K., and Wilt, F. H., "Action of actinomycin D on exocrine pancreas cell differentiation." *J. Mol. Biol.* **13**, 767 (1965).
453. Rutter, W. J., Wessells, N. K., and Grobstein, C., "Control of specific synthesis in the developing pancreas." *Natl. Cancer Inst. Monograph* **13**, 51 (1964).
454. Kallman, F., and Grobstein, C., "Fine structure of differentiating mouse pancreatic exocrine cells in transfilter culture." *J. Cell Biol.* **20**, 399 (1964).
455. Wessels, N. K., "DNA synthesis, mitosis and differentiation in pancreatic acinar cells *in vitro*." *J. Cell Biol.* **20**, 415 (1964).
456. Yaffe, D., and Feldman, M., "The effect of actinomycin D on heart and thigh muscle cells grown *in vitro*." *Develop. Biol.* **9**, 347 (1964).
457. Klein, N. W., and Pierro, L J., "Actinomycin D: Specific inhibitory effects on the explanted chick embryo." *Science* **142**, 967 (1963).
458. Jainchill, J., Saxen, L., and Vainio, T., "Studies on kidney tubulogenesis. I. The effect of actinomycin D on tubulogenesis *in vitro*." *J. Embryol. Exptl. Morph.* **12**, 597 (1964).
459. Revel, M., and Hiatt, H. H., "The stability of liver mesenger RNA." *Proc. Natl. Acad. Sci. U.S.* **51**, 810 (1964).
460. Cozzone, A., and Marchis-Mouren, G., "Messenger ribonucleic acid stability in rat pancreas and liver." *Biochemistry* **6**, 3911 (1967).
461. Sussman, M., and Sussman, R. R., "The regulatory program for UDP-galactose polysaccharide transferase activity during slime mold cytodifferentiation: Requirement for specific synthesis of RNA." *Biochim. Biophys. Acta* **108**, 463 (1965).

462. Halvorson, H., "Physiology of sporulation." *In* I. C. Gunsalus and R. Y. Stanier, eds., *The Bacteria.* New York: Academic Press, 1962, Vol. 4, pp. 223–264.

463. Aronson, A. L., and Rosas del Valle, M., "RNA and protein synthesis required for bacterial spore formation." *Biochim. Biophys. Acta* **87**, 267 (1964).

464. Doi, R. H., and Igarashi, R. T., "Genetic transcription during morphogenesis." *Proc. Natl. Acad. Sci. U.S.* **52**, 755 (1964).

465. Pollock, M. R., "The differential effect of actinomycin D on the biosynthesis of enzymes in *Bacillus subtilis* and *Bacillus cereus.*" *Biochim. Biophys. Acta* **76**, 80, (1963).

466. Martinez, R. J., "The formation of bacterial flagella. II. The relative stability of messenger RNA for flagelin biosynthesis." *J. Mol. Biol.* **17**, 10 (1966).

467. Nakada, D., "Formation of ribosomes by a 'relaxed' mutant of *Escherichia coli.*" *J. Mol. Biol.* **12**, 695 (1965).

468. Woese, C., Naono, S., Soffer, R., and Gros, F., "Studies on the breakdown of messenger RNA." *Biochem. Biophys. Res. Commun.* **11**, 435 (1963).

469. Levinthal, C., Keynan, A., and Higa, A., "Messenger RNA turnover and protein synthesis in *Bacillus subtilis* inhibited by actinomycin D." *Proc. Natl. Acad. Sci. U.S.* **48**, 1631 (1962).

469a. Zimmermann, R. A., and Levinthal, C., "Messenger RNA and RNA transcription time." *J. Mol. Biol.* **30**, 349 (1967).

469b. Mangiarotti, G., and Schlessinger, D., "Polyribosome metabolism in *Escherichia coli.*" *J. Mol. Biol.* **29**, 395 (1967).

470. Nakada, D., and Magasanik, B., "The roles of inducer and catabolite repressor in the synthesis of β-galactosidase by *Escherichia coli.*" *J. Mol. Biol.* **8**, 105 (1964).

471. Fan, D. P., "Decay of intact messengers in bacteria." *J. Mol. Biol.* **16**, 164 (1966).

472. Fan, D. P., Higa, A, and Levinthal, C, "Messenger RNA decay and protection." *J. Mol. Biol.* **8**, 210 (1964).

473. Kepes, A., "Kinetics of induced enzyme synthesis." *Biochim. Biophys. Acta* **76**, 293 (1963).

474. Dresden, M. H., and Hoagland, M. B., "Polyribosomes of *Escherichia coli* breakdown during glucose starvation." *J. Biol. Chem.* **242**, 1065 (1967).

475. Dresden, M. H., and Hoagland, M. B., "Polyribosomes of *Escherichia coli,* re-formation during recovery from glucose starvation." *J. Biol. Chem.* **242**, 1069 (1967).

476. Hartwell, L. H., and Magasanik, B., "The molecular basis of histidase induction in *Bacillus subtilis.*" *J. Mol. Biol.* **7**, 401 (1963).

477. Tschudy, D. P., Marver, H. S., and Collins, A., "A model for calculating messenger RNA half-life: short lived messenger RNA in the induction of mammalian δ-aminolevulinic acid synthetase." *Biochem. Biophys. Res. Commun.* **21**, 480 (1965).

478. Villa-Trevino, S., Farber, E., Staehelin, T., Wettstein, F., and Noll, H., "Breakdown and reassembly of rat liver ergosomes after administration of ethionine or puromycin." *J. Biol. Chem.* **239**, 3826 (1964).

479. Trakatellis A. C., Axelrod, A. E., and Montjar, M., "Studies on liver messenger ribonucleic acid." *J. Biol. Chem.* **239**, 4237 (1964).

480. Blobel, G., and Potter, V. R., "Studies on free and membrane-bound ribosomes in in rat liver." *J. Mol. Biol.* **26**, 279 (1967).

481. Howell, R. R., Loeb, J. N., and Tomkins, G. M., "Characterization of ribosomal aggregates isolated from liver" *Proc. Natl. Acad. Sci. U.S.* **52**, 1241 (1964)

482. Blobel, G., and Potter, V. R., "Ribosomes in rat liver: An estimate of the percentage of free and membrane-bound ribosomes interacting with messenger RNA *in vivo.*" *J. Mol. Biol.* **28,** 539 (1967).

483. Shapot, V., and Pitot, H. C., "Isolation and factionation of ribonucleic acid from the smooth endoplasmic reticulum of rat liver." *Biochim. Biophys. Acta* **119,** 37 (1966).

484. Pitot, H. C., "Altered template stability: The molecular mask of malignancy?" *Perspectives Biol. Med.* **8,** 50 (1964).

485. Penman, S., Sherrer, K., Becker, Y., and Darnell, J. E., "Polyribosomes in normal and poliovirus-infected HeLa cells and their relationship to messenger-RNA." *Proc. Natl. Acad. Sci. U.S.* **49,** 654 (1963).

486. Scherrer, K., Latham, H.,and Darnell, J. E., "Demonstration of an unstable RNA and of a precursor to ribosomal RNA in HeLa cells." *Proc. Natl. Acad. Sci. U.S.* **49,** 240 (1963).

487. Girard, M., Latham, H., Penman, S., and Darnell, J. E., "Entrance of newly formed messenger RNA and ribosomes into HeLa cell cytoplasm." *J. Mol. Biol.* **11,** 187 (1965).

488. Girard, M., Penman, S., and Darnell, J. E., "The effect of actinomycin on ribosome formation in HeLa cells." *Proc. Natl. Acad. Sci. U.S.* **51,** 205 (1964).

489. Philipson, L., "Chromatographic separation, and characteristics of nucleic acids from HeLa cells." *J. Gen. Physiol.* **44,** 899 (1961).

490. Latham, H., and Darnell, J. E., "Distribution of messenger RNA in the cytoplasmic polyribosomes of the HeLa cell." *J. Mol. Biol.* **14,** 1 (1965).

491. Pitot, H. C., Peraino, C., Lamar, C., and Kennan, A. L., "Template stability of some enzymes in rat liver and hepatomas." *Proc. Natl. Acad. Sci. U.S.* **54,** 845 (1965).

492. Marchis-Mouren, G., and Cozzone, A., "Inhibition by actinomycin D of valine incorporation into specific proteins of rat pancreas *in vivo.*" *Biochemistry* **5,** 3684 (1966).

493. Forchhammer, J., and Kjeldgaard, N. O., "Decay of messenger RNA *in vivo* in a mutant of *Escherichia coli* 15." *J. Mol. Biol.* **24,** 459 (1967).

494. Davidson, E. H., "Hormones and genes." *Sci. Am.* **212,** 6, 36 (1965).

495. Lieberman I., Abrams, R., and Ove., P., "Changes in the metabolism of ribonucleic acid preceding the synthesis of deoxyribonucleic acid in mammalian cells cultured from the animal." *J. Biol. Chem.* **238,** 2141 (1963).

496. Clark, M. F., Matthews, R. E. P., and Ralph, R. K., "Ribosomes and polyribosomes in *Brassica pekinesis*" *Biochim. Biophys. Acta* **91,** 289 (1964).

496a. Williams, G. R., and Novelli, G. D., "Ribosome changes following illumination of dark-grown plants." *Biochim. and Biophys. Acta* **155,** 183 (1968).

496b. Stout, E. R., Parenti, R., and Mans, R. J., "An increase in RNA polymerase activity after illumination of dark-grown maize seedlings." *Biochem. Biophys. Res. Commun.* **29,** (1967).

497. Biggers, J. D., Whittingham, D. G., and Donahue, R. P., "The pattern of energy metabolism in the mouse oocyte and zygote." *Proc. Natl. Acad. Sci. U.S.* **58,** 560 (1967).

498. Brinster, R. A., and Thomson, J. L., "Development of eight-cell mouse embryos *in vitro.*" *Exptl. Cell Res.* **42,** 308 (1966).

498a. Daniel, J. C., Jr., "The pattern of utilization of respiratory metabolic intermediates by preimplantation rabbit embryos *in vitro.*" *Exptl. Cell Res.* **47,** 619 (1967).

499. Kaempfer, R. O. R., and Magasanik, B., "Mechanism of β-galactosidase induction in *Escherichia coli.*" *J. Mol. Biol.* **27**, 475 (1967).

500. Kidson, C., and Kirby, K. S., "Selective alterations of mammalian messenger-RNA synthesis: Evidence for differential action of hormones on gene transcription." *Nature* **203**, 599 (1964).

501. Means, A. R., and Hamilton, T. H., "Early estrogen action: Concomitant stimulations within two minutes of nuclear RNA synthesis and uptake of RNA precursor by the uterus." *Proc. Natl. Acad. Sci. U.S.* **56**, 1594 (1966).

502. Kidson, C., "Kinetics of cortisol action on RNA synthesis." *Biochem. Biophys. Res. Commun.* **21**, 283 (1965).

503. Roychoudhury, R., Datta, A., and Sens, S. P., "The mechanism of action of plant growth substances: The role of nuclear RNA in growth substance action." *Biochim. Biophys. Acta* **107**, 346 (1965).

503a. Johri, M. M., and Varner, J. E., "Enhancement of RNA synthesis in isolated pea nuclei by gibberellic acid." *Proc. Natl. Acad. Sci. U.S.* **59**, 269 (1968).

504. Jacob, F., and Monod, J., "Genetic repression, allosteric inhibition, and cellular differentiation." *Symp. Soc. Study Develop. Growth* **21**, 30 (1963).

505. Moore, J. A., "Nuclear transplantation and problems of specificity in developing embryos." *J. Cellular Comp. Physiol.* **60**, Suppl. 1, 19 (1962).

506. Demerec, M., "A comparative study of certain gene loci in *Salmonella.*" *Cold Spring Harbor Symp. Quant. Biol.* **21**, 113 (1956).

507. Hartman, P. E., "Linked loci in the control of consecutive steps in the primary pathway of histidine synthesis in *Salmonella typhimurium.*" *Carnegie Inst. Wash. Publ.* **612**, 35 (1956).

508. Pette, D., Luh, W., and Bücher, T. "A constant-proportion group in the enzyme activity pattern of the Embden-Meyerhof chain." *Biochem. Biophys. Res. Commun.* **7**, 419 (1962).

509. Mier, P. D., and Cotton, D. W. K., "Operon hypothesis: New evidence from the 'constant proportion' group of the Embden-Meyerhof pathway." *Nature* **209**, 1022 (1966).

510. Pontecorvo, G., *Trends in Genetic Analysis.* New York: Columbia University Press, 1958.

511. Giles, N. H., Case, M. E., Partridge, C. W. H., and Ahmed S. I., "A gene cluster in *Neurospora crassa* coding for an aggregate of five aromatic synthetic enzymes." *Proc. Natl. Acad. Sci. U.S.* **58**, 1453 (1967).

512. Fink, G. R., "A cluster of genes controlling three enzymes in histidine biosynthesis in *Saccharomyces cerevisiae.*" *Genetics* **53**, 445 (1966).

513. Webber, B. B., and Case, M. E., "Genetical and biochemical studies of histidine-requiring mutants of *Neurospora crassa.* I. Classification of mutants and characterization of mutant groups." *Genetics* **45**, 1605 (1960).

514. Jacoby, G. A., and Gorini, L., "Genetics of control of the arginine pathway in *Escherichia coli.* B. and K." *J. Mol. Biol.* **24**, 41 (1967).

515. Kiho, Y., and Rich A., "A polycistronic messenger RNA associated with β-galactosidase induction." *Proc. Natl. Acad. Sci. U.S.* **54**, 1751 (1965).

515a. Slayter, H., Kiho, Y., Hall, C. E., and Rich, A., "An electron microscopic study of large bacterial polyribosomes." *J. Cell Biol.* **37**, 583 (1968).

516. Leive, L., and Kollin, V., "Synthesis, utilization and degradation of lactose operon messenger RNA in *Escherichia coli.*" *J. Mol. Biol.* **24**, 247 (1967).

517. Imamoto, F., Ito, J., and Yanofsky, C., "Polarity in the tryptophan operon of *Escherchia coli.*" *Cold Spring Harbor Symp. Quant. Biol.* **31**, 235 (1966).

518. Imamoto, F., and Yanofsky, C., "Transcription of the tryptophan operon in polarity mutants of *Escherchia coli*. I. Characterization of the tryptophan messenger RNA of polar mutants." *J. Mol. Biol.* **28**, 1 (1967).

519. Yanofsky, C., and Ito, J., "Nonsense codons and polarity in the tryptophan operon." *J. Mol. Biol.* **21**, 313 (1966).

520. Imamoto, F., and Yanofsky, C., "Transcription of the tryptophan operon in polarity mutants of *Escherichia coli*. II. Evidence for normal production of tryptophan messenger RNA molecules and for premature termination of transcription." *J. Mol. Biol.* **28**, 25 (1967).

521. Martin, R. G., Silbert, D. F., Smith, D. W. E., and Whitfield, H. J., "Polarity in the histidine operon." *J. Mol. Biol.* **21**, 357 (1966).

522. Martin, R. G., "The one operon-one messenger theory of transcription" *Cold Spring Harbor Symp. Quant. Biol.* **28**, 357 (1963).

523. Goldberger, R. F., and Berberich, M. A., Sequential repression and derepression of the enzymes for histidine biosynthesis in *Salmonella typhimurium*. *Proc. Natl. Acad. Sci.* **54**, 279 (1965).

524. Jacob, F., and Monod, J., "On the regulation of gene activity." *Cold Spring Harbor Symp. Quant. Biol.* **26**, 193 (1961).

525. Ames, B. N., Hartman, P. E., and Jacob, F., "Chromosomal alterations affecting the regulation of histidine biosynthetic enzymes in *Salmonella*." *J. Mol. Biol.* **7**, 23 (1963).

526. Lee, N., and Engelsberg, E., "Coordinate variations in induced synthesis of enzymes associated with mutations in a structural gene." *Proc. Natl. Acad. Sci. U.S.* **50**, 696 (1963).

527. Stent, G. S., "The operon: On its third anniversary." *Science* **144**, 816 (1964).

528. Beckwith, J. R., "Regulation of the lac operon." *Science* **156**, 597 (1967).

528a. Ippen, K., Miller, J. H., Scaife, J., and Beckwith, J., "New controlling element in the *Lac* operon of *E. coli*." *Nature* **217**, 825 (1968).

529. Berberich, M. A., Venetianer, P., and Goldberger, R. F., "Alternative modes of depression of the histidine operon observed in *Salmonella typhimurium*." *J. Biol. Chem.* **241**, 4426 (1966).

530. Engelhardt, D. L., Webster, R. E., and Zinder, N. D., "Amper mutants and polarity *in vitro*" *J. Mol. Biol.* **29**, 45 (1967).

531. Beckwith, J. R., "A deletion analysis of the lac operator region in *Escherichia coli*." *J. Mol. Biol.* **8**, 427 (1964).

532. Jacob, F., Ullman, A., and Monod, J., "Le promoteur élément génétique nécessaire à l'éxpression d'un opéron." *Compt. Pend.* **258**, 3125 (1964).

533. Steers, E., Craven, G. R., and Anfinsen, C. B., "Comparison of β-galactosidases from normal (i^-, o^+, z^+) and operator constitutive (i^-, o^c, z^+) strains of *Escherichia coli*." *Proc. Natl. Acad. Sci. U.S.* **54**, 1174 (1965).

534. Bourgeois, S., Cohn, M., and Orgel, L. E., "Suppression of and complementation among mutants of the regulatory gene of the lactose operon of *Escherichia coli*." *J. Mol. Biol.* **14**, 300 (1965).

534a. Imamoto, F., "On the initiation of transcription of the tryptophan operon in *Escherichia coli*." *Proc. Natl. Acad. Sci. U.S.* **60**, 305 (1968).

534b. Baker, R. F., and Yanofsky, C., "The periodicity of RNA polymerase initiations: A new regulatory feature of transcription." *Proc. Natl. Acad. Sci. U.S.* **60**, 313 (1968).

534c. Bauerle, R. H., and Margolin, P., "Evidence for two sites for initiation of gene expression in the tryptophan operon of *Salmonella typhimurium*." *J. Mol. Biol.* **26**, 423 (1967).

535. McClintock, B., "Some parallels between gene control systems in maize and in bacteria." *Am. Naturalist* **95**, 265 (1961).

536. Gilbert, W., and Müller-Hill, B., "Isolation of the lac repressor." *Proc. Natl. Acad. Sci. U.S.* **56**, 1891 (1966).

536a. Gilbert, W., and Müller-Hill, B., "The lac operator is DNA." *Proc. Natl. Acad. Sci. U.S.* **58**, 2415 (1967).

537. Ptashne, M., "Specific binding of the λ phage repressor to λ DNA." *Nature* **214**, 232 (1967).

538. Ptashne, M., "Isolation of the λ phage repressor." *Proc. Natl. Acad. Sci. U.S.* **57**, 306 (1967).

538a. Riggs, A. D., Bourgeois, S., Newby, R. F., and Cohn, M., "DNA binding of the lac repressor." *J. Mol. Biol.* **34**, 365 (1968).

538b. Riggs, A. D., and Bourgeois, S., "On the assay, isolation and characterization of the lac repressor." *J. Mol. Biol.* **34**, 361 (1968).

539. Loomis, W. F., and Magasanik, B., "The catabolite repression gene of the lac operon in *Escherichia coli*." *J. Mol. Biol.* **23**, 487 (1967).

540. Hiraga, S., Ito, K., Hamada, K., and Yura, T., "A new regulatory gene for the tryptophan operon of *Escherichia coli*." *Biochem. Biophys. Res. Commun.* **26**, 522 (1967).

541. Baumberg, S., Bacon, D. F., and Vogel, H. J., "Individually repressible enzymes specified by clustered genes of arginine synthesis." *Proc. Natl. Acad. Sci. U.S.* **53**, 1029 (1965).

542. Roth, J. R., Anton, D. N., and Hartman, P. E., "Histidine regulatory mutants in *Salmonella typhimurium*. I. Isolation and general properties." *J. Mol. Biol.* **22**, 305 (1966).

542a. Anton, D. N., "Histidine regulatory mutants in *Salmonella typhimurium*. V. Two new classes of histidine regulatory mutants." *J. Mol. Biol.* **33**, 533 (1968).

542b. Ursprung, H., Smith, K. D., Sofer, W. H., and Sullivan, D. T., "Assay systems for the study of gene function." *Science* **160**, 1075 (1968).

543. Marushige, K., and Bonner, J., "Template properties of liver chromatin." *J. Mol. Biol.* **15**, 160 (1966).

543a. Stevenin, J., Samec, J., Jacob, M., et Mandel, P., "Determination de la fraction du genome codant pour les RNA ribosomiques et messagers dans le cerveau du rat adulte." *J. Mol. Biol.* **33**, 777 (1968).

544. Bonner, J., Dahmus, M. E., Fambrough, D., Huang, R. C., Marushige, K., and Yuan, Y. H., "The biology of isolated chromatin." *Science* **159**, 47 (1968).

545. Church, R. B., and McCarthy, B. J., "Ribonucleic acid synthesis in regenerating embryonic liver." *J. Mol. Biol.* **23**, 477 (1966).

546. Mirsky, A. E., and Pollister, A. W., "Chromosin, a desoxyribose nucleoprotein complex of the cell nucleus." *J. Gen. Physiol.* **30**, 117 (1946).

547. Dounce, A. L., and Hilgartner, C. A., "A study of DNA nucleoprotein gels and the residual protein of isolated cell nuclei." *Exptl. Cell Res.* **36**, 228 (1964).

548. Wang, T. Y., "The isolation, properties, and possible functions of chromatin acidic proteins." *J. Biol. Chem.* **242**, 1220 (1967).

549. Mirsky, A. E., Unpublished experiments (1967).

550. Leveson, J. E., and Peacocke, A. R., "Studies on a complex of deoxyribonucleic acid with non-histone protein." *Biochim. Biophys. Acta* **123**, 329 (1966).

551. Leveson, J. E., and Peacocke, A. R., "Complexes of non-histone protein in calf thymus chromatin" *Biochim. Biophys. Acta* **149**, 311 (1967).

552. Busch, H., *Histones and Other Nuclear Proteins*. New York: Academic Press, 1965.

553. Allfrey, V. G., Daly, M. M., and Mirsky, A. E., "Some observations on protein metabolism in chromosomes of nondividing cells." *J. Gen. Physiol.* **38**, 415 (1955).

554. Wang, T. Y., "Incorporation of ^{14}C amino acids into ribonucleoprotein fraction of isolated thymus cell nuclei." *Biochim. Biophys. Acta* **49**, 108 (1961).

555. Wang, T. Y., "Role of the residual nucleoprotein complex and acidic proteins of the cell nucleus in protein synthesis." *Proc. Natl. Acad. Sci. U.S.* **54**, 800 (1965).

556. Hnilica, L. S., and Kappler, H. A., "Biosynthesis of histones and acidic nuclear proteins under different conditions of growth." *Science* **150**, 1470 (1965).

556a. Holoubek, V., and Crocker, T. T., "DNA-associated acidic proteins." *Biochim. Biophys. Acta* **157**, 352 (1968).

557. Patel, G., and Wang, T. Y., "Protein synthesis in nuclear residual protein." *Biochim. Biophys. Acta* **95**, 314 (1965).

558. Bonner, J., and Ts'o, P., eds., *The Nucleohistones*. San Francisco: Holden-Day, 1964.

559. Ciba Foundation Study Group No. 24, *Histones, Their Role in the Transfer of Genetic Information*. London: Churchill, 1966.

560. Allfrey, V. G., and Mirsky, A. E., "Mechanisms of synthesis and control of protein and ribonucleic acid synthesis in the cell nucleus." *Cold Spring Harbor Symp. Quant. Biol.* **28**, 247 (1963).

561. Littau, V. C., Burdick, C. J., Allfrey, V. G., and Mirsky, A. E., "The role of histones in the maintenance of chromatin structure." *Proc. Natl. Acad. Sci. U.S.* **54**, 1204 (1965).

562. Zubay, G., "Nucleohistone structure and function." *In* J. Bonner and P. Ts'o, eds., *The Nucleohistones*. San Francisco: Holden-Day, 1964, p. 95.

563. McEwen, B. S., Allfrey, V. G., and Mirsky, A. E., "Studies on energy-yielding reactions in thymus nuclei III. Participation of glycolysis and the citric acid cycle in nuclear adenosine triphosphate synthesis." *J. Biol. Chem.* **238**, 2579 (1963).

564. McEwen, B. S., Allfrey, V. G., and Mirsky, A. E., "Studies of energy-yielding reactions in thymus nuclei. I. Comparison of nuclear and mitochrondrial phosphorylation." *J. Biol. Chem.* **238**, 758 (1963).

565. Allfrey, V. G., Littau, V. C., and Mirsky, A. E., "On the role of histones in regulating ribonucleic acid synthesis in the cell nucleus." *Proc. Natl. Acad. Sci. U.S.* **49**, 414 (1963).

566. Bonner, J., and Huang, R. C. "Histones as specific repressors of chromosomal RNA synthesis." *In* Ciba Foundation Study No. 24, *Histones, Their Role in the Transfer of Genetic Information*. London: Churchill, 1966, p. 18.

567. Attardi, B., and Attardi, G., "A membrane-associated RNA of cytoplasmic origin in HeLa cells." *Proc. Natl. Acad. Sci. U.S.* **58**, 1051 (1967).

568. Harris, H., "Rapidly labelled ribonucleic acid in the cell nucleus." *Nature* **198**, 184 (1963).

569. Harris, H., "Breakdown of nuclear ribonucleic acid in the presence of actinomycin D." *Nature* **202**, 1301 (1964).

570. Attardi, G., Parnas, H., Hwang, M-I. H., and Attardi, B., "Giant-size rapidly labeled nuclear ribonucleic acid and cytoplasmic messenger ribonucleic acid in immature duck erythrocytes." *J. Mol. Biol.* **20,** 145 (1966).

571. Ellem, K. A. O., and Sheriden, J. W., "Tenacious binding of the bulk of the DNA-like RNA of metazoan cells to methylated albumin columns. *Biochem. Biophys. Res. Commun.* **16,** 505 (1964).

572. Yoshikawa-Fukada, M., Fukada, T., and Kawade, Y., "Characterization of rapidly labeled ribonucleic acid of animal cells in culture." *Biochim. Biophys. Acta* **103,** 383 (1965),

573. Warner, J. R., Soeiro, R., Birnboim, H. C., Girard, M., and Darnell, J. E., "Rapidly labeled HeLa cell nuclear RNA. Identification by zone sedimentation of a heterogeneous fraction separate from ribosomal precursor RNA." *J. Mol. Biol.* **19,** 349 (1966).

574. Soeiro, R., Birnboim, H. C., and Darnell, J. E., "Rapidly labeled HeLa cell nuclear RNA. II. Base composition and cellular localization of a heterogeneous RNA fraction." *J. Mol. Biol.* **19,** 362 (1966).

575. Houssais, J. F., and Attardi, G., "High molecular weight nonribosomal-type nuclear RNA and cytoplasmic messenger RNA in HeLa cells." *Proc. Natl. Acad. Sci. U.S.* **56,** 616 (1966).

575a. Edstrom, J. E., and Daneholt, B., "Sedimentation properties of the newly synthesized RNA from isolated nuclear components of *Chironomus tentans* salivary gland cells." *J. Mol. Biol.* **28,** 331 (1967).

576. Warner, J. R., Knopf, P. M., and Rich, A., "A multiple ribosomal structure in protein synthesis." *Proc. Natl. Acad. Sci. U.S.* **49,** 122 (1963).

577. Burney, A., and Marbaix, G., "Isolement du RNA messager des reticulocytes de lapin." *Biochim. Biophys. Acta* **103,** 409 (1965).

578. Yamana, K., and Shiokawa, K., "Occurrence of an inhibitory factor of ribosomal RNA synthesis in embryonic cells of *Xenopus laevis.*" *Exptl. Cell Res.* **44,** 283 (1966).

579. Johns, E. W., and Butler, J. A. V., "Specificity of the interactions between histones and deoxyribonucleic acid." *Nature* **204,** 853 (1964).

580. Murray, K., "The basic proteins of cell nuclei." *Ann. Rev. Biochem.* **34,** 209 (1965).

581. Hnilica, L. S., "Studies on nuclear proteins. I. Observations on the tissue and species specificity of the moderately lysine-rich histone fraction 2b." *Biochim. Biophys. Acta* **117,** 163 (1966).

582. Hnilica, L. S., and Kappler, H. A., "The specificity of histones and other nuclear proteins in different conditions of growth." *Federation Proc.* **24,** Part I, No. 2, 601 (1965).

582a. Beeson, J. L., and Triplett, E. L., "Localization and characterization of rat and chicken histones." *Exptl. Cell Res.* **48,** 61 (1967).

583. Dingman, C. W., and Sporn, M. B., "Studies on chromatin." *J. Biol. Chem.* **239,** 3483 (1964).

584. Goodwin, B. C., "Histones and reliable control of protein synthesis." *In* Ciba Foundation Study Group No. 24, *Histones, Their Role in the Transfer of Genetic Factors.* London: Churchill, 1966, p. 68.

585. Ciba Foundation Study Group No. 24, *Histones, Their Role in the Transfer of Genetic Factors.* London: Churchill, 1966, pp. 77–80.

586. Allfrey, V. G., Faulkner, R., and Mirsky, A. E., "Acetylation and methylation of histones and their possible role in the regulation of RNA synthesis." *Proc. Natl. Acad. Sci. U.S.* **51**, 786 (1964).

587. Allfrey, V. G., Pogo, B. G. T., Pogo, A. O., Kleinsmith, L. J., and Mirsky, A. E., "The metabolic behavior of chromatin." *In* Ciba Foundation Study Group No 24, *Histones, Their Role in the Transfer of Genetic Factors.* London: Churchill, 1966, p. 42.

588. Phillips, D. M. P., "The presence of acetyl groups in histones." *Biochem. J.* **87**, 258 (1963).

589. Kleinsmith, L. J., Allfrey, V. G., and Mirsky, A. E., "Phosphoprotein metabolism in isolated lymphocyte nuclei." *Proc. Natl. Acad. Sci. U.S.* **55**, 1182 (1966).

590. Kleinsmith, L. J., Allfrey, V. G., and Mirsky, A E., "Phosphorylation of nuclear protein early in the course of gene activation in lymphocytes." *Science* **154**, 780 (1966).

591. Langan, T. A., and Smith, L. K., "Phosphorylation of histones and protamines by a specific protein kinase from liver." *Federation Proc.* **26**, 603 (1964).

592. Langan, T. A., "A phosphoprotein preparation from liver nuclei and its effect on the inhibition of RNA synthesis by histones." *In* V. V. Koningsberger and C. Bosch, eds., *Regulation of Nucleic Acid and Protein Biosynthesis.* Amsterdam: Elsevier, 1966, p. 233.

593. Vogel, F., "Genetics: A preliminary estimate of the number of human genes." *Nature* **201**, 847 (1964).

Author Index

Numbers in parentheses are reference numbers and indicate that an author's work is referred to, although his name is not cited in the text. Numbers in italics show the page on which the complete reference is listed.

A

Abrams, R., 279(495), *350*
Ackerman, G. A., 258(446), *348*
Afzelius, B. A., 100, *336*
Aggarwal, S. K., 196, 197(359), *343*
Ahmed, S. I., 288(511), *351*
Aitkhozhin, M. A., 70, 71(133), 87 (172), 91(172), 95(133), *332, 333, 334*
Alfert, M., 177(328), 224(328), *342*
Allfrey, V. G., 9, 10(21, 22, 23, 24), 44 (93), 50(93), 53(93), 78(155), 161 (155), 204(380), 206(21, 300), 207 (380), 208(385), 209(385), 212 (385, 394), 225, 226(385), 228, 233 (394), 235(394), 247(429), 304 (553), 304(560), 305(385, 563), 317 (24), 318(587), 319(561, 587), 320 (589, 590), *326, 327, 330, 334, 344, 345, 347, 354, 356*
Amaldi, F., 214, *345*
Ames, B. N., 290(525), *352*
Amma, K., 168, 169, *341*
Ananieva, L. N., 9(28), 296, 297(28), 302(28), *327*
Ancel, P., 143, *340*
Anfinsen, C. B., 292(533), *352*
Anton, D. N., 292(542a), 293(542), 297 (542), *353*
Atwood, K. C., 7, *326*
Attardi, B., 307, 309(570), 322(570), *354, 355*
Attardi, G., 214, 307(567), 309(570), 322(570), *345, 354, 355*

B

Arnstein, H. R. V., 258, *348*
Aronson, A. I., 58(113), 264,(463), 298 (113),*331, 349*
Auclair, W., 97, 98(187), *335*
Augusti-Tocco, G., 83, 85(165), *334*
Axelrod, A. E., 271, 275(479), *349*

B

Bacon, D. F., 293(541), *353*
Baca, M., 15(37), *327*
Bachvarova, R., 44(93), 50(93, 103), 53, 61(103), *330, 331*
Baker, R. F., 292(534b), *352*
Baker, T. G., 177, 177(327b), *342*
Baltzer, F., 18(39), 19, 20, *328*
Bard, S. G., 100(197), *336*
Barker, G. R., 249(434), *347*
Barros, C., 30, 33(77), 83(77), *329*
Bauerle, R. H., 292(534c), *353*
Baumberg, S., 293(541), *353*
Bautz, E. K. F., *331*
Beatty, B. R., 209(383), *345*
Becker, Y., 272, 274(485), 314(485), *350*
Beckwith, J. R., 291(531), 292(528, 528a), *352*
Beermann, W., 78(161), *334*
Beeson, J. L., 316(582a), *355*
Belitsina, N. V., 70, 71(133), 87(153, 172), 91(172), 95(133), *332, 333, 334*
Bell, E., 72, 99(190, 191), 252, 255, 256 (438), 276(437), 313(438), *333, 335, 347, 348*

357

Subject Index

A

Accessory cell functions in oogenesis, 193–201

Actinomycin, *see also* Actinomycin D
effect of, on dCMP activity during development, 84
treatment of embryos, *see* Actinomycin-treated embryos
use of, in template half-life studies, 274–275

Actinomycin D
effect on HeLa cells, 273
on polyribosomes, 254–255
on macromolecule synthesis, 270

Actinomycin-treated embryos, 255
comparison with species–hybrid experiments, 26–30
development of, 26–30
protein synthesis in, 35–38

Alkaline phosphatase, activity of, in aggregating cells, 142

Altered cell fate experiments, 4–5

Ambystoma, 153, 154, 211
nucleoli in developing oocytes, 212
pigmented vegetal cytoplasm in, 153

Amphibian oocytes, RNA synthesis in, 208–209

Amphibians, *see also* specific genus
DNA content of oocyte, 244
genome control in hybrids, 21–23
transcriptions underlying morphogenesis, 32, 33

Amphioxus, 71, 135

Arbacia, 18, 19, 35, 66, 81, 98, 146
electrophoresis of embryo proteins, 36

Arenicola, 116

Ascaris, 6–7, 15–17, 75, 76, 91, 118, 123–125, 127, 167, 190, 191, 244, 252
RNA synthesis in, 81

Ascidia, 23, 71
RNA synthesis in, 80

Asterias forbesi, 30

Auxin, 284

B

Bacillus cereus, 264, 265, 276, 298

Bacillus subtilis, 8, 264, 266, 267, 269, 282

Bacteria, *see also* specific species
gene regulation systems in, 264–269, 286–294
rapidly decaying template RNA, 267–269

Bar gene, in *Drosophila,* 4

Beröe, 121, 154, 170

Bird
DNA content of oocyte, 244
oogenesis in, 176–177
ribosomal RNA synthesis in embryo, 72, 80

Blastomeres
isolated, capabilities of, 117–122
specifications of, in egg cytoplasm, 122–127

Blood cells, sedimentation pattern of RNA from, 308, 310–311

Bufo, 214

C

Calligrapha bigsbyana, 126

Calliphora, 199

Camarodonta, 24

Cell differentiation, *see also* Differentiation
definition, 12
DNA in, 5–7
differences in DNA sequences, 7–9
as function of variable gene activity, 3–11